THE LITTLE ENTENTE

THE LITTLE ENTENTE

By

ROBERT MACHRAY

NEW YORK

Howard Fertig

1970

First published in 1929

HOWARD FERTIG, INC. EDITION 1970
Published by arrangement with George Allen & Unwin, Ltd.

Library of Congress Catalog Card Number: 68:9665

PRINTED IN THE UNITED STATES OF AMERICA
BY NOBLE OFFSET PRINTERS, INC.

TO

THE NEW EUROPE

PREFACE

THIS book aims at presenting an accurate and fairly full account of the origins, objects, and activities of the political organization known as the Little Entente, one of the most striking and significant outcomes of the period of travail, anguish, and rebirth that brought the New Europe into being. Written from the point of view that this New Europe, notwithstanding defects, is far better, politically and ethnically, than was pre-War Europe, the story unfolded in these pages is that of a large part of Central and South-Eastern Europe during the last ten years. In the course of the decade, despite some obstinate questionings, peace has been consolidated, and the status established on the basis of the Peace Treaties has increasingly taken on the character as well as the appearance of permanence.

Anyone who remembers the aspect of the Continent towards the close of 1918, in 1919, and even in 1920, and compares it with that of 1928, or who recalls the prophecies of disaster and doom, including the swift coming on of another Great War that would overwhelm civilization, which were made so frequently nine or ten years ago, and contrasts the gloom of those vaticinations with the peace, order, and returning prosperity of Europe to-day, cannot but realize that a process of normalization has been and is at work, and moves on to more and more complete achievement. In this process the Little Entente has been a great factor—a greater factor than has been generally understood, partly because of the persistent misrepresentations of its enemies, and, much more, because of the public's lack of knowledge of the subject, a lack this book is intended to remedy.

An alliance of Czechoslovakia, Yugoslavia, and Rumania, the chief Succession States of the former Habsburg Empire of Austria-Hungary, the Little Entente was projected towards the close of 1918, was active during 1919 though not formally established, and was definitely constituted in 1920–21 by three treaties. The first of these was the Czechoslovak-Yugoslav Convention of Defensive Alliance of August 14, 1920 (prolonged and substantially extended on August 31, 1922); the second was the Czechoslovak-Rumanian Convention of Defensive Alliance of April 23, 1921; and the third was the Yugoslav-Rumanian Convention of Defensive Alliance of June 7, 1921. The name of "The Little Entente" was given to the combination of the three States first in derision by a Hungarian journal, but soon afterwards found general acceptance as an appropriate appellation.

The Little Entente was not a unitary alliance, as its scope was restricted to certain specific aims which were stated in the Preamble of each treaty. These were to safeguard the peace obtained by much sacrifice and provided for by the Covenant of the League of Nations, and to maintain the status laid down in the Peace Treaties—particularly in their case the Treaty of Trianon as regards Hungary, which affected all three States, and the Treaty of Neuilly as respects Bulgaria, with which Yugoslavia and Rumania were directly concerned. The contracting parties agreed to assist each other against an unprovoked attack by Hungary, while Yugoslavia and Rumania were to take steps in common concerning all questions of foreign policy relating to Hungary and Bulgaria. The Little Entente treaties have been prolonged from time to time, and remain the political and juridical foundation of the organization.

This alliance did not come into existence fortuitously nor could it properly be said to be artificial; it had its roots in the past. Its main business was to conserve in Central and South-Eastern Europe the new régime that had issued from the dissolution of the Habsburg Empire under the impact of the War and the revolutionary movements of the Nationalities of which it had been composed. Thus, this book begins with a description of the clash of these Nationalities of Austria-Hungary up to the outbreak of the War, and this is followed by a chapter dealing with the downfall and disappearance of the Habsburg Empire and the emergence in Central Europe of the new régime in the three last months of 1918. The Succession States of which the new régime consisted were Czechoslovakia, Yugoslavia, Greater Rumania, Poland, Italy, "Austria," and "Hungary," and what happened to them at the Peace Conference is narrated in the third chapter. These three chapters taken together serve to indicate the real historicity of the Little Entente; if it was new, it had long been foreshadowed. M. Mitilineu, a former Rumanian Foreign Minister, once said that if the Little Entente had not existed it would have been necessary to create it; but in the situation of the three States comprised in it, nothing was more in the very nature of things than its formation and declared policy.

Next are passed in review the negotiations that resulted in the signing of the first Little Entente treaty—between Czechoslovakia and Yugoslavia—and the assurance of collaboration given by M. Take Jonescu, then Rumanian Foreign Minister. Lengthy but very interesting quotations are made from an exposition by Dr. Benesh, the Czechoslovak Foreign Minister, of the reasons why the Little Entente had been constituted. *Mutatis mutandis* this remarkable speech might have been delivered in 1928, for the aims of the Little Entente have never changed at all. Very early in its history it had to contend against Anschluss—the union of Austria with Germany—and Magyar schemes of irredentism and Habsburg restoration, as the narrative states. In 1921 it was tested by the two attempts of the ex-Emperor Charles to regain the throne of Hungary, and proved its value in preserving the peace of Central Europe, though mobilization had to be resorted to by Czechoslovakia and Yugoslavia—the only instance of the kind to be recorded.

Thenceforward the story, as it is set down in this book, shows the expansion of the influence of the Little Entente in two directions, both well in keeping with its policy, though not prescribed by its treaties. First, the Little Entente took a prominent part in safeguarding the interests of Central Europe in the general international situation as it developed under the leading or the reverse of the Great Powers; for example, the three States took action in common at the Genoa Conference, where Poland ranged herself by their side, and at other great international conferences, as well as in the meetings of the League of Nations. Secondly, the Little Entente expanded by the making of friendly treaties, economic as well as political, with neighbouring and other States, while at the same time its States concluded treaties with one another for the betterment of their commercial relations. Its overriding purpose being the consolidation of the New Europe, with its own place in the new order as assured by the Peace Treaties, it did not stop at holding in check the forces working for disintegration, but tried to find, found, or kept on trying to find, bases for cooperation with its neighbours and others.

In 1923 the occupation of the Ruhr, and what was called on the Continent the "Anglo-French conflict" that arose out of it, gave very grave concern to the Little Entente, which had seen and still saw in the Big Entente, especially in the enduring collaboration of Great Britain and France, the most solid guarantee of peace and of the New Europe. If the Little Entente was oriented to France, as it was, it none the less looked to England as being with France the "necessary authority," as President Masaryk termed it, for the preservation of the *status quo*. It could not but deplore the tension between the two Powers, and therefore was vastly relieved when the Dawes Plan was formulated and accepted. It supported the Geneva Protocol, and when that fell through, it rejoiced in Locarno, with its seven interlocking treaties making for the consolidation of peace; still more did it rejoice in the Kellogg Pact, with its ban on war as an instrument of national policy. The last chapters of this book are devoted to a study of the reactions of the Little Entente to the general situation as it worked out on the foregoing lines; but they also picture the internal problems, difficulties, and happenings in the Little Entente itself and in its individual States that affected them during the years 1923–28, such as the Italo-Yugoslav controversy, the recrudescence of the question of Anschluss, and the campaign for the revision of the Treaty of Trianon.

For sins of commission and omission in the book I apologize, but I trust they are neither numerous nor flagrant; certainly none of them is to be charged against those who kindly assisted me with material or in any other way. I have written for many years articles on foreign affairs in the reviews, and in this connexion it may not be out of place to say how I came to write this particular book. In the middle of April, 1926, much surprise and speculation were occasioned throughout the world by the news that Germany was about to sign a treaty with the Soviet. The Locarno Treaties had been signed, but difficulties had arisen respecting the admission of Germany to the League of Nations; the news, therefore, appeared to have a curious, not to say sinister, significance. The treaty was signed at Berlin and its terms were made public. A leading English paper attacked Dr. Benesh, Czechoslovak Foreign Minister continuously since 1918—and for all these years the chief spokesman of the Little Entente—for having addressed a *questionnaire* to certain Powers with a view to elucidating the exact bearing of the treaty. To such a degree did this proceeding excite the ire of the paper, which had pro-German leanings, that it asserted that he had "dropped the mask," the inference being that he had been guilty of double-dealing. This journal has a reputation for accuracy; the strange thing was that Benesh had himself advocated the recognition of the Soviet, and had even gone to the length of concluding a commercial treaty with it four years before. I decided to look into the matter for myself.

It was a little difficult, because apart from general information derived from articles in newspapers, reviews, encyclopedias, and so forth, nothing on the Little Entente of an authoritative kind was to be found in English. Enough material, however, was obtained for an article which was published in the *Fortnightly Review* for June, 1926, under the title, "The Little Entente and Its Policies," and which demonstrated that Benesh could not be guilty of the odious charge that had been brought against him. It was at that time, then, that I became interested specially in the Little Entente. Reflecting on the highly important rôle played by the Little Entente in Europe and how little there seemed to be known about it, particularly in England, I thought it a great pity that there was no book on the subject. The idea of writing it myself came to me, but I put it away—as I imagined; it came back, however, and the result is this volume.

In accumulating material for it, I soon came upon an excellent book in French entitled *La Petite Entente: ses Origines, son Histoire, ses Connexions, son Avenir*, by M. Albert Mousset, and published in Paris in 1923 by Bossard. It brings the history of the Little Entente up to the end of 1922, and gives much detailed information on the beginnings on the organization and of its first year or two. It made my task a good deal easier, and I gratefully make my acknowledgments to M. Mousset, to whom I must also render my thanks for the help obtained from two other of his books, *Le Royaume Serbe, Croate, Slovène*, published in 1926, and *L'Europe balkanique et danubienne de 1925 à 1928*. A bibliography of books consulted and sometimes quoted from will be found towards the end of this volume, but I must make special mention—in the order in which they were read and made use of in the text—of President Masaryk's *The New Europe*, of all of Professor Seton-Watson's books dealing with various aspects of Central Europe, of Mr. Wickham Steed's books, particularly his *Through Thirty Years*, of Masaryk's *The Making of a State*, and the companion book by Benesh, *My War Memoirs*. It may be said that these works, important though they are, are all on one side—which, of course, is true; but this does not mean that I failed to acquaint myself with the literature on the other side; for instance, I read very carefully the three immense volumes on *The Hungarian Peace Negotiations*, published by the Hungarian Ministry of Foreign Affairs, as well as other works presenting the Magyar case.

For the period of the Peace Conference an extensive range of books exists, but I am chiefly indebted to Major Temperley's standard work, *History of the Peace Conference of Paris*, Steed's *Through Thirty Years*, and Professor Seymour's fourth volume of *The Intimate Papers of Colonel House*. With the shining exception of M. Mousset's book, works on the Little Entente itself are still to seek, but my own would be very much poorer were it not for the various *exposés* delivered by Benesh before the Foreign Affairs Commission of the Czechoslovak Parliament in Prague. Of these expositions, the more important for my purpose are his speech on September 1, 1920, and his address on "Five Years of Czechoslovak Foreign Policy," on February 6, 1924; considerable quotations are made from both. While statements corresponding to those in all of these documents were made by the other chief representatives of the Little Entente in their own Parliaments or to their newspapers, they are not so easily accessible, but the text contains many quotations from and references to their deliverances as reported in the British and Continental Press. In presenting them a certain amount of repetition has, quite naturally, been unavoidable, because of the consistency of the policy and the uniformity of the action of the Little Entente, which are thus emphasized.

With regard to the order in which the three States, when referred to together, are mentioned, it should perhaps be said that while it may be held that the treaties by which they constituted the Little Entente should date that order, I have not always observed this arrangement, which in any case involves no precedence of one or another of them. Nor is there intended any notion of precedence in the order in which the chief representatives of the Little Entente are placed in this book. The Index contains short biographical notes in supplement of the text, in which the omission, except in quotations, of titles, as, for example, Beust for Count von Beust, implies no discourtesy or disrespect, but was made solely to save space in the story itself. Footnotes have been avoided altogether, references, where essential or desirable, being provided in the body of the narrative. Concerning the spelling of some foreign proper names, it may be noted that an attempt has been made to English them, instead of use being made of hooks and other diacritic signs which, as a rule, have to be explained in a special table or list. Benesh is an illustration. Benes, with a hook over the last letter, is doubtless good Czech, but the English language is innocent of this hook, and in English works the name is best spelled Benesh, the hook merely representing the letter *h*. *The Times* has long printed the name of this eminent statesman as Benesh. Where the spelling of such proper names has become standardized among us, as, for instance, Palacky, it has been retained. Generally the term Yugoslavia is used, except in quotations, throughout the book for the Kingdom of the Serbs, Croats, and Slovenes, the official designation of the triune State.

ROBERT MACHRAY

December, 1928

A delay in publishing this book gives me the opportunity of bringing the narrative succinctly, in a short Postscript, pp. 357 ff., up to the close of the tenth regular Little Entente Conference, which was held on May 20th–22nd at Belgrade.

R. M.

June 1, 1929

CONTENTS

CHAPTER IV

CHAPTER V

CHAPTER VI

CHAPTER VII

CHAPTER VIII

CHAPTER IX

ILLUSTRATIONS

THE LITTLE ENTENTE

CHAPTER I

CLASH OF THE NATIONALITIES IN THE HABSBURG EMPIRE

TO 1914

FROM amidst the welter of international relations in 1919–20 after the World War, the political organization which soon came to be known as the Little Entente emerged as a serious effort to establish settled conditions and provide a solid guarantee of peace in Central and South-Eastern Europe. It was in this large and highly important area that the greatest changes had taken place, owing to the dissolution of the Empire of the Habsburgs and its replacement by a series of new or new-old States in 1918, under the pressure of the War and the revolutionary movements induced by or associated with that gigantic conflict. Of the Succession States, as they were generally termed, the three chief States were Czechoslovakia, Yugoslavia, and Rumania, and these were precisely the States which composed the Little Entente.

Also from the point of view of being Succession States, Poland came next; then Italy; and, in rather a different way, Austria and Hungary, which were severed politically from each other and so reduced in size and significance as to do scarcely more than suggest by their names the Austria-Hungary, the Dual Monarchy, that had been one, and not the least considerable, of the six Great Powers of Europe, but that had disappeared, in all probability for ever, from the map. For it was not so much that the Habsburg Empire fell, as fall it did; it went to pieces and ceased to exist as a State, as a political entity. Four Empires crashed in the World War: Russia, Turkey, Austria-Hungary, Germany, in the order of occurrence. But Russia, Turkey, and Germany, though they lost dynasties and territories, remained States which were still readily recognizable as Russia, Turkey, and Germany respectively, and the history of each went on without break or pause. Far otherwise was it with Austria-Hungary; she passed, and with her passing her history came to a close. Long familiar landmarks were swept away. *Fuit Ilium!*

Apparently sudden and undeniably swift and convulsive towards the end, the demise of this great State, with a population of upwards of fifty millions, was a most remarkable and indeed, in modern times, an unprecedented event, but it was scarcely so sudden as it seemed, nor was there anything about it that was mysterious or really inexplicable. What was strange and striking enough was the amazing completeness, the singular finality of the thing. After lasting for centuries the Habsburg Empire became within a span of a few days as a tale that was told. Why and how was it, then, that it perished in this way? And why and how was it replaced, as in fact it was replaced, almost overnight?

These questions, however, resolved themselves into virtually one and the same question—the question of the divers Nationalities of which Austria-Hungary consisted; and the answers were summed up virtually in one and the same answer—the living will to be independent, the fixed determination to be free on the part of those of her Nationalities which had long been oppressed under her rule, and which found opportunity to give that will and determination full expression in and through the World War. Moreover, question and answer alike foreshadowed the formation of just such a combination as the Little Entente, which was a new organization, but had its roots in history.

The Mixture of Races

When the War broke out, as for many years before, Austria-Hungary was far from being a compact, homogeneous State, though more or less unified politically by the Habsburg system, which was a continuation of a medieval, dynastic, militaristic absolutism, the abiding reality behind an elaborate but deceptive Constitutional façade of two Parliaments and various provincial Diets. The State was composed of a mass of heterogeneous Nationalities, at least nine in number: German, Magyar, Czechoslovak, Polish, Ukrainian or Ruthenian, Serbo-Croatian, Slovene, Rumanian, and Italian. By separating the Slovaks from their kinsmen the Czechs, and the Croats from their relatives the Serbs, eleven Nationalities were counted. A more minute division, including the Jews, gave thirteen or more.

It was this extraordinary mixture of different races and tongues that caused Austria-Hungary to be called, not altogether unjustly, a political monstrosity and a ramshackle Empire. The most notable thing was that whatever number of Nationalities were enumerated, an Austrian Nationality was not included; there was no such Nationality. Austria, Latinized from *Oesterreich*, and originally the *Östmark*, the Eastern march of the Empire whose Northern march was Brandenburg, was German and her people were German, whereas the rest of the Habsburg dominions, and much the larger part of them, was Magyar, Latin, and, predominantly, Slav—Czech, Slovak, Polish, Ukrainian or Ruthene, Serb, Croat, and Slovene. Earlier in their history the Habsburgs, who held the German crown for centuries, had tried to transform the various Nationalities into a united, centralized, solidly German State, but they failed, mainly because of the stubborn resistance of their non-German peoples to that policy

The Principle of Nationality

In 1526 the Turkish peril brought about the free union of Austria, Bohemia, and Hungary, but under dynastic domination the union soon lost its freedom, and both Bohemia and Hungary were oppressed by Austria. The Czechs of Bohemia rebelled, but were crushed in the Battle of the White Mountain in 1620, nor did they recover their national consciousness till after nearly two hundred years of devastating tyranny. The Magyars of Hungary, long preyed on and weakened by the Turks, rose repeatedly and sometimes successfully to a certain extent against their Habsburg masters and Germanization; at other times they supported the Habsburgs, and were not always rewarded for their pains; their devotion to Maria Theresa did not prevent her son Joseph II from fresh and determined efforts to Germanize them.

With the French Revolution, the pivotal period of the modern era, the principle of Nationality, of which there had been some previous manifestations, made itself felt more and more as a great political force in Europe. In the Habsburg Empire was seen a national awakening, a renaissance of the Magyars, the Czechs, the Slovaks, and the Southern Slavs, or Yugoslavs, generally. But this uprising of national spirit and sentiment was premature, and was followed by an intense reaction under the long and heavy régime of Metternich. The Nationalities were sternly repressed—even the German Nationality suffered under absolutist rule, to which an end was put only by the Revolutions of 1848–49. The principle of Nationality had been scotched, not killed. For a time it became so active again that the Habsburg Empire appeared to be on the verge of dissolution, but it was fated to last seventy years longer.

Struggle against Absolutism

When Revolution broke out in Paris early in 1848, it had a violent repercussion throughout Austria-Hungary. In Vienna a dangerous riot caused the retirement of Metternich and compelled the Emperor, Ferdinand V, to call a Constituent Assembly to abolish absolutism, an object sought, at any rate at first, by Germans and Czechs in common. Even more serious was the Revolution of which Budapest was the scene, and soon all Hungary was aflame under Kossuth; her aim was independence, and she nearly achieved it. In Bohemia and Croatia strong revolutionary movements looking towards securing autonomy were on foot. Lombardy and Venice fell away. The Nationalities were up! At the outset of the struggle the Emperor, a weakling who had trusted entirely to Metternich, was forced to yield on all sides. On April 8 he issued the Charter which recognized the right of Bohemia to independence.

Two months later a Pan-Slav Congress, summoned by the Czechs and attended by Czechoslovaks, Yugoslavs, Poles, and Ukrainians, was held in Prague under the presidency of Palacky, the foremost historian of Bohemia and the Czech people. This congress, met in such circumstances, was for ever memorable as a coming together of the Nationalities, and if it achieved little or nothing at the moment, marked a tendency and suggested the trend of events in the future.

Palacky was the man who uttered the famous saying, "If Austria had not existed it would have been necessary to invent her." The words, important from such a source, were often quoted as an argument against the breaking up of the Habsburg Empire. Attempts were made by fervid partisans of his to explain them away, but their meaning was perfectly plain, and the truth was simply that he was mistaken. A view different from his was expressed by Havlicek, another prominent Czech leader, who, when inviting the Poles to participate in the pan-Slav Congress, wrote: "An understanding between us Czechoslovaks and Poles would be to our advantage, especially under present circumstances, when everything, even the break-up of Austria, may be anticipated. I am sure that if the Government continues its policy, Austria will fall to pieces before next winter and the Czechs are not going to save her. The Czechoslovaks, Poles, and Yugoslavs, united politically and supporting each other, will surely sooner or later attain their object, which is to procure full independence, national unity, and political liberty." In the congress the dismemberment of Austria was openly advocated by Bakunin, the Russian revolutionary. On June 12 a manifesto was published appealing to Europe for justice, for the restitution of a united Poland, and against the oppression of the Slavs by the Magyars and the Turks.

Austria, however, was not to fall to pieces just then. It was the congress itself that was broken up, for it came to a premature end because of riots in Prague, which led to the intervention of the military and its summary closing. But in those days the great majority of the Czechs looked for redress to a federalist Austria, and in the Austrian Parliament, 1848, their deputies stood for that idea as against German centralism. When after further troubles in Vienna the Parliament was transferred from that city to Kremsier, the Czechs, Yugoslavs, Ukrainians, and some Poles formed a block of 120 members. On December 2 Ferdinand abdicated and was succeeded by his nephew, Francis Joseph, who dissolved Parliament in March, 1849, and imposed a Constitution by imperial decree. Reaction soon triumphed and absolutism was in force once more.

In Hungary the conflict of the Magyars with the Habsburgs was much more severe and much longer protracted than the struggle against them in Austria. As was their wont, the Magyars fought bravely and well, inflicting several defeats on the Imperial armies. But the problem of Hungary was complicated by the attitude assumed towards her by the non-Magyar peoples in Croatia, Dalmatia, the Banat, and Transylvania, an attitude which was inspired by the same principle of Nationality as inspired herself, but which was not one of friendliness to her because of the oppression they endured at her hands. "We hoped," said the Croats to the Emperor, "that in the new world of liberty the Magyars would recognize the other races as their equals, but we have been disillusioned." And Jellachich, who had been made Ban, or Governor, of Croatia, demanded in his declaration of war on the Magyars "equality of rights for all the peoples and Nationalities living under the Hungarian Crown." Through his instrumentality the feudal Croatian Diet became a popular assembly, which proclaimed as one of its chief aims the turning of the Habsburg Empire into a federation on the Swiss model. In the Banat the Serbs rose to assert the rights of the non-Magyar races, as also did the Rumanians in Transylvania.

To overcome all this hostility and defeat at the same time the Imperial forces was no mean achievement, but the Magyars proved equal to it. In the spring of 1849 the measure of their success was shown when on April 14 they declared their country independent, pronounced the forfeiture of the Throne by the Habsburgs, and converted the Kingdom of Hungary into a Republic. But their triumph was short-lived. In his extremity Francis Joseph called on his brother autocrat, the Tsar Nicholas I, for help, and a large army from Russia, after heavy fighting, subjugated the Magyars, with the result of the renewal of absolutism in Hungary—as in Austria. Nor did the Yugoslavs receive any better treatment than before. The Nationalities were in evil case.

One thing, however, stood out above all. By calling in the Russians the Habsburg Empire demonstrated its inherent lack of strength and solidity to the world. From 1849 to 1859 a strenuous and sustained effort was put forth by Bach, an Austrian politician, to unify the State by the old methods of centralization, Germanization, and repression, but it failed. He had been active in promoting the revolutionary movement in 1848, but soon afterwards figured as a Government official, subsequently being, first, Minister of Justice and then Minister of the Interior. In the upshot his policy was even less successful than that of those who had previously attempted to unify the State, for it only the more estranged the Nationalities, particularly the Croats, from the dynasty. Increasing financial difficulties and, in 1859, the war with France and Sardinia, accompanied by the disasters of Magenta and Solferino, emphasized again the Empire's weakness. Some other policy had to be tried. Bach resigned, and a series of experiments in Constitution-making was essayed.

Absolutism appeared to be abolished in 1860 by the "October Diploma" purporting to grant a "lasting and irrevocable Constitution," but doing in reality nothing of the sort, for the Emperor replaced it early in 1861 by another known as the "February Constitution" setting up a so-called unitary Government, but patently designed to give the Germans control of the other Nationalities. The Reichsrat, or central Parliament, the Council of Ministers, and the new electoral system were so devised as to place the balance of power in German hands. The Czechs protested in vain. The Magyars and the Croats refused to recognize the Reichsrat from the first, and after a time the Czechs and the Poles ceased to attend it. Severe pressure was put on all of them, nor was it relaxed till 1865, when Francis Joseph, dismissing the German Ministry because it claimed to regulate the budget, dissolved the Reichsrat and suspended the Constitution. He had formed another plan.

The Ausgleich

The Emperor intimated that he had decided to "come to an understanding with the legal representatives of his people in the Eastern regions," and this was taken, rightly, to mean the introduction of a system of Dualism in which the Germans and the Magyars would be predominant. Little did he think that in making this statement he was pronouncing what was to seal the fate of the dynasty and the Empire alike. Not that no warnings were uttered. Palacky foretold that this would soon or late but inevitably unite all the Slavs against such a combination, and would lead to the wreck and ruin of the Habsburgs. "We Slavs were before Austria existed, and we shall be when she no longer exists," he said. Later he declared, "I myself give up all hope of a long preservation of the Austrian Empire, not because it was not desirable or had no mission to fulfil, but because it has permitted the Germans and the Magyars to grasp the reins of government and found on it their racial tyranny." In November, 1866, the Bohemian Diet asserted that Bohemia had the same right to independence as Hungary, and warned the Emperor of the danger of Dualism.

The majority of the Czechs still thought a federation possible, but the Emperor never seriously or for long entertained the idea. The Dual Monarchy, as it was widely designated, endured for upwards of half a century, for all the rest of the long life of Francis Joseph—there was that, whatever its worth, to be said for it; but if the Empire had been federalized, it would hardly have broken down as it did in 1918. Any doubt or hesitation the Emperor might have had disappeared after the loss of the war with Prussia in 1866 and the exclusion of Austria from the old German Confederation. The battle of Königgrätz, or Sadowa, gave the death-blow to the unitary State. Francis

Joseph determined to make very great concessions to the demands of the Magyars.

Beust, appointed Foreign Minister by the Emperor in the autumn of 1866, negotiated with Deak and Andrassy as representing Hungary, and he concluded an agreement with them in February, 1867. This resulted on December 21, of that year, in the Ausgleich, or Compromise, by which the Habsburg realm was divided into two States, the Austrian Empire and the Kingdom of Hungary, officially styled in international relations the Austro-Hungarian Monarchy or, more generally, the Dual Monarchy. According to the settlement the two States were independent of each other. Each had its own Constitution and legislative powers, with separate Departments for most branches of internal administration. But the closest political connexion was established between Austria and Hungary by their having the same Sovereign, who retained his dynastic rights, and by joint Ministries for Foreign, Army, and Naval Affairs, the necessary funds being contributed by the two States in common with fixed proportions for each. A customs and commercial union, the terms of which were renewable, subject to revision if required, every ten years, provided economic consolidation, supplemented, as it was, by the same coinage, measures, and weights, and bank of issue.

Externally the Habsburg Empire was the same, indivisible State as before, as was shown, most conspicuously perhaps, by its having one and the same Diplomatic and Consular Service all over the world. Internally, within the Empire, the political position of Hungary had been vastly improved, evidence of which was seen in the crowning, with much pomp and ceremony, at Budapest of Francis Joseph as "Apostolic King of Hungary." This could not but gall the Czechs. More than once he had promised to be crowned at Prague as King of Bohemia, but he never kept his word, though legally and historically Bohemia was a Kingdom in the same sense as Hungary, and had equal title to consideration. By 1867 Lombardy and Venetia had been lost, and in that year the Dual Monarchy, as regarded its Austrian part, consisted of

Upper and Lower Austria, Salzburg, Styria, Carinthia, Carniola, the Coastland, Tirol and Vorarlberg, Bohemia, Moravia, Silesia, Galicia, the Bukovina, and Dalmatia; and its Hungarian part was made up of Hungary (including Slovakia and Transylvania) and Croatia-Slavonia. The Ausgleich handed over the Slavs and Italians of Austria to the Germans and the Slavs and Rumanians of Hungary to the Magyars. As Nationalities, the Germans and Magyars, subject to the dynasty alone, were supreme over the others.

Reactions of the Nationalities

Dualism, represented statutorily by what came to be called the "December Constitution," exasperated the Czechs, and they refused to take part in either the Reichsrat or the Diet of Bohemia. In 1868 they issued a public declaration to the effect that they would never accept Dualism, and they laid stress on the right of Bohemia to independence. Great anti-Austrian demonstrations were made throughout the country. But Czech opposition was broken by the military—martial law was proclaimed in Prague, and repression was again general till 1870, when the shadows cast by the Franco-German conflict induced the Emperor to try to conciliate the Czechs. In September, 1871, Francis Joseph solemnly "recognized the rights of the Bohemian Kingdom," and in response the Czechs formulated a demand for the reinstitution of the "October Diploma" in the Austrian part of the Monarchy—only, however, to have it rejected, and military rule and repression reimposed.

The Poles in Galicia, where the political position was complicated by the problem of the Ukrainians, or Ruthenians, were divided in their views of the new régime. Some of their leaders advocated boycotting the Reichsrat and supported the federalist idea. A struggle for complete autonomy as against German centralism went on, in fact, for some years. But moderate opinion was less hostile, and became even friendly when it was apparent that the Polish vote in the Reichsrat, which was a necessity if the Vienna Government was to have a working majority in the House, could be used for gaining further concessions. Goluchowski, a Pole and the first Governor of Galicia during this period, succeeded in making that province so Polish in almost every way that Poles from Russian Poland, where everything was very different, went there in order to "breathe," as they said, "Polish air." On the other hand, the Ausgleich had an oppressive effect, not only on Bohemia, but also on Southern Austria, which was partly Italian and partly, but to a larger extent, Yugoslav—Slovene, Serb, and Croat.

When in 1867 Hungary was definitely, though with qualifications, installed as the other member of the Monarchy, the area assigned to her included Croatia-Slavonia. The relations between the Magyars and the Croats were far from cordial; the Croats, under their Ban, had had a certain amount of autonomy; and the project of a Yugoslav State was not new, but was anathema to the Magyars. Racki, the Croat historian, who had accompanied Strossmayer to Budapest when the negotiations were proceeding in 1866, said, "The idea of a Yugoslav State, arising in Croatia or in Bosnia or Serbia, would always find in Hungary a most determined foe." The Magyars, however, were careful to give the Croats a good deal of self-government with respect to educational, legal, and religious matters, but they reserved to themselves, to the Parliament in Budapest, where the Croats had only a small representation, the control of all financial, transport, fiscal, and commercial affairs. Naturally the Croat Nationalists strongly objected to such an arrangement, but they were overborne by Rauch, a new Ban appointed by the Magyars, who altered the electoral law in such a way as to reduce to an impotent minority the Nationalist representation in the Diet of Croatia. At Rauch's dictation a pliant majority made terms with Hungary, which were not at all favourable or even just to Croatia.

The Rumanians of Transylvania fared worse. Like Croatia-Slavonia, Transylvania had had a long, though not unbroken, connexion with Hungary. After various vicissitudes the province had been separated from Hungary in 1849 and had become an Austrian crownland; some ten years later it was given autonomy, with a Diet which had considerable powers.

In 1863 the Diet at Sibiu, or, in Magyar terminology, Nagyszeben, the German Hermannstadt, voted for separation from Hungary and union with Austria, but this decision was reversed by the Diet which met at Kluj or Kolozsvar, the German Klausenburg, in 1865, the Magyars being then in the majority. With the Ausgleich, Transylvania was deprived of all autonomy, and was fully incorporated with Hungary. The Rumanians in Transylvania, though much the most numerous element in its population, were thenceforward subjected to an intense process of Magyarization, despite their bitter opposition. These Rumanians, however, refused to be denationalized, and no doubt their determination was greatly stiffened by the fact that on the other side of the mountains their brothers in Wallachia and Moldavia had in 1860 united these principalities, after some forty years of semi-independence, in the one State of Rumania. There was a real, living Rumania to which these oppressed people could look with hope, as look they did.

In addition to the Serbo-Croat and Rumanian Nationalities, Hungary had a third Nationality in the Slovaks, who were Slavs. For centuries they had been separated politically from their kinsmen, the Czechs, nearest to them geographically as well as racially, and they spoke a language that differed only slightly from Czech. Though they were regarded with the utmost contempt by the Magyars, who had a familiar saying that "a Slovak was not a man," they were as heavily oppressed as the Transylvanian Rumanians, and were made to undergo Magyarization in an even harsher form. Bordering on Slovakia on the east was Sub-Carpathian Ruthenia, and it supplied the fourth of Hungary's subject Nationalities to be Magyarized in accordance with the general plan, but numerically it was small and otherwise insignificant.

Hungarian Action

In December, 1868, the Hungarian Parliament passed a measure known as the Law of Nationalities, which had some appearance of an endeavour to satisfy the "subject races." In its preamble it stated that all citizens of Hungary, no matter their Nationality, formed under the Constitution one nation, the "indivisible unitary Hungarian nation." But this statement was one which of course no Nationality other than that of the Magyars accepted. Yet the provisions of the law, which dealt with law courts, churches, schools, and public institutions, gave everyone the right to obtain instruction in his mother tongue up to the time when his university education began, and to use his mother tongue in his dealings with the State or his fellows. As Magyarization always had meant the enforced learning of the Magyar tongue upon those to whom it was not native, the law seemed to promise relief, but in practice this was not the case, for it was the law itself that was not enforced by the Magyars and it virtually became a dead letter.

As the great mass of the other Nationalities not only did not desire, but on the contrary strongly objected, to learn Magyar, the effect of the Magyar policy which permitted the law to be valueless was to deny any adequate education to them at all, and hence their illiteracy was appalling. The Magyars maintained that the Nationalities were unfitted by their backwardness to participate in political life, but they took care to keep them in that condition, from which submission to Magyarization was the only way out. The root of the trouble lay in the fact that the Magyars were in a minority in Hungary, and therefore sought to turn it into a majority by assimilating the other Nationalities or, failing in that, to hold them in thrall. "*Gardez vos hordes*," Beust had said to Andrassy, "*nous garderons les nôtres*." But in this matter the Magyars showed themselves to be more proficient than the Germans of Austria. They held the reins of political power entirely in their own hands by electoral laws ensuring their always having a large majority in the Hungarian Parliament, whereas in Austria the Germans in the Reichsrat had to rely on unstable coalitions with the Nationalities, who were played off against each other on the *Divide et impera* principle.

In Hungary the conservation of political power was immensely facilitated by the cohesion of the Magyar nobility and gentry as a ruling caste. Whether Conservative or Liberal by party label, they were one in their Nationalism. Passionately conscious of their own Nationality and most tenacious in fighting for it, they seemed to be absolutely incapable of understanding that what had fired their own courageous and resolute hearts worked like a flame in the hearts of the other Nationalities too. As Cavour said, the Magyars fought for their own liberty but would not allow liberty to others. In return for administrative and other concessions, which included a university teaching in their own language, the Czechs were induced in 1879 to abandon the passive resistance they had maintained for several years, and to attend the Reichsrat. Most of them still believed in a federalist solution of the problem of the Nationalities, at least in Austria, but they were in sympathy with the aspirations of the Slovaks and the other non-Magyar races of Hungary—the Yugoslavs, as well as the Rumanians, but more particularly the Yugoslavs. By that time the whole Yugoslav question had attained larger dimensions.

Occupation of Bosnia and Herzegovina

In the previous year, 1878, there occurred an event which was destined gravely to increase the difficulties that beset the Dual Monarchy, and led, together with other factors, to its destruction. This was the occupation by Austria-Hungary—it was a joint undertaking—of Bosnia and Herzegovina, two provinces of the decrepit Turkish Empire and almost entirely peopled by Yugoslavs, mostly Serbs, Moslem in some measure by religion, the Begs or chiefs with their retainers having gone over to Islam to save their property, while the bulk of the peasantry remained Christian-Orthodox. At first and for a term of years the occupation, attended, as it was presently, by a distinct improvement in the material conditions of the provinces, appeared to vouch for the increased strength and stability of the Habsburg Empire. But as time went on and the occupation was followed by annexation it became clear that Bosnia-Herzegovina had given added force to the Nationalities movement by deepening the menace that was implicit in the Yugoslav question.

From about the end of the eighteenth century the Turkish Empire had also felt the disruptive action of Nationalism. Though it was determined to limit, as far as was possible, the results of Russia's victory over Turkey, which had been crystallized in the Treaty of San Stefano, the Congress of Berlin, 1878, recognized the principle of Nationality in acknowledging Serbia, Montenegro, and Rumania as independent States, absolutely free from all political connexion with their former masters the Turks. A further extension of the principle was the setting up of Bulgaria as a self-governing principality. As against these recognitions of the principle there was the handing over to the Dual Monarchy of Bosnia and Herzegovina, both Yugoslav or rather Serb countries. The congress shut its eyes to the existence of the general Serb problem and its explosive potentialities; it quite missed the significant thing, which was that Serbia, from racial sympathy with the risings in Bosnia and Herzegovina in 1876, had not hesitated to declare war on Turkey; Serbia was beaten, and preserved from complete defeat only by Russian intervention, but the significance of her action remained as a guide for the future.

With all the other Great Powers on her side, Austria-Hungary thought she could afford to disregard the biggest Slav State, Russia, and to say nothing at all about Serbia, who was weak and could be handled fairly easily. The statesmen of Vienna advocated conciliatory measures, while those of Budapest characteristically preferred the use of violence. At that time neither imagined that the Yugoslav question embodied a genuine danger to both. "The troops are about to cross the frontier," ran the proclamation of the Dual Monarchy to the Bosniaks and the Herzegovinians. "They come as friends to end the evils that have disturbed not only your lands but the adjoining lands of the Empire for years. The Emperor could no longer look on and see violence reigning in the vicinity of his territories. At the Berlin Congress it was unanimously resolved that the Monarchy should restore order and well-being, and the Sultan has entrusted you to the care of the Empire." But it was not so very easy. Both Bosnia and Herzegovina offered a stout resistance in 1879 and again in 1882, and it was not till the summer of the latter year that the two provinces were pacified. There followed twenty years, however, of peace and progress, though political freedom was unknown.

Serbia and the Empire

Serbia, like Rumania, became a kingdom soon after the Berlin Congress, but her first king, Milan, was not exactly a heroic figure. His people were Russophil, but his whole policy was oriented towards Austria-Hungary. In 1881 his Foreign Minister signed a secret treaty with the Habsburg representative in Belgrade. By its second clause Serbia agreed not to tolerate political, religious, or other intrigues which, taking her territory as a point of departure, might be directed against the Monarchy, including Bosnia, Herzegovina, and the Sanjak of Novibazar; Austria-Hungary undertook similar obligations with respect to her and the dynasty. By the fourth clause Serbia agreed not to conclude any political treaty with another Government, without a previous understanding with Austria-Hungary, and not to admit into her territory a foreign armed force, regular or irregular, even as volunteers. Further, it was provided that if either State was threatened with war, or was at war, the other was to observe friendly neutrality, and where military cooperation was necessary the details were to be regulated by a military convention. It was also agreed that if circumstances were favourable, Serbia might expand to the south.

Milan added a personal declaration that he would not enter into any negotiation of a political nature between Serbia and a third State without obtaining the consent of Austria-Hungary. Serbia derived some advantage from this alliance, for when she was defeated by Bulgaria in 1885, the Dual Monarchy came to her rescue. All through his reign till his abdication in 1889 in favour of Alexander, his son, Milan was at least consistent in his attitude to the Habsburg Empire, whose friendship he believed to be essential for the security of his country. There were many Serbians, however, who were of a totally different opinion; they declared that friendship with the Habsburgs, coupled with their occupation of Bosnia and Herzegovina, made perfectly impossible the realization of the national ideal of a Great Serbia. This feeling steadily grew in intensity during the reign of Alexander, and when, after the shocking murder of this last of the Obrenovitch line and his wife, Peter Karageorgevitch succeeded to the throne in 1903, it was no more than natural that the new King should turn away from Austria-Hungary and look for support to her great rival in the Balkans —Russia, who, in fact, had long been trying for ascendancy at Belgrade, but who, every whit as little really interested in the application of the principle of Nationality, was bent on serving her own ends. Temporarily her attention was chiefly fixed, not on the Near East, but on the Far East, where she had embarked on a great adventure that in 1905 brought her into collision with the rising Japanese Empire and ended in disaster. This failure had the consequence of diverting the main stream of her policy to the Balkans again.

Professor Masaryk

In the Austrian Reichsrat the Czechs long championed the Yugoslav cause within the framework of the Habsburg Empire, but for the most part their thoughts dwelt on their own Nationality. When in 1879 they abandoned passive resistance and attended the sessions of Parliament in Vienna, they still maintained their hostility to Dualism, but their leaders were inclined to be too conservative and opportunist, and not sufficiently combative. These were styled the Old Czechs, and from them the Young Czechs split off in 1887, with a much more forward programme. The opportunity of the latter came in 1890, when the former concluded an agreement with the Germans, known as the Punctuations and unfavourable to Bohemia, which excited general resentment throughout the country, and occasioned the collapse of the Old Czech Party. The Young Czechs began a radical anti-German policy in the Reichsrat, and openly attacked the Triple Alliance in 1891, the Alliance of Germany, Austria-Hungary, and Italy, with the tacit support of Great Britain, which led to the counterbalancing Dual Alliance of Russia and France.

In that year a Professor in the new Czech University of Prague, by name Thomas Masaryk, was elected to the Reichsrat as a member of the Young Czech Party, in which he, Dr. Kramarsh, and Professor Kaizl, formed the "Realist" fraction, defined as "a philosophic effort for a regenerated democratic national policy." Fated to play a most distinguished rôle in the history of the Czechs and all unconscious then of it, he showed the way in which his mind was working by a sharp criticism of the Vienna Government, which was German, for its anti-Yugoslav action in Bosnia, and by so outspoken a defence of the right of Bohemia to State independence that a German deputy called him a traitor to Austria, a statement that was untrue, for Masaryk at that time was a federalist who accepted Palacky's famous epigram about the necessary existence of the Habsburg Empire. In 1892 some members of the Young Czech Party started a Radical movement which called itself Omladina, or Youth. It aimed at rousing the young generation against the Germans, and in 1893 organized demonstrations against the dynasty. Martial law was once more proclaimed in Prague; there were many arrests and sixty-eight of the prisoners were sentenced to long terms of imprisonment for high treason.

During the previous year the Rumanian Nationalists in Transylvania, despairing of getting any redress from the Magyars, addressed a Memorandum to the Emperor setting forth their grievances, including the inequitable working of the electoral laws of Hungary. The Rumanian students of the University of Bucarest published a pamphlet reciting the wrongs which the Rumanians of Transylvania were compelled to endure; when the students of Budapest University replied, they were answered by the Rumanian students of Transylvania, who bitterly denounced Magyar rule in the *Réplique*, which was published in Vienna. The result was that the executive members of the Rumanian National Party in Transylvania and the students who had written the *Réplique* received savage sentences, and the Rumanian National Party was dissolved by ministerial decree. All this did not pass unnoticed among the Czechs. In 1893 Masaryk, disgusted with the way in which things were going, resigned from the Reichsrat, to return to it, however, some years later. In 1900 he founded a democratic progressive party, but it did not attract many adherents.

Empire Strained

Meanwhile the fabric of the Dual Monarchy underwent periodically a severe straining when the arrangements for revision of the Ausgleich did not function smoothly. Difficulties arose in 1877 over financial matters, but were obviated by a compromise after heated discussion. In 1887 another crisis occurred, which also was resolved. Ten years afterwards, when the Ausgleich came up again for renewal, the differences between the two parts of the Empire were of the most serious nature. Badeni, a Pole of Galicia, was then Prime Minister of Austria-Hungary. In the hope of quelling, or at all events dominating, the conflicts of the Nationalities that scarcely ever ceased in the Reichsrat, he made an attempt at enfranchising the masses in Austria in 1896, but general and equal suffrage was not instituted till 1907. With a view to appeasing the Czechs, he issued in 1897 Language Ordinances, which put on a footing of equality the Czech and German languages in Bohemia and Moravia, but this step encountered the fiercest opposition from the Germans, supported by the Socialists, in the Reichsrat, in which tumultuous scenes took place, and obstruction was so determined that even any appearance of Parliamentary Government became impossible. Badeni resigned, and his decrees were rescinded. The Emperor thereupon handed the control of affairs to the Germans, to the intense indignation of the Czechs.

In Hungary also the appearance even of Constitutional Government broke down, not so much because of the other Nationalities, as from the violence of those Magyars who clamoured for the absolute independence of their country and abolition of the Ausgleich. No agreement was reached between Austria and Hungary in 1897 or 1898, and while this period of dislocation and strife continued the business of the Empire was carried on by imperial decrees in place of the ordinary methods. Finally a settlement was arrived at and the Ausgleich was renewed in 1899. The consent of the Magyars was obtained by commercial and financial concessions. An imperial decree sufficed for Austria; her peoples were not consulted, and all their protests were ignored. The Magyars had scored again.

In Hungary the Independence Party, whose objective was the dissolution of the tie with Austria, grew stronger, more insistent and intransigent in their demands on the Crown during the next few years. The tension was terrible from 1903 to 1906, and seemed to suggest a repetition of the revolution of 1848–49. The struggle centred in the persistent claim made by the Independents that Magyar must be the language of command for the Hungarian regiments of the Dual Monarchy. This claim, which the Emperor resisted as infringing his rights, was a popular one, as was manifested by the elections in 1905, when Tisza, who sided with Francis Joseph, was defeated, and the Independence Party, who had formed a coalition with other Parties, swept the country. A remarkable feature of the strained situation was the emergence of a Serbo-Croat Coalition composed of the Serbs and Croats of Dalmatia and Fiume, as well as of Croatia-Slavonia. To this coalition the Hungarian Coalition offered the bait of free elections in Croatia-Slavonia and the appointment of officials agreeable to the Serbo-Croats. The Hungarian Coalition took office in April, 1906, granted the promised free elections, but refused to appoint the officials desired.

But before the Hungarian Coalition took over the Government the crisis had passed—in a way that illustrated the mentality of the Magyar aristocracy. Tisza retired in June, 1905. Kristoffy, Minister of the Interior in the interim administration of Fejervary, proposed the establishment of universal suffrage by imperial decree. His notion of universal suffrage was to give the vote only to Hungarians who could read and write Magyar, and not to the Nationalities. This measure, however, would have increased an electorate well under a million to one of two and

PRESIDENT MASARYK

three-quarter millions, including large numbers of Magyar peasants. More than two million Slovaks, Serbo-Croats, and Rumanians were left out of the scheme. But it caused the liveliest apprehension in the coalition. The very existence of the privileged classes appeared to be threatened. Tisza himself deprecated universal suffrage. It was too much for the coalition, which straightway capitulated with respect to the language of command in the Army, though it did agree to extend the franchise. In Austria there had been for some time a Socialist agitation for universal suffrage, and in 1907 the Emperor yielded to it, but for him it was merely a political move in the dynastic game, another way of enabling him to manœuvre the Nationalities, across the principle of which Socialism completely cut.

After the introduction of universal suffrage the Reichsrat consisted of 259 Slav deputies, of whom 108 were Czechs, and 257 non-Slav deputies. All the Nationalities were split up into small groups; thus, of the Czechs the Social Democrats outnumbered the Young Czechs, and the Agrarians were still more numerous; the Germans, too, were divided. But, with the annexation of Bosnia and Herzegovina by Austria-Hungary in 1908, the question of the Nationalities—the racial question—came to the front once more and resumed its dominance as *the* problem of the Habsburg Empire. Both the Germans of Austria and the Magyars of Hungary approved of the annexation. The Czechs opposed it, as did most of the other Slavs of the Dual Monarchy, with the exception of the Poles, who saw in it a blow at hated Russia. Neither they nor anyone else could foresee that it was a prelude to mighty and far-reaching events.

Bosnia-Herzegovina Annexed

Under the Emperor, Aehrenthal had directed the foreign policy of Austria-Hungary from 1906, and it was he who engineered the annexation of Bosnia and Herzegovina, in defiance of the Treaty of Berlin, which provided for no more than the occupation and administration of the provinces by the Dual Monarchy, the Sultan remaining their suzerain. Though no one supposed that his suzerainty was other than nominal, or that these territories would ever be restored to Turkey, the announcement of the annexation on October 6, 1908, created a storm throughout all Europe, a storm which later was seen to be the precursor of the far greater storm, the cataclysm that shook the world. The two groups of Great Powers that fought the World War openly arrayed themselves against each other; Germany and Austria-Hungary on one side, and Great Britain, France, and Russia on the other. With the Central Powers, Italy was joined in the Triple Alliance, but she was ever an uncertain factor. The Triple Entente was newer and less tried, for the Anglo-Russian Entente had been made only in 1907, three years after the Anglo-French Entente. At first Germany was inclined to disapprove of the annexation, but soon came into line with the Dual Monarchy.

The question was international, and as such had little to do with the question of the Nationalities, though it did eventually contribute materially to the success in Austria-Hungary of the liberating principle of Nationality. Great Britain took exception to the annexation without the consent of the contracting Powers as a breach of an international treaty and therefore contrary to international law. Despite the Triple Alliance, the King of Italy described the annexation as a stab at the Berlin Treaty, though Titoni had spoken in favour of it. Russia was angry; it did not transpire till later that her Minister Isvolsky had been outplayed by Aehrenthal in a game of their sinister diplomacy, but this defeat had made her all the more angry. Relations between the Dual Monarchy and Russia became so tense that both States began mobilization secretly. France, though not eager for war, stood by Russia. Bulgaria, who had proclaimed her independence and whose Prince had assumed the title of King on October 5—the day before the annexation—took sides against Austria-Hungary. In Turkey, where the Young Turk movement was making its influence increasingly felt, there was hostility to the Habsburg Empire, one sign of which was a boycott of all Austro-Hungarian goods; but Aehrenthal succeeded in squaring the Turks by agreeing to pay an indemnity and by other concessions.

It was on and in Serbia that the annexation had the most serious repercussion, as was to be expected. And it was here that the principle of Nationality came in, for the Serbians rose as one man to protest against the passing into the Habsburg hands permanently of Bosnia and Herzegovina, lands peopled by Serbs like their own land. Further, with the backing of the Western Powers and Russia, they lodged a definite protest against the annexation, demanded autonomy for these territories under the guarantee of the Great Powers and for themselves an outlet to the sea—the Adriatic—with a strip connecting the port with their country.

From the international point of view, Serbia was highly important as the natural gateway from Europe to the East by way of Constantinople and Asia Minor—one of the immemorial highways of the world. It was across Serbia, through Belgrade, that the pan-Germans had drawn the line of the Berlin–Baghdad Railway—with its large series of ulterior implications, which had alarmed Great Britain, France, and Russia, and which had conduced to an appreciable extent to the formation of the Triple Entente. Serbia was thus a meeting-point of international interests, with their inevitable cross-currents, their ceaseless ebb and flow. With the unification of the German Empire and of Italy, the path of expansion for Austria-Hungary, if such a path was open to her, was in South-Eastern Europe; this meant that Serbia might, and in fact did, block the road. Apart from Austria-Hungary, the Great Powers were not concerned in the pan-Serbian aspect of the question, which affected her policy so profoundly and dominated that of Serbia.

After the accession to the Serbian throne of Peter Karageorgevitch and the orientation of Serbia to Russia, the attitude of the Dual Monarchy became more and more hostile to the small State, whose existence it had been willing to tolerate so long as this involved dependence on Vienna and Budapest under an appearance of independence. But the Serbians wanted a real independence, not only for their own sake, but for the sake of Great Serbia, the prospective unified State of all the

Serbs of which Belgrade dreamed and for which it incessantly agitated and schemed. Regarding all this as an insolent challenge, Austria-Hungary had met it by raising a customs barrier against Serbian exports, the largest of which consisted of pigs, and there followed what was known as the Pig War, 1905–07, which hurt Serbia but was not without benefit to her, as it made her seek and find new markets for her live stock and grain. Such a struggle could not but embitter further the relations of the two countries to each other; the Austro-Hungarians were angry because of their failure to coerce the Serbians, and the Serbians were enraged because the Austro-Hungarians had struck what they thought must be a fatal blow to the whole economic life of Serbia. Nor would the feelings of the Serbians be rendered less keen by the knowledge of the passing in Hungary of the Apponyi Laws in 1907 with the design of curbing the Nationalities—Serb, Croat, Slovak, and Rumanian—and promoting their Magyarization. The position was not and could not be improved by the manner in which the crisis of 1908 over the annexation was solved.

Serbia armed, but she found no support from Russia other than diplomatic; exhausted by her war with Japan, Russia was unable to face so soon another long conflict. Austria-Hungary reinforced her troops in the south-east of the Monarchy, and Germany stood firmly by her side. The odds were too great, and though the Serbians hated giving in to the Habsburg bully, prudence prevailed. On March 31, 1909, Serbia presented a Note at Vienna which declared that she had not suffered any injury to her rights through the annexation, and that, changing her attitude to the Dual Monarchy, she would maintain good neighbourly relations with it. Ostensibly Serbia yielded at the behest of the Great Powers, but it was all a diplomatic camouflage, the plain truth being that she had been browbeaten into submission, while Russia had been humiliated, a thing which she neither forgot nor forgave. The international situation remained unaltered; the curtain had been rung down on the first act of the drama, and that was all.

A High Treason Trial

In 1909 the Habsburg Empire seemed to have attained a new height of power, but if it was flushed with triumph there were unmistakable flaws in its splendour. The annexation of Bosnia and Herzegovina, which it proceeded to organize as one province with a very restricted autonomy, irretrievably embroiled it in the Balkans; and whether it was the conscious or unconscious tool of pan-German aims in the Near and Middle East, that it would be used by Germany in any way that suited her best in pursuance of the *Drang nach Osten* or *Drang nach Suden*, as in this case, was inevitable. Besides, the question of the Nationalities continued to be for Austria-Hungary as intractable and as devastating a problem as ever. This was thrown into high relief by two trials, one in 1909 at Zagreb, then officially called Agram, and the other in Vienna in 1910. Both trials became famous and through them the names of some prominent Slav leaders were well known throughout Europe—that of Masaryk most of all.

In August, 1908, fifty-three Serbs of Croatia-Slavonia were imprisoned at Zagreb for high treason, the charge being that they were members of a pan-Serb revolutionary organization, the "Slovenski Yug," or the South Slav, with headquarters at Belgrade. These men had been denounced by an Austro-Hungarian *agent provocateur* called Nastitch in a pamphlet published at Budapest. Their trial began on March 3, 1909, and lasted for seven months. The proceedings were so scandalous as to excite unfavourable criticism in other countries; they were vigorously assailed by Masaryk—he had re-entered the Reichsrat in 1907—and pungently commented on by him in the Austrian Parliament in May, 1909. Nastitch was the chief witness for the prosecution, but his testimony was discredited; in spite of this, the accused were sentenced to long terms of imprisonment, which were evidently justified so little that after a short time the men were set free. The real object of the trial had been to drive a wedge between the Serbs and the Croats in order to break up the Serbo-Croat Coalition founded in

1905, but the Croats remained true to the Serbs, supported them throughout the trial, and provided for the families of the poorer prisoners. The efforts of the Austro-Hungarian authorities not only completely failed in this matter, but also led to an exposure of the curious judicial methods of the Habsburg Empire.

A second and worse exposure followed hard on the first. In December, 1909, the Serbo-Croat Coalition brought in Vienna a libel action against Dr. Friedjung, the Austrian historian, and others, who had accused the coalition of being in the pay of Serbia on the strength of official documents, some of which had been supplied by the Austro-Hungarian Ministry of Foreign Affairs and the rest had come from the Archduke Francis Ferdinand, the Heir Presumptive to the throne. The Archduke earlier in his career had played with the idea of a federalized Austria-Hungary and of replacing Dualism by Trialism—of creating a Yugoslav State within the Empire as a counterpoise to the States of Austria and Hungary—but had abandoned it as being only too likely to encourage agitation in Serbia, and strengthen pan-Serbism. In the trial it was proved that all the documents were forgeries, the grossness of which was demonstrated by Masaryk, who had come to attend the proceedings, as did many others owing to the attention that had been drawn to the Zagreb affair. Masaryk did more, for he went to Belgrade to get the originals of the forgeries, procured them, and as a result publicly accused Aehrenthal of being privy to their publication and deeply implicated in the campaign against the coalition. Though thus discredited, the Minister did not resign, but all Europe knew what had happened.

One of the chief figures in both affairs was Supilo, who, with Trumbitch and other Nationality leaders, had formed the coalition in 1905; they were to be heard of again in the final struggle. But it was Masaryk who stood foremost. He had long been recognized as a great Slav prophet, teacher, and guide, as a man who understood and loved the Yugoslavs. The Zagreb and Friedjung trials placed him on a pedestal in their regard from which nothing could ever cast him down. Later this was to be most influential in helping to bring about the fall of the Habsburg Empire, in the redistribution of its parts among the Nationalities, and in the formation of the Little Entente.

THE BALKAN WARS

Hardly were these two trials over and had gone on the record when there occurred the first of a series of events of the utmost importance internationally. In July, 1911, Germany dispatched a cruiser to Agadir in southern Morocco, at once a threat to France and a challenge to the Triple Entente, which was answered by a fighting speech from Lloyd George that left no doubt of how Great Britain regarded the action of the German Emperor and of the cleavage between the Great Powers. Two months later the Italian-Turkish War opened with the sudden descent of Italian forces on Tripoli. One consequence of this conflict was the liberation of Albania, whose tribes had risen in revolt on attempts of the Young Turks to Turkify them; with war with Italy on her hands, Turkey came to terms with the brave mountaineers, and all unwilling illustrated the triumph of the principle of Nationality. In October, 1912, the Turks, after losing Tripoli, the last of their old African conquests, and the Dodecanese Islands, were compelled to make peace with the Italians, in presence of the alliance of Bulgaria, Greece, Serbia, and Montenegro, and the war it declared on them in that month. Two "Balkan" wars ensued.

In the First Balkan War the Turks were beaten in several great battles by the allies, whose success had scarcely been regarded as probable by the rest of Europe, though the Bulgarians had been expected to give a good account of themselves. The victories of the Serbians were particularly distasteful to Austria-Hungary, who had expected them to be smashed by the Turks with little difficulty; indeed, in this anticipation the Dual Monarchy had moved troops into Bosnia-Herzegovina and had ordered a part mobilization in Croatia-Slavonia and southern Hungary in order to protect, as it pretended, Serbia, by a military occupation, from the Turks in the event of her defeat. That the Serbian army had routed their enemy at Kumanovo and Monastir and had been able to send 50,000 men to support the Bulgarians in the siege of Adrianople was gall and bitterness alike to Vienna and Budapest: it was plain, at any rate, that the Serbians were no longer to be despised as soldiers; some comfort, however, was derived from the remarkable successes in the field of the Bulgarians, who were not believed to be true friends of Serbia, and who therefore might be made to serve the turn of the Habsburgs later, but even this sorry satisfaction was to be denied them, for despite their intrigues and much to their confusion, it was Serbia, not Bulgaria, that won the Second Balkan War.

Before the Serbians vindicated their superiority over the Bulgarians in the Balkans, various things occurred that showed clearly the bent of Austria-Hungary was for war on Serbia, and indicated again the alignment of the Great Powers. By the spring of 1913 the Dual Monarchy had mobilized a million men, vastly increased its artillery, and spent £40,000,000 on military preparation generally. It tried to get Italy to join in driving the Serbians and Montenegrins out of Albania, but in this it was disappointed. A second attempt to obtain Italian participation, while the Second Balkan War was going on, likewise came to naught. When the Balkan allies were disputing over the allocation of territory in Macedonia, Austria-Hungary signed a secret convention with Bulgaria, the effect of which was seen when the Bulgarians attacked the Serbians without warning and started the Second Balkan War in July, 1913.

All through this time it looked as if the Monarchy might at any moment begin hostilities. An ultimatum was, in fact, in course of preparation for submission, first to Germany, when the threatening attitude of Russia, determined not to accept another humiliation, counselled caution, and as Germany intimated that she was not ready, the ultimatum got no farther. Great Britain and France, anxious to keep the conflict from spreading, enjoined moderation on Serbia, who withdrew her troops, though very reluctantly, from Albania; this permitted Austria-Hungary to "save her face," as it was a gain for her, but it also militated against her declaring war. On August 9, 1913, the Peace of Bucarest terminated the fighting in the Balkans without her intervention, but with the definite aggrandizement of Serbia and a great strengthening of her prestige, and a corresponding decline in the prestige of the Dual Monarchy, in South-Eastern Europe. These results had a direct and an enormous bearing on the question of the Nationalities. The victory of Serbia was welcomed in Croatia-Slavonia, whose autonomy had been autocratically suspended two years before. All the Slavs of the Empire were delighted with the Serbian success, which some of them had helped to secure by enlisting in the Serbian army.

It was natural that the idea of a Great Serbia should grow and swell, and that the Germans of Austria and the Magyars of Hungary should be more and more enraged. Their anger was intensified by the agitation, continuous and increasing throughout this period, in Rumania in favour of the liberation of the Transylvanian Rumanians from the oppression under which they groaned. Afraid of an alliance of Serbia and Rumania directed against herself, Austria-Hungary sought to ensure Rumania's adhesion to the Triple Alliance; King Carol was willing enough, but the bulk of his people fastened their eyes on the Triple Entente and made his position difficult. The whole situation in the Balkans was intolerable for the Monarchy. In a Memorandum for Germany, Berchtold, the successor of Aehrenthal, who had died in February, 1912, urged that every effort should be made to form a new Balkan League under the leadership of the Central Powers for the suppression of Serbia as a political power. But before this paper was sent to Berlin the Archduke Francis Ferdinand and his consort were murdered in Sarajevo—a detestable crime only too much in keeping with the tragedies that stained the Balkans. This occurred on June 28, 1914. Exactly one month later Austria-Hungary declared war on Serbia.

World War Begins

Nothing else could be expected than that the Dual Monarchy, unless absolutely prevented from doing so, would seize the opportunity for a final settlement with Serbia, by force of arms if other means failed. Though there was not sufficient proof, Serbia was held to be guilty of the crime of Sarajevo. What Francis Joseph thought was expressed in a letter to the German Emperor in which he said the murder of his nephew was the direct outcome of the Russian and Serbian pan-Slav agitation, which aimed at weakening the Triple Alliance and disrupting the Empire. Though it might not be possible, he continued, to prove the complicity of the Serbian Government, there could be no doubt that its policy, the object of which was the union of all Yugoslavs under the Serbian flag, encouraged such crimes, while at the same time endangering the Habsburg Empire. His efforts, he added, must be concentrated on isolating Serbia and reducing her territory. He concluded by voicing his conviction that an agreement between Serbia and Austria-Hungary was impossible, and that peace was out of the question in Europe so long as Belgrade, the centre of criminal agitation, went unpunished. The German Emperor, in reply, assured Francis Joseph of his full support. A strong, but not too strong, Habsburg Empire was what Germany required for her plans, which would be thwarted by a Great Serbia. "Our own interests," the German White Book stated, "were menaced by the Serb agitation."

Relying on German assistance, Berchtold said in the Council of Ministers on July 7 that the time had come for a military reckoning with Serbia, and all agreed with him, except Tisza, the Hungarian Prime Minister, who favoured diplomatic negotiations and terms not impossible of acceptance; in a subsequent statement he stressed his fear of international complications. A week later it was decided to send an ultimatum to Serbia; Tisza concurred, but recommended making a declaration that, apart from rectifications of the frontier, Austria-Hungary would take no territory from Serbia, but

Berchtold maintained that Serbia must be made smaller. A Note was prepared and after some modification was presented to Serbia on July 23, with a time limit of forty-eight hours. The burden of it was that since the Great Serbia movement against the Monarchy had continued for years with the object of separating from it certain parts, and since the Serbian Government, contrary to its declaration in 1909, had not suppressed but had encouraged this agitation, the Austro-Hungarian Government, in order to end this state of affairs, demanded the condemnation of the movement and the suppression of all pan-Serb associations and propaganda, the dismissal of the officials and teachers compromised, and the participation of Austro-Hungarian officials in the steps which the Serbian Government must undertake to terminate the whole business.

Negotiations began at once between the Triple Alliance and the Triple Entente for an extension of the short time limit, but the Dual Monarchy refused a prolongation. On July 25 Serbia replied to the ultimatum by accepting the majority of its demands, but made reservations respecting Austro-Hungarian participation and the dismissal of officials. This answer was not deemed satisfactory, diplomatic relations were broken off, and on July 28 Austria-Hungary declared war on Serbia. Ineffective attempts to localize the conflict were succeeded by the breaking out of the World War, the Great Powers being grouped against each other as had been anticipated, but this did not obscure the truth that the immediate origin of the long and terrible struggle which ensued was found in the question of the Nationalities, though the relevancy of the question to the issue was not clearly, if at all, understood in some quarters, as, for example, in Great Britain and France, where everyone thought of Austria-Hungary as a durable State and Great Power, despite internal dissensions—their significance was not realized. Yet the drums of war had hardly begun to beat when above their sound was heard the call of the combatants to as typical a Nationality as any in the manifestos of Austria and Germany, as well as Russia, addressed to the Poles.

CHAPTER II

HABSBURG EMPIRE DISSOLVES

1914–1918

When the Dual Monarchy declared war on Serbia, its action was enthusiastically endorsed by its Germans and Magyars; its Poles viewed it with mixed feelings, for though they abhorred Russia they could not forget that Austria-Hungary was fighting by the side of Germany, another oppressor of their countrymen; the response of the other Nationalities was hostile and immediate, if not at first profoundly impressive. From the outset it was evident that the struggle was not popular among the Yugoslavs of the Empire or among the Czechs, for they did not conceal their sympathy for the Serbians. Vienna said that mobilization had proceeded smoothly, but this was not true; on leaving Prague, Czech soldiers expressed themselves bitterly at the prospect of having to support Austria.

In Paris, Czechs hauled down the Austro-Hungarian flag at the Embassy; in Russia, Czechs drew up a scheme for a Czech Legion, which they submitted to the Tsar, and before the close of August, 1914, they formed the *Druzhina* or League of Czechs in Russia. In Croatia the Croats, whose hatred of the Magyars had not diminished while Rauch continued to be their Ban, lost no opportunity of manifesting their antagonism and of obstructing, in every way possible, the operations of the Imperial troops. After the first Austrian invasion of Serbia had come to its ignominious close, the Serbians and Montenegrins invaded Bosnia, but they were forced back from before Sarajevo; their retirement was the signal for severe reprisals among the Bosniaks by the Austro-Hungarian Command, on the plea that they had succoured the enemy, as no doubt was the case, for they, too, were Serbs. Throughout the area of the War, where the armies of the Monarchy were engaged, there was to be observed a widespread movement of opposition in the shape of insubordination and desertion on the part of the Slav regiments—a movement which grew mightily as the War went on.

All these things were signs and portents, not wonders; without control or direction the spirit thus shown could not do much to affect the course of the conflict in general, and had the serious disadvantage of providing easy opportunities for severe retaliatory measures, the result being a reign of terror in Bohemia and elsewhere, with imprisonments and many executions. The Czechs and the Yugoslavs needed leaders at home and abroad, particularly abroad, where their cause was little known, to coordinate and make the most of these scattered efforts, often blind and blundering and therefore of scant effect. Leaders presented themselves, notably in foreign lands, where they were wanted most and could render the greatest service. In their own country there also were leaders, but they had to move warily and secretly in presence of the terror. Armed revolution on any scale was impossible because of the overwhelming strength locally of the Imperial troops, who rigorously enforced martial law. In Austria open political action was out of the question as the Reichsrat was kept closed, nor was it convoked again till the end of May, 1917. It was the campaign of the Nationalities' leaders abroad that told more and more effectively against the Dual Monarchy.

Campaign Abroad of the Nationalities

This campaign was started early in August, 1914, in Italy by some Yugoslavs, including a few members of the Austrian or Hungarian Parliaments and Diets, with Trumbitch at their head. Other prominent Yugoslavs there were Popovitch, Mestrovitch, Goritchar, and Zhupanitch. Rome was their headquarters, and there the Serbian Legation provided them with a natural and convenient centre. All had the same programme—the unification of the Yugoslav or South Slav race—but all were not of one mind regarding the manner in which it was to be worked out. There was doubt of the exact place to be held by Serbia in or to the future State of Yugoslavia;

some spoke of a Great Croatia, others of a Great Serbia. But it was of hopeful augury for a real unity of the Southern Slavs that the Serbian Government at Nish, to which it had retired from Belgrade, proclaimed in the Skupshtina or Parliament in November, 1914, the carrying on of the War until "we have delivered and united all our brothers who are not yet free, Serbs, Croats, and Slovenes." When Tisza praised the Croat troops of the Dual Monarchy for their "true-hearted bravery in the fight for the common Fatherland," the Yugoslavs in Rome published in the chief Italian newspaper a protest by "The Croatian Committee," no names being signed, to preclude reprisals at home.

Succeeding in escaping from Prague, Masaryk was in Rome in December. Of all the Slavs of the world, he was the most acceptable to the Yugoslavs, not only because of his courageous and successful action in the Zagreb, or Agram, and Friedjung trials, but also because of his profound understanding and deep sympathy. He let it be known that he thought the unity of all the Yugoslavs could best be achieved under the aegis of Serbia. As he himself said, "The heroic struggle of Serbia created a living programme for all the Southern Slavs." Masaryk was in Rome for only a few days, but he spent them profitably with his Yugoslav friends and in examining the position of Italy with respect to the War, his conclusion being that the Italians would either remain neutral or, if they did not do so, they would not side with Austria-Hungary. In January, 1915, he went to Switzerland, where he began systematic work for the liberation alike of Czechs and Yugoslavs, in accordance with plans he had already drawn up in collaboration with Benesh, Shvehla, and others in Prague, plans which could be realized only by the dissolution of the Habsburg Empire and the substitution for it of a series of States on the basis of Nationality, free and independent as units, like the Czechoslovakia of his hopes, or as parts of other States, also free and independent, such as the Yugoslavia to whose existence he looked forward, on the same basis. In any case, the whole history of his country, as he saw it, placed the Czechs on the side of the Allies, who, in his view, were fighting the battle of humanity against oppression.

Masaryk at Work

There were some colonies of Czechs in Switzerland, and from Geneva, where Masaryk settled awhile, a secret messenger service was soon established which kept him in touch with Prague, bringing him news of all that was happening in Austria-Hungary, and telling his people there of the progress of the campaign for their liberation. The first effort was to create a single organization for the Czechs in all the Allied countries, and by the summer of 1915 it was practically achieved. In Paris papers such as *L'Indépendance Tchèque* were published and a National Council of Czech Colonies was formed; in May Dennis began the issue of the periodical *La Nation Tchèque*, the influence of which was considerable. In Petrograd and Kieff papers were published advocating the Czech cause. The first Congress of the delegates of Czechoslovak Societies in Russia was held at Moscow, and a General Association founded. In the United States, where both Czechs and Slovaks had journals of their own before the War, a Congress of the "Czech National Association in America" met at Cleveland and made a centre for common work. England, too, had Czechoslovak organizations.

In April Masaryk, who was recognized everywhere as leader, spent some time in London as well as in Paris. For Sir Edward Grey, afterwards Lord Grey, the British Foreign Secretary, he wrote a memorandum, vindicating the historical right of the Czechs to independence and the movement that was being carried on against the Dual Monarchy, and deprecating the allotment of a large part of Dalmatia to Italy, as he had heard was proposed by the Allies. Czech cooperation with the Yugoslavs had continued, for many of their prominent men, Supilo among them, visited Geneva and discussed the situation; the division of opinion respecting what Yugoslavia was precisely to be still persisted, though all alike spoke of national unity. Then came the signing of the Treaty of London on April 26,

1915, concluded after lengthy negotiations between the Triple Entente and Italy, and allotting with other territory about half of Dalmatia to Italy—causing thereby indignation and excitement among the Yugoslavs. The Yugoslav Committee transferred its headquarters from Rome to London in May, and issued a statement to the effect that Serbia and Montenegro were not engaged in a war of conquest, but of defence and liberation. "We are fighting," declared the committee, "to liberate our people from a foreign yoke and to unite them in one free nation. To perpetuate the separation of these territories by leaving them under the Austro-Hungarian domination, or another foreign domination, would be a flagrant violation of our ethnographic, geographic, and economic unity; our people would, without any doubt, oppose to it an energetic and justified resistance."

But the War at the moment was far from being won; the position of the Allies in the field was not favourable; and Masaryk thought that in the circumstances the moral, political, and military significance of Italy coming out against Austria-Hungary—Italy did not declare war on Germany till August of the following year—was of overriding importance. German and Austro-Hungarian propaganda was strong in Switzerland, and of course painted the successes of the Central Powers in the most brilliant colours. The action of Italy in separating herself from the Triple Alliance and changing over to the Triple Entente at this juncture appeared to be a vital matter, and certainly was a great discouragement to enemy propaganda.

Effect of Russia's Collapse

Perhaps the most striking feature in 1915 of the War was the defeat of Russia. Warsaw and Vilna fell, and all Russian Poland was occupied in the course of the summer by the Central Powers. How deplorable was the situation was indicated when the Tsar, Nicholas II, who had no particular competence for anything, took over the supreme command in person. The failure of Russia had a great effect on the Czechs and the Yugoslavs, who had regarded her as the Big Slav

DR. TRUMBITCH

Protector of all the smaller Slav peoples. Many Czechs had believed that the Tsar, with his mighty armies, would set Bohemia free, though why the replacing over them of one absolutist sovereign by another was to bring it about was not at all clear; in truth they saw Russia through a golden but obscuring haze.

Masaryk knew Tsarist Russia and had disclosed in his book, *The Spirit of Russia*, her true character years before the War, but he had made little impression on the Czech Russophils at the time; later his knowledge of Russia, and the view he had consistently taken of her, were to stand him in good stead and to be of immense service to the cause of his country and its people; even in 1915 they remembered what he had said about Russia being a rotten prop on which to lean, and they turned their thoughts away from her, with the idea of depending more on their own efforts. In Yugoslavia the attitude towards Russia was determined largely by religious or rather Church considerations—the Orthodox Slavs looked to Russia, but the Roman Catholic Slavs did not. And when the Tsar talked of his "Slav Brethren," he was referring to the Orthodox Slavs, as, for instance, those of Serbia; he had no comprehensive policy for the Yugoslavs at all. The supreme aim of Russia was the possession of Constantinople, and it recked little of the Catholic Yugoslavs or Czechs; all the Slav States were to serve the purpose of Holy Russia in her great "mission." In fact, it was very plain that Russia would do nothing for the Nationalities of Austria-Hungary from the first, for Nationality was not a principle she had ever encouraged, and 1915 made it plainer still.

But it was on the Poles that the defeat of Russia had the most remarkable effect. By the conquest of Russian Poland by the Germans and the reoccupation of Galicia by the Austrians, the territories of Old Poland were united in a sense once more, but subject to the will of the Central Powers, which was not in the least agreeable to the Russian Poles. The political energies of the Poles were divided. Strange as it seemed, many Poles supported Russia under the impression that she would grant, through the influence of her Western Allies, self-government to a unified Poland. Other Poles held to the idea of a united Poland which would form a part of the Habsburg Empire on terms similar to those that joined Hungary to Austria.

In brief, there was a dissipation of Polish activity, centres of the conflicting elements being established in Petrograd, Moscow, Kieff, Paris, and London on the one hand, and in Warsaw, Cracow, Berlin, and Vienna on the other. Pilsudski's legions fought for Austria-Hungary, other Polish legionaries fought for Russia, and not a few Poles enlisted in the French armies. But none of them then envisaged the free, independent Poland, with the full expression of her Nationality, that was to come. As things were, some Poles worked for the Allies, others for the Central Powers, but all hoped for some resuscitation of their national life, some sort of national reunion. This they found in the following year was not going to be accorded to them by the Central Powers, who, when they proclaimed an independent Poland on November 5, 1916, created it out of Russian Poland only, and placed it in a federative union with themselves, which meant being under Germany, for, of course, she was far stronger than Austria-Hungary.

"The Problem of Small Nations"

It was on November 14, 1915, that Masaryk issued a public declaration of hostility to Austria, of open war on the part of the Czechs. This manifesto was signed by "The Czech Committee Abroad" and by representatives of all the Czech foreign colonies. Masaryk stated that it was published because of the excitement in these colonies and of their fears lest he should fail to make a public stand, but especially to prevent the Czechs at home from being tempted to give way—he was afraid that the defeat of Russia might have an unfortunate effect. He had received in advance the assent to the manifesto of the leading members of the "Maffia," the secret organization which soon after the opening of the War had been established in Prague and in other parts of Bohemia with a view to fighting Austria. By this time Masaryk was in London, where he remained, except for short visits to Paris, till April, 1917. Before leaving Geneva, he had been joined by Benesh, the second greatest name among the Czech liberators abroad, and they apportioned the work between them—Masaryk taking London as his centre and Benesh taking Paris, Masaryk still being recognized as the head of the whole movement.

He had arrived in London at the end of September, and was almost immediately offered a Slavonic professorship in King's College. His inaugural lecture on October 19, 1915, made history. His subject was "The Problem of Small Nations in the European Crisis," and the lecture was a great political success. Mr. Asquith, the British Prime Minister, had promised to take the chair—in itself a striking tribute to the importance of Masaryk—but as Asquith fell ill, Lord Robert Cecil, afterwards Lord Cecil of Chelwood, represented him. Of his lecture Masaryk wrote: "It brought out for the first time the political significance of the zone of small peoples in Europe that lies between the Germans and the Russians. It enabled me to put both the German *Drang nach Osten* (the Urge towards the East) and Russian policy in a new light, and to show the essential characters of Austria-Hungary and Prussia. In this light the breaking up of Austria-Hungary by the liberation of her peoples was revealed as the main requirement of the War. Finally, I argued strongly against the fear of the so-called Balkanization of Europe and urged, convincingly, I think, that small nations are capable of and have a right to independent development as States, each according to its own culture." After this manner, then, did Masaryk preach the gospel of the Nationalities, which, if it was not absolutely new in England, was little understood, and certainly had never been presented so authoritatively and yet persuasively before. "Henceforth," said Masaryk, "the small peoples and the possibility of their independence were seriously talked and written about. The positive side of the War—reconstruction—came into the foreground, replacing the conception that its object was either defence against the Germanic Powers or their overthrow, and placing the War in its true light as the beginning of the great refashioning of Central and Eastern Europe and, indeed, of Europe as a whole."

Among those who helped Masaryk in his work, Wickham Steed, of *The Times*, and Seton-Watson, whose books, such as *Racial Problems in Hungary*, were well known, stood out prominently in London; both rendered great service to the cause of the liberation of the Nationalities. In the *Edinburgh Review* for October, almost simultaneously with Masaryk's lecture, Steed published a programme for the radical transformation of the Dual Monarchy as a condition of permanent peace, and called for the unification of the Southern Slavs in a State of Yugoslavia, as well as for a "Czech-Moravian-Slovak State." In another article he foreshadowed a United States of Yugoslavia, an autonomous Poland under the suzerainty of Russia, an autonomous, if not independent, Bohemia, with Moravia and Slovakia, and a united Rumania. It was at least a very good guess at what was to come about. But all such happy imaginings were clouded as the year closed by the overrunning of Serbia by the Central Powers and Bulgaria, who, Slav though she was, had allied herself with them in the previous September; as the new year opened Montenegro also was occupied; the lot of the Yugoslavs in their homelands was bitter in the extreme.

Progress of Liberation Campaign

Meanwhile the campaign for liberation made good progress in France under the able direction of Benesh, who also had the assistance of Shtefanik, the third most important of the Czech leaders abroad. In agreement with Benesh, Masaryk went to Paris in February, 1916, for a month's visit. During it he saw Briand, then Prime Minister of France, and placing before him a small map of Europe, illustrated from it his thesis that the division of Austria into her historical and natural elements was a condition of the reconstruction of Europe and of the real weakening of Germany, or, in other words, of French security. The force of the argument was grasped by Briand at once; he accepted Masaryk's policy and promised to carry it out. Masaryk followed up this interview by publishing in the *Matin* a statement of his campaign against the Habsburg Empire, a statement which he said "hit the mark not only in Paris but in all Allied countries. The Allies began to understand that it would not be enough to overthrow the Central Powers and to penalize them financially and otherwise, but that Eastern Europe and Europe as a whole must be reorganized."

Beginning to understand was much, and if a very great deal had still to be done, the visit was thus a fruitful one. Isvolsky, then Russian Ambassador to France, was impressed by Briand's reception of Masaryk, and promised his support. Direct cooperation between the Czechs and the Yugoslavs began in Paris and continued uninterruptedly. On Masaryk's return to London, where Briand's action had also had a good effect, the campaign was prosecuted with the utmost energy, one of the most striking of its manifestations being a great public Czech and Yugoslav demonstration against Austria-Hungary in the summer. On its expository side the cause derived marked benefit from Seton-Watson's periodical, *The New Europe*, in itself an illuminating title, and from other publications. Many articles, not a few of them written by Masaryk, dealing with the subject, appeared in the British Press.

The sufferings of Serbia had drawn special attention to South-Eastern Europe and the Yugoslav problem, and this was augmented when Alexander, the Serbian Crown Prince, accompanied by Pashitch, the veteran statesman of the Balkans, came on a visit to London. Pashitch and Masaryk were old and tried friends and they took counsel together. Pashitch was a protagonist of a Great Serbia, but just then a Great Serbia or a united Yugoslavia seemed as remote from realization as a Czechoslovakia, so discouraging was the situation in the field for the Allies. Nor did it improve as the year advanced. A brilliant renewal of the Russian effort, with a sweeping victory at Lutsk, relieved the pressure on the French and Italian fronts, but the Russians were held up and then thrown back.

Their successes had helped to bring Rumania into the War alongside the Allies; the Rumanian forces drove rapidly across the passes into Transylvania, where they had numerous sympathizers, but soon were checked, defeated in several battles, and compelled to withdraw from most of their territory; by the end of 1916 the Central Powers were in possession of Bucarest.

Francis Joseph, an incarnation of dynastic absolutism, died on November 11, 1916, and as an idea had long been current that his death would be the signal for the break up of the Habsburg Empire, many among the Nationalities regarded it as an omen of the collapse of the Dual Monarchy, though at the moment there seemed little to suggest anything of the sort. Masaryk and the other leaders did not lose heart, but, on the contrary, worked harder than ever. In the course of the year a Czech National Council, a kind of Government, with Masaryk as President and Benesh as Secretary-General, was established in Paris, and was recognized by the Czech foreign colonies and their organizations, including the Czechoslovak National Association of the United States. This National Council was particularly significant when questions respecting the Czech Legions fighting in the War were considered.

The Czech Legions

While negatively the refusal of many thousands of Czechs in the Austrian Army to fight was an assistance to the Allies, the organization of Czech prisoners of war—in reality they had gone over, sometimes whole regiments of them, in voluntary surrender to the opposing troops—was positively helpful by furnishing them with fresh combatants; as the war proceeded Czech Legions were formed in Russia, France, and Italy. Of 70,000 prisoners taken by Serbia during the first months of the struggle, half of them were Czechs who had surrendered and who thereafter fought for her. Upwards of 300,000 Czechoslovaks likewise surrendered to Russia, where in the *Druzhina*, composed of Czechs who were Russian subjects or living in Russia, there was a nucleus of a distinctively

Czech force. From the beginning of the War one of Masaryk's greatest objects was to create an army from among the Czech prisoners of war, though the notion of forming an army abroad was, as he said, so natural that Czechs outside Austria began everywhere to act spontaneously on it.

With the sure instinct of political genius, he saw from the start that it was of infinite importance for the liberation of his country that the Czechs, in the largest numbers possible, should fight for and with the Allies. First, this was done by enlistment in the British and French ranks, and afterwards by the formation of contingents, regiments, legions; there they were, and the Allies could not overlook their existence or their meaning. In after days Masaryk wrote: "All our arguments would have served us little had not our political position been changed for the better by the recognition of the National Council in Allied countries, thanks to the formation of our Legions in three of them." The fighting Czechs were the supreme argument for the independence of their native land.

Nor were these Czech forces devoid of significance to the Yugoslavs and the Rumanians, for they forged a fresh bond between them all. The Russian Government was suspicious for some time of the Czechs, who were not Orthodox, and it made difficulties, which the formation of a Serbian Legion, the Serbians being Orthodox, did not have to encounter. Several detachments composed of Serbians and other Yugoslavs, prisoners of war, were sent from Russia to Serbia as early as 1915. After the overrunning of Serbia by the Central Powers a Serbian Division was dispatched to aid the Rumanians, and it was joined by many Czechs tired of waiting for some action by a real Czech army, which was prevented by the obstacles put in its way by the Russian authorities. Under the leadership of the Serbian general, Zhivkovitch, the Division fought with great gallantry in the Dobrudja against Mackensen's advance. If it fought in vain, as it did, it strengthened the ties between the Czechs, Yugoslavs, and Rumanians in the struggle for their common freedom.

Here perhaps was to be discerned the first faint hint of the combination of the nations afterwards called the Little Entente. When Masaryk was in Jassy, in Moldavia, and temporarily the Rumanian capital, in October, 1917, he came to that conclusion: "Politically my stay at Jassy bore good fruit. Our personal acquaintance and cooperation with the Rumanians were the germ of the Little Entente. When Rumania decided to make war, Benesh, Shtefanik, and I had sent Bratianu a telegram saying that Rumania was fighting for the liberation of our people."

United States Intervention

The year 1917 was marked by two events of the most far-reaching military and political importance—the intervention of the United States on the side of the Allies, and the absolute collapse of Russia through two Revolutions, the first of which led to the fall of Tsarism and the second to the Bolshevik régime of Lenin. Both events powerfully affected the struggle of the oppressed Nationalities of the Habsburg Empire and eventually made for their liberation. In December, 1916, President Wilson issued an invitation to the belligerents to state their war aims; in the Message he emphasized the right of small peoples to self-determination and proposed a League of Nations. Germany declined, though politely, to accede to the invitation. The Allies, accepting it, replied: "We find no difficulty in answering the request. The civilized world knows that they imply, first of all, the restoration of Belgium, Serbia, and Montenegro, with the compensation due to them; the evacuation of the invaded territories in France, Russia, and Rumania, with just reparation; the reorganization of Europe, guaranteed by a stable régime and based at once on respect for nationalities and the right to full security and liberty of economic development, and upon territorial conventions and international settlements such as guarantee land and sea frontiers against unjustifiable attack; the restitution of provinces torn from the Allies by force or against the wish of their inhabitants; the liberation of the Italians, as also of the Slavs, Rumanians, and Czechoslovaks from foreign domination; the setting free of the populations

M. PASHITCH

subject to the bloody tyranny of the Turks; and the turning out of Europe of the Ottoman Empire as decidedly foreign to Western civilization." There was a reference to the intentions of the Tsar with respect to Poland, which had been indicated by manifesto.

Masaryk, Trumbitch, and the other leaders of the Nationalities considered that the Reply of the Allies was a brilliant success for their cause; this was also the view of the Central Powers, who told their peoples that the Allies were bent on conquest and disruption, and who, a few weeks later, resumed unrestricted submarine warfare, in consequence of which Wilson broke off relations with Germany on February 3, and two months afterwards declared war. About a month earlier Petrograd and Moscow were in the throes of revolution; on March 15 the Tsar abdicated, and the Tsardom was at an end. The new Government announced that Free Russia did not aim at dominating other nations, but wished the establishment of a durable peace on the basis of the rights of nations to decide their own destinies; amongst other things, it "removed the chains that weighed upon the Polish people." On March 20 the Czech brigade in Russia proclaimed the Czechoslovak State, with the National Council in Paris as the Provisional Government and Masaryk as Dictator, in accordance with the new Russian doctrine of the self-determination of peoples. But the day of the Czechoslovak State was not yet.

Reichsrat in Turmoil

After being closed for three years, the Reichsrat was convoked by the Emperor Charles, who had succeeded to the throne on the death of his grand-uncle, Francis Joseph. It met at Vienna in May, 1917, and hardly had it opened when the representatives of the Nationalities gave utterance to their opposition to the Dual Monarchy as then constituted. Parliament met when shadows were beginning to fall over Austria-Hungary. The general military situation was still favourable, but nowhere had her armies distinguished themselves except when stiffened by German troops. Her dependence on Germany became more and more visible to all the world, as the military and economic resources of the Monarchy were increasingly drawn upon and their exhaustion drew near. In many of the towns of Austria there was a lack of the necessaries of life. The Russian Revolution, with its cry of self-determination, boded no good to the Habsburgs.

The Nationalities interpreted the Emperor's announcement of Constitutionalism which prefaced the meeting of the Reichsrat as a sign of weakness, and if they still talked of a federalist Austria-Hungary, they did so with quite extraordinary boldness. At the opening Stanek, a Czech leader, made a striking declaration "In the name of the Czech Union," which threw down the gauntlet to Dualism: "The delegation of the Bohemian nation is entirely convinced that the present dualist form of the Monarchy has divided it into dominating and oppressed Nationalities, to the clear detriment of the general interest, and that in order to abolish every sort of national privilege and ensure the full development of each Nationality in the interest of the whole Empire, and of the Dynasty itself, the conversion of the Habsburg-Lorraine Monarchy into a Federal State, composed of free national States with equal rights, is absolutely essential. At this historic moment, therefore, we take our stand upon the natural right of peoples to self-determination and free development—a right which in our case is, apart from everything else, further consolidated by indefeasible and recognized Acts of State; and we shall strive at the head of our nation for the union of all branches of the Czechoslovak people into a democratic State—a union which cannot leave out of account the Czechoslovak branch which lives in proximity to the historic frontiers of our Bohemian Fatherland." From this it was evident that the State contemplated by the Czechs took the Slovaks away from the Magyars and broke up Hungary in that direction, while at the same time it included the Germans resident within the old frontiers of Bohemia.

The Czech Declaration was followed by a Yugoslav Declaration with the like demand for a federation of the Empire and the "union of all territory within the Monarchy inhabited by Slovenes, Croats, and Serbs into an independent State, free from all external domination and established on a democratic basis under the sceptre of the Habsburg-Lorraine dynasty." This was voiced by Koroshetz, the leader of the Slovenes. The Polish deputies expressed their decision to separate from Austria in order to create a unified and free Poland, and the Italian members claimed to be joined territorially to their co-nationals in the Kingdom of Italy. All this was striking enough, but it was heightened when Kalina, denying all responsibility on the part of the Czechs for the War, spoke of their sympathy with the Entente Powers, and Strshibrny told the terrible story of the persecution which the Czechs had had to endure from Austria since the War had begun. The effect of the various Declarations and speeches was to isolate and arraign the Germans of Austria and the Magyars as distinguished from the other Nationalities.

Further trouble in the Reichsrat induced the Emperor to decree an amnesty with a view to reconciling the malcontents, but it did not have that result, for as soon as the prison gates were opened to Kramarsh and the other Nationalities' leaders who had been incarcerated, the campaign in Austria-Hungary herself took on fresh life and vigour. What might have seemed an act of magnanimity on the part of Charles disclosed itself as a retreat from a too formidable position and as providing, moreover, further opportunity for attacks on the Empire and undermining its political constitution.

Nationalities Abroad Increasingly Active

While the federalist solution of the Habsburg Monarchy still held the chief place, at all events ostensibly, in the activities in Austria-Hungary of the Nationalities other than German or Magyar, the campaign in the Allied countries, which sought nothing less than the break-up of the Empire, continued with unabated zeal. In March, 1917, Dmowski, the leader of the Poles in the West, presented to Balfour, British Foreign Secretary, an important Memorandum. It began by stating that as there was now no chance of a Russian solution of the Polish problem, and as the aim of the War was to reduce power to limits allowing the re-establishment of European equilibrium, an independent Poland was a necessity. He then went on to point out that this Poland must be sufficiently large and strong to be sure of economic independence, with an outlet to the sea, if it was to take its proper place in Europe; it should consist of Galicia and Teschen from Austria-Hungary, of Russian Poland, and of German Poland, including Danzig.

In May, 1917, Masaryk went to Russia, to see at first hand the working of the Revolution and its probable bearing on his plans and, above all, to carry through the creation of an army among the Czech prisoners of war. Benesh remained in Paris, in close touch with the statesmen of France, who exhibited the greatest friendliness to the cause; he was in constant contact with the Yugoslavs, Rumanians, and Poles. A Polish National Committee was organized in Paris; at Cracow resolutions had been passed demanding a united Poland with access to the sea—the Russian Revolution had caused many Polish hearts to beat high with hope: it was not forgotten that Wilson had spoken of a free and united Poland in a peace proposal made before the entrance of the United States into the War. On June 4, 1917, a Decree of the French Republic, signed by Poincaré as President, created a Polish army in France for the duration of the War, under the orders of the French High Command, but fighting under the Polish flag. This force consisted of Poles who had enlisted in the French armies and of other Poles who joined up. The Polish National Committee in Paris was recognized by the French Government on September 20, 1917, in a letter from Ribot, then Foreign Minister as well as Prime Minister, addressed to Dmowski, Piltz, and other members.

Particularly memorable was the Declaration of Corfu of July, 1917, for Yugoslavia, for in it Pashitch and Trumbitch, as the authorized representatives of all the Serbs, Croats, and Slovenes, testified to the unity of their peoples in their common determination to constitute an independent national State, and adopted as its designation the "kingdom of the Serbs, Croats, and Slovenes." It provided for the unification of flag and Crown, and for religious equality. Declaring that the Adriatic should be a free and open sea, it stated that the kingdom would be composed of "all territory compactly inhabited by our people," and that "it could not be mutilated without detriment to their vital interests." It added: "Our nation demands nothing that belongs to others but only what is its own. It desires freedom and unity." The Czech leaders abroad considered this joint Declaration as making for their success too, and equally as an important international manifesto of Yugoslav unity necessarily involving the dissolution of the Dual Monarchy. But in Italy it was not well received, as it was regarded as hostile to the Treaty of London, as unquestionably it was; yet the words, "all territory compactly inhabited by our people," left room for negotiation and a settlement. The Caporetto disaster in October showed both Italians and Yugoslavs where their common "vital interests" lay; the triumph of the Central Powers could be nothing else but their common ruin.

In November, 1917, the Bolshevik Revolution occasioned confusion and anxiety throughout Europe; if the complete withdrawal of the Russians from the War favoured Germany and Austria-Hungary, it also introduced new and difficult problems even for them. Masaryk narrowly observed the rise of the Soviet, and what he saw determined him to send to France the Czech army that, after much delay, had been formed in Russia. During the brief offensive of Kerensky against the Central Powers the Czechoslovak soldiers had proved at the battle of Zboroff that they were first-class fighting men. Masaryk succeeded in keeping most of them from the infection of Bolshevism. "My whole care," he said, "was to hold the Army together and prevent it from being drawn into the Russian chaos." He had arranged that a force consisting of 30,000 Czech and Yugoslav prisoners of war should go to the French front; part of it was dispatched direct; to send the rest in that way was found impossible, and he ordered all the Czechoslovak troops to go to Vladivostok, there to await transports which were to be provided by the Allies.

While he was in Russia several congresses of Czechoslovak Societies took place, and differences that had arisen were composed. He was one of the chief figures in the Congress of the Oppressed Nationalities of Austria-Hungary which was held in Kieff in November, and was attended by Czechs, Slovaks, Slovenes, Serbs, Croats, Poles, Rumanians, and Italians—representatives of all the non-German and non-Magyar races of the Dual Monarchy; there were special delegates from the Czechoslovak Legions and other armed units of the dissident Nationalities. The meeting was held in the Great Hall of the Kieff circus, and was attended by more than 5,000 people. It was opened by Bartoszevics, chairman of the Polish Executive Committee in the Ukraine, who explained in several languages what its object was. Maxa, president of the Czech Legionaries' Committee, was elected chairman of the meeting. Masaryk expounded the reasons for which these Nationalities were opposed to Austria-Hungary and the aims which they pursued. This congress was the forerunner of the greater Congress of the Oppressed Nationalities held some months later in Rome. Travelling in advance of the Legions, Masaryk arrived at Fusan, in Korea, whence he sailed to Japan, reaching Tokyo on April 8, 1918; the Vladivostok route was then impracticable. By the end of the month he was in Washington in intimate contact with the American Government.

Before Masaryk's arrival in America, the work of Benesh in France had been crowned with a most distinguished success. While in Russia Masaryk had requested him to negotiate with the French Government about the Czech army being formed there to go to France and to conclude a treaty with respect to it. In August, 1917, Benesh made an agreement with France, and on December 16, following, the French Government issued a decree which recognized that the Czechoslovaks had a right to form an army of their own—a right appertaining to a sovereign and independent nation—and had a right to fight on the side of the Allies, thus identifying them with the Entente. Further, France recognized the Czech National Council as having the control of this army, a right usually accorded only to the Government of an independent State. A summary of all this was given in the Decree itself when it said: "The Czechoslovaks organized in an autonomous army will fight under their own flag against the Central Powers." In a comment accompanying the Decree, Poincaré, then President of the Republic, wrote: "France has always supported by all means in her power the national aspirations of the Czechoslovaks." It was a great thing for Benesh and for the cause; there was joy in Bohemia, rage in Germany and Austria-Hungary.

On most of the War fronts, however, the situation favoured the Central Powers at this stage; only a week before Rumania, owing to the defection of the Russians, had been compelled to ask for an armistice—and so was out of the conflict. Nevertheless the first week of the new year showed how things were moving in Austria when the Czechs issued in Prague what was known as the "Three Kingdoms' Declaration" in the name of the "Czech nation and of its enslaved and politically disfranchised Slovak branch in Hungary." No longer was there mention of a federal State; condemning the oppression of the people by the Germans of Austria and the "oligarchy of a few Magyar noble families," the Czechs openly demanded that the future of the Czechoslovak State should be settled internationally—at the Peace Conference at the close of the War—and not by Austria-Hungary alone. It was no wonder that Seidler, the Austrian Prime Minister, said of this Declaration: "While the Declaration of May 30 of last year was of a character reconcilable with the fundamental dynastic and patriotic conceptions of the Austrians, one may search the Prague Declaration in vain for the remotest reference to the dynastic unity of the various Nationalities."

The Fourteen Points

It was perhaps no more than a mere coincidence, but certainly it was not a little disconcerting, that President Wilson, only two days after the Prague Declaration was published, should proclaim his categoric "Fourteen Points," the Tenth of which ran: "The peoples of Austria-Hungary, whose place among the nations we wish to see safeguarded and assured, should be accorded the freest opportunity of autonomous development." The other Points that concerned the Nationalities were the Ninth, the Eleventh, and the Thirteenth; the first of them called for a readjustment of the Italian frontiers along clearly recognizable lines of nationality; the second stated that Rumania, Serbia, and Montenegro should be evacuated, occupied territories restored, Serbia accorded free access to the sea, and the relations of the Balkan States determined along historically established lines of allegiance and nationality; and the third postulated that an independent Polish State should be erected which should include the territories inhabited by indisputably Polish populations, which should be assured a free and secure access to the sea, and whose political and economic independence and territorial integrity should be guaranteed by international covenant.

Here was not much encouragement for Austria-Hungary, but it was crystal clear that Wilson, while contemplating changes in the internal political structure of the Dual Monarchy, had in his mind no thought of the dissolution of the Empire. And it was just as plain from a speech made by Lloyd George, the British Prime Minister, three days before the publication of the Fourteen Points, that the British Government was of much the same opinion. He said: "The break-up of Austria-Hungary is no part of our war aims; but genuine self-government must be granted to those Austro-Hungarian Nationalities who have long desired it." As against that he stated it was a vital matter that the legitimate claims of the Italians for union with those of their own race and tongue should be satisfied, and that an independent Poland, comprising all genuinely Polish elements, was an urgent necessity for the stability of Western Europe; justice was to be done to men of Rumanian blood and speech in their legitimate aspirations.

These pronouncements of Wilson and Lloyd George could not but cause disappointment to the leaders of the movements for independence, such as Masaryk and Trumbitch. Wilson changed his views later when he had a fuller comprehension of the position, owing partly to the representations of Masaryk. Lloyd George privately explained that he had been influenced by tactical considerations. In England there was undoubtedly a certain friendliness to Austria-Hungary; many English people had some knowledge of Austria and especially of Vienna, whose *Gemüthlichkeit* had its appeal; others, particularly among the British nobility and gentry, had had fairly intimate associations with the corresponding classes among the Magyars and had felt at home in Budapest. To the British Government there appeared to be a chance of separating the Dual Monarchy from Germany, and its policy reflected this idea up to the spring of 1918, encouraged as it was by various peace-feelers emanating from the Emperor Charles, who realized the increasing weakness of the Monarchy and resented its dependence on Germany.

But all negotiations for a separate peace completely failed—leaving Austria-Hungary to her fate, a significant sign of which was beheld in the Congress of the Oppressed Nationalities of the Habsburg Empire, which was held in Rome in April, chiefly the work of Benesh, who organized it and brought it to success, notwithstanding many difficulties, such as the getting together of the Yugoslavs and the Italians, a task in which he was much assisted by the reconciling efforts of Wickham Steed and Seton-Watson. A preparatory French and Italian Committee included Franklin-Bouillon, Fournol, Torre, Gallenga, and Amendola, while Dmowski represented the Poles and Florescu the Rumanians. Trumbitch stood aloof for some time, but at last a common formula was evolved.

Congress of Oppressed Nationalities at Rome

This historic congress, a landmark in the struggle for liberation, was held on April 10–12, 1918, and it was not too much to say that, as coming events cast their shadows before, it indicated a positive departure in the policy of the Allies, for, unless they were defeated, there could be only one issue—the dissolution of Austria-Hungary. As its President the congress had Senator Ruffini, an Italian ex-Minister; the delegates were

Benesh and Shtefanik, of the Czechoslovak National Council; Trumbitch, Mestrovitch, and others of the Yugoslav Committee; Zamorski, Skirmunt, and other representatives of the Poles; Draghicescu, Lupu, and other Rumanians; and twelve deputies from the Serbian Parliament. Among the visitors taking an intense interest in the proceedings were Franklin-Bouillon, Fournol, Pierre de Quirielle, Wickham Steed, and Seton-Watson. The Italian Government, in which Sonnino was Foreign Minister, was not represented at the congress, but towards its close sent a message to the effect that it was in hearty sympathy with its aims.

Three Resolutions were adopted: the first proclaimed that each of the Oppressed Nationalities had the right to constitute its own Nationality and State unity, or to complete it, and to attain full political and economic independence; the second recognized in the Austro-Hungarian Monarchy the instrument of German domination and the fundamental obstacle to the realization of the aspirations and rights of these Nationalities; and the third, which was the most significant, recognized the necessity of waging a common struggle against the common oppressors, in order that each Nationality might attain complete liberation and national unity as a free State unit. An agreement also was reached between the Italians and the Yugoslavs, which declared that the unity and independence of Yugoslavia was a vital interest of Italy, and *vice versa*. A Memorandum on the future of Poland was submitted which maintained that no compromise was possible between Prussia and Poland, as neither could willingly renounce the mouth of the Vistula, and that Poland would either be saved with the Allies or become dependent on Germany; the way to counter this, it went on, was the reunion in one independent State of all Polish lands; a State of Czechoslovakia and a strong Rumania would help Poland. The principal speakers of the Nationalities were Zamorski, for the Poles, Lupu and Minorescu for the Rumanians—the Rumanians of Transylvania had at this time only a small organization without any prominent leaders, and Rumanians from the Regat spoke for them;

Trumbitch spoke for the Yugoslavs, and Benesh for the Czechoslovaks.

Amongst the most important utterances was that of Franklin-Bouillon, who, as President of the Parliamentary Committee for Foreign Affairs at Paris, announced that he was authorized by the French Government to give its sanction to the action of the congress, and an assurance that France would never conclude a separate peace, without Italy and the other Allies, great and small. "The congress," wrote Benesh, "was an undoubted success. The whole Italian public, the Press, Parliament, and Government, all diplomatic circles, and the Governments of all the Allied countries, followed its proceedings with interest and appreciation, the political results of which were soon manifested."

After the congress was over Orlando received a joint delegation of the Nationalities which had taken part in it, and emphasized the readiness of Italy to cooperate with the Yugoslavs and the other oppressed Nationalities; he also referred to the Czechoslovak Legion that had been recently organized in Italy. To a delegation who waited on him in Paris, Clemenceau expressed his approval of the findings of the congress and his agreement with some plans for further action that were placed before him. But in London there still was hesitation, which, however, passed when on May 25, Lansing, the American Secretary of State, declared officially in public that the proceedings of the congress had been followed with great interest by the United States Government, and that the nationalist aspiration of the Czechoslovaks and Yugoslavs had the earnest sympathy of his Government. The leaders of the liberation movement held this statement as tantamount to the adhesion of America to their programme; it undoubtedly represented a great advance in Wilson's views.

More was necessary, and this was achieved, thanks mainly to Masaryk, who was immensely active in America. On June 28, 1918, Lansing supplemented his former declaration: "Since the issuance by the American Government on May 29 of a statement regarding the nationalist aspirations for freedom of the Czechoslovaks and Yugoslavs, German and Austrian officials have sought to misinterpret and distort its manifest interpretation. In order, therefore, that there may be no misunderstanding concerning the meaning of the statement, the Secretary of State to-day further announces the position of the United States Government to be that all branches of the Slav race should be completely freed from German and Austrian rule." Here was the greatest triumph so far of the non-German and non-Magyar Nationalities. It was as if the doom of the Habsburg Empire had been pronounced—and so it was.

On June 30, France, through Pichon, then Foreign Minister, sent to Benesh a Letter in which he said that his Government considered it just and necessary to proclaim the right of the Czechoslovak nation to its independence and to recognize publicly and officially the National Council as the supreme organ of its general interests and the first step towards a future Czechoslovak Government. The French formula of recognition was taken to London by Benesh a few weeks afterwards. He had gone to the British capital to participate in a great meeting held in the Mansion House and organized by the Yugoslavs for July 25. Among other notabilities Balfour was present and made a speech from which it was clear that the British Government supported the Yugoslavs in the programme announced by Jovanovitch, the Serbian Minister, the first item of which was: "The independence and unity of all Serbs, Croats, and Slovenes in a single State." Benesh also spoke, and next day went to the Foreign Office to obtain official recognition of the Czechoslovak National Council as the Provisional Government of future Czechoslovakia, and had the satisfaction of receiving it on the following day, the National Council being described as the "trustee" for the Czechoslovak people, which was a distinction without a difference, as was proved by the setting up in Prague of a new Czechoslovak National Committee having the closest relations with the National Council in Paris, and as other events were very shortly to demonstrate in the most convincing way.

Nationalities Abroad Recognized as Belligerents

In the meantime the War had been running its terrific course. After enduring severe defeats with a serious loss of ground, the British armies in France stood "with their backs to the wall," and on receiving reinforcements began to move forward again. American troops poured into the field in large and impressive numbers. Late in the day, though fortunately not too late, the High Command on the Western Front was unified, and on July 18, 1918, the great Allied counter-offensive under Foch was launched on the Marne, with results that did not end till final success was achieved. It was the certainty that now possessed the Allies of their ultimate victory that emphasized the value of their recognition of the Czechoslovak National Council, with its implication of the recognition of similar bodies among the Nationalities contending for their liberation from the yoke of the Habsburg Empire. On August 9 the British Government published officially the exact terms of its recognition, the second paragraph of the pronouncement being most striking: "In consideration of their efforts to achieve independence, Great Britain regards the Czechoslovaks as an allied nation and recognizes the unity of the three Czechoslovak armies (in France, Italy, and Russia) as an Allied and belligerent army waging regular warfare against Austria-Hungary and Germany." On September 3 the United States, by a Declaration of the Secretary of State, recognized that a state of belligerency existed between the Czechoslovak forces in the field and the German and Austro-Hungarian Empires, and that the Czechoslovak National Council was a *de facto* Government, clothed with proper authority, and said that it was prepared to enter formally into relations with this *de facto* Government. A week later the Japanese Government followed suit.

In all these Declarations it was very noticeable that the Allies found the basis for recognition in the Czechoslovak fighting forces. Masaryk's perspicacity, to give it no higher name, was abundantly justified. The Yugoslavs of the Dual Monarchy were not nearly so well organized as the Czechoslovaks, and dissensions between them and the Serbians, which had broken out once more because of the attitude Pashitch had again assumed, did not make a good impression. After America had recognized the Czechoslovaks the Yugoslavs, who could absolutely count on his thoroughgoing support, asked Masaryk to approach the United States Government in order to obtain recognition too; Trumbitch sent the same request from Paris; it was not acceded to, for one reason or another, and in the end the thing did not matter, for the cooperation with them of the Czechoslovaks and the others ensured the success of the Yugoslavs, as of the cause generally, speaking broadly. On September 15, Masaryk organized a meeting of the Oppressed Peoples of Austria-Hungary on the model of the Rome Congress, Paderewski representing the Poles, Hinkovitch the Yugoslavs, and Stoica, a Transylvanian, the Rumanians. Paderewski and Masaryk were the principal speakers, and the Carnegie Hall, where this congress was held, was crowded, many sympathetic Americans being present. The long-struggling Nationalities, however, were now articulate everywhere, and all the world knew what was their common aim.

The Fated Empire

Nowhere were the Nationalities more articulate than in the Habsburg Monarchy itself by this time. The shadows were swiftly lengthening and deepening over the fated Empire. A sudden offensive against Italy in June, 1918, had achieved nothing. The number of effective soldiers and the supply of munitions had alike decreased; hunger and want stalked the land; here and there mutinies and risings took place; the bitter cry was for bread—a Bread-Peace! The recognition of "Czecho-slovakia" by the British and American Governments stiffened the attitude of the Czechs to the Dynasty, which till then had retained something of its integrating power. Hussarek, who had succeeded Seidler as Prime Minister of Austria, invited the Czech leaders to meet him—at the moment when they were conferring with the Yugoslav leaders! Stanek came, and when told that the Czechs must reject all declarations of recognition, refused to agree. The Czech Union denied the possibility of forming a federation—the day was past for that. When Hussarek talked tentatively of creating a South Slav State within the Monarchy, the Magyars shrilled opposition, and spoke fiercely of the "Integrity of Hungary."

On September 15, 1918, the Emperor Charles, behind the back of Germany, made peace proposals to the Allies, and asked them to send delegates, with full powers, to a meeting in a neutral country, but the proposal was declined. And on the very day that he made this offer an Allied offensive was opened on the Bulgarian front, and in a fortnight all was over, an armistice being granted on September 29 to Bulgaria. Hussarek made a last effort to bring all the Austrian parties into a coalition cabinet, but the Czechs would have none of it. As for the Magyars, they would not hear of a South Slav State as independent as their own—the very notion was blasphemy; yet Tisza went into Croatia to see what was taking place, and he was confounded when he was confronted by the Yugoslav Committee and a Memorandum demanding independence. Tisza was furious, and in his rage said to some Yugoslav delegates at Sarajevo: "It may be that we shall go under, but before we do, we shall summon enough power to grind you to pieces." Later he agreed that there might be a South Slav State, but organized in such a way that the "integrity" of Hungary would be untouched.

Now the end of the Habsburg Empire was fast approaching, event following event with lightning rapidity. Germany and Austria-Hungary offered to the United States an armistice, with negotiations for peace, but Wilson did not hurry his reply, and on October 16, 1918, the Emperor Charles issued a Manifesto in which he proclaimed that Austria, in consonance with the will of her peoples, was to be made into a federal State, in which every Nationality would be free to establish its own form of government in the territory it occupied. He declared that the union of the Polish districts of Austria with the independent Polish State was not precluded, but, on the other hand, he said that the integrity of territory belonging to the

Hungarian Crown would not be interfered with, and this meant that the Yugoslavs of Hungary would not get what they wanted—liberation from the Magyar State altogether. Except for the tie of personal union with the sovereign, the Magyars were to be free from Austria and her Nationalities, but their own "subject" Nationalities were not to be free. The rising tide swept all this away.

How the End Came

On October 18, 1918, President Wilson replied to the Austro-Hungarian proposal for an armistice which had been made on October 7, the basis suggested being acceptance of the Fourteen Points. Wilson said that since his announcement of them the situation had changed so radically that they no longer applied. The United States had recognized the Czechoslovaks as belligerents and the Czechoslovak National Council as a *de facto* belligerent Government, with full authority to direct the military and political affairs of Czechoslovakia, and it had also recognized the justice of the nationalistic aspirations of the Yugoslavs for freedom. As this was so, Wilson continued, the United States could no longer accept autonomy for these peoples, but must insist on these peoples themselves being the judges of what action was required to satisfy their conception of their rights and destiny as members of the family of nations. Wilson had progressed from autonomy to independence for the Nationalities; the advance could be seen quite clearly in his various addresses to the Americans and his Notes to the Central Powers.

Meanwhile the Czech leaders abroad had forestalled the Manifesto of Charles. On October 14, Benesh informed the Allied Governments that the Czechoslovak National Council had been transformed into a Provisional Czechoslovak Government, with Masaryk, who was still in America, as President, Shtefanik as Minister of War, and himself as Minister for Foreign Affairs and of the Interior, and that a Chargé d'Affaires had been appointed to each of the British, French, Italian, and American Governments. Benesh stated that these decisions had been taken in agreement with the political leaders at home, that Stanek, president of the Czech Union in the Vienna Parliament, had authoritatively declared that the Paris Czechoslovak National Council was entitled to represent the Czechoslovak nation in the Allied countries and at the Peace Conference, and that Zahradnik, another deputy, had said that the Czechoslovaks were definitely quitting the Parliament in Vienna, thereby breaking for ever all their ties with Austria-Hungary. France recognized the Provisional Government next day, and the other Allied Governments did so soon afterwards. On October 18 the new Czechoslovakia published a Declaration of Independence, in which, towards its close, occurred the words, "The longed-for age of humanity is dawning." But what actually was dawning, and more than dawning, was the liberation of the Nationalities.

On October 19, 1918, the South Slav National Council issued a Manifesto from Zagreb, demanding, as an application of the right of self-determination, a single independent South Slav National State, embracing all territory inhabited by Slovenes, Croats, and Serbs, without reference to State or provincial boundaries and solely on the basis of ethnic affinity. It rejected in advance all suggestions "of whatever nature that came from the side of Hungary." On the previous day Vaida Voyed, in the Hungarian Parliament, had announced that the Rumanians of Transylvania would from then onward "look after their own welfare," a notice of "Hands Off" to the Magyars; the Rumanian leaders had met together a week earlier at Oradea Mare or Nagyvarad, and come to the conclusion that the time had arrived to strike for freedom. Also, in the Parliament at Budapest, Juriga had spoken of the formation of the National Council of the Slovaks. It was obvious that Hungary, no less than Austria, was breaking up, though the Magyars at the moment derided even the thought of such a thing. But the writing on the wall was plain except to eyes that would or could not see. On October 21 a revolution broke out in Vienna; a German-Austrian National Assembly was set up, and its constituency was to include all "territories settled by

Germans within Austria." The Socialists clamoured for a republic; in Prague the same cry echoed. Polish independence was proclaimed and established in Western Galicia; in Lemberg, or Lwow, in Eastern Galicia, a Ukrainian Constituent Assembly proclaimed an independent "Ukrainian State extending over all territory ethnically Ukrainian." In Budapest, Karolyi was beginning the Revolution which was identified with his name, and was demanding the withdrawal from the front of the Hungarian regiments. Soon weary and dispirited soldiers were streaming homewards from all the Austro-Hungarian fronts—why fight any longer for this dissolving, dying Empire?

Yet after a fashion the Habsburg Empire still held together, but it was a mere *simulacrum*. Charles was still Emperor and King, at least in name; most of the high functionaries of State were at their posts, and the army, though depleted, was an army in being. On October 20 Charles notified the German Emperor that he had come to the irrevocable decision to sue for peace. But four days later, before his request was presented to the United States Government, to whom it was addressed, Diaz took the offensive on the south-western front, and his Italian, British, and French forces, after encountering a stubborn resistance at the start, marched rapidly and victoriously forward, the battle turning into a rout for Austria-Hungary.

This was the final catastrophe, but before Diaz granted an armistice on November 3, other notable events had occurred within the Monarchy. On October 27 a National Council was set up at Arad by the Transylvanian Rumanians which overthrew the Magyar authorities and took over the control of the country. Next day a bloodless Revolution in Prague resulted in the transference of Bohemia to the Czechs by the Austrian authorities, who withdrew their troops, according to a convention concluded with the Austrian Command. "The ties with Vienna, Budapest, and the Habsburg Dynasty," commented Masaryk, "were very definitely cut," though it took more than a fortnight to complete the Revolution, formally and materially, despite there being no opposition of any consequence. On

October 31 Budapest was in the hands of the revolutionaries, and Karolyi was about to be President of the Republic of Hungary. At a conference held in Geneva early in November, Pashitch for Serbia, now evacuated by her enemies and triumphant, agreed with Trumbitch, Koroshetz, and other representatives of the Yugoslav peoples who had belonged to the Dual Monarchy, on a programme of territorial and racial unity.

On November 11 the Emperor Charles, born under an unlucky star if ever a man was, renounced all share in the government of Austria, and the Lammasch Ministry, the last Habsburg Government, resigned. On the following day a Republic was proclaimed in the National Assembly of the new Austria in Vienna, while two days afterwards in the National Assembly at Prague Kramarsh proclaimed the dethronement of the Emperor and the establishment of the Republic of Czecho-slovakia, with Masaryk as President—elected by acclamation. Next day the Kingdom of the Magyars became a Republic too. Blow after blow, crash upon crash; all was over! The Empire of the Habsburgs had dissolved. The liberation of the Oppressed Nationalities was achieved. But if it was an end, it was also a beginning. *Incipit vita nova!*

CHAPTER III

THE SUCCESSION STATES

1919–1920

The Succession States materialized against the background of the World War won by the "Allied and Associated Powers." Without the collapse of Russia and the defeat of the Central Powers, this would have been impossible. But the dissolution of the Habsburg Empire occurred not because of the overthrow of Austria-Hungary and Germany, but because that overthrow provided a favourable opportunity to the Oppressed Nationalities, already struggling for freedom, to shatter their chains. On and off the conflict had lasted for seventy years—from 1848 to 1918. Now, the Dual Monarchy was dead, but the Nationalities that had composed it were alive. They fell into two groups. The smaller consisted of the defeated Nationalities—the Germans in the new Republic of Austria and the Magyars in the new Republic of Hungary, both practically organized though not delimited as States, but completely dissociated politically from each other, in November, 1918. The second and much larger group comprised the victorious Nationalities—the Czechoslovaks, the Yugoslavs (Serbs, Croats, and Slovenes), the Poles, the Ukrainians, and the Italians.

In this group a common aim had inspired common action; the aim attained, the next step was the making or completing of States distinctly expressing the Nationalism of each of its members. Thus, the Czechoslovaks formed Czechoslovakia; the Yugoslavs united with the Serbians in the Kingdom of the Serbs, Croats, and Slovenes, otherwise Yugoslavia; the Poles of Western Galicia joined with the other Poles in the Republic of Poland, which, after a time, absorbed the Ukrainians of Eastern Galicia; and the Italians of Tirol and the Coastland were incorporated with their nationals in the Kingdom of Italy. The very enumeration of these political changes or rearrangements, so strikingly natural when thus recited and eminently proper in themselves, was a vindication of the principle of Nationality, as it showed how under the New Order peoples of the same racial stock were once more being drawn together. The frontiers of this group had not yet been delimited definitely, but the main outlines and most of the details were already sufficiently clear.

As was bound to happen, differences, some of them acute, caused trouble in and between the States, and in a measure gave a certain colour to the oft-repeated charge, due, however, chiefly to hostile propaganda, that Central and South-Eastern Europe were becoming "Balkanized." Unjust as this accusation was, it had been foreseen, and preparation had been made to meet it. This was one of the origins of the Little Entente, though the combination foreshadowed at the instant had a wider reach, as appeared from a statement published by one of its founders, Take Jonescu.

Little Entente Projected

Writing in the November, 1921, number of *Eastern Europe*, a serial publication edited by Crawfurd Price, Take Jonescu, then Prime Minister of Rumania, said: "The conception of the dangers of the future, and the necessity of preventing the splitting up of Central Europe from becoming dangerous to the general welfare, imposed themselves on the politicians, who, in 1918, saw that with the materialization of their secular dream, heavy responsibilities would forthwith weigh upon their nations, now recalled to national life and liberty but obliged henceforth to work for the maintenance of order and the liberty of all. It was in such a spirit that as early as the autumn of 1918 negotiations commenced between Benesh, Venizelos, Pashitch, and me at Paris and London. At one time Venizelos, Pashitch, and I discussed the future order of the Balkan Peninsula; at another Benesh, Pashitch, and I examined our future relations as heirs of the Habsburg Empire. . . . We elaborated the project to unite our countries by definite and permanent ties. . . . We had but one immediate ambition: to appear before the future Peace Conference with our differences regulated, if necessary, by arbitrators chosen by us, but in any case determined to show the Powers that there was no need for them to intervene in our disputes. I shall never forget the day when Professor Masaryk, elected President of the Czechoslovak Republic, passed through Paris, on which occasion I had a conversation respecting the future. I spoke of the necessity of enlarging our Entente till it stretched from the Baltic to the Aegean Sea, thereby introducing Poland and Greece respectively. I asked him to meet Venizelos, and he offered to go to see him. The great Cretan preferred to visit President Masaryk, so we three met at the Hôtel Meurice. During that conversation we discussed the desirability of appearing before the Conference with our questions agreed on."

The idea Jonescu expressed of an Entente of States from the Baltic to the Aegean had had its echo elsewhere, for, speaking in the Reichsrat at Vienna in the autumn of 1918, Stanek, the Czech leader, had said, "We want a union of the three Slav States from Danzig via Prague to the Adriatic," the three Slav States being Poland, Czechoslovakia, and Yugoslavia. In his book, *The Making of a State*, Masaryk, referring to his talks with Jonescu and Venizelos, said that, in accordance with the situation then existing, "we contemplated a close understanding with the Southern Slavs and the Poles, as well as with the Rumanians and the Greeks. Though we were fully aware of the obstacles in our path, and particularly of the territorial disputes between the Southern Slavs and the Rumanians, we agreed to clear the ground for ulterior cooperation during the impending Peace Conference. The idea of the Little Entente was, so to speak, already in the air." This idea, he went on, had been developed by joint work with Yugoslavs, Rumanians, and Poles, and by common enterprises like the Rome Congress of the Oppressed Nationalities; and it was on the basis of that experience that he put forward in his book, *The New Europe*, the demand that alongside the Big Entente similar groups should be formed, above all among the Little States of Central Europe.

In one of his opening speeches as President—he had been

chosen President by acclamation at Prague on November 14, 1918—he observed at Prague: "We shall easily unite with the Rumanians and the Yugoslavs on the question of securing intimate contact. The Greeks also appreciate this unity through their leading men, especially Venizelos. When the difficulties between the Yugoslavs and the Italians have been smoothed away, as I hope they will be, then the Central Europe of the pan-Germans would be replaced by an *entented* group of States extending from the Baltic to the Adriatic and farther to Switzerland and France." When the Little Entente, however, was organized, it did not include Poland, though she cooperated, nor Greece, who was still at war with the Turks.

Liquidation of Habsburg Empire

Before the Peace Conference assembled at Paris in January, 1919, the situation in Central and South-Eastern Europe had been further clarified in some ways. In Czechoslovakia a Government functioned, with Kramarsh as Prime Minister and Benesh as Foreign Minister. On December 4, 1918, the Allies gave it plenary powers to unite Slovakia with the Republic, the Hungarian Republican Government under Karolyi having been ordered to evacuate its forces from "North Hungary," as the Magyars called Slovakia. With the assistance of French troops the whole area of Slovakia was occupied by the Czechs from the Danube to the Carpathians by the beginning of January, 1919. But on May 1, 1918, representatives of the Slovaks had declared themselves in favour of union at Liptovsky St. Nicholas, and they repeated the declaration, on a more important scale, at Turchansky St. Martin on October 30; on June 30 Masaryk had signed at Pittsburg the Convention between the Slovaks and the Czechs of America, which accepted an autonomous administration, a Diet, and Law Courts for Slovakia within the framework of the State of Czechoslovakia. Some Slovaks advocated complete independence in a separate State of Slovakia, others some kind of union with Russia, but the great majority favoured union with the Czechs, and, later, the Constitution of

Czechoslovakia was adopted by the Slovaks as well as the Czechs.

With the dissolution of Austria-Hungary, the unification of the Yugoslavs proceeded apace, victorious Serbia being the natural nexus. On November 19, 1918, Croatia-Slavonia, Dalmatia, Bosnia-Herzegovina, and Slovenia decided in a National Council at Zagreb for union with Serbia, to which Kingdom were united Montenegro, by vote of a National Council at Podgoritsa on November 24, and the Voivodina, by the decision of the National Assembly at Novi-Sad on the following day. Alexander, the Prince Regent, proclaimed on December 1, in the name of his father, King Peter, the "union of Serbia with the provinces of the independent State of the Serbs, Croats, and Slovenes in the unitary kingdom of the Serbs, Croats, and Slovenes." Thus Yugoslavia became a reality; many dreams had come true. The first Yugoslav Government was constituted on December 21 under the presidency of Protitch, among other leaders present being Trumbitch, Petritchitch, Spaho, and Pribitchevitch. Shortly afterwards the new Government informed the Entente Powers of the union of all the Yugoslavs under the Karageorgevitch dynasty. Troubles had still to be faced with Italy and much less seriously with Rumania, but the great fact stood forth in all its impressiveness that the Yugoslav Nationality question was solved, and solved in consonance with the principle of Nationality. Of course national consolidation remained to be accomplished.

In the meantime Rumania was also undertaking her unification. On the plea of an infraction of the Treaty of Bucarest—the German peace treaty of March 5, 1918—Rumania had again declared war on the Central Powers on November 9, 1918, and was advancing into Transylvania when the Armistice to Germany two days later put a stop to the World War generally. Her troops marched on to the line of the Maros, which had been fixed by the armistice concluded by d'Esperey with the Magyars, and on December 17 the Rumanians were allowed to occupy the rest of Transylvania and other territory

M. TAKE JONESCU

inhabited by Rumanians except the Banat, about which there was a dispute with the Yugoslavs. By the end of the year the Rumanian occupation of the country was completed. Political union had been achieved on December 1 at a convention held at Alba Julia, which proclaimed that Transylvania and other portions of land adjoining and inhabited by Rumanians were part and parcel of the Kingdom of Rumania. A fortnight earlier a National Council at Cernauti, or Czernowitz, had added the Bukovina, latterly an Austrian duchy but formerly included in Moldavia, to Rumania. Already in possession of Bessarabia, Great Rumania was twice the size of the Regat or "Old Kingdom." So Czechoslovakia, Yugoslavia, and Rumania, three of the Succession States, had now attained what was practically their final shape.

Poland, the fourth Succession State, had proclaimed her independence in a united State on November 9 in a republic comprising Austrian as well as Russian and German Poland; five days afterwards Pilsudski arrived in Warsaw and took over the government, but some little time elapsed before harmony was established between him and the National Committee in Paris by the conciliatory activities of Paderewski, who succeeded in forming a Coalition Ministry. As regards Italy, the fifth Succession State, the possession of some of the Austro-Hungarian lands to which she laid claim, especially under the Treaty of London, 1915, was a matter of sharp contention with the Yugoslavs, but no one disputed her right to Tirol and a considerable share of the coastland. Italy, too, was unified. The Habsburg Empire was completely "liquidated."

The Peace Conference

When the Peace Conference was held in Paris in January, 1919, it was presented with accomplished facts arising out of the dissolution of the Dual Monarchy and the redistribution, territorially and politically, of Austria-Hungary: these were, first, a species of survivals in the Republics of Austria and Hungary, which in a way were Succession States, but which in the view of the Allies were mainly regarded as representing the second of the enemy Great Powers defeated in the World War; and, secondly, the other Succession States—Czechoslovakia, Yugoslavia, Rumania, Poland, and Italy. All these seven States had assumed what was approximately their places respectively on the map of the New Europe, but ratification was required from and by the conference, which comprised twenty-seven Allied States with seventy representatives. Italy, as one of the Great Powers, had a specially strong position; her representatives were Orlando and Sonnino. Czechoslovakia had Kramarsh and Benesh, the latter of whom was now well known to the statesmen of France and Great Britain, and had already established a considerable reputation in Europe. Yugoslavia was represented by Pashitch and Trumbitch, the former much more typically Serbian than Yugoslav, and the latter much more Yugoslav than Serbian, but together standing for the new Kingdom of the Serbs, Croats, and Slovenes. John Bratianu headed the Rumanian Delegation, another notable member of it being Vaida Voyed, the leader of the Transylvanians. Take Jonescu had been invited to join it, but had declined. Dmowski and Paderewski represented Poland. Greece had a tower of strength in Venizelos, who was a favourite of the Allies and could count on a good reception: "What he asked," Lansing testified, "was granted because he asked it." Accompanying these stars in the firmament of Central and South-Eastern Europe was a multitude of satellites. Delegates for Austria did not attend until summoned some months later; it was December, 1919, when Hungary was invited to send representatives to Paris.

The first plenary session of the conference was held on January 18, 1919, and was opened by a speech from Poincaré, then President of France; among other things he urged the members to seek nothing but justice and apply the principle of national self-determination. But it was very soon apparent that the decisions would be taken by the five Great Powers—Great Britain, France, Italy, Japan, and the United States, the first three of which were represented by the Prime Minister and the Foreign Minister of the respective States, Japan by two distinguished statesmen, and America by President Wilson and Lansing, Secretary of State; the ten chief figures came to be styled the "Council of Ten." Clemenceau was chosen President of the conference, and his attitude to the minor Allies was not cordial, but harsh and bullying, as was unpleasantly evident at the second plenary session when he told them bluntly that the conference was chiefly the concern of the Great Powers, who had invited them to participate more as an act of grace than anything else. Nor did he respond to the challenge of Hymans, the Belgian Foreign Minister, who asked him how what he had said squared with the repeated declarations of leading Allied statesmen that the War had been fought to uphold the rights of small nations. In the upshot, however, the minor Allies secured representation on the various commissions. Throughout the conference the liberated Nationalities, now ranged under the respective State banners, acted in unison as far as was possible, and maintained a common front against their enemies; in this way they pursued a common fundamental aim. But among themselves there were these differences, previously alluded to in part, which called for adjustment either by themselves or by the conference.

Differences among the Succession States

These differences sprang out of the apportionment of certain parts of the defunct Austro-Hungarian Monarchy. The first was concerned with the division of territories on the Adriatic between the Italians and the Yugoslavs; the second related to the Banat, possession of which was claimed by both the Rumanians and the Yugoslavs; the third was the question of Teschen in Austrian Silesia, about which the Czechoslovaks and the Poles were in opposition. The first and second arose out of the Secret Treaties made by the Allies in the course of and under pressure of the War with a view to obtaining the entrance into the field of Italy and Rumania respectively. The first had already embroiled the Italians and the Yugoslavs while the War was proceeding, but was supposed to have been settled by the agreement arrived at during the Rome Congress of the

Oppressed Nationalities. The Italian Government plainly indicated, however, that it did not regard the matter, the main point of which was possession of Dalmatia and Fiume, as closed, and tension increased between the Italians, who demanded that, according to the Treaty of London, 1915, more than half of the province should be assigned to them, and the Yugoslavs, who asserted that it was theirs, as the vast majority of its population was indubitably Yugoslav. Ill-feeling had been deepened on the one hand by the surrender of the Austro-Hungarian fleet to the Yugoslavs, and, on the other, by the harsh treatment in Italy of some Yugoslav naval officers who had crossed the Adriatic with the news of the surrender. Almost from the start of the Peace Conference the status of the Secret Treaties engaged attention and led to difficulties. Great Britain and France had signed the treaties and were prepared to stand by them if held to their bond, though they were well aware that they violated the principle of Nationality by doing so. Italy was disposed to hold them to their bond.

The United States was in a different position from Great Britain and France, as it was not a party to these treaties and disliked them exceedingly. A suggestion that Wilson should arbitrate between the Italians and the Yugoslavs fell through owing to the hostility of Orlando and Sonnino. In April Wilson published his Declaration on the question of the Adriatic—Dalmatia and especially Fiume—which gave great offence to the Italians, as he maintained that the interests of small States were to be safeguarded quite as much as those of Great Powers, and that the principle of Nationality must be applied to a settlement; consequently Fiume could not be allocated to Italy. As a result, Orlando and Sonnino left the Peace Conference and went to Rome, where they were enthusiastically received; they returned within a few days, and negotiations were resumed, but in the end no agreement was reached, the relations between the Italians and the Yugoslavs remaining embittered for years.

Towards the end of January the second of these differences respecting the redistribution of Habsburg territories came up before the Council of Ten—the rival claims of Rumania and Yugoslavia to the Banat, which consisted of three counties that had belonged to Hungary, and was inhabited by Rumanians on the east, Suabians or Germans and Magyars in the middle, and Serbs on the west. In consonance with the Secret Treaty made in 1916 between Rumania and the Allies, Bratianu put forward a claim to the whole of the Banat. To this Vesnitch, the Serbian Minister in Paris, replied that Serbia had not been consulted by the Allies when they concluded the treaty with Rumania, and therefore it was impossible for Serbia to recognize it as valid. Vesnitch was supported by Trumbitch on behalf of the Yugoslavs; they could not recognize the treaty either, he declared, but were ready to agree that the part of the Banat inhabited by the Rumanians should go to Rumania on the understanding that the part inhabited by their own nationals should be incorporated in the new Serb-Croat-Slovene State, while the Suabians and the Magyars should be consulted about their future. Orlando and Sonnino, in opposition to the eight members of the Council of Ten, who approved the proposal of Trumbitch, would not accept it; they were backing Bratianu, because he had promised to uphold the Treaty of London. Thereupon Trumbitch made his proposal in official form, stating at the time that Yugoslavia adhered to the principle of Nationality, meaning thereby to imply the inadmissibility for the same reason of the Treaty of London. Ultimately the Banat was divided between Rumania and Yugoslavia.

While this controversy was going on a serious dispute between the Poles and the Czechs developed over Teschen in Austrian Silesia. An agreement had been made in the district itself by which part went to Poland and part to Czechoslovakia. France, however, had privately recognized the right of the Czechoslovaks to the whole of it, but when the local Czechoslovak troops advanced into the territory inhabited by the Poles they met with opposition. It seemed as if war could not be avoided between Poland and Czechoslovakia, but the immediate crisis was tided over owing to the tact and skill of Paderewski and Masaryk. The Peace Conference dispatched a commission to

Warsaw, where an arrangement was made and accepted by the Czechs temporarily. This difference, like the two other matters in dispute, was settled, but not till two years passed; until it was finally adjusted by a partition of Austrian Silesia between the two States, their feelings towards each other could not be described as friendly.

Bolshevism in Hungary

For several reasons, among them the quicker dispatch of business and greater secrecy, the Council of Ten became, on March 25, 1919, the Council of Four—Wilson, Clemenceau, Lloyd George, and Orlando; when Orlando was temporarily absent, it was reduced to a Council of Three. The four dictators found themselves faced by a grave crisis over the Bolsheviks. Strong influences emanating from the regions of high international finance, and active from the beginning of the Peace Conference, had been working for the recognition of the Soviet Government. Chicherin, the Bolshevist Commissar for Foreign Affairs, or Soviet Foreign Minister, had offered large commercial concessions in exchange for recognition. Actual hostilities against the Soviet were being undertaken in Europe and Asia with little success by the forces of the Counter-Revolutionaries, though assisted and encouraged by the Allies. A small American mission had been sent to Moscow to investigate and report; it returned in an optimistic mood and with a definite proposal for the virtual recognition of the Lenin régime. Recognition by the Big Four appeared to be assured—to the general dismay, which expressed itself so forcibly that Wilson paused, and recognition was not accorded.

Before this conclusion was reached, the Bolsheviks were giving a demonstration of their methods and aims in a country much nearer Paris than was Russia. On March 22, 1919, Karolyi's Government fell, and a Soviet Government was set up in its place under Bela Kun, a lieutenant of Lenin from Moscow. The ostensible cause of the resignation of Karolyi was the boundary suggested by the Allies for the Republic of Hungary, but Bolshevik intrigue and propaganda also accounted for his overthrow. General Smuts, representing the Big Four, arrived in Budapest on April 4 to examine the position of affairs, but his stay was short; next day he left for Prague, where he saw Masaryk, and then returned to Paris. Bela Kun and his Soviet Republic did not get recognition, much to their disappointment, and doubtless to that of Lenin, who had had some hope of undermining from Budapest the Peace Conference and everything else that promised stability and reconstruction in Europe. Czechoslovakia and other neighbouring States, in which Bolshevik agitation was at work to some extent, as in most of the other countries of Europe, felt alarmed at the Bolshevik hold on Hungary, and in the last days of May, 1919, the Czech Army commenced a campaign against Hungary with the object of driving Bela Kun and the Soviet Government out of the country. At first this offensive did not thrive, and Kositse, or Kassa, the most important town in Eastern Slovakia, was taken by the Red forces from the Czechs. Then the Reds began an advance against Bratislava or Pressburg, the Poszony of the Magyars.

Bela Kun's operations took on the character of a national war, for many Magyars, who had little or no love for him, but who hated the Czechs, enrolled themselves in his ranks. Even those Magyars who were plotting against him secretly held their hand for a while in the hope that he would succeed in restoring Slovakia to Hungary. On June 8 the Council of Four addressed an ultimatum to Bela Kun bidding him stop his campaign against the Czechs, but he temporized and did not obey. Nine days later a second and peremptory ultimatum was sent from Paris ordering him to withdraw from before Bratislava at once, otherwise the French troops concentrated at Szeged and the Rumanian forces at Arad would march on Budapest. This threat made Bela Kun retire in order to defend the capital, but before he withdrew he set up a Slovakian Soviet Republic; it lived but a few days, for the Czechs speedily reoccupied all Slovakia. Next Bela Kun turned his attention to opposing the Rumanian advance from the Tisza, which started on July 28 in force; despite resistance the Rumanians crossed the river on

August 1 and occupied Budapest on August 4. On July 31 Bela Kun had fled to Vienna, and the Hungarian Soviet Republic collapsed. A "White" Terror succeeded the "Red" Terror, and the country was more distracted than ever.

The Peace Treaties

But the Peace Conference had had many other things to deal with, above all the settlement with Germany. On April 28, the day on which the fifth plenary session saw the creation of the League of Nations, the German Delegation began to arrive in Paris, and finally the Peace Treaty was signed in the Palace of Versailles on June 28, 1919. Germany recognized the Succession States. The provision touching the independence of Czechoslovakia covered the inclusion in that State of Carpathian Ruthenia, a small territory chiefly inhabited by Ukrainians which had formed the north-eastern corner of Hungary; the extension of the new State to the east was thus formally indicated in an international agreement. Poland obtained the definite cession of what had been German Poland, or most of it, and a commission was appointed to trace on the spot the boundaries of Poland and Czechoslovakia.

Next to the settlement with Germany came that with Austria. The Peace Treaty with Austria was signed in the Château of St. Germain-en-Laye on September 10, 1919, the Austrian National Assembly in Vienna having agreed to accept it two days earlier. Both the Yugoslavs and the Rumanians had dissented to parts of the treaty. The latter persisted, and the matter was postponed. After some sharp exchanges between Paris and Bucarest, the Rumanian Government intimated in November that it would sign without reservation. Naturally the St. Germain Treaty possessed a greater interest for the Succession States than the Versailles Treaty, as it materially affected all of them. The introduction to the treaty significantly noted that the War originated in the Declaration made against Serbia by Austria-Hungary, that Austria-Hungary had ceased to exist, and that the States of Czechoslovakia and Yugoslavia had been recognized. By the treaty Austria recognized the independence of Czechoslovakia, Yugoslavia, Poland, and Hungary, and accepted their frontiers and those of Rumania as these had been or were ultimately to be determined; commissions were appointed to delimit the boundaries. The fate of the Klagenfurt area was to be settled by plebiscite—ultimately it went to Austria. Provision was made for the protection of racial Minorities. Eastern Galicia was transferred to the Allies, and the Trentino, Southern Tirol, Trieste, and Istria went to Italy, the line of the common frontier with Yugoslavia being left for settlement at a later date. Among other provisions were the internationalization of the Danube and the prohibition of the union of Austria with Germany without the consent of the Council of the League of Nations; the pre-War National Debt was to be shared by the Succession States, and Austria was to pay reparation for thirty years from 1921.

This treaty did not come into existence without a great deal of discussion, criticism, and controversy in the Peace Conference and outside it. Austria still had friends in Great Britain and France, and these, with others who regarded the subject from a colder point of view, considered the terms of the treaty unduly severe on various grounds. Even in the Peace Conference itself a tendency to deal leniently with Austria had been noticeable at times. Propaganda minimized her share in the War and spoke of the dire effects of destroying the economic unity which was alleged to have been a very important and exceedingly valuable feature of the former Empire; it was maintained that reduced to a small State of six millions, overweighted with Vienna and its two million inhabitants, the Austrian Republic could not long survive. A project was mooted for the formation of a Danubian Federation, with Vienna and Budapest as its central points, which would have been in essence a reconstruction of Austria-Hungary, and might even have led to the return of the Habsburgs, but the Succession States concerned, with the exception of course of Austria and Hungary, could see no advantage in it to them, but much the reverse; as Masaryk tersely put it, "They were too well satisfied with the freedom they had obtained to think of resuming their chains." In any case, all ideas that aimed at the resuscitation of the Empire failed to take into account the fundamental fact that it had been broken up by the majority of the Nationalities which composed it, and not by the Allies, though their success contributed greatly to the result.

Pribram, the Austrian historian, in his book *Austrian Foreign Policy, 1908–18*, phrased it: "Austria-Hungary broke down in consequence of the disastrous War. She might, but for the War, have existed as a Great Power for many years longer. The World War was therefore the immediate occasion of the downfall of the old Monarchy. But the deeper causes of its collapse lay in the irreconcilable antagonism of the different Nationalities, which aimed at an independence incompatible with the idea of imperial unity and of the ascendancy which the Germans had enjoyed for hundreds of years. Regrets, however, are of no avail. History has pronounced its verdict. Austria-Hungary is no more." The simple truth was that the final blow to the Dual Monarchy was dealt by the peoples who had been oppressed by the Habsburgs—the Czechoslovaks, the Yugoslavs, the Rumanians of Transylvania, and the Poles of Galicia. And as this was the case, no scheme for reviving the Empire, such as the Danubian Federation, had the slightest chance of being considered by those who had been freed from the onerous political servitude it had imposed.

Anschluss

On a different plane was the idea of the union of Austria with Germany—*Anschluss an Deutschland*. Politically the Austrian Republic was divided nearly equally between the Christian Socialists and the Social Democrats; most of the former party opposed the union, but the great bulk of the latter party favoured it. The Austrians who still hoped for a Habsburg restoration saw in it an end to their dreams; on the other side were arrayed the pan-Germans still faithful, despite the issue of the World War, to the pan-German plan. While the ultra-clerical party disliked too close an association with

Protestant Germany, the Social Democrats advocated Anschluss because it held out the prospect of their gaining support from the German Social Democracy. Bauer, the Foreign Minister of the Austrian Republic, and a protagonist of the union with Germany, entered into negotiations at Weimar and Berlin with the authorities of the Reich, and together they produced a scheme which was to be laid before the National Assemblies of Germany and Austria, and on ratification was to bring about the object desired.

This, too, figured among the excursions and alarms of which the Peace Conference was the theatre; to the Council it suggested a resurgence of the Mittel Europa programme with its vast implications; to the Succession States, especially to Czechoslovakia, almost islanded among German populations, it bore a much more direct and immediate menace. And this had resulted in the insertion of clauses in both the Versailles and St. Germain Treaties categorically forbidding the union, a policy that was reinforced by pressure from the Allies on Vienna and its Government. Bauer was dismissed, and at least temporarily Anschluss fell into the background. This and other matters of common interest were kept steadily before the Peace Conference by the representatives of the Succession States, who often acted as a unit. A striking instance of this occurred during the discussion of the financial clauses of the Treaty of St. Germain. The question under review was concerned with pre-War reparations and War debts, and the members of the Czechoslovak, Yugoslav, Rumanian, and Polish Delegations agreed on a joint course of action. At the plenary session of the Reparations Commission on May 26, 1919, which dealt with the reparation terms of the proposed treaty with Austria, Trumbitch accordingly appeared as the spokesman of the four States, and announced that they jointly rejected any claim from them of reparations and accepted only a share of the pre-War debt of the Monarchy; this had the consequence of there being a revision of the clause to which they had taken objection. The collaboration of Czechoslovakia, Yugoslavia, and Rumania in this case, as in many others, again foreshadowed the formation of the Little Entente, with Poland also cooperating.

Habsburg Reaction

During August, 1919, while the terms of the Peace Treaty with Austria were still under consideration, the actual situation in Hungary after the disappearance of Bela Kun and his Soviet Republic caused renewed disquiet and apprehension. For about a week after the flight of Kun, at the end of July, the Government was in the hands of the moderate Socialists under Pedl, but on August 7 a *coup d'état*, organized by the counter-revolutionaries at Arad and Szeged, established a new Government which appointed the Archduke Joseph Governor of State, with Friedrich as Prime Minister. The Archduke was the only member of the Habsburg family who was beloved by the Magyars, among whom he lived as one of themselves. But he was a Habsburg, and that was sufficient to condemn him in the eyes of the Succession States, for they saw in him the head of a reactionary movement in favour of the restoration of the Habsburg dynasty and all for which it had stood. It could not be forgotten that the Emperor Charles, while renouncing any share in the Government of the Monarchy, had never abdicated in the sense of renouncing the Throne. There was the fact, moreover, that the Allied missions in Budapest had accepted, for the time being, the new Government. Besides, on August 9, the Supreme Council requested Rumania to arrest the advance of her troops, and this, too, could be interpreted as something in the nature of recognition. In an article entitled "The Little Entente," Benesh wrote of this time: "The Habsburg menace became acute as early as August, 1919, when the Archduke Joseph Habsburg seized the reins of power. Czechoslovakia at once sent a very emphatic Note to the Peace Conference on the dangers of a Habsburg restoration for Central European peace. The sequel to this step was the Note of the Supreme Council of August 21 announcing the opposition of the Allied States to a Habsburg Government in Hungary. The Archduke's designs were thus checked."

The Council made it clear that no Habsburg could have any place in any Hungarian Government, but a few months afterwards it was called on to make its verdict still clearer, without succeeding in putting a permanent stop, however, to the Habsburg movement. The Archduke's reign, if such it could be called, was of the briefest, but Friedrich contrived to remain Prime Minister till the departure of the Rumanians and the entry of Horthy into Budapest on November 16. In his Note to the Peace Conference, Benesh pointed out that the fears of a Habsburg restoration which were felt by the Czechoslovaks were shared equally by the Yugoslavs and the Rumanians. The menace was common to all, and it was their business to meet and overcome it. As the understanding grew of the danger which went on threatening them, an alliance of the three States became inevitable and the Little Entente was the outcome. The monarchist agitation in Hungary increased. In January, 1920, negotiations began at Paris for the Peace Treaty; in that month elections were held throughout Hungary for a National Assembly, and while they were proceeding the movement in favour of the Habsburgs attained large proportions. But a month earlier Benesh had started the conversations with the Yugoslavs that were the immediate origin of the Little Entente, its primary object being the safeguarding, as against Hungary, of the liberation of the Nationalities that had been achieved.

Treaty of Neuilly

Before the Peace Treaty was presented to Hungary, Bulgaria had signed her Peace Treaty with the Allies at Neuilly on November 27, 1919, after negotiations extending over three months. This treaty included the parts of the German and Austrian Peace Treaties that applied to Bulgaria; its preamble was identical with that in the Austrian Treaty. The Succession States mainly interested, though not on the ground of their being Succession States, were Yugoslavia and Rumania. The former gained small portions of territory on her eastern frontier, while the latter had restored to her the Dobrudja, which the Central Powers had assigned to Bulgaria by the Treaty of

Bucarest, 1918. The Treaty of Neuilly had afterwards a certain bearing on the internal and external relations of the Little Entente, inasmuch as Yugoslavia and Rumania entered into a treaty with respect to the fulfilment of the terms of the Peace Treaty by Bulgaria. In addition to that, this treaty fell into the general category of the Peace Treaties, and therefore to that extent came within the wider scope of the international affairs in which the Little Entente had an abiding concern, as making for the pacification and reconstruction of Europe. Any agreement that held in it the promise of peace in the explosive area of the Balkans was in itself a highly desirable thing. No one could forget, or was likely to forget, that it was in that region that the first shots in the World War had been fired. Like Austria, Bulgaria submitted to the Peace Treaty perforce; doubtless it was bitter to see her erstwhile rival Serbia aggrandized into Yugoslavia. Yet though not included in Yugoslavia, she herself was of the Southern Slavs, and an entente between them was not precluded in the course of time, as in the interest of both countries.

That it was well within the bounds of possibility that those who had been enemies should arrive, if not at an entente, at least at an accommodation and make the best of the situation, was effectively demonstrated when Benesh, as Foreign Minister of Czechoslovakia, invited Renner, the Austrian Chancellor, to Prague in January, 1920, for the purpose of discussing various important subjects which had their own attraction for the two statesmen, as being material to the welfare of their two peoples. Therein was revealed another of the aims which animated the far-seeing policy of Benesh, and with which the Little Entente was to be informed: a policy of friendly collaboration with other nations, above all with neighbouring States. No doubt it could be represented, as equally no doubt it was, that it was easy for him to talk in that way as he had got, or was about to get, all he wanted for Czechoslovakia, but he showed that his words were not an insufferable pose, for not only did he sincerely desire to bury the hatchet and discard all hatreds, but he offered to assist actively and substantially in ameliorating the hard lot, as hard it unquestionably was, of former foes. Therefore he said to Austria, with the full approval of Masaryk, whose disciple he was, "We Czechoslovaks will help you." As things were, it was not possible for him to say that to Hungary. The Magyars themselves, believing their hostility was absolutely justified, made it impossible.

Treaty of Trianon

For the three chief Succession States the Peace Treaty with Hungary was the most important of the series of treaties—for Czechoslovakia because of Slovakia; for Yugoslavia because of Croatia-Slavonia and the Adriatic question; and for Rumania because of Transylvania. The loss of these territories to Hungary meant a reduction of her pre-War area by about two-thirds; it was proper, however, to observe that she had already lost them before the Peace Treaty was presented to her, for by that time they were already in the possession of the three Succession States respectively. The treaty with Hungary, like that with Austria, confirmed, broadly speaking, the possession of these territories by these States, but in addition filled in or made provision for filling in details respecting the delimitation of frontiers. The Hungarian Delegation to the Peace Conference arrived in Paris on January 7, 1920. At its head was Apponyi, who, since the murder of Tisza by revolutionaries in Budapest in November, 1918, stood out as the foremost Magyar of the day. He was supported by Teleki and Bethlen, both Magyar leaders, and both subsequently Prime Ministers of Hungary; and with them was associated a large number of commissioners, experts, and councillors.

It was safe to say that no enemy State, everything considered, was more amply or ably represented than was Hungary at the conference. On January 15 the Supreme Council handed to the Delegation the terms of the treaty, and next day listened to a long speech by Apponyi setting forth what he declared to be the true situation of Hungary past and present. Two days later most of the members of the Delegation returned to Budapest for consultation with the Government on the reply to be made regarding the various conditions laid down in the treaty. Meanwhile the members who remained at Paris delivered to the Council preliminary Notes dealing with the question of the Nationalities and the "invasion of the country by the neighbouring people," as the action of the non-Magyar Nationalities and their friends was described. These Notes, of which there were many, were necessarily written from the Magyar point of view, and though they did not refer specifically to the terms of the treaty—some of the Notes had been drawn up in advance—they discussed at length every possible aspect of the "Hungarian problem." Observations on the treaty itself were elaborated at Budapest, and on February 12 those members of the Delegation who had gone there went back to Paris. Part of the Reply-Notes were handed to the Council, and the remainder were delivered later.

All these Notes, with their annexes, taken together ran into hundreds of documents, some of them of considerable length and many of them bristling with statistics. They completely covered the whole ground of controversy, no smallest corner of it being left untouched. The Supreme Council therefore was seized of the fullest information about Hungary from the Magyar standpoint, and was thus able to evaluate the arguments urged in her favour by the Delegation. No case for the defence was ever more strongly presented nor was one ever more carefully considered; but it failed to convince the Supreme Council. The core of the defence was the plea of the "Integrity of Hungary"—that the thousand-year-old State was a geographical, historical, and economic unit, and therefore should not be broken up. Further, in a Memorial on the Frontiers, it was pleaded that if Hungary was dismembered, as the peace proposals postulated, "State-formations would spring into being which every expert geographer would condemn to death in advance, for geographical absurdities never last long. The part of Hungary left would be surrounded by such frontiers as cannot by any means be called natural, and would therefore be the causes of eternal feuds, political disturbances and, moreover, of cultural and economic decadence. The process of dismemberment must be disastrous to the peoples living on both sides of the new frontier." The Council rejected these pleas.

If the Hungarian Delegation was active, the representatives at Paris of the three Succession States were certainly not less busy in the work of rebutting the statements and statistics, which they characterized as tendentious, that had been submitted by it to the Council. In February, 1920, the delegates of these States entered, automatically as it were, on common action, and Osusky, the Czechoslovak delegate, proposed that a joint reply should be drafted and sent to the conference in answer to Apponyi. This was accordingly done, the Memorandum being signed by Ghika for Rumania, by Zolgger for Yugoslavia, and by Osusky for Czechoslovakia. The emission of this official document was immensely significant, for it more than hinted at the formation of the Little Entente; it might indeed be said to be the first document produced by the Little Entente, though that organization had not been actually constituted. The meaning of the conjunction was a matter of general comment in the Press. On February 19 *The Times*, in an article, had stated on authoritative information that the Governments of Rumania, Yugoslavia, and Czechoslovakia had decided to make *démarches* in common concerning every question connected with the Hungarian Peace Treaty. Apponyi and the other Hungarian delegates heard the news; they also learned of the Memorandum signed by the three States and handed to the Council; and they requested to be permitted to reply to it orally, but such a method had been disallowed in the case of the other Peace Treaties and was refused in this case too.

Name of Little Entente

The Magyars were disposed to laugh at the combination of the Succession States; it was this very derision which led to that political combination receiving what became its distinctive appellation. On February 21, 1920, the Budapest daily paper *Pesti Hirlap* published an article in which it spoke contemptuously of the small and insignificant Little Entente as a ridiculous analogue of the Big Entente. The expression *la Petite Entente* soon became popular in Paris, and the delegates of the three States speedily adopted it among themselves. Though Benesh in a speech later referred to the "so-called Little Entente," the name stuck and came into general use even among the Succession States as an honourable and adequate designation.

It was not the first time that a term given in derision had been accepted and changed into a badge worn proudly by those at whom it had been thrust. So was it with *Les Gueux*, the Beggars of the Flemish League, with the *Sans-Culottes* of the French Revolution, and with the names Tory and Whig, originally abusive epithets applied by the two British political parties respectively to each other, but subsequently cherished by both as much esteemed labels. As often, history was repeating itself. The Little Entente, if not yet under that name, was in process of formation by the exchange of messages between the Foreign Ministers of the three States in that same month of February when the Peace Treaty with Hungary was being discussed and the battle of arguments continued. On May 6 the definite conditions of peace were put before the Hungarian Delegation, and showed no essential modification.

Millerand's Letter

In a covering letter, Millerand, the President of the Supreme Council, stated that the Allies had studied with the most scrupulous attention the Notes in which the Delegation had set forth its observations, with the result that they found it impossible to adopt the point of view of the Delegation. While the Allies hoped that the Hungary of the future would become an element of stability and peace, they could not forget the share of responsibility falling on Hungary with respect to the World War and in general the imperialistic policy pursued by the Dual Monarchy. They had not answered the propositions formulated in the numerous documents presented by the Delegation relating to the frontiers of Hungary. "It is not without ripe reflection that the Allied and Associated Powers have adopted the standpoint of not modifying any of the territorial clauses in the conditions of peace," said Millerand. "In coming to this resolution they have been guided by the consideration that any modification of the frontiers fixed by them would lead to inconveniences graver than those proclaimed by the Hungarian Delegation." Ethnographic conditions in Central Europe were such that it was impossible for the political frontiers in their total extent to coincide with the ethnical frontiers; thus certain isles of Magyar population would pass under the sovereignty of another State. "But no statement pretending that it would have been better not to modify the former territorial status can be based on this situation. A state of affairs, even if millennial, was not meant to exist when it was recognized as contrary to justice."

The Delegation had asked for a plebiscite, but the Council thought it quite unnecessary. "The will of the people was expressed in October and November, 1918, at the collapse of the Dual Monarchy, when the populations, oppressed for so long, united with their Italian, Rumanian, Yugoslav, and Czechoslovak kindred. The events occurring since that epoch constitute so many more proofs of the sentiments of the Nationalities formerly subjected to the Crown of St. Stephen. The tardy measures taken by the Hungarian Government to satisfy the need felt by the Nationalities of an autonomy is not able to create any illusion; they do not change at all the essentials of historic truth—notably that during long years all the efforts of Hungarian policy were directed to stifling the voice of the ethnical Minorities." The question of the actual lines of the frontiers, Millerand went on, had been deeply studied by the Council, but it was possible that an inquiry held on the spot might make apparent the necessity of making some changes of the limits provided by the treaty. In that case, if the Delimitation Commission found that the "provisions of the treaty in some spot create an injustice which it would be to the general interest to remedy," then it was permissible for the Commission "to address a report on the subject to the Council of the League of Nations," which might, at the request of one of the parties concerned, offer its services for an "amicable rectification of the original demarcation." The Allies expressed their confidence that this method of procedure would correct all injustices in the demarcation of the frontiers "against which objections not unfounded" could be raised.

Alluding to Carpathian Ruthenia, Millerand noted that the union of it with Czechoslovakia had been recognized by the Allies in a treaty with that State which contained special guarantees for the autonomy of the Ruthenians. Towards the close of his letter Millerand said: "As to the isles of Magyar population passing under another sovereignty, the treaties for the protection of the Minorities already signed by Rumania and the Serb-Croat Slovene State, and ratified by Czechoslovakia, guarantee their entire safeguarding." In the Reply itself it was stated under the heading of "Protection of Minorities": "The rules to be imposed for the protection of Minorities in all the Western States of Europe which have suffered great territorial readjustment have been made the subject of lengthy discussion and study. Those proposed by Hungary would, if adopted, carry in their train insurmountable complications." Finding the treaty still inacceptable, the Hungarian Delegation placed its resignation in the hands of the Budapest Government, which accepted it. When informing the Peace Conference of this, the Hungarian Government intimated that it would sign the Peace Treaty "owing to the pressure of political circumstances." The treaty was signed in the Château of Trianon, June 4, 1920, and the series of treaties in which the Succession States were vitally interested was concluded.

The Little Entente States

Although all the details of the frontiers of the chief Succession States were not finally settled till 1921, the area, composition, and political status, with competent organization, of these States were established by the summer of 1920. Of the three, Czechoslovakia early showed herself the most advanced politically and economically in the art and practice of government. Her Constitution was passed by the National Assembly in Prague on February 28, 1920; on May 28, 1920, Masaryk,

President from the beginning of her existence, was elected President for a term of seven years. The dispute with Poland over Teschen was decided by the Ambassadors' Conference on July 28, 1920, part of the district being assigned, as already stated, to Poland and the other part to Czechoslovakia. Consisting of Bohemia, Moravia, part of Silesia—the Czech National Historical Lands—Slovakia, Carpathian Ruthenia, and of various small German and Austrian territories allotted to the Republic by the Peace Conference, Czechoslovakia had an area of 54,207 square miles and a population of about thirteen and a half millions. The census of February 15, 1921, made the population 13,613,172, placing her tenth on the list of the States of Europe as regarded numerical strength; the figures roundly were much the same in 1920. The population included upwards of three million Germans and about three-quarters of a million Magyars, the former mainly in Bohemia, and the latter in Slovakia; there were also nearly 76,000 Poles.

These Minorities, especially the large German minority, constituted a serious problem in the consolidation of the country that had to be faced; a long step towards its solution was made by giving them full representation in the Parliament; in 1920 the Chamber of Deputies, the popular House, comprised 199 Czechoslovaks, 72 Germans, and 7 Magyars. The Constitution safeguarded all racial groups, big and little, and assured to them the maintenance of their schools. A new State, Czechoslovakia had to build up her whole system as a political and economic entity from the foundations. At the outset and for a time unrest, uncertainty, and confusion were seen in some quarters, but order was well maintained generally, and the work of consolidation steadily progressed. With respect to State-structure, both Yugoslavia and Rumania were in a different position from Czechoslovakia. Rumania had been an organized State for years, as Serbia had likewise been. The great enlargement of these States brought with it some difficult problems of national consolidation, but at any rate much more than foundations were in existence. There was Rumania with her King and Government, and the Rumanians of Transylvania joined themselves and their country to Rumania in the most natural way in the world. It was not quite so simple in the case of Yugoslavia.

On December 1, 1918, the Prince Regent Alexander of Serbia had proclaimed the unitary Kingdom of the Serbs, Croats, and Slovenes, but while doing so he referred to Serbia on the one hand, and to the independent State of the Serbs, Croats, and Slovenes, on the other. Pashitch and Trumbitch had agreed at Geneva in November, 1918, that a unitary Government for Serbia and the Southern Slavs should be elected alongside of the individual Serbian and Southern Slav Governments. Serbia was invited to the Peace Conference as an independent Allied State, but some time passed before Yugoslavia was definitely recognized by the Allies. The first Yugoslav Parliament, held at Belgrade on March 1, 1919, was not elected at all, but consisted of some eighty members of the Skupshtina of Serbia and representatives of the organizations in the territories severed from Austria-Hungary. In a speech the Prince Regent said that his replies accepting the resolutions for union voted by the various National Councils and Assemblies had been received with enthusiasm in "Sarajevo and Belgrade, Zagreb and Novi-Sad, Ljubljana (Laibach), and Cettinge, Split (Spalato), and Skoplie"; these were the capitals of the country. Great Britain, on May 9, and France on June 5, 1919, formally recognized the Serb-Croat-Slovene State—Yugoslavia.

The provisional Government prepared the way for the meeting of a Constituent Assembly, and this met at Belgrade; the Constitution, commonly called Vidovdan, was passed on June 28, 1921, and all Yugoslavia was unified. In 1920 this State consisted of Serbia, Montenegro, Bosnia, Herzegovina, Dalmatia, Croatia-Slavonia, Slovenia, the Voivodina, and some small portions of territory formerly Austrian or Hungarian, its total area being 96,134 square miles, and its population, according to a census taken at the end of that year, a little more than twelve millions. After long and difficult negotiations a settlement of the frontier with Italy was reached on

November 12, 1920, except as regarded Fiume. Like the other Succession States, Yugoslavia was confronted from the start with the heavy problem of national consolidation, the trouble arising not nearly so much in her case from questions relating to Minorities as from differences among the Yugoslavs themselves springing naturally enough from wide variations in the political, legal, economic, cultural, and other conditions in which they had lived in Serbia and Austria-Hungary in the old days. During the War, Pashitch, the representative of Serbia, and Trumbitch, the leader of the Yugoslavs belonging then to Austria-Hungary, were often on different sides; even at the Peace Conference they did not always see eye to eye. The Constitution of Yugoslavia put Serbians, Croats, and Slovenes on a footing of absolute political equality, but Zagreb, the headquarters of the Croats, preferred a federal system, and accused Belgrade, the centre of the Serbians, of pursuing a too-decided centralist policy.

The issue of federalism as against centralism was subordinated to another question in which Zagreb was quite as deeply interested as was Belgrade—the controversy with Italy; this exerted so strong a unifying influence that a separatist policy on the part of either Zagreb or Belgrade was completely outside even contemplation. The settlement with Italy left about three-quarters of a million Slovenes and Croats in the territories added to that Kingdom. The Peace Treaties left, on the other side of the account, more than a million Germans, Magyars, and Rumanians in Yugoslavia, whose interests, however, were safeguarded by a Minority Treaty signed in December, 1919, and also protected by the Constitution under which the representation in Parliament of the Minorities was guaranteed.

Enlarged Rumania, after the Peace Treaties, consisted of the Old Kingdom or Regat, Bessarabia, the Bukovina, Transylvania, Crisana, Maramuresh, and part of the Banat, the total area being 122,282 square miles, with a population of 17,400,000. The Minorities comprised about two millions—1,305,000 Magyars and Szeklers (akin in race to the Magyars) in Transylvania, and upwards of half a million Germans in Transylvania and the Banat. At the Convention held at Alba Julia on December 1, 1918, which proclaimed the union with Rumania of Transylvania and the other lands in Hungary inhabited by Rumanians, a series of resolutions was passed, including a statement of the principles to be followed respecting Minorities; these were remarkably liberal. In December, 1919, Rumania signed the Minority Treaty imposed, much against her will, by the Peace Conference, but in her Constitution, not adopted, however, till March, 1923, she pledged herself to observe its stipulations. As in the other chief Succession States, Rumania was also confronted with the problem of internal consolidation, but it was not vexed by differences such as subsisted between the Serbians and the Croats, for there was no question between Transylvania and the rest of Rumania that at all suggested separatism. Her most disturbing problem internally was concerned with the Minorities, notably the large Magyar Minority in Transylvania.

Poland

Poland's independence had been recognized by the Versailles Treaty on June 28, 1919, but all her frontiers did not assume their definitive lines for nearly two years afterwards, delimitation on the east being reached by the Peace Treaty with Soviet Russia signed at Riga on May 2, 1921. When thus constituted the Polish State contained various Minorities which together formed a large proportion of its total population, and it had signed a pledge at the Peace Conference to protect them; the Polish Minorities Treaty came into force on January 10, 1920. In 1921 Poland consisted of Congress Poland—the Poland delimited and assigned to Russia by the Congress of Vienna, 1815—Galicia, German Poland, Upper Silesia, and the Vilna district, with a total area of about 150,000 square miles, and a population upwards of 27,000,000, one-third of which was Polish neither in race nor speech, one of the largest compact Minorities being composed of three million Ukrainians in Eastern Galicia. In former days it had been the policy of the Habsburgs to play off the Ukrainians against the Poles, and in the Galician Provincial Diet there had been constant disputes between the two Nationalities. Before quitting Galicia, Austria placed the Ukrainians in power at Lwow, or Lemberg, and a struggle for possession ensued between them and the Poles. The Peace Conference, in effect, settled the quarrel and the fate of the region by placing it under the administration of Poland, for this led to the absorption of Eastern Galicia by that State.

The Peace Treaties, including that of Riga, left Poland the difficult problems of her relations with Germany and Soviet Russia, but her great internal problem was the same as that of the other Succession States—national consolidation. Of Italy, the remaining aggrandized Succession State to be considered, it was the case that this problem of national consolidation after the World War troubled her the least, for in comparison with the immense bulk of her purely Italian population, her Minorities, partly German but more largely Croat and Slovene, were inconsiderable—36,000,000 to less than a million. What gave special importance to the Slav part of the Minorities was its connexion with the Adriatic question and its sympathy with Yugoslavia.

Austria and Hungary

By the St. Germain Treaty, Austria consisted of Lower and Upper Austria, Salzburg, Styria, Carinthia, Tirol, and Vorarlberg, with a total area of about 31,000 square miles and a population of upwards of six millions—predominantly German. A Constitution was passed in October, 1920, by the National Assembly. Hungary ratified the Trianon Treaty on November 13, 1920; her area was then about 36,000 square miles and her population nearly eight millions, including a large German Minority, a considerable Czechoslovak Minority, a smaller Serbo-Croat Minority, a still smaller Rumanian Minority, and an inconsiderable number of Ukrainians. According to the census taken at the close of 1920 the Magyars formed nearly ninety per cent. of the whole population, but the rights of all the Minorities were guaranteed by the Peace Treaties, as in the other States.

Elections on the basis of universal suffrage took place in Hungary during January and February, 1920, and a coalition of the parties of the Right was returned to power. The new Parliament elected a Regent in Admiral Horthy, his official title being "Protector of the Magyar Republic." On March 23, 1920, a Government Order decreed that Hungary should become a Monarchy, that the Cabinet be called the "Royal Hungarian Ministry," that Hungary be styled a Monarchy in all official documents, and the Royal Arms adopted again. Teleki became Prime Minister in July, in succession to Huszar, by whose Government the Treaty of Trianon was signed. Under the cloak of legitimism, Habsburg propaganda had continued active, and was not checked even by a Note sent by the Supreme Council on February 10, 1920, supplementing its previous Note of August 21, 1919, announcing that the Allies were opposed to a Habsburg Government in Hungary. During the Teleki régime the monarchist reactionaries became bolder and bolder, and in December his Government decided in favour of a purely national kind of elective monarchy, but though this action was stated to be taken against the legitimists, it was widely believed to be merely a cover for a Habsburg restoration. But the negotiations which had been progressing for some time between Czechoslovakia, Yugoslavia, and Rumania had already resulted in the definite formation of the Little Entente, and its invincible determination to oppose all such plans was a political certainty that every Magyar had to take into account.

CHAPTER IV

THE LITTLE ENTENTE FORMED

1920

ALTHOUGH the three chief Succession States had by the middle of 1920 their frontiers coloured on the map of Europe and their internal consolidation in process of accomplishment, they yet could not escape sharing to the full the feeling of uncertainty and insecurity, stressed by chaotic economic and financial conditions, that permeated the political atmosphere of the Continent at the time. Besides the direct consequences of the War shown in impoverishment, want, and misery in many lands, the precariousness of the general situation was emphasized in Germany, where the young Republic contended against monarchist reaction; in Poland, still fast in her death-grips struggle with the Bolsheviks; in Soviet Russia, with her threat of world revolution and incessant propaganda and intrigues in foreign countries, despite her own anarchy; in the Baltic, with its fringe of new small States enmeshed in difficulties; in Austria, apparently on the verge of final collapse; in Hungary, with her angry and defiant Magyars; in Italy, menaced by a Communist upheaval; and in Greece and Turkey, where the War could scarcely be said to have terminated.

All the Peace Treaties, except that with Turkey, had been signed; there had been what Masaryk had called the "great refashioning of Central and Eastern Europe and of Europe as a whole." But vast numbers of people in most States, old or new, and not a few even in Czechoslovakia, seriously doubted whether the sweeping changes covered by the Treaties would or could be permanent; and all such doubts were being skilfully exploited by Red Communism in its fight against stabilization and reconstruction. The dearth of money and credit, as well as the high tariff walls raised by exaggerations of nationalism between State and State, added still darker tones to the dreary and discouraging picture. America was in full retreat from Europe. But Great Britain and France held together, and also held the rest of the Continent together; so long as the Anglo-French Entente lasted there was hope of better days to come. Then there was the new and untried League of Nations, the Covenant, with its programme of peace, being incorporated in the Peace Treaties. The Covenant spoke of international cooperation and international security, but each and every State, which was in an unstable position for any reason, feared that it would not do to attach a high value to the Tenth Article, though it was fundamental, as it provided: "The Members of the League undertake to respect and preserve as against external aggression the territorial integrity and existing political independence of all Members of the League. In case of any such aggression, or in case of any threat or danger of such aggression, the Council shall advise upon the means by which this obligation shall be fulfilled."

The trouble, of course, was that the League had no force at its disposal capable of imposing its decisions on anybody, and therefore might be disregarded by everybody. Many people, indeed, disbelieved in the League, while others saw in it a panacea for the ills from which Europe was suffering, the truth being that the League was then quite an "unknown quantity." It was out of this flux of confusion and doubt that the Little Entente emerged, to become at once an instrument making for peace and reconstruction in Central and South-Eastern Europe, and hence of all Europe; as making for peace, it took its stand once and for all on the Peace Treaties, and as making for reconstruction, it definitely pursued a policy of helpful collaboration with neighbouring and other States.

Aims of the Little Entente

In an article contributed to *Eastern Europe*, December, 1921, Benesh wrote: "The Little Entente came into being not only for the purpose of supervising and assuring the application of the terms of the Treaties of Peace, but, above all, to safeguard the heritage of the revolution, of that terrible convulsion, to lay definitely the foundations of a New Order, and to reconstitute politically, economically, and socially the Central Europe of the future. Such is the deep significance of the Little Entente. It is not a military enterprise, nor is it a project of conjectural politics. It is something infinitely more: it is the expression of the constructive forces which are at work in Central Europe. It is, as it were, the vertebral column of the new political and economic system in those regions. It is an instrument of collaboration offered to a world which is trying to reconstruct itself."

Writing in the same number of *Eastern Europe*, Take Jonescu viewed the subject from a slightly different angle when he said: "To every man who does not deceive himself it is evident that after such a war as we have just suffered, and which has turned the past upside down, the nations will fall into two groups—the satisfied and the dissatisfied, those interested in safeguarding what they have justly gained, and those who dream only of destroying what has been obtained by their victorious adversaries. A war which, as Viviani has said, has been a revolution, does not end with the signature of peace treaties. It is continued in the very souls of peoples, and the duty of statesmen is to create and maintain such a condition of things as shall convince those who would reverse the newly-established order of the inanity, and even the danger, of any such attempt. It is not a question of perpetuating the idea of war. It is no desire to disregard the determination of humanity to maintain the peace of the world. But it is not sensible to imagine that the vanquished of yesterday, who likewise provoked the catastrophe, have accepted, or will accept, the judgment before which they have been compelled to bow by force of arms."

Jonescu's range was restricted to the necessity that pressed for immediate attention—the safeguarding of the new political status brought about by the War and the action of the Nationalities, which had been confirmed by the Treaties of Peace. The range of Benesh was wider; it also considered the stage that had been reached, but it looked to the future and its developments—to lay the foundations of a New Order, but foundations on which should arise the splendid fabric of a reconstituted Central Europe. Safeguarding the heritage of the

Revolution which had overthrown the Habsburg Empire inevitably came first with the three chief Succession States; it was a matter of far deeper interest to all of them taken together than anything else; and the logic of things just as inevitably brought them to combine to meet any attack on the heritage of which they had entered into possession. And safeguarding that heritage was the same as maintaining the Peace Treaties, so far as they applied to them in common. All three were vitally concerned with the maintenance of the Treaty of Trianon; all three were faced from the very outset by the determined hostility of the Magyars, which had, in fact, begun months before the Little Entente was formed, as was indicated in the previous chapter.

The Negotiations

Published by the Czechoslovak Ministry of Foreign Affairs in 1923 at Prague, a White Book containing "Diplomatic Documents relating to the Conventions of Alliance concluded by the Czechoslovak Republic with the Kingdom of the Serbs, Croats, and Slovenes, and the Kingdom of Rumania," illustrated very clearly the progress of the negotiations that led up to the formation of the Little Entente, as well as the scope of these conventions. Implicit in the correspondence disclosed in these documents was the preparation for the Little Entente by discussion and action in common during the Peace Conference by the leaders of the Succession States. Of the documents, the first, and as typical as any of the series, was dated Paris, December, 1919, and addressed to Benesh at Prague. It recorded a conversation between Trumbitch and Osusky, the Czechoslovak Minister to France, who sent the dispatch to his chief. It stated that Trumbitch and the Yugoslav Delegation to the Peace Conference were in favour of collective action against Hungary, in the event of the Magyars making an attack; it added that Trumbitch had referred to his Government at Belgrade the proposal for a defensive convention which evidently Benesh had submitted to him during a visit to Paris shortly before, and which had afterwards been approved by

President Masaryk and the Czechoslovak Government. The second document, dated Prague, January 5, 1920, and sent by Benesh to Vaida, the Prime Minister of Rumania, at Bucarest, was of special importance. Benesh suggested that so far as Hungary was concerned the interests of Rumania and Czechoslovakia were absolutely identical, and that the time had come for the two States to take action in common respecting the Magyar menace—of which he reminded Vaida they had often spoken when they had met at Paris. He went on to say that he was in close touch with Yugoslavia in this matter, and he concluded by maintaining, "Yugoslavia, Rumania, and Czechoslovakia can easily reach an agreement guaranteeing themselves against the Magyar danger."

Hungary was not the only preoccupation of Rumania; there was Bulgaria, and, far more threatening, there was Soviet Russia, who persisted in regarding Bessarabia not as reunited to, but as annexed by Rumania. With these two questions Czechoslovakia had no direct concern, and Benesh's policy was to make alliances only with States having the same direct interests as his own State; this was possible in his view, the other was not, at any rate at the start—*L'art politique c'est l'art du possible*. Rumania, however, had a direct interest with Poland in Soviet Russia, and similarly had a direct interest with Yugoslavia in Bulgaria, but Czechoslovakia had a direct interest in neither Soviet Russia nor Bulgaria, and her attitude to both was one of neutrality. The only interest Czechoslovakia, Yugoslavia, and Rumania had in common was Hungary, and Benesh stuck to this point when the Little Entente was in course of formation. In February, 1920, Chermak, the Czechoslovak Minister at Bucarest, informed him that his proposal for defence in common was accepted in principle by Rumania, and Osusky sent word from Paris that while Trumbitch favoured the alliance the actual convention would have to be negotiated direct by Yugoslavia and Czechoslovakia. On February 12 the Yugoslav Government produced a draft of a defensive convention and handed it to Kalina, the Czechoslovak Minister at Belgrade.

Things were thus well in train when in March they were disturbed by the probable repercussions of the monarchist reaction in Germany—the Kapp *putsch*. Dr. Kapp's Government was a short-lived affair, but at the outset it seemed serious enough, when taken in connexion with what was going on in monarchist circles in Austria and Hungary, to induce Benesh to telegraph to Kalina at Belgrade on March 14 his fear that the reaction might extend to Vienna and might lead, "on the part of the Magyars," to an attack by the "reactionary Magyars and Austrians" on the Czechoslovaks, the Yugoslavs, and other neighbours. He could not foresee what a complete fiasco the Kapp *putsch* was going to be in two or three days, but in Hungary he knew well there were sufficient grounds for considerable apprehensions. Scarcely five weeks before, the monarchist reactionary parties in Budapest and other Hungarian centres, encouraged by mendacities to the effect that the Allies had changed their policy and were in favour of a restoration of the Habsburgs, had gone to such lengths as to draw from the Conference of Ambassadors a scathing Note, which said:

"The Principal Allied Powers consider it their duty to deny the reports which have been circulated abroad and are calculated to mislead public opinion. They are represented as ready to recognize or to favour the restoration of the Habsburg dynasty to the throne of Hungary. The Principal Allied Powers believe that the restoration of a dynasty which personifies in the eyes of their subjects a system of oppression and of domination over other peoples, in union with Germany, would not be compatible either with the principles which were fought for or with the results achieved through the War for the liberation of peoples till then in bondage. It is not within the intention, nor can it be regarded as the duty of the Principal Allied Powers, to intervene in the internal affairs of Hungary or to dictate to the Hungarian people what form of Government or of Constitution they shall adopt. Nevertheless, the Powers cannot allow the restoration of the Habsburg dynasty to be regarded as a question concerning the Hungarian nation alone. They declare, therefore, that a restoration of this nature would be in conflict

DR. BENESH

with the very basis of the peace settlement, and would be neither recognized nor tolerated by them."

Having this in his mind, and aware that the Note had failed to bring about any marked improvement in the situation, Benesh in his dispatch to Kalina asked him to inform the Yugoslav Government that the Czechoslovak Government held that their agreement for action in common against Hungary, though not yet completely worked out in its details, should come at once into force, as it was necessary for both Governments to be prepared to deal with the Magyars at any moment. In his reply to Benesh, Kalina stated that the Yugoslav Government desired the Czechoslovak Government to apprise the Allies of the danger in the Kapp *putsch* to the two States, and said that Belgrade awaited the early acceptance of the defensive convention that had been previously submitted by it to Prague. Benesh, however, had objected to this agreement because it was to be "secret." Protitch, the Yugoslav Prime Minister, thereupon suggested that the convention itself might be short and "open," but that the military dispositions contingent on it must be kept secret.

Yugoslavia had been passing through a severe political crisis over her internal policy—another phase of the centralist-federalist controversy—and the Davidovitch Cabinet, with which Benesh had been negotiating, was replaced by an administration under Protitch, who assured Kalina that he regarded the convention in the same light as his predecessor, and that Yugoslavia would take joint action with Czechoslovakia against Hungary if the situation called for it. As it happened, the situation did not call for it, because of the swift failure of the Kapp attempt; but on April 17 Kalina was able to intimate to Benesh that Protitch approved the defensive convention, as modified, and that Yugoslavia bound herself to act on it whenever necessary.

Meanwhile negotiations had been proceeding with Rumania. On April 23, 1920, Benesh informed Kalina that when he had asked the Rumanian Government whether it would join with Czechoslovakia and Yugoslavia in combating the Magyar danger, and whether it would agree to a defensive alliance of the three States *vis-à-vis* Hungary, the answer had been favourable. But for some time nothing of a more definite nature was achieved. As a matter of fact, Czechoslovakia and Yugoslavia had practically no difficulty in reaching agreement, closely connected as they were by ties of race and by the living memory of the oppression they had endured at the hands of Austria-Hungary. Rumania, with her Latin rather than Slav sympathies, was in a different position, and she knew very little of the Czechs, though she did not forget Masaryk and the assistance rendered by the Czechoslovak legionaries in the Dobrudja during the War. Some of her political groups looked askance at the idea of an alliance with the two other States, and Take Jonescu himself had advocated that alliance as part of a larger combination, including Poland and Greece. Some of the Rumanians seemed to favour even the plan for a Danubian Federation. Negotiations therefore tarried somewhat.

In June Averescu became Prime Minister of Rumania, with Jonescu as Foreign Minister, and on June 12 Chermak told Benesh that Averescu was ready to resume discussion of his proposals for a defensive alliance. In July it was announced in the Belgrade papers that Benesh would shortly visit that city for the purpose of direct negotiation with the Yugoslav Government for the completion of the convention between their two States. Another turn in the internal politics of Yugoslavia had put Vesnitch in power, and Raskano, the Rumanian Minister at Belgrade, just come from a trip to Bucarest, informed him that the Rumanian Government desired the closest relations with his Government, and that Jonescu approved and wished for a "union" of the three States, first by an entente between Yugoslavia and Czechoslovakia, and afterwards by the direct negotiation with himself of a threefold agreement. Jonescu's ideas did not harmonize altogether with those of Benesh, but before anything further was done in this matter there was a curious interlude. This came in the shape of a suggestion to the Supreme Council from Hungary that, in view of the Soviet's attack on Poland, four Magyar divisions should be armed by the Allies or by France alone, and sent against the Bolsheviks. The report in Prague was that these troops were to occupy Eastern Slovakia and Carpathian Ruthenia. As such a proposal was entirely inacceptable to Czechoslovakia, the representatives of that State abroad made an emphatic protest against its acceptance, and it was dropped. On August 14, 1920, Benesh arrived in Belgrade, and the defensive convention was signed the same day by him for Czechoslovakia and by Nintchitch, the Yugoslav Minister of Commerce and acting Minister of Foreign Affairs.

First Little Entente Treaty

This convention, which was the political and juridical foundation of the Little Entente, began by stating that the two States were firmly resolved to maintain the peace which had been obtained at the cost of such great sacrifices, and which was embodied in the Pact of the League of Nations, and also to maintain the order established by the Treaty of Trianon between the Allies and Hungary. The First Article read: "In case of an unprovoked attack by Hungary on one of the High Contracting Parties, the other Party binds itself to co-operate in the defence of the Party attacked, in accordance with the arrangements mentioned in the Second Article"—which was to the effect that the "competent technical authorities" of the two States would, by agreement between themselves, take whatever measures were necessary for carrying out the purpose of the convention. The Third Article forbade the conclusion of an alliance with a third State without previous notice; the Fourth Article gave the convention a life of two years; and the Fifth said that the convention would be communicated to the League of Nations. The Sixth and last Article provided that ratifications of the convention were to be exchanged at Belgrade as soon as possible—and the familiar phrase meant exactly what it said. The points to stress about this convention were that it was bilateral, involving Czechoslovakia and Yugoslavia alone, was concerned only with the relations of the two States to Hungary, and, for the rest, made much of the League of

Nations, though it contained no reference to Article XXI of the Covenant, which recognized the validity of "regional understandings like the Monroe Doctrine for securing the maintenance of peace," and which might well have been taken to apply in this case.

In the mind of Benesh, no partisan of secret engagements, the important thing was to make the convention known to all the world, and this he conceived was best done by anchoring it to the League and its programme of peace, which was also the programme of the Big Entente. On the day after the signing of the convention Benesh gave an interview to the correspondent in Belgrade of the *Journal des Débats*, in which he said that now that the territorial status of Czechoslovakia had been fixed, his principal aim was to ensure its continuance. "We have no intention of launching out on foreign adventures," he went on, "but now that our State has been consolidated, our desire, profiting by that circumstance, is to collaborate with the Entente (the Allies) in the definite re-establishment of the general peace. This is the object of my visit. We stand for a policy of large horizons—one that aims at the stabilization of Central Europe. It is a policy that will help the Allies, because it will add to their strength. We are glad to show to those who regret the dismemberment of Austria, or who dream of a Danubian Federation, that Central Europe is quite able to consolidate itself by an understanding between the principal heirs of the Dual Monarchy. Besides, we desire particularly that the Magyars would learn wisdom and cease to foment troubles. And in this we are not guided by egoistic national interests, but by considerations of the peace of Europe as a whole."

The Press of the two States welcomed the signing of the convention. The *Chas* of Prague pointed out, in answer to an objection that was being made, that the "so-called Little Entente"—the name was still, so to speak, unofficial—"far from being in opposition to the Big Entente, actually strengthened and completed it." The Yugoslav newspapers dwelt on the fact, as they conceived it, that if the Czechoslovaks lost the freedom they now possessed, it would not be long before the freedom of Yugoslavia would also be in jeopardy; and on the other hand, if Yugoslavia should be broken up, then Czechoslovakia would become a prey to the Magyars, Slovakia falling to Hungary, and Bohemia being left at the mercy of the Germans of Austria. Said the *Demotrika* of Belgrade: "Even if there did not exist a feeling of Slav solidarity rooted in the hearts of the two peoples, the community of interests would lead them towards an alliance, the only question being to hit upon the best way of forming it." To judge by the Yugoslav papers the way had been found. The practical bent of the Czechoslovaks was seen in the demand of their leading journals that the political convention should be supplemented by an economic one, the manufactured products of their own country being exchanged against the agricultural products of the other.

Rumanian Cooperation

Satisfied with the results of his visit to Belgrade, Benesh went on to Bucarest. On August 16 he had informed President Masaryk that the convention with Yugoslavia had been signed, "everything having gone off very well and in the best order," and that Jonescu had given him a pressing invitation to visit Rumania; "I believe I can do some good there," he added. Benesh's large horizons never seduced him into missing an opportunity; with him, as with Masaryk, the real was not lost to sight while pursuing the ideal. He arrived in the Rumanian capital on August 17, and was warmly greeted by Jonescu, to whom he communicated the news of the signing at Belgrade of the defensive convention by Yugoslavia and Czechoslovakia with a view to the maintenance of the Treaty of Trianon, and stated that if Rumania would join them, the two States would be well pleased. These facts were mentioned in a Memorandum drawn up by the two statesmen on August 19, with the addition that, as the aim of Rumania's policy was to bring about an alliance of the "five States sharing in the common victory" —Poland, Czechoslovakia, Yugoslavia, Greece, and Rumania— Jonescu was not at the moment in a position to accept fully the suggestion offered by Czechoslovakia and Yugoslavia. Jonescu, however, agreed, without entering into a formal treaty, to give "reciprocal military assistance" if Hungary without provocation attacked any one of the three States—Czechoslovakia, Yugoslavia, and Rumania.

Jonescu had been particularly desirous of seeing Poland in the new alliance, but the Teschen question between Czechoslovakia and Poland was still unsettled, and Czechoslovakia in any case, as has been said, had not that direct interest in Soviet Russia which Rumania and Poland had in common. It had been asserted by the Vienna Press that the Russian problem would keep Rumania and Czechoslovakia apart, but both Jonescu and Benesh very wisely came to the conclusion to leave it alone, and to concern themselves with concentrating on the Magyar problem, in which they were both equally interested. Benesh thus expressed the net results of his journey: "The Defensive Convention concluded between Czechoslovakia and Yugoslavia provided that these two States should help each other in case of an unprovoked attack by Hungary. That convention, supplemented by the assurance on the part of Rumania, given on the occasion of the Bucarest negotiations between Take Jonescu and myself on August 19, that Rumania acknowledged a similar obligation, even though no formal treaty was concluded created a strong and permanent bulwark against the execution of the Habsburg plans."

Benesh on the Little Entente

Thus, then, was the Little Entente formed. As soon as it became known that the Little Entente was actually in existence, the whole Press of Europe commented on it. While most newspapers admitted that its formation was a political event of importance, a number of journals were, or seemed to be, ill-informed regarding its real character, and others, again, thought it would or could not last very long. In a lengthy speech in the Czechoslovak Parliament on September 1, 1920 —almost immediately after his return to Prague from Bucarest —Benesh stated very clearly what were the reasons for the formation of the Little Entente; on this occasion he spoke of it as the "so-called Little Entente." His first reason was found in the unrest prevalent throughout Europe. "Under the influence of the War, of the negotiations at the various international Conferences, of the latest events in Russia and in the East, the whole of Europe is still in a state of unrest, which, with the resultant feeling of insecurity, produces a certain nervousness, an irritation in the nations and States, and in the end a sense of fear and anxiety about the future. This unrest and anxiety manifest themselves especially in all the small States of Central Europe, in both their internal and external politics —fears of a social revolution, economic upheaval and anarchy, fears of an armed conflict with one of the neighbours, of the ruin of the State, of a return to old conditions, and in particular fears of a monarchist or other reactionary movement. Neither individuals nor nations can live long in such a feverish state —eventually it would spell complete moral ruin and the destruction of all political, social, and economic order. This is one of the reasons which have led us to try to bring about an atmosphere which would do away with this psychology, inspire the people with confidence, and produce order before long...We wanted to begin reconstruction, and to begin it in agreement with those who have identical interests and aims, and feelings similar to our own."

Benesh found the second reason in the economic situation, "difficult not only in Czechoslovakia, but throughout Central Europe." That situation was better than some of its critics supposed, but it was not satisfactory, because there were no direct economic relations between States and nations, and because of the problems of the exchange. "All this," said Benesh, "leads to revolutionary tendencies, economic misery, and sometimes to social anarchy, and cannot be solved except by the establishment of normal relations as quickly as possible between States which complete each other. When in such conditions a political agreement has been reached between three States which are so near each other, this agreement cannot remain restricted to political questions alone. It is clear that the basis for the agreement is also the manifold economic needs on the one side and on the other. The satisfaction of these needs would bring these countries to a more normal economic and financial position, and through that to more consolidated moral, political, and social conditions. The Czechoslovak Government realizes that there is only one effective and just policy against all the difficulties that have sprung from the War, and this policy we have carried on up to the present, and finally incorporated it in the idea of the so-called Little Entente between ourselves, Rumania, and Yugoslavia. The meaning of this policy is (1) external security, (2) the rapid establishment of intimate political and economic relations between the three States, and (3) the establishment of internal order in the three States to facilitate the undisturbed working out of political and social reforms in them."

Then Benesh gave a third reason for the formation of the Little Entente, and in doing so replied to certain objections urged against it. "From time to time," he said, "we hear from different sides regrets that old Austria-Hungary has been destroyed. The various difficulties of the different national States are emphasized and held up as illustrations of the incorrectness of anti-Austrian policy during the War, and this serves as a plea for the various plans for a Danubian Federation, or at least of a Customs Union of the former Austro-Hungarian territories. It is absolutely useless to be afraid to-day of these tendencies, for they will never be attractive enough to cause a repetition of a history which was so fatal to us, Yugoslavia, and Rumania. There is no doubt, however, that the nations of Central Europe have many common interests; and we would play into the hands of our adversaries if we pretended not to see the plausible side of these tendencies clamouring for a federation. They were started solely because the importance of the common interests was overrated to such an extent as to make it appear that new confederations should be established. A reconstruction of such formations, whether in a political or an economic sense, would always be dangerous to us. On the other hand, it is necessary to examine judiciously the real common political and economic interests of these States and

DR. NINTCHITCH

to work for a *rapprochement* in regard to those matters in which a *rapprochement* is possible. By doing so we shall give a sufficient guarantee to Europe that we are able to maintain political order, build up necessary economic relations, and make possible a general European consolidation.

"Our present agreement with Yugoslavia and Rumania is a first step on the way towards the construction of a new political and economic system in Central Europe. It is a system which will be much more elastic than any other formation, federation, or union, whether political or economic. The aim of our policy is the establishment of a new political system in which the individual States will be able to create political and economic unions in the form of bilateral agreements—short-termed and renewable, but corresponding to the change in the international situation, and to the different political, economic, and social structures of the three States. The interests and needs of the three will thus be coordinated, and in this way Europe in general and the Allies in particular will have a sufficient guarantee that there will be real order in Europe. It would be a basic error to establish in Central Europe any merely political military alliance. Our aims must be different, higher, more important. Only in that way will the union between us remain constant, because it will correspond not only to our feelings of friendship and sympathy, but also to our vital interests. It is evident that the Entente between the three States will function properly only when its traditions are firmly established and its idea will have penetrated the entire philosophical systems of the three States. Only in that way will the alliance be permanent and really beneficial. It is understood that it will be open also to other new members in the future, in agreement with the present members—all that is work for the future." What mattered now was to take the first step, always the most difficult, and the most important.

Attitude to Hungary

Having considered these three general reasons, Benesh passed on to deal with Hungary, the pressing concrete reason why the Little Entente was formed; in that light, this was the most significant part of his speech. He said: "All three States are neighbours of Hungary, where there is still a régime which is a danger for us all. The agreements to which we came concerning the enforcement of the Peace Treaty of Trianon have to ensure first of all peace in Central Europe against all surprises on the part of Hungary. This was the central point of our whole negotiations; but it would be a great mistake for anyone to overrate the importance of Hungary as a political factor. It is clear that all three States are interested in the competent enforcement of the Trianon Treaty, which was signed by Hungary, and in preventing any military danger on the part of Hungary. On the other hand, we must not forget that there are to-day only about eight million Hungarians in Hungary, whereas the three neighbouring States have a population in all of nearly forty-five millions. In our coming to an agreement about the Treaty of Trianon, it was never a question of imposing on Hungary something unjust or incorrect. The question was rather to create a new atmosphere, in which the Hungarians would realize what sort of policy it will be necessary for them to follow in the future.

"Hungary is a State in which the War has wrought only the slightest changes in its social structure, political opinions, and general notions of the international situation. The social structure of present-day Hungary is practically the same as before the War. The government is in the hands of practically the same people as before the War—of the people who were more or less responsible for the War. It is governed by the same cliques which governed there before the War, and there is no new political generation which could take over from the old gentry the leadership of the Hungarian nation, accept the situation as it is, and finally begin to carry out a loyal, honest, realist, and democratic policy towards its neighbours. The fantastic notions of political methods and the romantic hopes and opinions of a possibility of changing the present situation, the unreal conceptions of the various new political constellations in Europe, the non-serious Hungarian offers, now here, now there, to help and collaborate, which reduced to their true value are nothing more than unprecedented bluff—this was and still is to-day the Hungarian political method. To all this we must add the terrible social problem of Hungary. The Hungarian intelligentsia, the State employees, army officers, and a part of the industrial class have lost, through the catastrophe that overtook their country, practically completely their former means of subsistence. These people have become the most furious adherents of the old régime, of the terror, reaction, nationalism, and the old Imperialism—for on that they had lived. What to do with them is to-day the Hungarian problem, and the problem of the new generation in Hungary.

"This explains also the present Hungarian régime and the unrest resulting from it. A self-conscious and progressive small Peasant Party in Hungary has not yet enough force to change the condition of things, but the neighbours of Hungary must understand that condition, know it, and by that knowledge show how it may be changed. It is not sufficient just to proclaim antipathy to Hungary. It is necessary to look for ways out of this situation, and to help them and ourselves so as to bring about friendly relations in the future. If we came to an agreement with Yugoslavia and Rumania concerning the Treaty of Trianon, it was not only in order to defend what had been signed and agreed upon, and to prevent any Hungarian adventures, but also to point out in an educational sense the future development of Hungary. There is nothing left to Hungary but to change all the political and national conceptions which she has held up to the present, to change her structure and political methods. Should that come to pass, it will help to create a situation in which it will be possible to stretch out a hand to Hungary towards a reasonable cooperation with all her neighbours. These neighbours are naturally always ready to live on friendly terms with Hungary and to collaborate with her in peace towards a consolidation of conditions and the development of friendly neighbourly relations between us all in Central Europe."

The Little Entente and Europe

With respect to the general European situation, Benesh said he thought it an illusion to suppose that there would be any rapid change. The Allies would, he hoped with all his heart, preserve their unity; it was in the interest of Europe that those who had contributed most to the existing state of affairs should also have the greatest possible moral and material authority to finish the work of peace. The Germans were consolidating their State and preparing to play a rôle proportionate to their strength. Despite her anarchy, Russia would always have a tremendous influence in determining events in Europe, though that anarchy was likely to last a long time. "We must endeavour to reach proper relations with these three big European factors, and build up, step by step, these relations. . . . If Central Europe," he continued, "is to be preserved from the upheavals which are now taking place in Poland and Russia, we and Yugoslavia and Rumania must try to create a common sphere of interests and common political tendency. In politics and economics we have certain common Central European interests; in geography we also form a certain community; and the Peace Treaties which have been signed bring us very closely together. The task of this community is therefore to define our real interests and mutual needs, not only between ourselves, but also with regard to general European conditions. By the fact that we reached an agreement in regard to a number of questions which are already known to the public, and that we have kept mutual independence, we shall create in future a certain common political life, and keep always in view that we are working for the general consolidation of Europe. With a population of nearly forty-five millions our three States represent an important strength, both politically and economically; together we are strong enough to defend our interests and to be useful to a real European peace. Our relations to the Big Entente are clear. It is always in the interests of England, France, Italy, and America to see the situation in Central Europe consolidated in such a way that the States of Central

Europe may not be at the mercy of events, or become the victims of some expensive policy which could provoke a new world catastrophe. All that has just been concluded in Belgrade and Bucarest falls well within the general policy of the Western Allies, as was pointed out in our public declarations in these cities. In the same way Italy finds satisfaction that our action aims at making impossible any confederations and any renewal of the old Austro-Hungarian Monarchy. It is necessary in particular to stress the fact that the central point of the Little Entente's whole relations to the Big Entente is to keep all its deliberations within the scope of the Peace Treaties, and this means, in brief, the unity of the Little Entente with the Allies."

Turning to the subject of Soviet Russia, Benesh said he believed that a genuinely neutral policy in the Russian-Polish conflict and in Russian things in general was in every way possible for the Czechoslovaks, Yugoslavs, and Rumanians under all conditions, now that they had come to a real agreement concerning their common problems. "It falls within the frame of the Czechoslovak peaceful and neutral policy to do everything which would enable us to enter into economic relations with Russia. The Russian-Polish conflict prevented this, but we hope that the present turn in events will make it possible (the Poles a fortnight before had decisively defeated the Bolsheviks in a great battle a short distance from Warsaw). "We trust that we shall be able to find a basis for a really friendly policy towards Russia in the future." After stating that the Little Entente's attitude towards Germany was expressed in the perfectly correct demand for her loyal carrying out of the Peace Treaties, and by the desire to collaborate with Germany in bringing about a peaceful and normal situation, Benesh proceeded to say that its relations with Poland "would certainly be friendly, honest, and open," and that it sincerely wished to see the conclusion of the Russian-Polish conflict on a basis that would make future wars between Poland and Russia impossible. "For we are convinced that there will be no peace in Europe if the relations between them are not friendly and based on a just solution of their territorial questions." He referred again to the fact that in their exchange of views Nintchitch, Jonescu, and himself had reached full agreement that their three States should maintain neutrality in the Russian-Polish War (which was terminated six months afterwards by the conclusion of the Treaty of Riga, March 18, 1921).

Having discussed these aspects of the policy of the Little Entente, Benesh turned to its relations with Austria. "During all our deliberations," he said, "we were unanimously of opinion that the relations of our three States to the Austrian Republic can and must be friendly. In its case we desire to continue a constructive policy, and to take as our common standpoint that its existence be made possible so that it may collaborate with us harmoniously and without danger to our interests. In this matter the views of the three States are absolutely identical. It will be a question especially of commercial treaties between us. Recently some steps were taken in this respect by Czechoslovakia and by Yugoslavia and Rumania. We are trying to harmonize our economic interests with those of Austria—Rumania recently concluded the first commercial treaty with her." Summing up, Benesh stated that the Convention with Yugoslavia was a full basis for common action in numerous political questions, as was plain from the declarations made by Vesnitch, the Yugoslav Prime Minister, and himself at Belgrade on the signing of the document; it was clear that the mutual and honest friendship of their two States ensured close collaboration. The declarations made at Bucarest by Averescu, the Rumanian Prime Minister, and himself, after the agreement had been reached, evinced the same sincere and friendly spirit, another sign of which was the settlement in principle of the question of the frontiers between Carpathian Ruthenia and Rumania.

Mistaken Views of Little Entente Aims

Although this lengthy speech, which was widely reported, covered the whole ground and made abundantly manifest what were the objectives of the Little Entente, as well as the spirit of peace and cooperation which informed its activities, there still prevailed mistaken views in some foreign circles of the true nature of the young organization. In October, 1920, Jonescu, accompanied by Titulescu, afterwards Rumanian Minister at London, Foreign Minister, and Minister at London again, made a tour of the Allied capitals, in the course of which he saw Giolitti and Sforza at Rome, Millerand and Leygues at Paris, and Lloyd George and Curzon at London, and laid before them the general scheme of the Little Entente. In Paris he was given a formal denial by Millerand of the existence of a treaty between France and Hungary—this was one of the tendentious rumours current at the time; further, Millerand expressed his cordial approval of the Little Entente and its plans. In London Jonescu was the guest of the Foreign Office at a banquet presided over by Curzon, the British Foreign Secretary, who congratulated Rumania on her enlargement and consolidation; replying, Jonescu said their aim was to build up such a combination of States in their part of Europe that other States which might be tempted to attack them would not dare to do so.

On October 15, 1920, *The Times*, in an editorial commenting on the visit of Jonescu, said: "The Little Entente, which is being arranged among the heirs and assigns of the old Dual Monarchy, is the outcome of the centripetal tendencies of commerce in the Danube lands, and forms a useful correction to the policy of splendid isolation which the centrifugal pressure of new-born national dignity tended to inflict on some States in that part of the Continent. It is to be hoped that the achievement of an amicable political understanding will be but the prelude, at short date, to a series of economic and commercial arrangements which will enable international trade to make use of the Danube in order to flow like a reviving flood over all riparian lands. They may in that way find a unity in the bonds of trade and common interest which they could only struggle to avoid when the Habsburgs sought to inflict it on them as a symbol of political domination." These sentences, with their curious adumbration of something similar to the idea of a Danubian Federation, showed that in the West, while the economic and commercial advantages that might flow from the Little Entente were understood, its high political value as a rampart of peace and a base for international cooperation was not as fully grasped.

As October closed Jonescu arrived in Prague, and told Benesh that as the result of the conversations he had had with the leading statesmen of the Allies all misunderstandings respecting the Little Entente had been dissipated, and that all proposals that might or would favour the Magyars were "definitively dead." In a Memorandum drawn up on October 30 by Jonescu and Benesh it was noted that they confirmed anew what they had agreed on at Bucarest in August. Jonescu was going on from Prague to Warsaw, and he undertook that when he was in the Polish capital he would emphasize the necessity of a definitive entente between Poland and Czechoslovakia, an entente which, Benesh asked him to say, was greatly desired by the latter State. The Memorandum also provided for mixed commissions, with experts, to settle once for all the common frontiers of Rumania and Czechoslovakia, and for a special commission to negotiate a commercial treaty between them, including some improvement in their railway, telegraph, and postal services. This document finished with the statement: "M. Take Jonescu and M. Benesh, in their declarations, particularly accentuated the fact that the agreement between the two States, now confirmed and made perfect from certain points of view, must be considered as durable and definitive."

Treaty of Rapallo

Jonescu, in the negotiations at Warsaw, recognized that Poland had no direct interest in the Little Entente, whose common direct interest was concentrated on Hungary, a State with which Poland had no direct contact, though she had a certain sympathy for her that was especially noticeable among the Polish nobility and gentry. Jonescu's conversations were concerned with the common interest his country and Poland had in Soviet Russia, and these eventually (March 4, 1921) led to a defensive treaty between Rumania and Poland of great importance to both. With Italy the position of the Little Entente was governed by the fact that both had a common interest in the maintenance of the Peace Treaties, more particularly the St. Germain and Trianon Treaties. But there had continued the quarrel between Yugoslavia and Italy which was the unfortunate legacy from the Treaty of London, 1915, and which might become very dangerous to any programme of peace and cooperation in that part of Europe. Therefore the situation called for compromise and settlement, nor was good will lacking.

In his first speech as Prime Minister of Yugoslavia, Vesnitch declared: "Neither the Government nor the elected representatives of the Serbs, Croats, and Slovenes ought to look on Italy as an enemy country. We have to settle important and difficult questions with Italy. . . . We must reduce all causes of friction to a minimum." Nor were there wanting voices in Italy calling for a friendly agreement; not all Italians were of the uncompromising D'Annunzio type. After long and sometimes stormy negotiations, a very considerable success was registered in the Treaty of Rapallo, November 12, 1920, which fixed the frontier. Italy renounced Dalmatia, with the exception of Zara, the Yugoslav Zadar, and several adjacent communes, while Fiume, the Yugoslav Rieka, was recognized as independent—to become later a bone of contention. The great thing, however, was that a settlement was reached of the main question which had divided the Italians and the Yugoslavs.

At the time this treaty was signed, there was also signed a convention having an important bearing on the Little Entente and its policy. This Convention of Rapallo, like the Treaty of Rapallo, bore the signatures of Giolitti, Sforza, and Bonomi as representing Italy, and of Vesnitch, Trumbitch, and Stojanovitch for Yugoslavia. The preamble set forth that the convention was made to ensure the benefits of the peace obtained at the cost of such great sacrifices by the victory over the Austro-Hungarian Monarchy. In the First Article Italy and Yugoslavia bound themselves to maintain the Peace Treaties with Austria and Hungary, and to take action in common to prevent the restoration of the Habsburgs; but this undertaking was, by the Second Article, limited to diplomatic action by Italy in any case that might arise. Further, the Governments of both countries were to inform each other of attacks directed against their security by Austria and Hungary, which for this purpose were to be kept under constant observation. The Fourth Article had a special significance for the Little Entente, for in it appeared the statement that the Italian Government had heard with satisfaction of the Convention of Alliance between Yugoslavia and Czechoslovakia for purposes similar to those of this convention, of the conclusion of which it wished Yugoslavia to notify Czechoslovakia. The convention was for two years and was renewable.

Commenting on this Italo-Yugoslav Convention, Benesh pointed out that it indicated that Italy had taken up an attitude towards Central European problems which was analogous or parallel to that of the Little Entente. In a speech on the foreign policy of Czechoslovakia delivered in the House of Deputies, Prague, on January 27, 1921, he mentioned that he himself was starting for Rome in a few days. "The road to Rome," he said, in view of the signing of this convention, "means the confirmation of the policy of the Little Entente and a direct understanding with Italy on the Austrian, Hungarian, and Habsburg questions, while as regards attempts to restore the *status quo*, whether in the economic or the political sense, we shall, I trust, come to an absolutely unanimous agreement. This means that our relations with Italy will be based on the Peace of St. Germain and the Peace of Trianon, and this will emphasize before all the world that the best basis of all agreements and understandings, the best work for the consolidation of Europe and the best work for peace and friendship between two nations, is a decision to give loyal and devoted aid to each other for the purpose of carrying out to their logical conclusion those treaties of peace which were signed by a common indivisible hand. It stands to reason that such a political agreement must be reinforced by actual economic interests and by co-operation in the field of finance and trade. We shall therefore, in the negotiations at Rome, do all that is necessary for the conclusion of a commercial treaty, which itself will be one more important stone in the fabric of our Republic and in the pacification of Central Europe. Our action in this matter will certainly give our people an opportunity of remembering with gratitude the great services which Italy rendered to us in the War, and will prompt them to devote more and more attention to the interests and friendship of Italy, to the Italian people, Italian culture, commerce, and industry. Before and during the War this was impossible. To-day it is our duty, a great and most agreeable duty."

While on his way early in February, 1921, to Rome, Benesh stopped at Linz, where he met Mayer, the Austrian Chancellor, and after an exchange of views on the situation, disturbed then by a recurrence of the Anschluss agitation, came to an agreement with him on certain points at issue. In his speech on January 27 Benesh had said that the question of incorporating Austria with Germany did not and could not arise, as the international situation did not admit of any change in the article in the St. Germain Treaty forbidding their union. "If this eventuality of incorporation is held out in certain quarters as a menace, it is done rather with the object of producing a certain atmosphere and of securing international assistance." In the same way, he said of the suggestion of a Danubian Federation, that "Such talk is carried on, not because the thing may be regarded as seriously possible of realization, but with the object of exerting a certain pressure upon us and our neighbours in order to extract various concessions." He referred to what Czechoslovakia had already done to help Austria: "We came to an agreement with Austria whereby we have done our utmost to provide our neighbour, in her difficult circumstances and according to treaty and our obligations, with our coal and other material; we have alleviated her position by supplies of our products and raw stuffs." As a matter of fact the Czechoslovaks had come to the assistance of the Austrians when no one else did, or perhaps could help them. In the first half of 1919 the value of goods exported from Czechoslovakia to Austria was 863 million Czechoslovak crowns against imports from Austria of 355 million crowns. From October, 1919, to March, 1920, Austria was supplied with 3,500 truckloads of Czechoslovak sugar. On April 1, 1920, a new agreement was made arranging for the delivery of 2,350 truckloads of sugar at the price of 13½ Czechoslovak crowns per kilogramme when the general market price was 30 crowns. It was thus evident that far from waging an economic war on Austria, as some asserted, Czechoslovakia, notwithstanding economic troubles of her own, was doing her best to succour her, and to enable her to live as an independent State.

In the speech alluded to Benesh mentioned that for months he had been "endeavouring to resume economic relations with Hungary." In view of the "uncertainty in the East and in Germany we must at all costs," he said, "have peace and quiet to the South of us. That means creating in Central Europe a new political and economic system by which that peace and quiet would be assured. That would entail a definitive understanding between us and Austria, between us and Hungary, between Yugoslavia and Austria, between Yugoslavia and Hungary, between Rumania and all these States, in the matter of communications, post, telegraphs, navigation, various finance and banking relations, the exchange of goods and commercial treaties generally, whether parcellary, short-termed, or renewable. It would entail entering by degrees upon a system of unfettered economics and freer trade, guarding, of course, at the same time all the essential and vital interests of this State." Though no complete and precise plan had been worked out, what was to be aimed at and achieved was clear. Touching the problem of Austria, Benesh maintained that it was a European and even a world problem, owing to the universal lack of credit, but exhibited in Austria in an extreme form. To solve that problem action should be taken not on philanthropic lines, or by granting temporary credits, as had been done, but by elaborating a great financial scheme for the economic recovery, not alone of Austria, but of a whole group of States, including Czechoslovakia, who then would be better able to assist her neighbour.

The Benesh-Sforza Letters

After his conference with the Austrian Chancellor Benesh went on to Rome, where he received a cordial welcome. How completely he was successful in attaining his object was shown by Notes in the form of letters exchanged between him and Sforza, the Italian Foreign Minister, and dated Rome, February 8, 1921. Sforza, writing to Benesh, said he was happy to declare that their conversations had disclosed a perfect identity of views and complete accord on the main lines of the foreign policy of their States, this identity being the consequence of the interests their peoples had in common, especially in the application of the Peace Treaties and the policy to be followed towards the Succession States of the Austro-Hungarian Monarchy, inasmuch as the objects sought—the security and prosperity of the two States—were in complete accordance. He regarded, he went on to say, the Declaration he was making as a more efficacious guarantee of the agreement and political collaboration of their two States than a special convention would be. But, he continued, seeing that the Italian frontiers had been fixed by the Treaty of Rapallo between Italy and the Serb-Croat-Slovene State, and that a special convention had been concluded at the same time which provided that that convention should be communicated to the Czechoslovak Government, it followed naturally that the agreements and engagements it contained had the same value for Italy and Czechoslovakia. In his reply Benesh repeated the actual words of Sforza's letter, and added that the Czechoslovak Government fully concurred. In brief, Italy had taken her stand with Yugoslavia and Czechoslovakia in opposing any breach of the Peace Treaties and any attempt at the restoration of the Habsburgs. The policy of linking up the States by a system of economic and trade conventions was illustrated by a commercial agreement between Italy and Czechoslovakia, March 23, 1921—some six weeks after the visit of Benesh to Rome. A few days earlier Benesh had met Teleki, the Hungarian Prime Minister, and Gratz, the Foreign Minister, at Brück, and had begun negotiations with them for a commercial treaty with Hungary.

Benesh had devoted a large part of his speech on January 27 to the Magyar question. "It is unthinkable," he said, "that we should not, as speedily as possible, renew economic and political connexions with Hungary, so as to avail ourselves economically of the conditions prescribed by Nature—conditions which compel us to seek a market in Hungary for our manufactures, to supply Hungary with various raw materials and necessities, and to get in return the agricultural and other products of that country. The very substance of things confirms all this, geographical proximity, and a long tradition coming to us from the past. History teaches us that we and the Magyars cannot live in permanent opposition and hostility to each other. Our task for the future is thus a simple one: we must resume our interrupted connexions with Hungary. . . . We must without delay arrive at an agreement respecting the Danube and transport by water. We must come to an arrangement regarding the supply of various articles indispensable for us and for Hungary. There is really no reason, after the ratification of the Peace Treaty, why we should not commence work on these questions."

Before dealing with the economic aspect of Czechoslovak-Hungarian relations, Benesh had touched on other features of the situation. It was necessary, he said, that the Magyars should put an end to their "senseless propaganda" carried on chiefly against Czechoslovakia in England, France, and America. That propaganda was followed closely and counteracted by the Czechoslovak Government, and the Magyars themselves were coming to see that it was not in that way that Hungary would recover her "Integrity." Therefore they had dissolved some of their propaganda organizations. He referred, too, to the widespread idea, which existed especially in the West, that in Hungary no other régime was possible except a monarchy. "There is talk of the ex-Emperor Charles, of his son, of the

Archduke Joseph, of other members of the House of Habsburg, of some Magyar noble, and finally of a foreign dynasty. If we analyse the situation correctly, we must say that the question of the restoration of the ex-Emperor Charles does not and cannot arise, for that would be a real *casus belli* for several of Hungary's neighbours." In a way Benesh was a little sanguine and optimistic. For when the negotiations begun at Brück were proceeding favourably, they were suddenly interrupted by the astonishing news that the ex-Emperor Charles had reappeared on the scene, and was bent on regaining the throne of St. Stephen. Here was the first testing of the Little Entente.

CHAPTER V

THE LITTLE ENTENTE TESTED

1921

WHILE the general situation in Europe exhibited little, if any, improvement during 1921, that year was packed with events of decisive importance for the Little Entente, which demonstrated its strength and vitality in the face of two Habsburg attempts to overthrow the New Order established by the Peace Treaties, and which further justified its existence by the increasing energy of its policy of cooperation with other States in the interests of peace and reconstruction. Its internal consolidation was manifested by the conclusion of two other defensive conventions—the first, between Czechoslovakia and Rumania in replacement of the understanding, the obligation, to take common action, acknowledged by Take Jonescu in his conversations with Benesh at Bucarest in August of the preceding year and expressed in their Joint Memorandum; and the second, between Rumania and Yugoslavia, with a new and significant development. These two conventions, together with the Convention between Czechoslovakia and Yugoslavia, signed at Belgrade on August 14, 1920, completed the political and juridical formation of the Little Entente. It was not, and never assumed the character of, a unitary alliance, but, resting, as it were, on its triangular base of the three conventions, had its restricted, though perfectly definite, ends in view.

Early in the year Italy and Czechoslovakia had affirmed their community of interest with Yugoslavia in the Convention of Rapallo as regards the Magyar danger. The external consolidation of the Little Entente was also seen in the conclusion of a political treaty with Austria by Czechoslovakia and of the treaties with Poland by Rumania and Czechoslovakia, the latter treaties being linked, to a greater or less extent, with the Franco-Polish and the Soviet-Polish Treaties of 1921 in the framework of the New Europe. While Poland did not join the Little Entente, her relations with Czechoslovakia, which had hitherto been troubled, became more friendly before the close of the year, and her military alliance with Rumania was a fact which the other members of the Little Entente could not but take into account, though each maintained its own attitude towards Soviet Russia. By the end of the year, too, Austria moved closer to the Little Entente by a commercial treaty with Czechoslovakia which permitted a fairly large measure of collaboration on the part of these States. Various efforts by Czechoslovakia for economic cooperation with Hungary which promised some degree of success were nullified by the course of events in the latter country.

Taken as a whole the Little Entente, in touch, as it was, with Italy and Austria on the south and Poland on the north, far from showing the Balkanization of Central Europe with which it was still unjustly charged, was at once a political substitute of considerable magnitude for the Austria-Hungary that had disappeared, and a solid, stabilizing force of high political value not only in Central Europe, but in Europe generally. In its economic aspect the Little Entente contributed to the recovery of the Continent by a series of commercial conventions and agreements made by its States between themselves and with other States besides Austria, and by its activities at the Rome and Porto Rosa Conferences. In short, the Little Entente, especially after the conclusion of the Austro-Czechoslovak Treaty, stood forth a living and irrefutable witness of the non-Balkanization of Europe, and, at the same time, of the possibilities of its reconstruction. Hungary was, and remained, a difficulty and a danger.

Charles's First Attempt

All Europe was startled when the ex-Emperor Charles appeared without warning in Budapest on March 27, 1921, and attempted to regain the throne of Hungary. There were some who said, on grounds that seemed good to them, that France was perhaps not really startled at all, but was merely dissembling when she joined in the general chorus of surprise and reprobation among the Allies that was the immediate result of this move of Charles. In his book *Five Years of European Chaos*, Maxwell Macartney, a representative of *The Times* in Hungary during this crisis, wrote: "Whatever may or may not have been the attitude of the French Government, it is everybody's secret that France for a long time coquetted, not to use a stronger term, with the idea of a Danube Confederation under some form of Habsburg overlordship. In her readiness to prevent at all hazards the union of Austria with Germany France was prepared to tolerate a return of the Habsburgs, and it was, in fact, largely owing to intrigues in this direction that the Czech Foreign Minister, Dr. Benes, called into being the Little Entente with its primarily anti-Habsburg policy."

Benesh said that this statement was simply not true; the most that could be alleged of France was that there was evident in that country a tendency, as shown in some of its newspapers, in the direction of favouring Charles on the ground indicated, namely, the strengthening of Hungary and the withdrawing of Austria from the German orbit. Boroviczeny, in his narrative of "The First Attempt of the Emperor Karl to Regain his Throne," which was published in Ashmead-Bartlett's book, *The Tragedy of Central Europe*, said that Charles "had absolute guarantees from Briand's Cabinet that he had nothing to fear from the Little Entente. The Great Powers would merely protest, as when King Constantine returned to Greece, their only aim being to avoid war." The statement respecting absolute guarantees—did Briand ever give an absolute guarantee?—was denied. What seemed probable was that the wish, father to the thought, coupled with the Magyar imaginativeness of some of Charles's friends, had magnified out of all proportion some articles in the French Press, or even some expressions of French politicians. Ostensibly, at any rate, France, as represented by her Government, came out against the ex-Emperor.

Among those most genuinely surprised were undoubtedly many of the chief supporters of Charles, the legitimists of Hungary, for he had given them no hint of his intentions. Horthy, the Regent, and the Hungarian Government were certainly taken by surprise. As was noted in the preceding chapter, Teleki, the Prime Minister, had, only a few days before, been engaged with Benesh in negotiating a commercial treaty between Hungary and Czechoslovakia with favourable results—which meant better relations between those States; the reappearance of Charles could mean nothing but the opposite. Nor were the vast majority of the people of Hungary in a state of expectancy that he was coming; indeed, it was plain that no attempt at organizing anything or influencing anybody had been made.

The Little Entente Startled

However it was with others, the Little Entente was startled and profoundly stirred by the unwelcome news of the arrival of the ex-Emperor in Budapest; it was felt as nothing less than a direct challenge, and it was taken up at once. Of the two questions at issue between Hungary and the Little Entente—the Magyar dogma of the "Integrity" of Hungary, and the restoration of the Habsburgs—the second was the more important because it was the more moving in its personal appeal, and in that way the more formidable. For here was a Habsburg—the head of the Habsburgs—back again! It was no wonder that instantly messages were exchanged between Belgrade, Bucarest, Rome, and Prague—and Budapest, the storm centre. What they heard at first was not particularly alarming, Charles having spent only a few hectic hours in the capital with Horthy and one or two others, and returning thereafter to the town in Western Hungary at which he had arrived unexpectedly two days before. It was sufficiently clear that he had received some check—exactly what and why were in some doubt. According to the story told by Boroviczeny, Charles had not informed Horthy of his coming, because the Regent was surrounded by people who were hostile to him. Nor had he been in communication with those men of whose loyalty he was sure.

Slipping quietly out of Switzerland, he had reached Vienna without incident; thence, accompanied by Count Erdödy, a childhood playmate, who had known nothing of the ex-Emperor's return till he actually saw him, he motored to Szombathely, arriving there on the evening of Good Friday, March 25, much to the surprise of Count Mikes, the Bishop of Szombathely, at whose palace he presented himself, and to whom he made his plans known. Teleki, the Hungarian Prime Minister, along with Grant Smith, the American High Commissioner, was staying for the Easter holidays at the country seat of Count Sigray, the Governor of Western Hungary, a few miles from the town; to their amazement Teleki and Sigray were summoned to Szombathely for a consultation with Vas, a member of the Hungarian Government included in the Bishop's Easter guests, and some other gentlemen. The meeting took place at two o'clock in the morning of Saturday, and it was decided, after much debate, that Charles should go on to Budapest, Teleki preceding him by two hours in a motor-car, "in order to prepare Horthy for the coming of the King." No one then appeared to doubt that the Regent would hand over the Government to Charles on his arrival in the capital.

As it happened, Teleki was delayed, and Charles reached Budapest before him; in any case, Horthy did not prove as compliant as had been hoped. He told Charles that he could not resign the Regency without the assent of the National Assembly which had elected him and before which he had sworn an oath of fidelity. Charles maintained that he was King of Hungary by right and had been crowned by Parliament; that the National Assembly had no power to alter the Constitution, and as a matter of fact had never dethroned him; and that Horthy himself was under oath of allegiance to him. Horthy replied that he considered the oath he had taken as Regent dispensed him from his oath to Charles. He strongly urged the danger of war with the Little Entente, and spoke of the inefficiency of the Hungarian army from its lack of equipment. He earnestly requested him to abandon the enterprise and quit the country. Finally, Horthy prevailed on him to return at once to Szombathely. There the ex-Emperor, who was suffering from a chill caught on his way back from Budapest, remained for more than a week.

England, France, and Italy promptly informed Horthy that they had not modified their view of a Habsburg restoration. On March 29 the Yugoslav Minister at Budapest told him that the Belgrade Government regarded the restoration of Charles or any Habsburg as an international question, and would oppose, by force of arms if necessary, any such attempt. The Rumanian Minister declared that his Government protested against the re-establishment of Charles, and expected the Hungarian Government to prevent it. To all of them Horthy replied that he had declined the proposals made by the ex-Emperor and had pressed him to leave Hungary. Next day the Czechoslovak Minister, who had been acting with the others, went to the Hungarian Foreign Office, and after an emphatic statement of the point of view of Prague concerning Charles, asked what was the actual position of the Hungarian Government in the affair. Gratz, the Foreign Minister, was absent, but his deputy said that the matter was one which was solely the concern of Hungary and was not international; an assurance, however, was given that the Hungarian Government had excluded from its programme the question of the kingship. The Czechoslovak Minister retorted that a Habsburg restoration was an international question, as was plain from the fact that the Big Entente and the Little Entente acted together in their proceedings in this respect. On the same day Benesh informed the British, French, and Italian Governments that the Hungarian Government had been told that measures would be taken in agreement with the friendly States to ensure the immediate departure of Charles—first, by a declaration of a blockade, to be followed, if that failed, by a military demonstration. The Czechoslovak Minister in Paris telegraphed that the French Government was opposed to a Habsburg restoration, and had ordered its representatives in Budapest to demand the withdrawal of the ex-Emperor from Hungary.

On April 1, 1921, the Hungarian National Assembly met in extraordinary session, expressed approval of the course which Horthy had taken as Regent, and declared he had acted in accordance with the Constitution in sending Charles about his business. Horthy was cheered, and the Hungarian National Anthem was sung. On April 1, too, the Conference of Ambassadors unanimously adopted a resolution which was communicated to the Hungarian Government. It said: "The events of which Hungary is the theatre compel the Principal Allied Powers to remind the Hungarian Government and people of the terms of the Declaration made on February 4, 1920. Faithful to the principles therein stated, the Allies must repeat that the restoration of the Habsburgs would jeopardize the very bases of the peace, and that it cannot be recognized or tolerated. The Allied Powers expect that the Hungarian Government, conscious of the gravity of the situation which would be created by the return to the throne of Hungary of its former sovereign, will take adequate steps to terminate an attempt of which even a momentary success would have for Hungary the most disastrous consequences."

Charles Leaves Hungary

But Charles, who was recovering from his indisposition, showed no signs of departing; he declared, according to Boroviczeny, that he would leave the country if his presence really meant danger to Hungary, but for the present he did not see that it did so, and he maintained that he had an indisputable right to remain on Hungarian territory to await a suitable moment to regain his throne. During the next two or three days the leaders of the Little Entente considered the sending of an ultimatum to the Hungarian Government demanding the withdrawal of Charles on or before the evening of April 7, and the representatives of the Big Entente were constantly impressing on Horthy the necessity for his immediate departure. Meanwhile the Hungarian Government secured the guarantee of the Big Entente for the safe passage of the ex-Emperor through Austria to Switzerland. On April 5 Charles took his departure, the reason, given by Boroviczeny, being: "When at last the secret reports of the General Staff told of the first sign of mobilization, namely, the appearance of a strong cavalry division of the Serbians in Szabadka, Hungarian territory occupied by the Serbs, his Majesty consented to travel back to Switzerland, and left on April 5 by special train under the protection of foreign officers."

So ended the first attempt of Charles, and with it passed the danger to the Little Entente which in other circumstances might have been sufficiently serious. There were moments when it did seem to be serious, and the fact that the Hungarian Government took no positive steps to enforce the withdrawal of the ex-Emperor, gave some grounds for the suspicion that it was insincere even in what it said with respect to his attempt; it was not a little curious that the Hungarian Government, in its Note to the Swiss Government concerning his future residence in Switzerland, should expressly recognize him as the legitimate King of Hungary, for this rather suggested that it considered that the restoration was feasible, but that this particular effort was to be condemned because it was evidently premature. Charles himself declined to admit that his defeat was final. He told the people at Szombathely that he would soon return, and in a proclamation to the Hungarian nation he expressed his confidence that the moment would come when he should "again be enabled to live" in his Fatherland and to unite his "strength with it in common work for the common ends." The Little Entente had thus fair warning, and it could not but be aware that though the immediate danger had disappeared, the Habsburg problem remained unsolved.

Commenting on the situation, Benesh said: "The Czechoslovak Government, which took the first steps at the Peace Conference to obtain the retirement of the Archduke Joseph" (from the Governorship of Hungary in 1919) "will in consequence of these events settle, in agreement with its Allies, several questions which threaten the peace of Central Europe: the question of Western Hungary, that of the Habsburgs, and that of giving assistance to the democracy of Hungary." The first of these questions was concerned with the continued occupation by Hungary of the Burgenland, which became acute later in the same year, and the third referred to curbing the power of the Magyar aristocracy by the real enfranchisement of the Magyar peasantry, though how this was to be done—it implied interference in the internal affairs of Hungary—was left studiously vague. What this abortive *coup d'état* of Charles demonstrated more than anything else was the solidarity of the Little Entente in its capacity for taking defensive action against the Habsburg menace, though in view of what took place six months afterwards—the second attempt of Charles—it was perhaps insufficiently peremptory in its treatment of the Hungarian Government.

As things were, it was realized by the Little Entente that the links that united it could with advantage be strengthened, and this led, after brief and quick negotiations, to the signing of a defensive convention, in place of the previous understanding, between Czechoslovakia and Rumania at Bucarest on April 23, 1921, by Take Jonescu for the latter State and Veverka, the Czechoslovak Minister to Rumania, for the former.

Second Little Entente Treaty

This convention was on lines identical with those of the Czechoslovak-Yugoslav Convention of August 14, 1920, except for the introduction of an Article, numbered IV, which read: "In order to coordinate their efforts for peace the two Governments" (of Czechoslovakia and Rumania) "bind themselves to take action together on questions of foreign policy bearing on their relations with Hungary." The new clause, obviously occasioned by the attempt of Charles, revealed the complete inclusion of Rumania in the Little Entente, and was in accordance with the unanimous desire of the Rumanian people, who now understood much more fully than before the reality of the Habsburg danger, which had certainly not been entirely eliminated. Another aspect of the convention was pointed out in the Press—that as an industrial Czechoslovakia and an agricultural Rumania were the natural complements of each other, the economic results that might be expected to flow from it would be not less important than the political; in fact, a commercial treaty was signed with the convention. The next move towards the completion of the Little Entente occurred in the negotiations between Belgrade and Bucarest for a defensive convention, having regard not only to Hungary, but also to Bulgaria, which began at this time.

Third Little Entente Treaty

Both Yugoslavia and Rumania had a direct interest in Hungary and Bulgaria through the Trianon and Neuilly Peace Treaties. The Bulgarian Government had shown a persistent unwillingness to fulfil the clauses of the Neuilly Treaty respecting disarmament and reparations, and was more than suspected of closing its eyes when the *komitadjis* raided across the Bulgarian frontiers on the two neighbouring States. Early in May Pashitch, then Prime Minister and Foreign Minister of Yugoslavia, invited Take Jonescu to come to Belgrade to discuss matters, and Benesh was informed by Veverka that Jonescu had told him that a defensive convention was being contemplated by the two States. Jonescu arrived in Belgrade on June 5, 1921, and was warmly greeted by the Yugoslav Government and Press, the latter laying stress on the fact that the Rumanians and the Serbians were the only two Balkan peoples who had never been at war with each other. The convention was signed on June 7; it completed and in a measure extended the Little Entente. It differed from the two other Little Entente Conventions in its preamble by omitting the allusion to the Pact of the League of Nations, and by including the Treaty of Neuilly alongside the Treaty of Trianon.

Its First Article read: "In case of an unprovoked attack by Hungary or Bulgaria, or by both those Powers, against one of the Contracting Parties, which aims at the destruction of the state of things created by the Treaty of Trianon, or by that of Neuilly, the other Party undertakes. . . ." In the Fourth Article, which corresponded to Article IV of the Czechoslovak-Rumanian Convention, the two contracting States bound themselves to take action together on questions of foreign policy bearing on their relations with Hungary and Bulgaria. Thus was the original framework of the Little Entente enlarged. While in Belgrade Jonescu availed himself of the opportunity of settling with Pashitch in a friendly manner some details of their common frontier which had been in dispute.

Of the results of his visit to Belgrade Take Jonescu said to an interviewer: "I have just concluded with the Serb-Croat-Slovene Government an agreement which aims, not at acts of hostility, but at the integral maintenance of the Peace Treaties in which our two nations are interested. We have taken advantage, moreover, of the occasion to settle various questions relating to our frontiers, commerce, railways, and shipping. The basis of the agreements which constitute the Little Entente has been direct interests; we realize the coordination of our political views by a series of limited understandings and mutual assurances. The object of this system is to avoid divergences of opinion which are natural even among neighbours, but which, if intensified, would present an opening to the intrigues of our enemies. To my mind this is the most important side of our agreements, because it is permanent, whereas the defensive guarantee becomes operative only in the case of attack upon us." Jonescu then spoke of what was always near his heart—an alliance of larger scope than that of the Little Entente, but inclusive of it. "My own desire," he said, "would be to discover a formula which would cover the indirect as well as the general interests of the peoples victorious in the World War. The Little Entente would then become the basis of an alliance of all the victors in Central and Eastern Europe for the maintenance of all the Peace Treaties against all assaults. It is my hope that what we have now done will develop in that sense in the future."

He might have added that he himself had made a promising start in that direction by the Defensive Convention between Poland and Rumania, signed at Bucarest on March 4, 1921, by himself for Rumania and by Prince Sapieha, the Polish Foreign Minister, for Poland. In Article VI of this convention the Polish Government specifically recognized the agreements made by Rumania with other States for the maintenance of the Trianon and Neuilly Treaties, while the Rumanian Government recognized the agreements concluded between Poland and

France. The most important of these Franco-Polish Agreements was that signed by Marshal Pilsudski at Paris on February 19, 1921, which provided for defensive action in common against unprovoked attack on the territories or legitimate interests of France and Poland. In the Fourth Article of this agreement the two Governments bound themselves to consult together before concluding new agreements affecting their policy in Central and Eastern Europe. All this was no doubt in the thought of Jonescu when he spoke to the correspondent who interviewed him. The Rumanian statesman was extremely desirous of bringing Poland and Czechoslovakia into intimate contact with each other; and if he found the propitious time had scarcely yet arrived, he helped to prepare the way for it.

Immediately after the signing of the Yugoslav-Rumanian Defensive Convention both Pashitch and Jonescu sent telegrams to Benesh telling him what had been accomplished, and regretting that he had not been able to be with them on this happy occasion. "We beg you to accept our most sincere congratulations," said Pashitch, "on the success of the common work in which you have collaborated with such great devotion." "You were never absent from our minds," said Jonescu; "I seize the opportunity to thank you once more for the great part you have taken in our splendid common work." Benesh was in London at the time, the main object of his visit being connected with an amendment of the Article in the Pact of the League of Nations referring to regional understandings, in the sense that agreements between members of the League, such as the conventions forming the Little Entente, might be not only approved by the League, but also promoted and negotiated under its auspices, "provided they were not inconsistent with the terms of the Covenant." Benesh was anxious there should be no misunderstanding of the thoroughly pacific aims of the Little Entente. Some of its opponents asserted that its defensive conventions, being essentially of a military character, were inconsistent with the terms of the Covenant; this was never the view of the leaders of the Little Entente, who, on the contrary, held that these conventions, all based on the Peace Treaties, were instruments for the preservation of peace, and therefore they made a point of registering them at Geneva. Their wish was to see similar conventions negotiated by other States and that this process might be made easier by Benesh's amendment.

Economic Conference at Rome

On June 15, 1921, this Conference of the Succession States, which had begun its sittings at Rome on April 6, and had been convened by the Italian Government, came to a close. The States taking part were Austria, Czechoslovakia, Italy, Poland, Rumania, and Yugoslavia. Hungary was represented in the earlier proceedings, but withdrew in the middle of May, when the conference was adjourned; she gave as her reason that she was not adequately prepared for an agreement. Dealing mainly with economics, the conference was a serious effort for the reconstruction of Central Europe. The work accomplished fell into three divisions: collective agreements and conventions which were to be concluded by all the Succession States; special agreements concluded by some of the delegations among themselves and forming a precedent for further temporary agreements between two or more States; and schemes concerning various problems in which it was found impossible to reach agreement at the time, and which were accordingly left for future discussion and settlement. The dissolution of Austria-Hungary had left many questions for solution. Of the seven collective agreements the first dealt with the distribution of public records, and was based on the relevant articles of the St. Germain and Trianon Treaties; the second was concerned with the method of acquiring or forfeiting State citizenship by individuals; the third, with estates held in trust; the fourth, with pensions of civil and military persons who had acquired the nationality of one of the States; the fifth, with private insurance companies and insurance contracts, involving delicate questions of the *valuta* or exchange; and so on. Among special agreements concluded between the States was a juridical convention between Italy and Austria, Italy and Yugoslavia, and Italy and Czechoslovakia. For example, the Italo-Czechoslovak juridical convention contained enactments on the legal protection of subjects of the two States concerned, and on the relationship between the legal authorities and the performing of notifications and requisitions in civil, commercial, and penal matters.

The extensive and difficult nature of the long programme of the Rome Conference naturally resulted in many questions remaining unsettled; some were removed altogether from the list, while others were postponed to an autumn session, among the latter being the question of the distribution of property in various areas of the Succession States, questions relating to commercial companies, banks and savings banks, and the formidable question of the settlement of debts and claims among subjects of the vanished Monarchy. The chief merit of the conference was that it attempted an amicable wholesale liquidation of complicated economic and financial problems, some of which had been left unsolved by the Peace Treaties, and in any case it ventilated by free discussion subjects of importance on which the views of the States concerned were in conflict but which were not incapable of adjustment.

Czechoslovak Negotiations with Hungary

Czechoslovakia resumed the economic negotiations with Hungary which had been interrupted by the Charles attempt. It had been arranged as an outcome of the meeting at Brück between Benesh and Teleki on March 14, 1921, that appropriate commissions should gradually apply the principles of the Peace Treaty and deal as experts with the various points at issue. Four commissions were appointed, and as soon as the situation improved after Charles's return to Switzerland, work was begun. On June 24 Benesh met Banffy, Hungarian Foreign Minister in succession to Gratz, at Marienbad, and agreed to scrutinize the results achieved by these commissions and to try to find a common basis for action in cases where difficulties had arisen. Difficulties had occurred in questions relating to the division of public records and the administrative resources formerly belonging to Hungary, and now applying to Slovakia and Carpathian Ruthenia, while other contested matters related to civil servants, the amnesty, and the racial Minorities. With regard to these Minorities it was decided to conclude a special agreement between Czechoslovakia and Hungary on the basis of the Peace Treaties, and another agreement defining the way in which the Minority Law was to be put into practice.

In a speech made in the Czechoslovak Diet at Prague, Benesh said of these negotiations: "The whole of these negotiations at Marienbad are essentially different from those which took place at Brück, where only general questions were considered. At that time the position of Hungary was different from what it is to-day, as the Peace Treaties had then not yet been ratified. The basis for our negotiations at Marienbad was the actual application of the Peace Treaties, so that the whole of the proceedings were concerned with concrete and entirely definite questions, and this is certainly a considerable advance. There is no doubt that thoroughly positive results will be achieved, and that in a very short time it will be possible to arrive at an agreement with our southern neighbour on all questions in such a way that we will be able to sign the agreement with Hungary as with Austria, and reach the same normal conditions in our dealings with Hungary as is now the case with Austria. This will mean a new step towards ensuring peace in Central Europe, and it is our desire that Hungary will appreciate our good will, and be as loyal in this matter as we are." At Brück the Habsburg question had been allowed to sink into the background, but at Marienbad, and at another meeting at Brno in September, Benesh made a point of impressing on Banffy the unalterable attitude of the Little Entente to Charles.

As after Brück, so at Marienbad and Brno, Benesh was just a little too sanguine and optimistic. At the moment of the Brück negotiations the minds of the leading Hungarian statesmen were set on improving their deplorable financial and economic position by entering into more cordial relations with the Czechoslovaks, whose position was much better. Then had come the affair of Charles; when it was past, the Magyar leaders were desirous of coming to terms with Czechoslovakia for the same reason as before. But Charles had still to be reckoned with. He had not renounced the throne of Hungary, and, indeed, kept up as active a campaign of propaganda and intrigue as his circumstances permitted. Besides, and more immediately to the point, strong political currents, not at all of a pacific character, were flowing in Hungary and threatening serious trouble, which presently developed in connexion with the Burgenland in Western Hungary.

Burgenland Affair

It was not till July, 1921, that the Allies ratified the Treaty of Trianon. Their long delay was variously interpreted; not a few saw in it a sign that the Allies held divergent views about the treaty, and others thought that it had encouraged Charles's venture. At any rate, two of its consequences were patent; one was that Hungary had not handed over to Austria the territory known as the Burgenland, though she had been bound to do so by the treaty, and the other, and not unconnected with the first, was that she was still maintaining under arms a much larger force than that to which she was entitled by the treaty—35,000 men. Czechoslovak estimates put the number of effectives at her disposal at seventy thousand bayonets, and the figures given by others were twice as high. After the ratification of the treaty the Allied Commission of Generals that had been in military control of Hungary was withdrawn, and replaced by an Inter-Allied Commission for the purpose of supervising the execution of the military clauses of the treaty; this commission arrived in Hungary in August, and proceeded to deal with the situation, but its work was slow.

At the request of Hungary the question of the evacuation of the Burgenland was coupled with the evacuation of the Baranya by the Yugoslavs. The Baranya was a county, or *comitat*, occupying the angle between the Danube and the Drave, which had been part of pre-War Hungary, and had been taken over in 1918 by Yugoslavia, to whom, however, the Treaty of Trianon attributed only the southern part of this territory. The northern portion contained the valuable mining district of Pecs, and the Magyars naturally were anxious to get it again. When the Ambassadors' Conference ordered the Yugoslavs to retire, Pashitch, the Yugoslav Prime Minister, complied, but showed resentment at the manner of the action of the Conference, which he thought should have first demanded the evacuation of the Burgenland by the Magyars, and, that being done, should then have asked for the evacuation of the Baranya. The Belgrade Press protested vehemently against what it regarded as a slight to their country and opposed the evacuation. Pashitch considered it likely that though the Magyars obtained what they sought, they would not withdraw from the Burgenland. The event proved that he was right, and the Burgenland question became of still greater international importance.

In Western countries little, if anything, was known of this territory, and it was to be said for them that Burgenland itself was a comparatively new name, having been recently manufactured by the Austrian Government to express the fact that some of the principal towns of the district had names ending in burg: for instance, Oedenburg, the Sopron of the Magyars. A small but rich country, the population of which was predominantly Austro-German, it continued to be occupied, for weeks after the ratification of the treaty, by bands of soldiers clad in Hungarian uniforms, who prevented by force of arms the Austrians from taking possession. The Hungarian Government officially protested that it was unable to control these bands, but the impression was widespread that it encouraged them; it was even said that the greater part of the Hungarian army was to be found in or near the Burgenland. When the Allies remonstrated with Hungary, she replied by proposing the opening of negotiations direct with Austria; the Conference of Ambassadors answered by an ultimatum threatening strong measures unless the district was evacuated without delay; when the evacuation was completed there would be no objection, it pointed out, to the conclusion of an agreement between Hungary and Austria on matters left unsettled. Evacuation did not take place, and when Austrian gendarmes appeared in the Burgenland in September they were driven out by rifle fire.

On September 12, 1921, Benesh dispatched a Note to the Ambassadors' Conference drawing attention to the state of things prevailing in this area. He said that grave events had occurred in Western Hungary, where were assembled thousands of former Magyar soldiers, volunteers, and bands, the character of which it was difficult to particularize, who fought pitched battles with those who wished to establish order and apply the Treaty of Trianon, and who terrorized the entire country. He declared that the neighbouring States were greatly perturbed by what was going on, and that their whole economic life, already deranged by the War, was suffering an intense strain from this fresh development, which, besides, was very dangerous for the peace of Europe. He asked that steps should be taken to terminate the anarchy in the Burgenland, which rendered more and more difficult the return to the normal that was the aim of the Allies. They should take prompt action, otherwise the idea would spread that international engagements could be broken and the Peace Treaties violated with impunity. In closing, he assured the Ambassadors that Czechoslovakia would act only in complete accord with the Allies. The Yugoslav newspapers, still bitter over the Baranya affair, commented in a very outspoken manner on the forcible-feeble dealings of the Ambassadors' Conference with the Hungarian Government.

At this stage an unexpected event occurred which both added to the dissatisfaction of the Yugoslavs and threatened the unity of the Little Entente. Hungary suddenly requested, in the most moving terms, the mediation of Czechoslovakia, who responded to the appeal. On September 23, 1921, Benesh discussed the situation with Schober, the Austrian Chancellor, and a few days later with Banffy, the result being a suggestion, as a compromise, that Austria might retrocede a part of the Burgenland—Oedenburg—to Hungary. Benesh then referred the suggestion to Belgrade and Bucarest for consideration. Take Jonescu approved it; not so Pashitch, who said that the Czechoslovak proposal was of such a nature as to create a precedent for the modification of the terms of the Treaty of Trianon, and he expressed the opinion that the question should be resolved by agreement of the States of the Little Entente among themselves. Referring to the matter at issue, the *Pravda* of Belgrade in an editorial did full justice to Benesh's strong desire to ease and end the situation in the Burgenland which perturbed the neighbours of Austria and Hungary, and increased the general *malaise* from which Europe was suffering. It said it was certain that he had believed his intervention had increased the international prestige of the Little Entente. But in this particular case he had proposed that Oedenburg should be handed back to the Magyars in contravention of the Treaty of Trianon—which was nothing less than a very serious departure in the policy of the Little Entente. Was this wise, in the circumstances of the time? He was reminded that the integral maintenance of the Peace Treaties was, and must remain, the fundamental idea of the Little Entente.

Italy, through Torretta, her Foreign Minister, now stepped in. Taking advantage of the small rift in the Little Entente's internal relations—Italy had regarded the rise and progress of the Little Entente with a certain jealousy—and having been appealed to by Budapest for mediation, Torretta intervened and invited the other Allies to collaborate in a rapid solution of the Burgenland dispute. Eventually a meeting was held at Venice on October 11–12, 1921, and an agreement signed between Austria and Hungary for a plebiscite to be taken in Oedenburg; this was done on December 17, and resulted in a large majority for Hungary. The Conference of Ambassadors agreed that Hungary should take over Oedenburg as from January 1, 1922. The rest of the Burgenland went to Austria, thus carrying out the compromise that Benesh had originally suggested when appealed to by Hungary. But a further turn in events quickly healed whatever differences existed within the Little Entente. A few days after the Venice meeting Oedenburg leaped again into the limelight as the place in which the ex-Emperor Charles began his second attempt to regain the throne of Hungary. On this occasion the Little Entente was not caught unprepared, as it had been on the first; it acted with energy and decision from the start.

Charles's Second Attempt

Breaking his parole to the Swiss Government—a breach which his partisans tried to excuse by "a conflict of conscience"—Charles, accompanied by the ex-Empress Zita, his consort, flew by aeroplane from Dubendorf, the Zürich aerodrome, at midday on October 20, 1921, and landed about half-past four in the afternoon near Denesfa, the castle of Count Cziraky, not far from Szombathely, the town in West Hungary which figured so largely in the first attempt. The story of the flight, the landing, and some of the events which followed were recorded by Boroviczeny, who was an eye-witness of many of the incidents he narrated, in his account of "The Second Attempt of the Emperor Karl to Regain his Throne, and his Untimely Death," which was published in Ashmead-Bartlett's book, *The Tragedy of Central Europe.*

In some prefatory paragraphs characteristic of his point of view, Boroviczeny said that the first attempt of Charles had the good result of reminding the Hungarian people that they had a crowned king in exile, whose return would be a great advantage to Hungary, and that "the strong dynastic movements in those parts of old Hungary under foreign occupation at the moment of the King's arrival, although not generally known, made it clear that the Emperor could restore the territorial integrity of the country much sooner than Horthy or any other President of the Republic. This spontaneous movement in the separated territories proved that the Emperor had a much larger following than the new régime." Horthy's régime was described as bringing "neither peace nor consolidation to mutilated Hungary. A silly persecution of Jews, many murders, and much stealing of the State's goods and money were its prominent features. The currency fell, and the country grew poorer and poorer. Political murders were frequent, and no attempt was made to bring the criminals to justice; there was little security before the law; the army did nothing except to maltreat the civilian population and steal goods in transport from the merchants, which they were supposed to guard, and yet no one was ever punished for these outrages and thefts. The sanctity of the private home was not respected, except the homes of the supporters of the Republicans, and the army became the guard of a political party instead of a defence to the nation. All these abuses under the Horthy régime made people long for the return of the legitimate King. In political circles the restoration was the chief topic of conversation, and the object of long negotiations with the Government, which pretended to be legitimist, and to wish as ardently for it as the legitimists themselves."

Boroviczeny stated that Charles had kept in close touch with the politicians, and that in August, 1921, there were negotiations between Bethlen, the Hungarian Prime Minister, and Horthy on one side, and Andrassy and Gratz acting for the ex-Emperor on the other; that an officers' organization resolved in October, 1921, to proceed with the restoration, and invited some of the most distinguished politicians to place themselves at the disposal of Charles on his arrival in Hungary; and that Charles himself remained in communication with some of the representatives of the Great Powers, as well as with his "partisans in the States of the old Monarchy so as to ensure the neutrality of the Little Entente." Boroviczeny concluded the introduction to his story with the words, "Thus in October the Emperor Karl decided to make his final effort to regain his throne."

Charles and Zita were conducted first to the castle of Cziraky, and during the same night to Oedenburg (Sopron), where they were joined by a battalion of soldiers and some of the Ministers of Charles's last Hungarian Government, and others. Next day General Hegedus, the commander of the troops in Oedenburg, assured Charles, according to Boroviczeny that the whole garrison and district acknowledged him as their rightful sovereign. Early on the following day, October 22, Charles and Zita reached Gyor, and in the evening were at Komarom, where he reviewed the garrison. While this inspection was going on Rakovszky, a former President of the Hungarian National Assembly, and now nominated Prime Minister by Charles, telephoned to Bethlen a summons to the Hungarian Government to hand over office to a new Cabinet Charles had chosen, and to maintain peace and order in Budapest till Charles had arrived there. Bethlen asked Rakovszky to keep Charles at Komarom to await the coming of Vas with a letter from Horthy, which proved to be a protest by Horthy against handing over the powers that had been legally conferred on him by the National Assembly.

Vas was received by Rakovszky and Andrassy, who had been authorized to read Horthy's letter; Charles was resting and did not see it. Vas asked for details of Charles's plans and how the international difficulties of the restoration were to be surmounted, but was given no information, on the ground that Horthy, to whom he was to report, had been indiscreet before. Vas motored back to Budapest. Next morning Charles resumed his march on the capital, but was held up between Torbagy and Kelenfold, on the outskirts of the city, where the railway lines had been torn up and forces had been hurriedly got into position to oppose his further advance. Some fighting took place, and a few were killed on both sides. Charles forbade his troops to shed further blood, and the firing immediately ceased. An armistice was agreed to, and a line of demarcation was drawn by Hegedus, the Commander-in-Chief of the guards of Charles.

Of the action of Hegedus, Boroviczeny wrote: "He himself (Hegedus) related in his statements, which were published in Parliament in November, 1921, that he premeditatedly betrayed the King, and drew the demarcation line in a way which was disadvantageous and intended to make possible the capture and disarmament of the loyal troops during the night. It was agreed that the armistice should last till the following morning, when the representatives of the Government at Budapest and of the King should meet. On the 23rd General Hegedus, under pretext of visiting his troops, went in to Budapest, gave an exact report to the Government of the position of the King's army, and received orders how to act. On his return he told His Majesty he had been to Pest to try to induce the Government to surrender, but could not persuade them, and had witnessed the most minute preparations to resist his advance. Hegedus persuaded the King to do whatever he was asked, and assured His Majesty of his loyalty once again, but begged him to dismiss him from the command, as his sons were on the side of the Government. His Majesty accepted his resignation, and told him that it was a strange sign of loyalty if he could not bring over his sons; besides, as there was no longer any fighting, he need not remain with the army. In spite of his dismissal, Hegedus figured as Commander at the moment when the line of demarcation was drawn." A very curious story, but with significant touches that made it appear entirely credible.

The Little Entente Active

Meanwhile the Little Entente had been extremely active. The arrival of Charles at Oedenburg on October 21, the taking of the oath of allegiance to him by the garrison there, the proclamation of the restoration, and the appointment of Rakovszky as Prime Minister were all reported in the columns of the Little Entente newspapers early on the following day, and caused a great sensation. A Belgrade journal asserted that the return of the ex-Emperor was tantamount to a declaration of war on the Little Entente States, the immediate mobilization of whose armies was called for by the Prague Press. These newspapers faithfully reflected the opinions and emotions of the people of these countries. It could not be said that the reappearance of Charles in Hungary had not been foreseen and provided for by the Little Entente; the Defensive Conventions had been supplemented, in accordance with their Second Article, by other conventions, a Czechoslovak-Rumanian Military Convention being signed on July 2, 1921, and a Czechoslovak-Yugoslav Military Convention on August 1, 1921. The three States were, in fact, ready to move, but before proceeding to mobilize they first pursued a course of energetic and resolute diplomatic action.

On October 22 Benesh, in a Circular Note to the representatives abroad of Czechoslovakia, defined the attitude of his

Government to Charles and the Habsburg question: "The presence of the ex-Emperor on the soil of Hungary is a *casus belli*. We are proceeding without delay to prepare for mobilization, and we shall not hesitate to take the most energetic measures in unison with the other States of the Little Entente. Even if Charles should withdraw from Hungary we shall have recourse to the necessary diplomatic steps and exercise the greatest pressure, if necessary by armed force, to obtain the liquidation of the Habsburg question in Hungary and to put a final end to the danger created by the House of Habsburg in Central Europe." It was thus made plain that the aim of the Little Entente was the absolute abrogation of the claims and pretensions, not only of the ex-Emperor, but of every member of the Habsburg family, to the throne of Hungary.

That this was not the standpoint of the Hungarian Government was shown by a Note, addressed by Banffy to the Czechoslovak representative in Budapest on the same day, declaring that Hungary stood by the principles of the Law passed in 1920—"King Charles not being able, according to these principles, to exercise the rights of sovereignty over Hungary, will be compelled to leave the country without delay. The Hungarian Government has already taken the requisite measures." The Little Entente demanded much more than that. In a strong message from Prague, dated October 23, Benesh impressed the Little Entente point of view on the Big Entente. This was followed up next day by a letter in the same sense to the Conference of Ambassadors signed by the Rumanian and Czechoslovak Ministers and the Yugoslav Chargé d'Affaires in Paris.

This document, which went to the root of the matter, read: "The Rumanian, Yugoslav, and Czechoslovak Governments consider the events occurring at present in Hungary to be a consequence of the events in the Burgenland. They see in these events an assault on the Peace Treaties, which these Governments themselves have executed loyally, trying in that way to keep the peace in Central Europe. They feel themselves to be menaced not only by the return of Charles, but also by the attitude of the Hungarian Government, which has favoured and defended openly the happenings in the Burgenland. Their Governments are convinced that the peace of Europe requires that all measures, even the most energetic measures, should be taken for the final liquidation of the Habsburg question and the execution of the Peace Treaties. They hope for the support of the Allies, especially in all matters relating to the strict application of the Peace Treaties. The Rumanian, Yugoslav, and Czechoslovak Governments, while thus informing the Allied Powers of their point of view, assure them that they will take all measures necessary for a rapid and definitive settlement of the said questions in order that peace may be finally re-established in Central Europe, as they are convinced that any solution that did not bring about a definitive settlement would have the greatest danger for Europe." The signatories were Ghika for Rumania, Osusky for Czechoslovakia, and Mihailovitch for Yugoslavia.

On the same day, October 24, 1921, the Ambassadors' Conference addressed a Note to the Hungarian Government, which said: "The Allied Powers recall to the Hungarian Government the terms of their Declaration of April 1. Seeing that the former sovereign persists in claiming the throne, on which his presence would have the gravest consequences for the peace of Central Europe, the Powers ask the Hungarian Government, first, to proclaim the forfeiture of the throne by the ex-King Charles, and secondly to hold the person of the ex-King till he quits Hungarian territory under conditions which the Allied Governments will fix. The Powers declare that if the Hungarian Government does not accede to this request immediately, they will decline all responsibility regarding the intervention in Hungary of the neighbouring States, and the consequences that may result from it." In acquainting the Little Entente Governments with this Note, the Ambassadors' Conference said that the Allied Powers were confident that, in a situation already so grave, the Little Entente would make no decision or take any action except in agreement with them.

Charles Fails Again

While these diplomatic exchanges were going on Charles had become the prisoner of the Hungarian Government. According to Boroviczeny's narrative, General Than, in command of the Government's troops, sent a letter to Charles's chief officers saying that the armistice, which had been agreed to on October 23, ended at five o'clock on the morning of October 24; it was half-past seven when the letter was delivered. Negotiations were begun between representatives of the Hungarian Government and of Charles, and a protocol was drawn up by them; it provided, among other things, for the written abdication by Charles of the throne, for the personal security of himself and the ex-Empress Zita as long as they remained on Hungarian soil, for the designation by the Hungarian Government of a residence for them in Hungary, after negotiations with the representatives of the Great Powers in Budapest, and for an agreement with the Powers concerning their future domicile abroad.

Boroviczeny stated: "During the negotiations the Government troops, which during the night had received big reinforcements, began to march into the rear of the King's Guard, who, conforming to the armistice, were camping in their previous position. As soon as the Commanders noticed this unfair movement, they endeavoured to make a last but hopeless defence. . . . The lives of their Majesties were in imminent peril when the Government's troops began to fire on the train. The position being hopeless, a high officer was left behind to rally those of the Guard who had not been captured, and the train containing their Majesties and their suites moved westwards to regain Western Hungary, where it was believed they would be safe for the time being. But the train could go no farther than Tata, as the lines had been torn up. The King and Queen therefore accepted the hospitality of the owner of the beautiful castle in Tata, Count Esterhazy, who, together with the greater part of the Hungarian aristocracy and the mass of the nation, remained faithful to their King, even in his powerless condition." Headed by Hegedus, soldiers of the Hungarian Government soon appeared at Tata to look after the "security" of Charles and Zita; they were virtually prisoners. According to Boroviczeny, an attempt was made during the night of October 24–25 to assassinate the ex-Emperor, but it was defeated owing to the watchfulness of Esterhazy and others. On October 25 the Hungarian Government arrested Rakovsky, Andrassy, Gratz, and Boroviczeny, "who figured as the political councillors of the King." Charles protested, and demanded to be arrested, too, whereupon Rakovsky and the three other gentlemen were allowed to remain with him as long as he was at Tata. On October 27 Charles, with his four councillors and Esterhazy, and the ex-Empress, accompanied by Countess Schönbrun, afterwards Mme. Boroviczeny, and Countess Esterhazy were removed to Tihany, a monastery on Lake Balaton. The Esterhazys were forced to return to Tata, but the others were kept as closely guarded prisoners by soldiers of the Hungarian Government.

On October 25 Banffy had announced that Charles would be interned at Tihany, where he would be compelled to abdicate, and this being the state of the case, Banffy said that Hungary resumed her freedom of action—the Habsburg question had lost its "actuality," as Charles would leave the country for ever. This, of course, was far from satisfying the Little Entente. On the preceding day both Czechoslovakia and Yugoslavia began mobilizing. In a week the former State mobilized 300,000 men, and the latter 200,000 men, a formidable force, which indicated a determination of the most convincing kind to bring about the settlement desired. The Rumanian Government authorized General Averescu to mobilize six infantry divisions and two cavalry divisions. The Italian Government, acknowledging the agreement with the Little Entente against the Habsburgs, proclaimed its solidarity with it in regarding any prolongation of the sojourn of Charles in Hungary as a *casus belli*, but asked that war should not be declared before Italy had been consulted; an agreement with her, it was said, would reinforce the position of the Little Entente both with

Hungary and the Big Entente. She thought, however, that the question of the complete and final liquidation of the Habsburgs should not be resolved by force of arms, but by diplomacy after the ex-Emperor had quitted Hungarian territory. This did not satisfy the Little Entente either.

What was in the mind of its leaders appeared in the correspondence between Benesh and Banffy, which was published in the White Book, entitled "Documents diplomatiques concernant les Tentatives de Restauration des Habsbourg sur le Trône de Hongrie, Août, 1919–Novembre, 1921," issued by the Czechoslovak Ministry of Foreign Affairs, Prague, in 1922. On October 23 Benesh reminded Banffy that at Marienbad and at Brno he had told him how he regarded the question of the ex-Emperor. Three days later Tahy, the representative of the Hungarian Government at Prague, informed Girsa, who was deputizing for Benesh, his chief, that Banffy was greatly surprised that Benesh should seem to have doubts of his good will and of the sincerity of his intentions. The attitude of the Hungarian Government showed that he (Benesh) was mistaken; Banffy said that the Hungarian Government was ready to take, even at the cost of great sacrifices, whatever measures were necessary for the peace of Central Europe, and to put down the attempted *coup d'état* of Charles by force of arms. In his reply next day Benesh thanked Banffy for his assurances, but went on to say that after what had taken place in Hungary the action of the Hungarian Government was considered insufficient in Yugoslavia and Czechoslovakia by their Governments and peoples. What was in the best interests of Hungary and what alone would safeguard peace must be done: "The whole dynasty of Habsburg must be deprived of its rights to the throne, and, in addition, the Hungarian Government must undertake in writing to carry out the provisions of the Trianon Treaty in all their rigour. If the matter is not solved in this way, nothing will remain but recourse to military measures." On October 26 Benesh sent a message to the Czechoslovak Ministers at Paris, London, and Rome, to be passed on to the Big Entente. This made the attitude of the Little Entente still clearer by presenting two new demands. He stated that the Big Entente was asked to accept the point of view, which was fundamental, that the simple prohibition of the accession to the throne of Charles, or eventually of his son, was not enough. Adequate guarantees must be given that the provisions of the Peace Treaty should not be eluded by Hungary concerning her disarmament; to this end the Little Entente should be called on to participate in the disarmament of Hungary, kept constantly informed of the progress of that disarmament, and supply whatever information it possessed with respect to that subject; this might be done, it was suggested, by a sub-commission auxiliary to the Allied Commission, as the Little Entente had no intention of impairing the prestige of the Big Entente, or of ignoring its rights. It was no longer, however, a question of any modification of the provisions of the Treaty of Trianon, but a question of applying in a practical manner its disarmament clauses. Further, the Big Entente was requested to endorse the claim for an indemnity from Hungary in payment of the expenditure incurred by the mobilization of the forces of the Little Entente. In a letter to Briand, Benesh stressed these points, and requested the immediate support of France for them in the Ambassadors' Conference.

Habsburg Question Vital

This letter concluded with the statement that the Habsburg question was a vital one to the Little Entente, and that if it was not settled in accordance with the views of the Little Entente it would be difficult to keep the peace. This was true. Excitement was increasing in the three States, especially in Czechoslovakia and Yugoslavia, where the impression was growing that the Big Entente, if it was not precisely favouring Hungary, was not acting in the peremptory fashion which the situation, in their opinion, necessitated. The actual situation was in fact pretty well understood in Prague, Belgrade, and Bucarest, as was evident from their newspapers.

On October 27 the Ambassadors' Conference sent a Note to the Hungarian Government expressing satisfaction with what the latter had done to terminate the second attempt of the ex-Emperor, and intimating that Charles should be handed over to the commandant of the British fleet at Budapest, who would protect him while the Allies settled where he was to reside. The Conference added that the forfeiture of the throne by Charles must be proclaimed without delay.

Banffy thereupon announced that the demands of the Allies would be fulfilled, and that the King, who was interned, was at their disposal. Early in the afternoon of October 29 the representatives in Budapest of France, England, and Italy, together with those of the Little Entente, met the British Commissioner Hohler, who informed them that a British monitor would convey the ex-Emperor and his consort to Galatz in the course of the next two or three days. On that day, too, the representatives of the Little Entente—Take Jonescu had specially enjoined the Rumanian Minister to participate in the *démarche*—told Banffy that the Habsburg question in its entirety must be settled immediately and finally, otherwise the consequences would be grave. In reply, Banffy declared that the liquidation of this second attempt of Charles carried with it the liquidation of the whole Habsburg question as a natural result, and conformably with the Constitution of Hungary. This, again, was not enough for the Little Entente.

In Western countries the importance of the points at issue was still but partially understood. Hungary was not without friends in Paris and London. In a section of the French and British Press sympathy was shown for Charles, and sentimentalists, bewailing his hard fate, saw something in his ill-starred career that they called romantic. There were people, to say nothing of newspapers, who accused the Little Entente of insolence in setting itself up against the Big Entente. Czechoslovakia was singled out for attack on the ground that she was busying herself in the internal affairs of Hungary, which were none of her business, and that she was trying to overthrow the Government that existed in Hungary and replace it by another of her own choosing. Reports to this effect were current in

England to such an extent that Benesh sent a message to the Czechoslovak Minister in London denying their truth emphatically, and characterizing them as sheer propaganda. It was some time before the fact was grasped in the West that the Little Entente regarded the Habsburg question as one of life or death, and the reason why it did so: that there could be no peace in Central Europe until this question was out of the way once and for all, and therefore must be finally settled—by war, if there was no other way. To many in the West this seemed a very drastic method; once more were heard statements affirming and deploring the Balkanization of Central Europe; again regrets were expressed for the disappearance of Austria-Hungary.

Where it did not spring from ignorance, nearly all of this was tendentious propaganda, and was meant to damage the Little Entente. Whether it had any influence on the Ambassadors' Conference or not, that body addressed a Note to Benesh, which he received on October 30, stating that it was of opinion that the forfeiture of the throne by "all the Habsburgs" could be demanded; that as the Conference was charged with the application of the Peace Treaties, it was its duty to see to that of the Treaty of Trianon and of the conventions which consequently had been made among some of the Powers which had inherited Austria-Hungary; that the control of disarmament was in the hands of the Commissions appointed for that purpose by the Great Powers, but that the Conference would be glad to have an exchange of information between the Commissions of Control and the Little Entente, as had been suggested; and that, whereas the Conference had invited the Little Entente States to refrain from doing anything without previous consultation with the Great Powers, and whereas the Hungarian Government had by its own efforts succeeded in ending the attempt of Charles to the satisfaction of the Powers, the Conference could not recognize the claim of the Little Entente to an indemnity from Hungary. This Note concluded by saying that the Great Powers held that the "present correct attitude" of the Hungarian Government justified in no way military action by the Little Entente, which, therefore, should proceed at once with the demobilization of its forces.

In line with part of this Note the Italian, British, and French representatives at Budapest placed before the Hungarian Government on October 31 a communication from the Conference, which said that, though that Government had put a stop to the attempt of the ex-King, it had not obeyed the Ambassadors' command to proclaim the forfeiture of the throne by him—procuring his abdication was insufficient. The Conference drew the attention of the Hungarian Government to the growing agitation in the neighbouring States; to calm it Hungary was asked to proclaim immediately the forfeiture by Charles of the throne, extending at the same time that forfeiture to all members of the House of Habsburg. On October 31 the Hungarian Government announced that Charles would be handed over to the Big Entente and dethroned, and that Hungary would accept whatever was the decision of the Great Powers, in whose hands she had placed her fate. The Hungarian Government, following the advice of the Great Powers, had not, it was pointed out, taken any military steps to oppose the Little Entente. Two days before, Benesh had proposed to Belgrade and Bucarest to defer military intervention for a few days, in the hope that as the Big Entente had acceded in part to the demands of the Little Entente, it might yet grant all of them. He did his utmost to "ginger up" the Conference of Ambassadors. On October 31 he addressed to it a long and important letter (No. 58 in the Czechoslovak White Book previously mentioned), which reviewed the whole situation from his standpoint and that of the Little Entente, in reply to the Ambassadors' Note, of October 30, to the Czechoslovak, Yugoslav and Rumanian Governments.

Benesh's Historic Letter

This historic document, of exceptional value to the student of conditions in Central Europe at this time, began by thanking the Ambassadors' Conference for its decision respecting the forfeiture of the throne of Hungary by the whole Habsburg family. The situation in Central Europe, it was remarked, had been highly critical, because public opinion in the Little Entente States had taken the view that the Trianon Treaty was not being applied with the same strictness as the Versailles and St. Germain Treaties; therefore the assurance given by the Conference that it would energetically apply the terms of the Trianon Treaty to Hungary was particularly important. Czechoslovakia attributed fundamental significance to the question of the disarmament of Hungary, for she had seen that so far the Hungarian Government had prevented the provisions of the treaty in this regard from being carried out. As neighbours knowing intimately all that was going on in Hungary, and the political methods of the Hungarian authorities, the members of the Little Entente would be able to collaborate usefully in the difficult task of disarming Hungary, without desiring to interfere in her internal affairs or to alter in any way the terms of the Peace Treaty. This collaboration having been admitted in principle by the Ambassadors, for which the Little Entente was grateful, the next step to be taken would be to state what form this collaboration would take.

So far, good. But the Conference had rejected the claim for an indemnity. Then followed various arguments for a modification of its action, the first of which was that the representations of the Allies at Budapest had had precious little effect until they were backed by the mobilization of Czechoslovakia and Yugoslavia, which alone really accounted for what was now described as the "correct attitude" of the Hungarian Government. In support, the occurrences in the Burgenland were adduced at considerable length, and stress was laid on the disregard by Hungary of the orders of the Ambassadors thereanent. It was obvious that in the present case it was the mobilization that had made all the difference. Another argument was that the mobilization had been justified to a great extent by the statement made by the Great Powers to Hungary that if she did not implement the command of the Conference, she would be left to be dealt with by the Little Entente—which had acted on the implication by mobilizing. Morally the Little Entente was entitled to an indemnity; if the principle of the thing was not recognized, then Hungary would be given a premium for the non-application of the Peace Treaty. It was all very well to speak of demobilizing; Czechoslovakia was willing to demobilize, but knowing thoroughly the political methods of the Hungarian Government, she was against an immediate mobilization, for, if that was done, the Hungarians would recommence their game of duplicity; the Czechoslovak Government had no confidence in the Magyars in this matter, but a short time might be granted to see whether they fulfilled the decision of the Ambassadors; if they were told they would have to pay an indemnity, that would hasten things. The Conference was thanked, in conclusion, for its understanding of this grave crisis in the life of the Little Entente, which again gave an assurance that it would do nothing contrary to the common interests of all the Allies.

Though couched in the most courteous language, the letter was firm in tone throughout. During the whole of this conflict with Hungary and the diplomatic controversy with the Ambassadors, Benesh acted as the chief spokesman of the Little Entente. Without ceasing to be Foreign Minister, he had become Prime Minister of Czechoslovakia on September 27, 1921, as head of a coalition of various groups in the Diet; all its groups united to uphold him in a firm policy. Similar unanimity was manifested by the Yugoslav Parliament; in its session of October 29 all its parties combined in demanding firmness on the part of their Government; Pashitch identified himself with Benesh. Jonescu, too, rendered great assistance. Rumania had not proceeded with her mobilization; on that account she did not join Czechoslovakia and Yugoslavia in asking an indemnity, but she supported their claims to one.

Habsburg Restoration Barred

Tension throughout Central Europe was relieved when the crisis was partially resolved on October 31 by a Note from Banffy to the Conference sent through the representatives of the Big Entente at Budapest. Hungary accepted without reservation the decision of the Conference respecting the forfeiture of the throne by Charles and all other Habsburgs, and stated that her National Assembly would be convoked within a week to pass the necessary legislation. On November 3 the Conference replied to Benesh's letter of October 31. In their response the Ambassadors noted that the Little Entente had agreed to conform with the decisions of the Conference; said that Hungary had placed herself in the hands of the Great Powers, would proclaim the forfeiture of the throne by the House of Habsburg, and that her National Assembly would be called together to give it legal effect; referred to the preparations for demobilization being made by the Little Entente; and absolutely rejected its claim to an indemnity, for which they could find no juridical foundation—even if such a foundation existed and the claim was recognized, the indemnity would rank after the payments for reparations as provided in the Peace Treaty, meaning thereby, of course, that the payment of the indemnity would be postponed indefinitely. A touch of spleen perhaps in the last observation, but it put the indemnity practically out of court.

On November 3, 1921, the Hungarian National Assembly met to consider a law abrogating the sovereignty of Charles and annulling the succession rights of the House of Austria (*Domus Austriaca*) under the Pragmatic Sanction of 1723, but maintaining a monarchical form of State-Government for Hungary according to ancient usage, the election to the throne being deferred to a later time. On Benesh's pointing out that the law did not specifically forbid the possibility of the restoration of the Habsburgs by way of an open election, the Ambassadors on November 5, through the Allied representatives at Budapest, directed the Hungarian National Assembly to make it quite clear by law that the Habsburgs were permanently excluded from the throne of Hungary, free election or not. This accordingly was done, the law having added to it on November 10 a declaration making impossible a Habsburg restoration on any pretext whatsoever, and providing against a candidate for the throne being selected till after consultation with the Great Powers. Thus the crisis was definitely solved. Czechoslovakia and Yugoslavia demobilized. The Conference declared that it was satisfied with the law, as altered, and further recognized it as an "International Act," thus furnishing, it considered, a stronger guarantee than that given by a law which some day might be revised.

The Little Entente, by its steady pressure on the Ambassadors, with that pressure unflinchingly emphasized by the mobilization of half a million men, had achieved its fundamental aim—the absolute liquidation of the Habsburg question. But it was gained at considerable costs, the expenditure on mobilization of Czechoslovakia alone amounting to 450,867,935 Czechoslovak crowns, which at the rate of exchange then current was about two million pounds sterling.

On November 1 Charles and his Consort had been conveyed on board the British monitor *Glowworm*, and later were taken by the cruiser *Cardiff* to Funchal in Madeira. There the ex-Emperor died on April 1, 1922, in pitiful circumstances, the last of a great dynasty that had ruled in Europe for several centuries.

CHAPTER VI

THE LITTLE ENTENTE EXPANDED

1921–1922

If the two attempts of the ex-Emperor Charles to regain the throne of Hungary rendered abortive the negotiations between Czechoslovakia and that country for an improvement in their relations, Czechoslovakia had at any rate the satisfaction of concluding a highly important political treaty with Austria on December 16, 1921. The way had been prepared for it by the meeting of President Masaryk of Czechoslovakia and President Hainisch of Austria at Hallstadt on August 10. The two statesmen were accompanied by their respective Foreign Ministers, Benesh and Schober, the latter also being Austrian Chancellor. Discussion centred in Austria's relations to the Little Entente and her attitude to the Habsburg question. Economic matters were considered, but not specifically, in the absence of economic experts. After the meeting it was officially stated that the relations between Austria and the Little Entente were excellent.

Comment in both Czechoslovak and Austrian newspapers was very favourable, the general view being that another stage had been reached in the consolidation of Central Europe; Yugoslav and Rumanian journals wrote in a similar strain. The *Chas*, Prague, in a leading article said that while the Czechoslovaks could not altogether forget the struggle with Austria for three centuries, the fact remained that Czechoslovakia and Austria were neighbours, separated, but not isolated, from each other. That their relations should be friendly was dictated by their common interest. The only drawback was the unfortunate economic situation in Austria—which some Austrians thought might be remedied by attaching Austria to Germany (Anschluss). The truth was, said the *Chas*, that Austria had to rely on her own resources, and must carry out the process of recovery, depending on herself, with the aid of the Big Entente as well as other neighbours—an indispensable condition. What was indicated was a treaty of good neighbourliness. Negotiations for such a treaty, for which the train had been laid by previous conversations between Benesh and Renner, were entered on at once. The Burgenland trouble and the second attempt of Charles caused some interruption, but in both these affairs the Austrian Government preserved a perfectly correct attitude, and there was no actual hitch in the negotiations.

Treaty of Lany

On December 15, 1921, Hainisch and Schober went to Prague, where on the following day the treaty, commonly called the Treaty of Lany, was signed by them for Austria and by Masaryk and Benesh for Czechoslovakia. By this treaty the two States bound themselves to carry out fully all the stipulations of the St. Germain and Trianon Treaties; to guarantee to each other the territorial status assigned to them by these treaties; to observe neutrality in case of a conflict with third parties; to prohibit in their territories the formation of any political or military organization directed against either of them; to aid each other in their opposition to any plan for the restoration of the former régime; to settle disputes among themselves by arbitration; to communicate to each other the political or economic agreements with third parties which either had made; and not to conclude any agreement in contradiction of the treaty. Benesh described the treaty as founded on a "policy of friendly coexistence on the basis of a recognition of the Peace Treaties," and said it "did not make Austria a member of the Little Entente, but it signified an accord between the policy of Austria and that of the Little Entente."

It was scarcely to be supposed that the pan-German element in Austria would approve of this treaty, seeing that it implied the recognition of the situation created by the Treaty of St. Germain, which, among other things, forbade the union of Austria with Germany without the consent of the Council of the League of Nations. In a speech in the Parliament at Vienna, Schober replied with vigour and success to all the attacks of the pan-Germans. He reminded them that Austria had several times already undertaken to execute loyally the provisions of the St. Germain Treaty, and the Treaty of Lany merely reaffirmed the undertaking; it introduced nothing new. It was to be expected that if Austria obtained further assistance by reason of the treaty, those giving that help would ask for a fresh and solemn recognition of the St. Germain Treaty. What could Austria do but give it? The only way in which she could ameliorate her position was by having good relations and economic *rapprochement* with the neighbouring States, particularly Czechoslovakia. That meant and could only mean a political *rapprochement*, which, he maintained, any statesman solicitous of the national interests could not well refuse, especially as it carried with it no attack on the rights of the nation, but improved both its internal and external situation.

The treaty was in fact a good thing for Austria. In Yugoslavia it was hailed as a great achievement. In pre-War days the bulk of the exports of Serbia had been taken by Austria-Hungary, with Vienna as a central clearing house alike for railway and river trade and commerce. After the War Austria still held the first place as a market for the produce of Yugoslavia; in 1921 the total value of the exports of the latter country was 1,320,600,000 dinars, of which Austria took nearly one-half—563,444,000 dinars, the figure rising to 882,300,000 dinars in 1921. At that time all transactions between Yugoslavia and Austria were based on a commercial treaty signed on June 27, 1920; it was of a provisional character, and had been extended several times, with the prospect of the conclusion of a definitive commercial treaty in the near future, a prospect that the Treaty of Lany could not but make easier of realization.

Rumania, the third member of the Little Entente, was not less well-disposed towards Austria. In an interview published in the *Neue Freie Presse*, Vienna, Take Jonescu, referring to Austria's relations with the Little Entente, said that he had given instructions to the Rumanian representatives, who at that moment were discussing economic questions at Vienna, not to regard Austria as an enemy State, but on the contrary to accord to her all the advantages that Rumania afforded to the

States of the Little Entente. He added that he would be delighted if Austria would join that organization; her adhesion to it was to take the only course which would benefit her international relations; this was the view of Rumania, nor would she alter it unless Austria manifested the desire to unite with Germany. Czechoslovakia showed her good will to Austria by opening a credit for her of five hundred millions of Czechoslovak gold crowns, a sum at that time equivalent to one hundred milliards of Austrian crowns (about £4,000,000 sterling). This action, which involved a considerable sacrifice on the part of Czechoslovakia, was of great assistance to Austria, and materially facilitated her financial sanitation by the League of Nations in 1922.

Poland and the Little Entente

The expansion of the Little Entente, exemplified by the Treaty of Lany, was also seen in the conclusion, a few weeks earlier, of a treaty between Poland and Czechoslovakia. This treaty was preceded by a treaty of commerce which was signed at Warsaw on September 20, 1921, and was similar to those commercial treaties which Czechoslovakia had already concluded with her allies. A visit to the Polish capital and Posen of Hottowetz, the Czechoslovak Minister of Commerce, had contributed to the success of the negotiations for the treaty, but other influences were at work in the same direction—a *rapprochement* between Poland and Czechoslovakia. As already noted, Take Jonescu worked incessantly to bring this about. Writing in the autumn of 1921, he said that neither Poland nor Czechoslovakia had been able to explain to him the reasons for the misunderstandings between the two nations; he had "heard memories of the recent past under the Habsburg revived," and he was "aware of the soreness provoked by the Teschen question." These matters were now history. "Therefore," he added, "I consecrated much of my time to bringing about an alliance between the Czechoslovaks and the Poles." But after the Teschen dispute was out of the way there appeared in the Press of the two peoples a distinct tendency towards finding some road to better relations, and this synchronized with a change in the attitude to Czechoslovakia of the Polish Government, under the administrations of Witos and Ponikowski, with Skirmunt as Foreign Minister.

Skirmunt, who had been one of the Polish representatives at the famous Congress at Rome of the Oppressed Nationalities in 1918, and afterwards was Polish Minister at Rome, was appointed Foreign Minister in the summer of 1921. Well-acquainted with the ideas current in the political circles of Western Europe, he announced a policy that corresponded with them—a policy of peace based on the Peace Treaties, an agreement with the Allied Powers, and an amicable settlement of all controversial questions with neighbouring States, especially with Czechoslovakia. The settlement concerning Teschen by the Ambassadors' Conference had undoubtedly left a feeling of soreness among the Poles and the Czechoslovaks. The Czechoslovak Government's foreign policy, however, was steadily directed to rendering public opinion throughout the country favourable to an agreement with Poland, for the same reasons that had led to the formation of the Little Entente, namely, the integral observance of the Peace Treaties, the consolidation of Central Europe politically and economically, and the general peace. When, therefore, some Polish journals criticized Skirmunt's policy towards Czechoslovakia as being equivalent to capitulation to that country's policy, the Czechoslovaks replied that his policy represented only the fulfilment of the obligations which Poland had entered into on the terms of the Peace Treaties, in the same way as Czechoslovak policy represented compliance with them. Further, it was urged that if Poland intended to carry out a policy similar to that of Czechoslovakia, this in itself was a proof that the Czechoslovak policy was a good one; with regard to Russia, the question in the background of the thoughts of the Poles, Czechoslovak policy, it was stated, while obviously Slavonic and democratic, did not permit an active part to be taken on either side of the Polish-Russian controversy.

These and other newspaper expressions of opinion did not

disguise the fact that very many Poles agreed with Skirmunt and regarded a Polish-Czechoslovak agreement as necessary. In consonance with his policy Skirmunt sent to Prague as Polish Minister Erasmus Piltz, who had previously been Minister at Belgrade, and was known to be friendly to the Little Entente. Another indication of that policy was given when, during the second attempt of Charles, the Polish Minister at Budapest, notwithstanding the traditional friendship of Poland for Hungary, associated himself with the Allies and the Little Entente in their opposition to the ex-Emperor and in their pressure on the Horthy Government. Skirmunt himself visited Prague early in November, and a Defensive Convention was signed by him and Benesh on November 6, 1921.

The terms of this convention, which differed a good deal from other pacts of the Little Entente, were: (1) Both States mutually guaranteed their territorial integrity on the basis of the treaties to which they owed their existence and independence; (2) In case of an attack on one of them by a neighbouring State, both agreed to observe a benevolent neutrality and to permit the free transit of war material; (3) Poland declared her disinterestedness in Slovakia and Czechoslovakia her disinterestedness in East Galicia; each State undertook to dissolve on its territory all organizations aiming at the severance of parts of the other State and to suppress propaganda to that end; (4) Both States recognized the treaties and conventions signed by their Governments with other States; (5) A commercial treaty was to be concluded; (6) Arbitration was provided for; (7) Treaties entered into by one party with a third State were to be communicated to the other; (8) Duration of this treaty was for five years.

In a statement published some time after the signing of this treaty Benesh said: "A significant extension of the political circle of the Little Entente was the treaty concluded by Minister Skirmunt and myself on behalf of Poland and Czechoslovakia respectively. That treaty definitively put an end to the unsettled relations existing between the two States as a result of the diplomatic controversies respecting Teschen, and laid the foundation of peaceful neighbourly existence and collaboration. Under the treaty the two States mutually recognized each other's territories as defined in the Peace Treaties, and undertook whenever necessary to agree on a common application of the terms of these treaties. They undertook mutually to observe neutrality and to settle disputes by arbitration."

As a matter of fact, however, this treaty was not ratified by Poland. Speaking of this in February, 1924, in the Committee of the Czechoslovak Parliament, Benesh observed: "You all know that this treaty has not been put into operation. I regret this, and meanwhile it remains merely as a document of our foreign policy. There was not enough understanding either amongst ourselves or in Poland. . . . I shall to-day say openly why I regret that we have not been able to arrive at a Czechoslovak-Polish Treaty earlier. People have spoken, and from time to time they will speak, of the entrance of Poland into the Little Entente. That is not correct. That is the way to hurt the sensibilities of Poland, and it does not have any material bearing upon the situation either. Between the Little Entente and Poland there has several times been close cooperation in questions common to both, and especially at the Genoa Conference. This collaboration is desirable and good, and it will certainly be put again strongly into practice. I wish it sincerely. But that has meant and will always mean the formula—Poland and the Little Entente. If one takes into account the general line of policy followed so far by Poland and the members of the Little Entente, one can see that no negotiations have ever been undertaken concerning the creation of a great territorial combination and allied block, but only of a limited understanding based on real interests and following concrete aims. This has always been expressed by the provisional formula—Poland and the Little Entente, a formula just and realizable despite various difficulties. . . . My aim has always been to come to an understanding with Poland before the entrance of the new Russia into European politics. The situation is such that an understanding will be much more difficult when Russia intervenes more actively in European politics, and it will be more difficult for all of us, for ourselves, for Poland, and for Russia. It seems that this has not been understood in time and sufficiently, either in Czechoslovakia or in Poland. Hence we have the intention to-day to resume as soon as possible the interrupted work and finally to come to an agreement."

It was not till April, 1925, that a political treaty was negotiated between the two States, which was ratified by both in due course. In the meantime the Skirmunt-Benesh Treaty of 1921 had had certain good results; its spirit of cordial cooperation was shown in an agreement to create a joint commission, composed of equal numbers of Poles and Czechoslovaks, to deal with all questions connected with Teschen, as well as Spiez and Orava, on a basis of equity and justice; and the cooperation of Poland with the Little Entente was most noteworthy at the Genoa Conference in 1922, and indeed was so intimate and constant that the four States were sometimes alluded to as the "Quadruple Entente."

Economic Conference of Porto Rosa

From the economic point of view the Conference of Porto Rosa, which was the sequel to that of Rome, described in the previous chapter, and which terminated on November 25, 1921, strengthened the position of the Little Entente and the Succession States in general by bringing about less abnormal conditions in Central and South-Eastern Europe. The first questions discussed related to the political aspects of trade. It was agreed that the system of prohibitions which prevailed was irrational. Some States were issuing fresh prohibitions or changing those current, and business men were never certain of receiving goods they had purchased, nor could manufacturers tell whether they could deliver goods that had been ordered. An arrangement was therefore reached by which the individual States of the defunct Austro-Hungarian Monarchy agreed to issue no fresh prohibitions for a long period; export and import licences once given were not to be cancelled. The railways, however, constituted the chief problem of the conference. It was solved by an agreement to introduce free transit of goods and to conclude special railway contracts. No arrangement was arrived at respecting the distribution of rolling stock, because this was a matter on which important decisions had yet to be made by the Reparations Commission, nor were provisional arrangements possible, as each State feared to prejudice its interests when the final distribution came about. But the conference did succeed in putting an end to the restrictions on the transit of rolling stock, which on many railways had resulted in delay and even in the complete stoppage of traffic. Satisfactory results were obtained in questions affecting postal, telegraphic, and telephone services. The chief purpose of the conference was to fix a date which would serve as the starting-point for decontrolling foreign trade in all the Succession States, but this was found to be impracticable, as the precise moment at which foreign trade would be decontrolled depended greatly on the trade policy of the Big States, as well as on the possibility of stabilizing the rate of exchange. In the circumstances it was thought best to leave each individual Government to take its own decision on this point. Arrangements were made for better Customs facilities at frontier stations. Taken as a whole, the Conference of Porto Rosa indicated a distinct advance. The fact that all the Succession States except Hungary, still intransigent, that is, Austria, Czechoslovakia, Poland, Yugoslavia, Rumania, and Italy, despite their political differences, agreed on the necessity of organizing this economic cooperation was a hopeful sign of the gradual consolidation of all that very considerable part of Europe.

The chief hindrance to trade had been the reluctance of the individual States to allow railway wagons with goods to proceed beyond their own frontiers, owing to the uncertainty of getting them back again. The delegates at this conference boldly decided on their own initiative, under reserve that their respective Governments must sanction such action, that from January 1, 1922, there should be an unrestricted circulation of wagons among the States concerned, but without prejudice to the final distribution by the Reparations Commission. Each State was to put a distinguishing mark on the wagons at its disposal, and this was to be duly respected by the other States until further notice, without any reservations whatever. In sum, the effort, not without a measure of success, of the Conference of Porto Rosa was to restore to some extent the economic unity which had been a feature of the Dual Monarchy and had been lost on the dissolution of that régime—this, however, without implying any such idea as that embodied in the phrase Danubian Federation.

The Genoa Conference

Replying to the congratulations of the leading members of the Czechoslovak Parliament on January 1, 1922, President Masaryk delivered a speech in which he summarized the position then of the Little Entente. "As regards our foreign policy," he said, "we have achieved successful results. The Little Entente, drafted at Paris in December, 1918, and carried into effect later, has proved its value. We have inaugurated valuable friendly relations with Poland and, more recently, with Austria, and in this way we have brought about a closer organization of a considerable part of Europe. The only country which remains is Hungary, and I hope that there also we shall arrive at an agreement. The organization of Central Europe is being carried out in agreement with the (Big) Entente. From the very beginning we have recognized it as a necessary authority for post-War Europe, and we desire this authority to continue. . . . Europe and in fact the whole of mankind is being caused grave concern by Russia. . . . To-day we can declare that our relations to our neighbours and to all States and nations are such as to ensure peace for us. We ourselves have no aggressive intentions. The Little Entente, the agreements with Poland and Austria, are purely for the purposes of defence and organization. They are intended to serve the cause of peace." The rest of Masaryk's speech dealt with the internal problems of his own Czechoslovakia. The earlier part of his observations, quoted above, referring to the necessary authority of the Big Entente, the desire that that authority should continue, and the grave concern caused by Soviet

Russia, touched on subjects which were profoundly agitating all Europe. Before that month of January closed they occupied the general attention to the exclusion of other matters when the Conference of Cannes virtually broke down owing to the divergence of views between Great Britain and France over the burning questions of Reparations, Reconstruction, and Soviet Russia. A deadlock was avoided by the postponement of the issues in debate to the Conference of Genoa, which sat from April 10 to May 19, 1922, and was designed to examine the best methods of restoring order and prosperity and of re-establishing credit, the exchanges, transport, and all the vast apparatus of trade and commerce throughout Europe, including Russia.

It was an ambitious programme, to say the least of it. It of course affected the Little Entente from the economic standpoint, but what was of great political importance was that any serious difference between Great Britain and France, if it developed, threatened the very existence of the Central European combination, which based itself fundamentally on the continuance of the Big Entente—the "necessary authority," as Masaryk rightly described it, in Europe. The preliminaries for the Genoa Conference made it abundantly clear that Great Britain and France held opposite views respecting German Reparations and the recognition of the Soviet. A divorce of the two Great Powers was the very last thing the Little Entente desired; but the position, owing to the antagonism between Lloyd George and Poincaré, who had succeeded Briand and was doing his utmost to crab the conference, was one of acute embarrassment for the Little Entente, as it did not and could not wish to take sides. It was necessary, therefore, for it to study the ground well in advance and prepare the policy to be adopted at Genoa.

Acting for the Little Entente, Benesh visited Paris and London in February, 1922, and had long conversations with Poincaré and Lloyd George. In an interview published in *The Times* on February 16 Benesh said: "The situation in Central Europe is such that we shall always cooperate with the Great

Allies, England and France, in the great questions of European policy, and for this reason we must know in what sense it is to be discussed. That is the question, and that is what I wish to ascertain here in London." A week later an interview with him in Paris, on his way back to Prague, appeared in the *Daily Telegraph*, and in it he explained that the object of his journey to London and Paris was to inform himself as to the intentions of the two Governments with regard to the Genoa Conference, not only from the political point of view, but as to the manner in which technical questions, such as exchanges, importation, and exportation between the various countries were to be considered. He said that he was "satisfied with the way he had been able to do his work." Certainly there was a larger measure of agreement between the British and French Governments after his visit. In some quarters it was stated that he had reconciled Lloyd George and Poincaré and was instrumental in bringing about their meeting at Boulogne on February 25.

The *Manchester Guardian* summed up the situation on February 28: "A new and more hopeful development for the prospects of the Conference is the large part which it now seems likely that the Powers of the Little Entente will play in it. Dr. Benesh, the youthful and distinguished Prime Minister of Czechoslovakia, has already done a great and unsolicited service in dissipating what now appear (*sic*) to be the imaginary differences between Mr. Lloyd George and M. Poincaré. He is the architect of the Little Entente, and has raised the financial and economic standing of his own country with extraordinary skill. . . . To the three Powers of the Little Entente it now seems that Poland will be added for the purposes at least of the Genoa Conference. If the union is close it will mean the emergence of a Power equal in size, numbers, and economic weight to that of a first-class State. Under the guidance of Dr. Benesh it should prove of incalculable advantage to the policy of economic liberalism which it is Mr. Lloyd George's aim to foster. For Dr. Benesh not only has set an example of economic toleration, but, by the intimate connexion which exists between his country and Russia, he will be able to interpret Russian needs with an authority which may be less readily accorded to the Russians themselves." On his return to Prague, Benesh, addressing the Czechoslovak Parliament, spoke hopefully of the results of his visit to the West and of the approaching conference.

Polish-Little Entente Block

While Benesh was in London and Paris the betrothal of King Alexander of Yugoslavia and the Princess Marie of Rumania at Bucarest afforded an opportunity of a meeting to other statesmen of the Little Entente. Pashitch and Nintchitch arrived from Belgrade on February 20, remained for four days, and had lengthy conversations with Bratianu and Duca, the latter having succeeded Jonescu as Foreign Minister when a new Rumanian Government had been formed shortly before. Benesh was represented by Veverka, the Czechoslovak Minister, and Skirmunt by Skrzynski, the Polish Minister. The main subject of discussion was the line to be taken by Poland and the Little Entente at Genoa, and a statement was published affirming the solidarity of the four States with respect to that conference, and stressing, among other points, the need of keeping to the programme formulated at Cannes; of holding a meeting of experts, Little Entente and Polish, at Belgrade for fixing a common economic policy; and of making proper agreements respecting the exchanges and transport, while safeguarding the independence of all the allied States and postulating fair treatment for them, with adequate representation at Genoa and participation in the discussions at the conference. At this Bucarest meeting there was a friendly and complete settlement of all matters still in debate about the Banat by Yugoslavia and Rumania; these States had signed a Military Convention on January 23, 1922, which supplemented the Defensive Convention of June 7, 1921.

The proceedings at Bucarest inevitably drew further attention throughout the world to the *rapprochement* of Poland with the Little Entente, and evoked a wide variety of comments in the Press. On March 2, 1922, Nintchitch went to Bratislava to see

M. DUCA

Benesh and to acquaint him with full particulars of the Bucarest meeting; in return Benesh told the Yugoslav Foreign Minister what had taken place during the former's recent visit to Paris and London. At Bratislava the two Ministers touched on the difficult question of relations with Russia. The Conference of Experts, Polish, Czechoslovak, Yugoslav, and Rumanian, opened at Belgrade on March 9 and closed on March 12. It was agreed that the four States should support at the Genoa Conference all measures aiming at the return to economic normality of the States represented there, the re-establishment of the means of communication and of international transport generally, the sanitation of the financial situation of Europe, and the furtherance of budgetary equilibrium in the different States. The striking result of this Belgrade meeting of experts was that Poland and the Little Entente determined on joint action at Genoa on whatever financial, economic, and commercial matters were to be considered there.

It had been arranged among themselves that the Prime Ministers and the Foreign Ministers of the Little Entente should meet shortly before the Genoa Conference, but at the last moment, as it fell out, neither Benesh, still Czechoslovak Prime Minister as well as Foreign Minister, nor Bratianu, Prime Minister of Rumania, was able to leave his own country at the time fixed. At Genoa the four States had two representatives apiece, the chiefs being Skirmunt for Poland, Benesh for Czechoslovakia, Nintchitch for Yugoslavia, and Bratianu for Rumania. As a rule they met together each morning before the opening of the daily sessions of the conference and decided on their common line of action for the day.

A preliminary meeting of the conference was held on April 9, 1922. The Little Entente and Poland were not asked to attend. France, whose leading representative was Barthou, wished them to be invited, but Great Britain and Italy were of opinion that only those should take part who had sent out the invitations to the conference. However, one of the French delegates was present during the same day at a meeting of the representatives of the four States which France recognized as forming a single block. Next day the conference was formally begun, 29 States, in addition to those of the British Empire, being represented. Germany and Russia were there—indeed, all Europe except Turkey might be said to be present. At the first plenary session four Commissions were appointed: the first commission to examine methods of putting into practice the principles enunciated at Cannes; the second, to deal with finance; the third, to consider economics; and the fourth, to regulate transport. It was the first, the Political Commission, that gave the conference its character.

The dominant issue was the renewal of relations with Russia, though, after all, that was only a part of the great problem of the economic reconstruction and recovery of Europe, and it was on this issue that the Genoa Conference virtually was wrecked. The bombshell that actually did the mischief was the announcement, a week after the opening of the conference, that Soviet Russia and Germany had on April 16 secretly signed an agreement which included both the abandonment of all War debts and plans for trade in common—the Treaty of Rapallo: this in fact was the salient outcome of the conference. Germany was censured, and took no part afterwards in the discussions concerning Russia. Chicherin and the other Soviet delegates were impenitent and remained intransigent. When the Allies stated the terms on which they would assist the recovery of Russia, and the Soviet representatives sent an unsatisfactory reply, the whole matter was postponed for consideration to another conference to be held at The Hague in June. Other results of the Genoa Conference were a non-aggression pact binding for eight months and a financial arrangement for stimulating European trade.

One of the things which kept that conference from absolutely devastating failure was the solidity of the Polish-Little Entente block; it appeared as almost the only stable political organization in the midst of the shifting sands of Europe. It was well-represented on all the Commissions and sub-Commissions, and its interventions in debate were neither infrequent nor jejune. Its influence was demonstrated, for example, when the resolute attitude of Skirmunt and Bratianu in support of Barthou in the Political Commission on the question of the reply that was to be sent to the Soviet Delegation was under consideration. On April 20, in the Economic Commission, another instance of the place held by this combination was shown when a Yugoslav delegate, Velizar Yankovitch, declared, in opposition to the British view, that long-term credits were requisite for international economic recovery. But the most striking instance of the growing power and prestige of the four States—this Quadruple Entente—was their acceptance by the members of the Big Entente on the same footing as they themselves stood: the Polish-Little Entente block, considered as one, took rank as a new Great Power by the side of Great Britain, France, and Italy, as was manifested on April 23, when the Great Allies, assisted by Skirmunt, Benesh, Nintchitch, Bratianu, and Mota, met in the Palais Royal to consider the terms of the Note to the German Delegation.

Bratianu, in the name of the four States, declared that the Soviet-German Treaty must be regarded as a menace to the peace of Europe, and that, this being the case, it was necessary for the Big Entente and the Little Entente to act in unison in future as they were acting together then. Lloyd George replied that there would be a close collaboration of the two Ententes henceforth. When, however, he announced the formula for the Pact of Europe, which in its spirit could not but disjoin the bonds that held the Big Entente together and make them useless, the four States demanded that this formula must be accompanied by a statement authorizing and legalizing regional groups like their own group. In this they had the support of France, "the only one of the Great Allies," said the *Pravda*, Belgrade, "which had remained faithful to the order of things created by the victory in the Great War." During the conference demands were made by Hungary and Bulgaria regarding the treatment of Minorities, and these were countered by Bratianu, speaking for the Little Entente.

"At Genoa," said Nintchitch, in an account of the conference given to the Yugoslav Parliament, "the Little Entente and

Poland filled an important political rôle. They always took a suitable initiative in contributing to the consolidation of the New Europe. The agreement which we had quickly established among ourselves enabled us to present a solid front against all attempts to modify the situation created by the Peace Treaties. Not only was there taken no decision contrary to our interests, but no questions were raised to our prejudice." In an interview published in the *Pravo Lidu*, a Czechoslovak paper, Benesh said that from the beginning he had not been optimistic regarding the conference. "The proceedings at Genoa will scarcely effect a change in the political or economic situation of Europe," he remarked. "The chief defect in the arrangement of the conference was that the Russian question, although not ripe for solution, was placed in the foreground. The chief economic problem in Europe at present is that of Germany, since it is necessary to devise a method of agreement between the economic condition of Germany and the reparation demands which it has to fulfil, always taking into account the bearing of this problem on the needs of economic restoration throughout Europe. The conference showed that Europe and Russia are not yet adequately acquainted with each other. Only subsequent developments will indicate what concessions Europe can grant to Russia, and *vice versa*. The preparations for the conference had not been sufficiently thorough, and it therefore was not surprising that the essential aim, namely, a decrease in the distrust among the various States and groups, had not been achieved. In this respect the horizon will be no clearer than it was before. Moreover, the attitude adopted by various delegates was prompted by the interests of their respective home policies. The Paris Peace Conference was far more independent in its action." Yet the conference had some good results—among them being the personal relationships between statesmen that were established at Genoa, which, he maintained, "would result in the disappearance of numerous misunderstandings and in the forming of connexions that would provide a solid basis for European peace. The Little Entente had demonstrated its complete internal solidity, and had shown its utility in the sphere of European politics by acting as intermediary on several occasions; the good will it had exhibited was greatly appreciated by the other States."

In a speech delivered on May 23, 1922, in the Czechoslovak Parliament, Benesh discussed at length what had taken place at the conference, and mentioned the interesting fact that, in accordance with his general policy, he had begun negotiations with the Soviet Delegation with a view to the conclusion of an economic agreement between Soviet Russia and Czechoslovakia; he had often expressed the opinion that the best way of dealing with the Russian problem was by "peaceful economic penetration." Speaking of the divergencies between Great Britain and France, he said that the Polish-Little Entente block had all along taken a moderate and mediatory attitude, and in any case the Little Entente had manifested itself as a consolidating element in the politics of Europe. He also stated that he and the other representatives of the group had taken advantage of the opportunity presented by their meeting at Genoa to discuss among themselves a "whole series of questions" in which the four States were particularly interested. Benesh would not have been Benesh if he had not made the most of the occasion: thus he had "political conversations," as he said in this speech, with Wirth and Rathenau, representing Germany; with Chicherin, the Foreign Commissar of Soviet Russia; with Banffy, the Hungarian Foreign Minister; with Schober, the Austrian Chancellor; with Schanzer, the Italian Foreign Minister; and so on. He noted as probable results of these talks the extension of the Czechoslovak commercial treaty with Italy and the renewal of the negotiations for political and economic relations with Hungary. Casting a critical eye over the whole Genoa Conference, he came to the conclusion that to say it had failed was "inexact." And considering the enhanced reputation of the Little Entente, which was the outstanding feature of the conference, he and the other statesmen of the group undoubtedly had grounds for satisfaction with what they had achieved.

Little Entente a Firm System

In nothing was the expansion of the Little Entente more distinctly exhibited than in the realization of its aim of making sure that its common Central European interests were safeguarded in the intricate network of European politics, both in their direct relations with the Great Powers and in the settlement of the various problems arising at international conferences, whether these problems had a direct or an indirect bearing on Central Europe. The distinction drawn at the Paris Peace Conference between the Principal Powers (*puissances principales*) and Powers with Limited Interests (*puissances à intérêts limités*) was in effect done away with. After the Genoa Conference the Little Entente had to be reckoned with as a firm political system, not only as regarded the Supreme Council, but in all questions which were in any way associated with the development of Central Europe. The joint action of the representatives of the Little Entente from June 15 to June 30, 1922, before and at the Hague Conference, June 26–30, 1922, confirmed the part which this system was to play in the future; the conference itself broke down on Soviet intransigence on the question of the restitution of foreign-owned private property in Russia, thus making absolute the failure of the Genoa Conference to establish relations with the Soviet Government.

The scope of the aim of the Little Entente disclosed at these conferences clearly went beyond the terms of the treaties on which that organization was based, even though the aim could be said to be included in the general programme outlined for the three States in the opening sentences of the treaties, which spoke of a determination to safeguard peace as embodied in the Covenant of the League of Nations and in accordance with the order established by the Treaty of Trianon, in the case of Czechoslovakia, Yugoslavia, and Rumania, and by the Treaty of Neuilly, in the case of Yugoslavia and Rumania. Something more was requisite. During their meeting at Bratislava on March 2 Benesh and Nintchitch had discussed the renewal and extension of the first Little Entente Treaty—

that of August, 1920, between Czechoslovakia and Yugoslavia. The marriage of King Alexander of Yugoslavia and the Princess Marie of Rumania at Belgrade on June 9, 1922, another link in the chain binding the Little Entente together, brought about a meeting of its leaders. Bratianu and Duca came from Bucarest, Benesh from Prague, and they talked about the situation with Pashitch and Nintchitch, and also with Okecki, the Polish Minister at Belgrade. Among other things, they came to a common understanding respecting the line they were to take at the Hague Conference, which was then only a few days away.

The strong position in which the Little Entente had placed itself so successfully now called for new methods of work. Hitherto an exchange of views through the ordinary diplomatic channels had been found sufficient, but the variety and multiplicity of the tasks which were now incumbent on the Little Entente required regular, frequent, and direct contact between its three Foreign Ministers. Thus it was that at this Belgrade meeting Benesh, Nintchitch, and Duca, the Foreign Ministers of the three States respectively at the time, made a formal agreement to hold periodical conferences in order to exchange views on the general political situation and to prepare for action in common whenever necessary; the intention was to hold these conferences twice a year. During this Belgrade meeting Benesh again discussed with Nintchitch the extension of the treaty of August, 1920, and also with Pashitch at Marienbad in August, 1922, with the result that the treaty was renewed and extended on August 31, 1922, at Marienbad, the signatures being those of Pashitch and Benesh.

New Czechoslovak-Yugoslav Treaty

This agreement was significant of the expansion of the Little Entente. It was not called a Defensive Convention, but a Treaty of Alliance. It began by stating that the Governments of Czechoslovakia and Yugoslavia, desirous of prolonging the agreement concluded between them on March 14, 1920, and of completing it by new stipulations, had as their object, first, the strengthening and maintenance of peace, and secondly, the consolidation and amplification of the political and economic ties between the two States. The First Article extended the life of the old treaty for five years, and in the Second the two States recognized the treaties, whether political or military, they each had made—Czechoslovakia with Rumania, Austria, and Poland; Yugoslavia with Rumania and Italy. By the Third Article the States undertook to find a solid basis for the collaboration of their economic, financial, and transport relations, and agreed, with that end in view, to conclude special arrangements, particularly a treaty of commerce. The Fourth Article covered an undertaking of these States to give assistance to each other, politically and diplomatically, in their international relations, and to confer in any case where their common interests were menaced. The duration of the treaty was five years.

It was obvious that the treaty widened very considerably the character and programme of the original Czechoslovak-Yugoslav Convention. "The signing of the first Treaty of Alliance on August 14, 1920, and the second on August 31, 1922," said Benesh, "was merely the external and formal side of a policy which was based on the logic of events. This conclusion of treaties happened at a time when external events made it psychologically possible and politically opportune. Formally and essentially it was a pre-eminently peaceful action. It confirmed the Peace Treaties and guaranteed, both externally and in accordance with the deep needs of the two nations, the security of the people, who needed peace in the highest degree and desired to stabilize conditions and follow the aims of the League of Nations." The treaty did not apply to Rumania. When the Czechoslovak-Rumanian Treaty of April 23, 1921, came up for renewal in April, 1923, there was no similar enlargement of the treaty relationship, nor were the ties of the members of the Little Entente expressed with equal symmetry in a political sense.

Little Entente Conference at Prague

A Conference of the Little Entente States took place at Prague on August 27–28, 1922; it was attended by the Foreign

Ministers, Benesh, Nintchitch, and Duca; Pilz, the Polish Minister to Czechoslovakia, was present; it was the first of the regular periodical conferences which had been arranged for at Belgrade in the previous June. At this conference Poland and the Little Entente came to an understanding as to the uniformity of their future political action, in view of the serious development of some Central European problems; it was felt once more that the maintenance of peace and order in Central Europe depended entirely upon an ever closer union of the four States. Moreover, it was ascertained that conflicts or differences, which were not to be under-estimated, but which were of a local character, between the individual States concerned, did not impair the fundamental identity of attitude towards the requirements of international politics, and that the chief tendencies of their foreign policy remained without change, because the community of their interests demanded it.

This conference was a preparation for the meeting of the Assembly of the League of Nations in the ensuing September; the Little Entente and Poland attached such importance to the Assembly that every single item on its agenda was closely scanned; this was the starting-point from which the discussion of the general political situation proceeded, together with the agreement as to the policy to be pursued in common at Geneva. The application of Hungary for admission to the League was mentioned, but decision was postponed, as there would be a better opportunity for this at Geneva, where the Foreign Ministers of the Little Entente would be at the time. The Prague Conference dealt with the problem of Austria very fully, and decided to advocate a financial and economic solution which would be workable in a practical manner. Shortly before Seipel, the Austrian Minister, had visited Prague, Berlin, and Verona in a desperate effort to get funds; this visit, together with the exchange of opinion which took place in consequence between Prague, Rome, and Paris, was considered most attentively, as were the possibilities inherent in the situation, such as the incorporation of Austria with Germany and the idea of a political-economic and currency union with Italy.

The Salvaging of Austria

Austria had gone from bad to worse financially and economically. At the end of 1921, 14 of her paper crowns had a value of only one-tenth of a penny; by August, 1922, ten times as many crowns were required for that value; 15,000 paper crowns went to the gold crown; the total of currency notes in circulation was in the trillions. And this despite the fact that the Austrians at the close of 1921 had determined to abolish food subsidies and to embark on a programme of self-help. The London Conference of February 21–March 14, 1921, had referred the Austrian problem to the League of Nations for solution. Great Britain, France, Italy, and Japan had agreed, as part of a general scheme, to release the liens they held on Austria through the Reparations Clauses of the Trianon Treaty. A plan embracing internal reforms, the raising of liens, and credits was worked out by the Financial Committee of the League, and was to be put into effect under the auspices of the League. At the moment it was not thought that Austria was in so bad a state as to warrant the belief that the essential credits could not be obtained, with the liens out of the way and the various reforms in force, and the whole under the financial control of the League. But the negotiations with the other Governments whose consent was needed for the raising of their liens were difficult and long drawn out, with the result that the condition of Austria became so grave, owing to the fall of the exchange and internal troubles, that by March, 1922, there was imminent danger of her entire collapse.

On August 7, 1922, Seipel made a despairing appeal to the Supreme Council for help, though in the meantime Great Britain, France, Italy, and Czechoslovakia had advanced considerable sums to tide over each emergent crisis, moneys, however, which were for the most part engulfed in current expenditure to "keep the wolf from the door," with practically nothing left to put the finances of the State on a sound basis. As, later, the Financial Committee of the League put it: "Austria has for three years been living largely upon public and private loans, which have voluntarily or involuntarily become gifts, upon private charity, and upon losses of foreign speculators in the crown. Such resources cannot in any event continue and be so used. Austria has been consuming more than she produced. The large sums advanced, which should have been used for the re-establishment of her finances and for her economic reconstruction, have been used for current consumption." It was in these circumstances that Seipel made his journey to Prague, Berlin, and Verona in a last desperate effort to obtain assistance. Berlin did not see its way to help, and the appeal seemed to lie between Prague and Rome, with the inevitable implication that whichever State assisted Austria would have the supervision of her political and other affairs. Neither Italy nor the Little Entente was willing that the other should gain control of Austria. Replying to Seipel's appeal to it, the Supreme Council, at a meeting held in London on August 15, 1922, decided to refer again the whole matter to the League, with a statement that no credits would be given unless as part of a general plan for the full recovery of Austria financially.

First of all, the Council of the League invited Austria and Czechoslovakia, under Article XV of the Covenant, to sit on the Council, with the same rights as had its regular members, while the problem was being discussed, and next, it appointed a committee consisting of the representatives of those two States—Seipel and Benesh—together with the representatives of Great Britain, France, and Italy—Balfour, Hanotaux, and Imperiali—to consider the political aspects of the question. It asked the Financial Committee of the League to draw up a comprehensive plan of financial assistance and administrative reform, and handed over other points to the Economic and Legal Committees. Helped by ample expert advice, the Council finally evolved a complete scheme, which was submitted to the Assembly—the Third—in September, 1922. Italy attended with a plan of her own, which was that the agreements come to at the Conference of Porto Rosa should be put into effect at once; this meant that all the Succession States would constitute a huge economic unity under the leadership practically of Italy.

As its experts declared that it was impossible to carry out immediately and fully the Porto Rosa agreements, the Little Entente strongly opposed the Italian plan, which was dropped.

On October 2, 1922, the League's plan for the financial restoration of Austria was unanimously approved. Three Protocols were signed by the British, French, Italian, Czechoslovak, and Austrian representatives at Geneva. By the First Protocol Great Britain, France, Italy, and Czechoslovakia, who guaranteed the loan that was to be raised for Austria, solemnly bound themselves to respect her political independence, territorial integrity, and economic independence, while on her side Austria undertook to respect strictly Article LXXXVIII of the St. Germain Treaty. The total amount of the loan to be given was 650 million gold crowns, or about thirty million pounds sterling, to be paid in instalments during the next two years; Great Britain, France, Italy, and Czechoslovakia agreed to cover eighty per cent. of the whole sum, the remainder being met by other States. The Second Protocol fixed the amount and the conditions of the loan, which took into account the successful accomplishment of the Austrian internal reforms —a difficult and painful task, but with self-support at its conclusion. The Third Protocol dealt with the obligations the Austrian Government had come under for the carrying out of these reforms, which the League deemed indispensable for the rehabilitation of the credit of Austria. It was provided that the League should be represented at Vienna by a Commissioner-General to control the payments made out of the loan. On November 3, 1922, the Austrian Parliament accepted the League's plan and passed the necessary legislation, which among other things definitely terminated the period of inflation.

The League appointed Dr. Zimmermann, formerly Burgomaster of Rotterdam, as Commissioner-General, and he began work in the following month. His and the plan's ultimate success, coupled with the sustained efforts of the Austrian Government and people, proved that Austria was viable as an independent State. Referring to the action taken at Geneva, Benesh said: "Our loan to Austria at a time when nobody wished to help, our decisive intervention in the League of Nations on behalf of the protection and financial sanitation of Austria, our financial guarantees and the signing of the Geneva Protocols—all that can be criticized, but one thing cannot be denied, namely, that we showed good will to our neighbour and applied the ideas of peace and the policy of reconstruction. I know the criticisms which have been made in connexion with this action. Those who voted against it are the very same people who reproached us for years with being unfriendly to Austria—I mean our German Opposition (in the Czechoslovak Parliament) and those who wished to see in our policy a support for reaction. To-day this already belongs to history, and history will speak in another way about the matter. Moreover, the Czechoslovak Government received from the Austrian Government, and from European public opinion, without exception, nothing but expressions of thanks and justified gratitude."

What Benesh did not mention, but what he might have mentioned, was that the point of view of the Little Entente, as distinguished from that of Italy, had triumphed in the Austrian question. On October 9, 1922, he had had a meeting with Schanzer, the Italian Foreign Minister, at Venice, where the latter came to the wise conclusion that it was quite possible for them to agree in the solution of the problem. Yet only a short time before the Press of Hungary and Italy had reported that an alliance was imminent between Italy, Hungary, and Austria! Thus, again in 1922, the expanding influence and power of the Little Entente was clearly demonstrated.

Hungary and the League

Although the reconstruction financially of Austria was the great work of the Assembly of the League in 1922, it had before it some other matters of outstanding importance, among them being the application of Hungary for admission to the membership of the League. In the previous year Apponyi had pleaded for admission, but without success. In September, 1922, Banffy represented Hungary before the League in support of the application; he insisted that the death of the ex-Emperor Charles had clarified the situation as between the Little Entente and his own country, which was determined, he maintained, to respect the League of Nations, the various treaties that had been concluded, and all its other international engagements. As the Little Entente concurred with all the other members of the Assembly, Hungary was admitted by a unanimous vote, September 18, 1922. The Little Entente plainly showed that it desired friendly relations with Hungary despite the continuance of a non-official irredentist campaign in that country. Czechoslovakia went so far as to conclude a commercial treaty with her on November 24, 1922, dealing with transport and Customs facilities in the interchange of goods, rules for commercial travellers, creation of courts of adjustment and arbitration, and the like.

It was a conspicuous venture of faith, and hardly seemed to be justified by the facts of the actual situation, for notwithstanding the efforts made by the Little Entente to have durable and at least correct relations with Hungary, there were during 1922 many unpleasant incidents engineered by the Magyars which interfered with any real development of neighbourly feeling and went a long way to frustrating anything of the kind on an international scale. Speaking on January 30, 1923, before the Czechoslovak Parliamentary Commission on Foreign Affairs, Benesh recalled numerous frontier incidents, attacks on Czechoslovak and other Little Entente officials in the course of their duty and on the frontier populations by irresponsible bands of armed Magyars, and many arrests and detentions of Czechoslovak and other nationals in Hungary in the most arbitrary fashion. To add to these were the intrigues of the legitimists, the systematic assaults at public meetings on the Peace Treaties, the action of open and secret irredentist organizations (such as that of the "Awakening Magyars") against the Little Entente. There were, besides, certain military measures on the part of the Hungarian Government itself which were contrary both to the letter and spirit of the Treaty of Trianon. "We follow attentively," he said, "everything that goes on in

Hungary. We cannot tolerate armaments and military measures which are aimed at upsetting the Peace Treaties. The position in Hungary is not such as to provoke a grave conflict, but it is such as to keep us always on our guard." As from the beginning, Hungary was a difficulty, and she had always to be kept in view by the Little Entente, however much its general policy, with its larger sweep, was concerned with other interests.

Conference of Lausanne

As has been seen, the inclusion of Greece in the Little Entente was a preoccupation of Take Jonescu (he died on June 21, 1922), but the fact that she had all along been at war with Turkey, coupled with the fact that her relations with the Yugoslavs had been tainted by what had taken place in the Great War, had militated against it. In September–October, 1922, the overwhelming defeat of the Greeks by the Turks, which seemed to involve once more the raising of the terrible Eastern question so familiar to the diplomats of Old Europe, caused grave anxiety to Yugoslavia and Rumania, who feared that the Treaty of Neuilly might possibly be compromised. The crisis brought Yugoslavia, Rumania, and Greece together, and this was facilitated by dynastic ties—the marriages of the Kings of Yugoslavia and Greece—King George, who had replaced his father, King Constantine, on the throne—with the Rumanian princesses, and the marriage of the Rumanian Crown Prince Carol with a Greek princess. In the negotiations between Yugoslavia and Greece that ensued, an agreement was reached respecting the Yugoslav Free Zone at Salonika, which had been under discussion in 1914, an agreement which was confirmed by a convention signed in May, 1923.

A more serious matter was that Yugoslavia and Rumania appeared to have to choose between the policy of Great Britain and that of France with respect to the Greco-Turkish conflict—the dilemma that confronted the Little Entente on some other major questions of the day; there was a lively exchange of Notes on this subject between Belgrade, Bucarest, and Athens, but without any particular result other than the expression of a strong desire for agreement between London and Paris. A development that was not without promise of furthering peace in the Balkans was that Stambolisky, the Bulgarian Prime Minister, went to Bucarest to take council with Bratianu, and then proceeded to Belgrade, where he had conversations with King Alexander, Pashitch, and Nintchitch. The Bulgarian statesman represented himself as being eager for a *rapprochement* between his own country and Yugoslavia, and asked for the latter's support of Bulgaria's claim to a port on the Aegean in accordance with the 48th Article of the Neuilly Treaty. Regarding the agitation in Macedonia, with the frequent raids of Bulgar komitadjis into Yugoslav territory, he suggested the appointment of a mixed commission to investigate matters on the spot, and to prepare a scheme that would be acceptable to the interested Governments. Taken in conjunction with the collaboration of Politis, the Greek Foreign Minister, with Nintchitch at Belgrade, the friendly interchange of views by these leading political figures in the Balkans augured well for the future.

The Conference of Lausanne, the object of which was the resolving of the whole crisis, opened on November 20, 1922, and found the Balkan States more or less united in their policy, much to the surprise of the Turks, who had counted on their being divided. Nintchitch, mediating successfully between Bulgaria and Greece, supported the fulfilment to the former State of the promise to assign to it an Aegean port; he stoutly repulsed every proposal to modify the Treaty of Neuilly, and in this he had the assistance of Duca. On November 28 Benesh arrived at Lausanne, and the three Foreign Ministers of the Little Entente met and considered the situation; they were of one and the same opinion concerning the issues at this conference. They also discussed, as was the way at all the meetings of the Little Entente leaders, other current questions in the high politics of Europe, such as the recalcitrance of Germany touching reparations and the growing impatience of France—which presently led to the occupation of the Ruhr, with its startling repercussions. Doubtless they considered, too, the rise of the Fascist régime and the meaning of Mussolini, and waited with some anxiety to see what he would do regarding the agreement which had been signed by Schanzer and the Yugoslav Minister at Rome on October 25, and was concerned with some particulars implementing the Italo-Yugoslav Treaty of Rapallo. During 1922 the Little Entente had immensely strengthened its position, but the year closed with heavy clouds overhanging Europe.

CHAPTER VII

THE LITTLE ENTENTE AND THE GREAT POWERS

1923–1924

EUROPE'S most difficult post-War period fell within the years 1923 and 1924. The clouds that were overhanging the sky as 1922 closed became heavier as the new year opened, and soon there broke a storm fraught apparently with irremediable disaster. The centre of the storm, which raged for months, was the question of Reparations, but with it was intimately associated the question of Security—that of Disarmament lay farther off. Among the Allies themselves opinions differed with respect to reparations, or, more specifically, the amount in cash or in kind to be exacted and extracted from Germany, whose capacity, though not her indisposition, to pay was in doubt. France saw in the recalcitrance of Germany the fixed determination of the latter to escape from the obligations imposed on her by the Peace Treaty; and France, under the leadership of Poincaré, was even more determined, if possible, that Germany should fulfil these obligations to the uttermost—should be forced, if necessary, to fulfil them. France wanted a guarantee; Poincaré demanded a "productive guarantee," and found, or thought he would find, it in the occupation of the Ruhr, that rich industrial region of Western Germany of which Essen was the capital.

OCCUPATION OF THE RUHR

While sympathizing with the claims of France to reparations, Great Britain was inclined to take a more lenient view, which was based on the belief that Germany was not in a position to comply with the French demands; the objection was not to enforcement in itself, but to the time and method of it. The proposals made by the British Government for dealing with the situation were not well received in Paris, the Press of which declared that they were tantamount to a revision of the Treaty of Versailles. Early in January, 1923, Poincaré intimated that France and Great Britain had agreed to disagree. In the Reparations Commission Germany was condemned as in default on her deliveries of wood and coal, that is, in her payments in kind. On January 10, 1923, Germany was informed by France that the Ruhr would be occupied as a "sanction"; 100,000 French and Belgian troops crossed into that district, occupied Essen, and proclaimed martial law throughout the area. Italy took the side of France, while Great Britain's attitude was neutral. Germany protested against the occupation, but made no armed resistance. Yet France and Germany were again locked in a deadly struggle. If there was no actual warfare, France was holding territory that was indisputably German, and Germany was replying by supporting the "passive resistance" made by the population of the Ruhr. In a word, it was war—war of a sort, but terrible enough, and fatal to the immediate prospect of the realization of any programme for the general recovery and reconstruction of Europe.

Though Great Britain officially was benevolently neutral, many of her people and a considerable number of her newspapers sharply criticized the action of France, and this all the more because it was manifested that France was losing rather than gaining on balance, and that Great Britain herself was injuriously affected by what was going on. This criticism of France, which was sharpened by French non-support of British policy in the Near East and at Lausanne, grew keener as the new Franco-German struggle proceeded. During a speech delivered in July, Baldwin, then Prime Minister for the first time in his career, significantly coupled the statements that, as a result of the occupation of the Ruhr, Germany was drifting towards economic chaos (as was shown by the fall of the mark to an unimaginably low figure), and that Great Britain was suffering heavily from bad markets, poor trade, and unemployment on a scale so gigantic that her economic position was being gravely jeopardized.

Some observers, and they were not confined to England, alleged that France was bent not so much on obtaining reparations as on the complete ruin of Germany, or on such a weakening of her that France would never have anything more to fear from that quarter—in proof, they pointed to French encouragement of Separatist tendencies in the occupied territory. Others again said that with her political and military alliances stretching from the Baltic to the Black Sea—Poland and the Little Entente States, who were described as her "vassals"—France was resolved on securing both the encirclement of Germany and an unchallengeable hegemony over Europe. And others again spoke of the fear that Germany, under this terrible pressure, would relapse into sheer anarchy, thus providing a favourable opportunity for the Soviet and fresh fuel for its World Revolution. What was clear was that the French occupation of the Ruhr threatened to demoralize all Europe. Great Britain and France, on whose alliance post-War Europe had founded such consolidation as was possible, seemed to be driving asunder, nor was the tension lessened till October, when, Germany having ceased to support passive resistance in the Ruhr, the proposal of the British Government that an economic conference should be held was accepted by France, Belgium, and Italy.

The Problem of Reparations

During this time of severe strain and the period of gradually reduced strain which followed and was marked by the negotiations leading to the consideration and the ultimate adoption of the Dawes Plan for dealing with Reparations, the Little Entente, while concerned as usual with its own immediate affairs, could not but be deeply affected in one way or another by the general political and economic situation consequent on the occupation of the Ruhr. Indeed, during 1923 and 1924 the relations of the Little Entente, as well as those of its individual States, to the Great Powers, particularly France, Italy, and Soviet Russia, came into special prominence and were the main preoccupation of its statesmen. At the start the Little Entente had based itself on two things—on the Peace Treaties and on the durability of the combination of the Great Allies, meaning thereby chiefly the effective continuance of the Entente between Great Britain and France. It was still based on the Peace Treaties. But it had come to act with a certain independence of the Great Allies; as was seen in the preceding chapter, the position of the Little Entente with Poland at Genoa became analogous to that of a Great Power. This was far, however, from being the same as the assumption by the Little Entente that it had any such power as that possessed by Great Britain or France, for it realized to the full that the status of the New Europe rested fundamentally on their concord.

The conflict over the Ruhr was therefore bound to cause its leaders and peoples no little anxiety; at first their anxiety was less, as prolonged resistance on the part of Germany was not anticipated, but, as the struggle grew in intensity, so did their anxiety. On January 30, 1923, Benesh delivered a speech on the international situation at a meeting of the Commission on Foreign Affairs of the Czechoslovak Parliament in Prague. Hardly a fortnight had passed since the Ruhr had been occupied, and the reaction subsequently of Great Britain to that event, as well as what took place later in the Ruhr, could not then be foreseen. He began by stating that as all the Allies could not agree on common action regarding reparations, France, in accord with Italy and Belgium, had decided to take action against Germany. England, while declaring herself benevolently neutral, had made it clear that there was no clash between the British and French Governments; there was only a divergence of view respecting the method to be employed for obtaining reparations from Germany.

According to his custom at such a critical time, Benesh presented to the commission an objective and detailed review of all that had occurred in the Ruhr up to the day when he spoke, and of the events that had led up to the occupation, tracing the "evolution of the problem of reparations" from the Agreement arrived at in London in May, 1921, to the Paris Conference in 1922, which was unable to reach an accord on the proposals submitted by the British Government on the one hand and by the French Government on the other, the upshot being the determination of France, in conjunction with Belgium and Italy, to take independent action. "At the moment the French Government," he said, summing up the results of this action, "is trying to exploit the natural riches of the basin of the Ruhr, to levy Customs on merchandise of German origin, and apparently proposes, with its Allies, to hold the occupied territories in pledge so long as Germany shall not have begun to fulfil in a regular manner the obligations imposed on her by the reparations." After branching off into a discussion of recent happenings in Hungary and of the Conference of Lausanne, with a reference to Soviet intervention at the latter, he returned to the subject of the occupation of the Ruhr, but more especially from the point of view of Czechoslovakia in particular and of the Little Entente in general.

"In the course of the last four years," he said, "we (Czechoslovakia) have created the tradition of our foreign policy, and have formulated very clearly our relations with our neighbours from the outset—our relations with our friends of the Little Entente and of France, and finally with Italy, England, and Poland." Nothing had occurred to change that policy. Earlier in his speech he had expressed his belief that the turn of events in the international situation had led, as if by fate, to what had happened in the Ruhr. "Recourse has not been had," Benesh averred, "to such extensive measures as those now taken by the Franco-Belgian forces except with reluctance, with regret, and only under extreme pressure. I myself have seen how French statesmen and parties come to their resolutions only after mature deliberation and painful effort."

What attitude was Czechoslovakia to take? "We are attached," Benesh continued, "to all the Allies of the War-time by the same ties of sympathy, friendship, and alliance as before—to Yugoslavia and Rumania by a special alliance; and with our other neighbours we have firm engagements founded on treaties and conventions with them; we hold to these engagements, which are based on the Peace Treaties. . . . The Czechoslovak Government favours peace. In present circumstances it considers its first duty to be the maintenance of order and peace in its immediate neighbourhood, that is, to do, in conjunction with its Little Entente Allies, everything that is necessary for keeping peace in Central Europe. In this way we shall be of the greatest service to ourselves, to our Allies, and to Europe. It is not true that we are making preparations for mobilization. We are, however, strong enough and ready enough to be able to ensure, against all those who might seek to gain some advantage from the present strained situation, the new state of peace which was established with so much suffering. Notwithstanding the difficulties of the international situation, we remain calm, in the confident hope of being able, without serious perturbation in our neighbourhood, to pursue our policy of reconstruction and peace, and we shall succeed in attaining our object, which aims at the reorganization of a new and peaceful Central Europe."

Hungarian Frontier Incidents

In the course of his review of the international situation, Benesh said that public opinion in the Little Entente States had been greatly stirred up, not only by the Ruhr affair, but also by what had been taking place in Hungary. He was alluding to the series of incidents that had occurred at points on the frontiers where those of Hungary marched with those of the Little Entente. He briefly touched on the fact that in a very flagrant instance—disturbances caused by Magyar contingents on the Rumanian frontier—the diplomatic representatives of both the Big and the Little Entente had intervened at Budapest; this was on January 13, 1923. Incidents in which Magyars were implicated took place on the Czechoslovak frontiers on March 15 and 24 and on April 10; in the last of these incidents Jan Sedlachek, a Czechoslovak frontier-guard, was killed by the Magyars. Intense feeling was aroused throughout Czechoslovakia, and there was a call for reprisals; the Czechoslovak Government made strong representations at Budapest and demanded compensation.

In reply to an interpellation on April 25 in the Commission on Foreign Affairs of the Czechoslovak Parliament, Benesh said : "After a year and a half we have not yet succeeded in establishing normal relations on the frontier; we were always being reminded that the lives of our frontier-guard were in danger.

It is plain that such a situation must be ended once for all. . . . The Czechoslovak Government is quite disposed to settle these (frontier) questions in a reasonable and amicable manner, but it insists on complete satisfaction for the murder of an innocent man, and for such measures as will guarantee tranquillity and peace to those living on both sides of the frontier." After stating that the Hungarian Government had proposed the appointment of a mixed commission to make a final inquiry into all the frontier incidents, he said that his own Government had already in hand the material for such an investigation, but had agreed to accept the suggestion; he thought it would also be a good thing if this commission could be given a more or less permanent character, for, if these incidents continued, there was the possibility of their developing into serious conflicts. He went on to say that the steps taken to put an end to these frontier affairs did not at all imply any change in the general policy of Czechoslovakia towards Hungary; on the contrary, the speedy conclusion of political and economic agreements between the two States would be encouraged and facilitated thereby. At the same time he protested against certain allegations made by the Hungarian Minister Daruvary to the effect that Czechoslovakia was trying to blacken Hungary before the other States of Europe. The sole aim of Czechoslovakia, Benesh declared once again, was to establish as soon as possible neighbourly relations with that country, but such relations presupposed calm and order on the frontier.

The mixed commission met on April 29–30, and it found a Magyar frontier-guard, on his own confession, guilty of the murder of Sedlachek; the result was less definite in the other cases. Under the title "The Conflict between Czechoslovakia and Hungary," a pamphlet was published at Prague by the Czechoslovakia Information Service in 1923, which gave a full account of the proceedings, together with a short narration of previous frontier incidents in which nine Czechoslovaks had lost their lives. A settlement in respect of the incidents and other matters was reached in the following September, in the course of negotiations between Benesh and Bethlen, Hungarian

Prime Minister, both then being in Geneva for the Assembly of the League of Nations; the amount of compensation to be paid to victims or their relatives was fixed, and propaganda was to be suppressed. One of the pleas put forward by the Hungarian Government in defence or mitigation of the incidents had been that they had occurred where the exact line of the frontier was not well defined or was still in dispute. In this connexion it should be noted that on April 23, 1923, the Council of the League of Nations, at the behest of Hungary, rectified the finding of the Delimitation Commission regarding the possession of the district of Salgo-Tarjan by Czechoslovakia. The Council decreed that it should go to Hungary, who thus gained the villages of Melmeko and Somosujfal, with the adjacent mines, the whole area having a population of about 1,800, of Magyar nationality. This decision was accepted by Czechoslovakia.

Yugoslav-Austrian Treaty

In February, 1923, relations between Yugoslavia and Austria took a decided turn for the better; up to that time they had had only provisional commercial agreements. On February 21 Seipel, the Austrian Chancellor, accompanied by Grünberger, Austrian Minister for Foreign Affairs, visited Belgrade and conferred with Pashitch and Nintchitch on all the points in debate between the two States, with the fortunate result of the signing of a Protocol containing four conventions to their common benefit. The first dealt with the abolition of the sequestration of properties of those under the jurisdiction of one of the two States on the territory of the other, and also was concerned with the problem of industrial businesses in which Austrian capital was invested. The second referred to the payment of obligations undertaken in Austrian crowns prior to March, 1919. The third settled the dispute regarding Austrian holdings of shares in enterprises in Bosnia-Herzegovina, and also dealt with the question of the property of the Yugoslav Legation in Vienna. The fourth regulated the transfer, in one of the two States, of the head offices of businesses having their field of work in the other State. In addition agreements were come to respecting passports, goods in transit, and so forth.

The negotiations, which terminated with the signing of the Protocol on February 26, were conducted with great good will on both sides, which again was conspicuous when in 1924 Nintchitch returned the Austrian visit by going to Vienna and conferring with Grünberger, several outstanding matters being arranged in a conciliatory way. In November of the previous year (1923) a mixed commission had been appointed to regulate communications and traffic on the frontier. These friendly meetings, with the resultant international understandings and consequent consolidation, were thoroughly in keeping with the whole policy and spirit of the Little Entente.

Little Entente Treaties Prolonged

Within the Little Entente itself further progress was registered when, on March 17, 1923, Czechoslovakia and Yugoslavia signed a convention for juridical assistance in common. Most notable was the unmodified prolongation of the Treaty of Defensive Alliance between Czechoslovakia and Rumania, which was signed at Prague on May 7, 1923, by Benesh for the former and Hiott for the latter State. It ran: "In view of the fact that the effects of the Agreement of Defensive Alliance concluded on April 23, 1921, have proved to be of benefit to the cause of peace, and as therefore a continuation of this Agreement is regarded as necessary, the undersigned Plenipotentiaries, furnished with full authority from the President of the Czechoslovak Republic and His Majesty the King of Rumania respectively, have agreed in good and proper form as follows: The Agreement of Defensive Alliance, concluded on April 23, 1921, shall remain in force for another three years from the date on which the ratifications of this Protocol are exchanged. After this period has elapsed, it will be possible to denounce it in accordance with the concluding stipulations of its Fifth Article. The validity of the Military Agreement arrived at on the basis of the Second Article of this Agreement is also prolonged for the same period. This

Protocol will be communicated to the League of Nations." The ratifications were exchanged at Prague on June 14, 1923, and the Protocol was registered by the Secretariat of the League in the following July.

A similar Protocol concerning the prolongation of the Convention of Defensive Alliance between Rumania and Yugoslavia was signed at Bucarest, on July 7, 1923, by Duca for the former and Tcholak-Antitch for the latter State. In like fashion it ran: "Whereas the Convention of Defensive Alliance of June 7, 1921, has been found to be advantageous to the cause of peace, and whereas its maintenance is therefore considered necessary, the undersigned Plenipotentiaries, furnished with full powers, found in good and due form, by his Majesty the King of Rumania and by His Majesty the King of the Serbs, Croats, and Slovenes, respectively, have agreed to the following provisions: The Convention of Defensive Alliance of June 7, 1921, shall remain in force for a further period of three years from the date on which the exchange of ratifications of the present Protocol takes place. When this term has expired, it will again be possible to denounce it according to the final provisions of the Fifth Article. The Military Convention concluded in accordance with the Second Article of the foregoing Convention shall be prolonged for the same period. The present Protocol will be communicated to the League of Nations." The ratifications were exchanged at Belgrade, but the Protocol was not registered with the Secretariat.

The original Convention of Defensive Alliance between Rumania and Yugoslavia, signed at Belgrade on June 7, 1921, was registered with the League of Nations only on September 2, 1926, and by that date a second Protocol, dated June 13, 1926, prolonging the Convention for a further three years, had been signed and ratified. Both Protocols, with the Convention, were published in 1927 by the League of Nations in *Arbitration and Security*, the systematic Survey of the Arbitration Conventions and Treaties of Mutual Security, deposited with the League, which was prepared by the Legal Section of the Secretariat.

Little Entente Conference at Sinaia

The unfriendly Magyar incidents on the frontiers of the Little Entente did not prevent its States from endeavouring to collaborate with Hungary in the economic field, as was clearly demonstrated when the Hungarian Government applied to the League of Nations for a loan, with the object of improving the internal condition of that country. On May 23, 1923, Hungary asked for the abolition of the general right of mortgage and the grant of a moratorium for the payment by her of reparations, in connexion with her application for the issue of an international loan. In the Reparations Commission the Little Entente drew attention to shortcomings in Hungary's disarmament and attempts to evade the terms of the Treaty of Trianon, but did not oppose the loan, provided its interests were safeguarded.

The proposed loan was one of the principal topics discussed at the regular, periodical Conference of the Little Entente, which was held from July 27 to 30, 1923, at Sinaia, the beautiful and romantic summer capital of Rumania. On this occasion Bratianu, Prime Minister, and Duca, Foreign Minister, represented Rumania, while Nintchitch appeared for Yugoslavia and Benesh for Czechoslovakia. On the day before the conference opened, Poland, through her Foreign Minister, had announced that she would not take part in it, and had also made it clear that she had no intention of entering the Little Entente, but she sent to Sinaia an observer in the person of Piltz, her former Minister at Prague. On July 30, 1923, the conference reported that it was the joint desire of the Little Entente States to facilitate an outlet to Hungary from her difficulties in the shape of an international loan, but on condition that the proceeds of the loan were used neither for new armaments nor irredentist propaganda. This condition was necessary because Hungary had not yet disarmed, and her Government had shown itself powerless to prevent irredentist propaganda leading to violence against the neighbouring States. The conference decided to obtain practical guarantees on these points.

In a declaration made to the Press, many of whose leading members had come to Sinaia, Duca said: "It has often been said that the Little Entente was against the floating of a loan to Hungary or, in other words, was opposed to financial measures designed to restore the terribly shattered economic situation of that country. These statements are inexact. Rumania, as well as Czechoslovakia and Yugoslavia, never showed any hostility to the idea of a Hungarian loan, but all three Powers asked for serious guarantees to be given to them that a Hungarian loan would not be used in Budapest against us, either by increasing their armaments or for financing irredentist propaganda."

The Czech journal *Venkov* wrote: "The Magyars have contrived to convince the Great Allies that they need a foreign loan for their economic reconstruction. They cannot obtain this until the mortgage rights of the Reparations Commission have been abolished, but, in order to do this, the consent of the States concerned must be got. The Little Entente at Sinaia once more emphasized its desire not to place obstacles in the way of the recovery of Hungary. Considering their experiences, however, with the present régime of Hungary, the Little Entente States have little confidence in the Magyar declarations, and demand there should be a strict control to prevent Hungary from misusing the grant of credits for the support of subversive activities against the neighbouring countries. This point of view will be communicated both to the Reparations Commission and also to the Allies, and it is for the Magyars to show, by accepting the conditions of the Little Entente, that they do not wish to disturb peace in Central Europe. Only then can they expect the desired improvements in the relations of the Little Entente towards them. According to our information, there is to be a discussion between the Little Entente States, the Allies and Hungary with a view to a special mutual agreement on the keeping of the Peace Treaties and reciprocal commitments, and thus all those concerned would guarantee among themselves peace in Central Europe, which would be a great advance towards consolidation in that area."

The Salvaging of Hungary

The Hungarian loan came up before the Assembly—the fourth—of the League of Nations at Geneva in September, 1923. Benesh met Bethlen on September 6, and the relations of Hungary to the Little Entente and the attitude of the latter to the question of the loan were discussed. Other discussions followed between them with satisfactory results, among them being, as stated above, the settlement regarding frontier incidents; agreements were also reached respecting the suppression of propaganda, easier conditions for the granting of visas, and a commerical convention. The representatives of Yugoslavia and Rumania were immediately informed of the course and conclusion of these negotiations, which fundamentally were carried on by Benesh on behalf of the Little Entente as a whole, so that there was no need for a formal meeting.

In his own account (in *Five Years of Czechoslovak Foreign Policy*) of the loan, Benesh wrote: "When the question of the reconstruction and financial sanitation of Hungary came to the front, we immediately adopted in this matter the same point of view as in the Austrian problem. At the last meeting of the League of Nations in September, 1923, we agreed in principle with Count Bethlen, the Hungarian Prime Minister, on the course of action to be taken, and we ourselves, together with the two other representatives of the Little Entente, sent in a request on our own initiative to the League of Nations, asking that body to begin the negotiations for the financial sanitation of Hungary. . . . So far as we are concerned, it was merely a continuation of our policy, from which we shall not diverge one inch. It is precisely this policy that has gained us international significance and respect in the world. We cannot renounce any of our rights and claims in regard to the Magyars, nor any of our democratic principles. We cannot give up the general line of this policy even in the Hungarian question." After referring to the various previous occasions on which he had stated that all the members of the Little Entente were anxious to see a change in the relations of Hungary to them, he said that when a reasonable agreement was concluded with that country the Little Entente would no longer be directed against it, just as the Little Entente had ceased to be directed against Austria.

With the participation of the Czechoslovak delegate, the Reparations Commission and the League of Nations worked out a plan for salvaging Hungary, which was similar to that which had been made for Austria. The Little Entente secured a share in the control of the loan, and the plan was approved by the Council of the League of Nations on December 20, 1903. In a Protocol, signed on March 14, 1924, by Great Britain, France, Italy, Rumania, Yugoslavia, and Czechoslovakia on the one hand and Hungary on the other, Hungary undertook to fulfil her obligations under the Trianon Treaty, in particular the military clauses, as also the other international engagements; and to abstain from any action contrary to the spirit of the Conventions drawn up in common for effecting the economic and financial reconstruction of Hungary, or which might prejudicially affect the guarantees demanded by the signatory Powers for the protection of the interests of the creditors. This Protocol was registered with the League of Nations on June 24, 1924. The loan, the amount of which was £11,000,000, was floated with the same success as the Austrian loan, both being under the auspices of the League.

Politically the Hungarian loan with the conditions attached to it meant that Hungary, which up to this time had been a source of unrest in Central Europe, was proceeding, under the prompting of her economic interests, along the path of consolidation. The internal situation of Hungary, however, remained unchanged, and gave but little hope that a more moderate attitude on her part towards the new régime contemplated by the granting of the loan would be permanent. Still, as a result of the discussions between Benesh and Bethlen at Geneva in October, 1923, negotiations were begun at Budapest in that month between Hungary and Czechoslovakia concerning a commercial agreement. In the previous month of July Czechoslovak-Hungarian agreements had been signed at Prague touching the release of deposits in banks, banking accounts generally, monetary claims, direct taxation, and private insurance companies—all to the good, so far as they went.

The Little Entente Conference at Sinaia in July, 1923, had in addition to the question of the loan to Hungary other topics of great importance before it. One of these was the question of the attitude to be taken towards Bulgaria, in which State Yugoslavia and Rumania were directly interested, and in which a new Government had been set up after the fall of Stambolisky through a *coup d'état* on June 9, 1923. Stambolisky had shown himself to be sincerely desirous of resuming normal relations with these two States, and had set his face against the Bulgar-Macedonian organizations and the komitadji incursions into Yugoslav territory. Soon after it had come into existence, the Tsankof Government, which followed that of Stambolisky, announced that it would scrupulously execute the obligations of Bulgaria under the Trianon Treaty and carry out the undertakings made by the late Government. The Sinaia Conference came to the wise conclusion that there was no objection to continuing normal relations with Bulgaria, so long as her Government kept its pacific promises. In some parts of the foreign Press it had been somewhat loosely stated that one of the objects of the conference was the extension of the Little Entente by the inclusion of Poland and Greece. But it was never intended that anything of the kind should be discussed at Sinaia. Naturally, there was an exchange of views on the present and future relations of the Little Entente to the two Powers.

Of Poland, *Venkov* said in the article already quoted from: "The question of an approach on the part of the Little Entente towards some neighbouring States has been raised in various quarters. At Sinaia it was decided that, for the time being, the extension of the scope of the Little Entente is not of immediate importance. Nevertheless, we are glad it was raised. It interests us (Czechoslovakia) in particular with respect to Poland. We hold the view that the character of the Little Entente would not be well served by the atmosphere surrounding the over-ambitious policy of Poland, and it was therefore not necessary for Polish circles to repeat so often their emphatic declaration that Poland does not propose to enter the Little Entente. Such declarations caused satisfaction to Poland's arch-enemies, who realize better than the Poles themselves whether Poland or the Little Entente would gain more by such a step. Polish public opinion allows itself to be carried away by fantastic statements abounding in the Polish Press, even in serious papers. In one instance it was inferred from some nebulous notion of a Rumanian-Yugoslav-Greek Alliance that the Little Entente is collapsing because it does not satisfy its members, while in another case the tainted sources of information in Rome are used by the *Kurjer Lwowski* to provide its readers with such attractive headlines as 'Against Czechoslovak Hegemony: Scheme for a Rumanian-Magyar-Bulgarian Alliance.' These are the best proofs that the question of extending the Little Entente, particularly as regards Poland, is not of immediate importance. In the meantime it will be enough to continue cooperation from point to point as the need arises." The irritation produced in some Czechoslovak circles by certain Polish newspapers found vent in articles like the foregoing, but the truth was that, while Poland did not actively cooperate with the Little Entente during 1923, there was no ground for saying that she was estranged from it.

Among the subjects discussed at the Sinaia Conference were economic questions directly interesting the three States, such as that of transport and the removal of obstacles to better economic relations generally among themselves. It was decided that Czechoslovakia should submit definite proposals to the two other States regarding these matters. The conference also closely scanned the programme of the coming session of the Assembly of the League of Nations, including the problem of ethnical Minorities, of which it reached a solution that the experience of the three States showed to be necessary. The fact was emphasized that, although from the very beginning the racial Minorities had been treated with great tolerance, yet representatives of these Minorities had distorted the truth in addressing themselves to the Great Powers. The stand taken by the conference was that, while the Minorities were assured of favourable conditions for their free development within the Little Entente as elsewhere, they must in return conduct themselves in a loyal manner and as good citizens of the country in which they lived, and give up all irredentist agitation. The rest of the agenda of the meeting of the Assembly was gone over with care, and a perfect understanding was reached with respect to it by the conference. But the proceedings throughout were of the most harmonious nature, the identity of view of the statesmen of the Little Entente being complete, as was of course stressed in the *communiqués* issued to the public, thus refuting the various calumnious tales of internal dissension.

Tension between England and France

The Sinaia Conference, however, had, as was usual at most of the conferences of the Little Entente, also under its survey the general political situation, particularly the occupation of the Ruhr at this time, the state of Germany, and the tension, then very great, between Great Britain and France. In the New Europe, which was based on the Peace Treaties, it was impossible for the Little Entente to disinterest itself from questions such as these. The conference began with a "detailed exchange of views on the general situation," according to the first *communiqué* that was published—which further announced that complete agreement had been come to on all points, the unity of the Little Entente being once again manifested as a factor making for general solidarity and peace. Duca, in his talk to the Press, put it succinctly: "The Little Entente group shows itself to be an important factor of peace and solidarity in the centre of a Europe which must endeavour to attain the consolidation of the state of things created by the Peace Treaties." Concerning Germany the conference, after prolonged discussion, found itself in unanimous agreement that the Little Entente should adapt its attitude to that of the Great Allies, but it took no decision in this matter; as everybody knew, the two Great Allies were scarcely in accord, and therefore the Little Entente marked time and adopted a waiting attitude. *Venkov* perhaps threw a little more light on the subject, when it said: "In the discussion on the general situation the possible difficulties in Germany were considered. The view taken was that, whatever events there may be in Germany, they will have no influence in changing the policy of the Little Entente, that is to say, the Little Entente will not intervene unless, of course, such events should transport themselves into the neighbouring States," i.e. Austria and Hungary.

No decision was come to at the Sinaia Conference regarding putting forward a candidate to represent the Little Entente on the Council of the League of Nations at the September meeting; this was left over till the occasion came and the Foreign Ministers of the three States were in Geneva, when Benesh, standing for the group, was elected as the Little Entente member of the Council, September 29, 1923, by thirty votes, a striking proof of the value attached abroad alike to this political organization and the man who had done so much for it. In addition to the Hungarian loan and his other preoccupations, Benesh took the deepest interest at Geneva in the League's activities on the question of Security. He acted as *rapporteur* both in committee and in the Assembly itself for the Treaty of Mutual Assistance, which he defended as an endeavour to solve that difficult problem. One of the principles on which this treaty was based was one that was dear to him and the Little Entente, for it recognized the necessity of regional treaties and alliances, though in this case they were to form the principal means of giving help to an attacked State, the treaty providing that all the States of the League undertook to assist any State in that plight.

In the following year Great Britain, of which MacDonald was then Prime Minister, rejected the principle of special regional treaties, demanding a universal pact in their place. The Treaty of Mutual Assistance was dropped, and this led, in turn, to the Geneva Protocol for the Pacific Settlement of International Disputes, September, 1924. What had been in the minds of the promoters of the Mutual Assistance Treaty was that Security would be obtained through it in a way that would satisfy France without antagonizing Great Britain, this being the greatest problem of the day. In September, 1923, the pacific rôle of the League of Nations had been deeply shadowed by Mussolini's attack on Greece and the shelling and occupation by the Italians of Corfu; many thought the League was hopelessly compromised and would break up. The general international situation seemed darker than ever, but the gloom was somewhat relieved when Germany surrendered to pressure and officially cancelled the policy of passive resistance in the Ruhr towards the end of that month.

On the invitation of Millerand, then President of France, President Masaryk, accompanied by his Foreign Minister, Benesh, paid a State Visit to Paris, arriving there on October 16, 1923. The reception of the venerable and venerated Masaryk was most enthusiastic by the French people; the French Government showered on him every mark of distinction and honour in its power. In a few days he crossed over to London, where he was handsomely entertained by King George and the British Government. The British Press, like the French Press, wrote long editorials in his praise. In England some wondered what was the specific object of these State Visits; the Heads of States did not visit other Heads of States without there being something in the wind, especially when their attendant Foreign Ministers were conferring together. That Masaryk was paying a State Visit for the first as President of Czechoslovakia to the two Great Allies suggested a kind of explanation, and a speech he made to representatives of the Press on October 23 appeared to confirm the idea. In this speech he emphasized the extreme importance and value of the Franco-British Entente, which he said should be maintained because it was essential for the peace and consolidation of Europe. He admitted that at the moment Europe was "a little bit demoralized," but he was confident that this was a transient state of affairs, and would pass away before very long. He said that when he was in Paris he had made certain representations with the object of reducing the tension between the two Great Powers. In language similar to that which he had employed in his speech on January 1, 1922 (p. 189), he declared that the Franco-British Entente was the "necessary authority" for post-War Europe, and that it was his desire and that of the Little Entente that this authority should continue to exist.

The President's words made a profound impression and were the subject of much favourable comment. There had been rumours that the main purpose of his visit with Benesh to Paris had been to prepare the way for a Franco-Czechoslovak Treaty, and that the reason for their going on to London was to smooth or soothe whatever British susceptibilities might be ruffled thereby. Masaryk made it perfectly clear by what he said of maintaining the joint authority of France and Great Britain that Czechoslovakia would make no treaty with France that could or would be hostile to Great Britain. After the return of Masaryk and Benesh to Prague, these rumours became more definite, and the implications of his speech were forgotten by not a few who could see nothing in any such treaty but support for French militarists and the policy of the encirclement of Germany by France and her "vassals." Their opinion appeared to be strengthened when, towards the end of 1923, France offered large credits to Poland, Yugoslavia, and Rumania for the purchase in France of munitions and military equipment —four hundred million francs to Poland, three hundred million to Yugoslavia, and one hundred million to Rumania. Poland and Yugoslavia accepted and Rumania declined the offers. In February, 1924, Benesh stated that France had never offered Czechoslovakia a loan, nor had Czechoslovakia asked France for one. What the British Government thought of the French credits was sufficiently shown when it inquired of the probable beneficiaries whether these loans or their War Debts would come first with them. When the same question was put to Poincaré, he returned a blandly evasive reply. On the other hand, the Dawes Plan was gathering some momentum, for the Commission was about to meet.

Little Entente Conference at Belgrade

It was in this disturbed atmosphere that the Little Entente held its next regular, periodical meeting, the place being Belgrade and the time January 10–12, 1924. Yugoslavia was represented by Pashitch, Prime Minister, and Nintchitch, Foreign Minister, while Rumania had Duca and Czechoslovakia Benesh, their respective Foreign Ministers. A large gathering of journalists from all quarters indicated how busy report had been about this conference and the importance attributed to it throughout Europe. By this time, moreover, the proposed Franco-Czechoslovak Treaty had formed the subject of much speculation, in general more or less ill-formed. Among other things, it was alleged that Benesh purposed to extend that treaty to the whole of the Little Entente. The first meeting of the Belgrade Conference was held on January 10 at the headquarters of Pashitch, and with him in the chair, but before it opened both Benesh and Duca on their arrival took pains to impress on newspaper correspondents how unlikely it was that the conference would produce any sensations. The *communiqué* given out of the first day's meeting was studiously vague. It merely intimated: "As at all previous conferences of the Little Entente, to-day's meeting"—the first of a series of meetings was what the words implied—" was concerned with the international political situation," and the members of the conference, as the result of their exchange of views, were able to record their complete agreement. "The Little Entente desires, as an organization for maintaining peace," it said, "to continue its friendly contacts with all the Allies, and, in view of the present situation in Europe, is all the more resolved to support that political tendency which makes for the maintenance of the Peace Treaties and for consolidation."

The second *communiqué*, which was issued next day at the close of the second meeting, was more informative in some respects: it was to the effect that: "The Foreign Ministers of the three States outlined the situation of their respective States as regards foreign affairs, and full agreement was reached.

Rumania, Czechoslovakia, and Yugoslavia are determined to continue this policy of peace, of attachment to the Peace Treaties and consolidation, which has always been the aim of the Little Entente. In the same spirit the Little Entente wishes to strengthen its amicable relations with all States. In this respect Dr. Benesh and M. Duca were able to point out with satisfaction that the difficulties between Yugoslavia and Italy are more and more retreating into the background, and that there is an increasing tendency towards a friendly settlement of various questions and a *rapprochement* between the two States. The Bulgarian and the Greek problems are viewed in Prague, Bucarest, and Belgrade in the same manner. Although the Little Entente does not desire to intervene in the internal affairs of Greece, it desires the consolidation of that country, and it hopes that Bulgaria will keep within the scope of the Peace Treaties and avoid doing anything that would disturb good relations with neighbouring States."

According to a *communiqué* issued on the evening of the same day after the meeting in the afternoon, the Foreign Ministers only concluded their discussions on various matters affecting the foreign policy of the three States at this third meeting of the conference, and next took up the question of the Hungarian loan, with regard to which, as it later appeared, they agreed to press the demand for concessions to the Little Entente States, in the matter of their financial obligations under the Peace Treaties, similar to those granted to the States whose liabilities had been, or were to be, reduced. Then the conference had something to say about Soviet Russia—each State was to "gang its ain gait," as before.

Press comment on this Belgrade Conference was copious; in France it was complimentary on the whole; in Italy it would have been much the reverse had word not gone forth that the coming agreement with Yugoslavia imposed some caution; in Great Britain it was restrained, because public opinion there, greatly exercised over the Franco-Czechoslovak Treaty, the terms of which had been made known immediately before the conference, was rather bewildered, and, speaking generally, was doubtful about the position of things; even in Poland misgivings regarding this treaty coloured the view taken of the conference. Before the conference the Press of the three States had fixed its attention mainly on the discord between France and Great Britain. *Politika*, the leading Belgrade paper, had recommended the conference to avoid at all costs making itself an arbiter in the Franco-British conflict, and had said that the Little Entente would make a grave mistake if it formed a "united front with France against England—therefore the conference must show that collaboration with France is solely for the maintenance of the treaties in Central Europe." The *Indépendance Roumaine* of Bucarest said: "Destined to assure respect for the Peace Treaties in Central and Eastern Europe, the Little Entente cannot dream of taking sides as a group with one or other of the Great Allied Powers, or aspire to the presumptuous rôle of arbiter. On the contrary, it should assist with all its power in maintaining agreement between the Great Powers, whose close union constitutes an essential guarantee of the peace of Europe."

After the conference the *Prager Presse* spoke of the erroneous interpretation of the Franco-Czechoslovak Treaty by a part of the European Press, who saw in it a step made by Czechoslovakia and the Little Entente "on the path of orientation to France in a sense hostile to England and Italy." On January 14, 1923, *The Times* published a dispatch from its Belgrade correspondent, which was dated the previous day, and which said: "The Little Entente Conference came to an end yesterday, after an incredible number of meetings, receptions, and banquets had been crowded into the space of 48 hours. . . . It is hardly necessary to add that the official *communiqués* have recorded the complete agreement of all three Ministers on all the subjects discussed. If it be considered," the correspondent continued dryly, "that the discussion covered the relations of the Little Entente with France, Great Britain, Italy, the Soviet Government, Hungary, Bulgaria, Greece, and Poland, and its policy in the matter of the Hungarian loan and reparations, as well as the effects of the recent British elections and the probable effect of the coming elections in France and Germany, this represents a considerable achievement."

The lengthy list of topics given a little derisively by the great London journal was discussed by the conference, but at it the emphasis had been transferred from the Franco-British dispute and the Franco-Czechoslovak Treaty to Italy and Soviet Russia. It was noteworthy, however, that Benesh left Belgrade for London immediately after the conference. His ostensible object was to participate in the negotiations then proceeding in London for the loan to Hungary, but he had the larger aim of getting into intimate touch with the new MacDonald Government, in office January, 1924, and of explaining to it anything it might think needed explanation.

The "Pact of Rome"

The truly significant feature of the Belgrade Conference was the news that instead of a Franco-Yugoslav or a Franco-Rumanian Treaty having been, or being about to be concluded, as had been prophesied, an Italo-Yugoslav Treaty held the field. Rumour, not entirely disinterested perhaps, had lied. But what was infinitely more important was the prospect opened up of a definite settlement between Rome and Belgrade, an excellent thing for the Little Entente, and a long step towards the pacification of Europe. The path had been strewn with difficulties, but these were overcome, largely owing to the determination and ability of Nintchitch, the Yugoslav Foreign Minister. On March 2, 1923, an Italo-Yugoslav Conference, looking to a revision of the Treaty of Rapallo, had been begun at Abazzia. When Benesh was in Rome in the following August for negotiations with Mussolini concerning various matters, he could not have failed to glance at least at the question of the Adriatic with the Duce. Before the Belgrade Conference, it had been asserted in part of the European Press that Benesh had been taken by surprise by the Italo-Yugoslav Treaty, whereas the truth was that he had been informed during the session of the League of Nations at Geneva in 1923 by Nintchitch of everything that was being done about it. "In like manner,"

Benesh said, "M. Nintchitch was informed with regard to our treaty with France."

The Italo-Yugoslav Treaty was signed at Rome on January 27, 1924, by Mussolini for Italy and by Pashitch and Nintchitch for Yugoslavia, but the negotiations were actually concluded on the first day of the Belgrade Conference in the course of conversation between Nintchitch and Summonte, the Italian Minister in Belgrade. The treaty, which was styled the "Pact of Rome," was in two parts; one was a "Pact of Friendship and Cordial Cooperation between the Kingdom of Italy and the Kingdom of the Serbs, Croats, and Slovenes," and the other was a supplementary Protocol, which stated that the Pact of Friendship contained nothing contrary to the alliances of Yugoslavia with the two other States of the Little Entente. The pact was entirely non-aggressive, its chief provisions being the guarantee in common of the Peace Treaties of St. Germain, Trianon, and Neuilly, and a pledge of neutrality by the one State in the event of an unprovoked attack on the other; there was also an undertaking that if the safety and interests of the one were threatened by forcible incursions from without, the other would afford political and diplomatic support "in the form of friendly cooperation for the purpose of assisting to remove the external cause of such threat." There was also an undertaking to consult together, "in the event of international complications, if the two States agreed that their common interests were, or might be threatened." The treaty was valid for five years.

It had a special supplement in an Agreement which recognized the annexation of Fiume by Italy, but attributed to Yugoslavia the Baros harbour, anciently part of Fiume, the Delta, and the Banchino—the Delta adjoined the purely Yugoslav (Croat) town of Sushak, which was divided from Italian Fiume merely by a narrow stream. Yugoslavia secured also a free commercial zone in the main harbour, with railway access. If it was not an ideal settlement, at least it was a settlement which went a long way to terminate that strife of tongues and pens, in both countries, that had made the Adriatic question a constant source of danger. Protests and criticisms came from the Raditchists in Croatia, but the treaty was ratified by the Skupshtina on February 19, 1924, by 123 to 21 votes, and five days later Italy handed over Sushak and the Delta to Yugoslavia. The Pact and the Agreement constituted an event of European importance. It was welcomed by the two other States of the Little Entente—"joyfully welcomed" were the words of Benesh.

A question which aroused considerable discussion at the Belgrade Conference was that of the recognition of Soviet Russia. The views of Benesh were well known; he favoured an economic *rapprochement* with Russia and *de jure* recognition of the Soviet Government when the time was ripe for it—not before. The attitude of Rumania continued to be influenced by the Soviet's hostility to her possession of Bessarabia, and among the rumours that beset the conference was one that represented Rumania as making overtures to the other Little Entente States for support against the Soviet. The Yugoslav Press had been strongly opposed to any such proposal; most Yugoslavs were Russophil, and though not enamoured of Bolshevism, they did not want to quarrel with Russia, no matter what her Government was. Opinion was divided on the question of recognition. Pashitch, who had been devoted to the Tsarist régime, was thought to be against it; one of his chief supporters, Spalajkovitch, then Yugoslav Minister in Paris, published in *Samouprava*, the official organ of the Radical Party of which Pashitch was the head, an article against recognition that was taken as an attack on Benesh and his Soviet policy. On the other side Balugdzhitch, then Yugoslav Minister in Berlin, argued in *Politika*, "that no Government which believes in a constructive policy in Europe can afford to remain without relations with Russia, whatever her régime," and he appealed for support to the ideal of Slav solidarity. Naturally it was not forgotten that the alliance with Rumania imposed no obligation concerning Bessarabia.

Here again rumour, fastening on the conflicting views of Soviet Russia within the Little Entente, was busy and mischievous; it was asserted that Benesh had suffered a severe rebuff at Belgrade. In his *Five Years of Czechoslovak Foreign Policy*, Benesh replied: "I learned from the newspapers that our policy in regard to Russia had come to grief at Belgrade, for I am said to have proceeded there to propose the recognition *de jure* of the Soviet Government, and that this scheme fell through. I may say that the Belgrade Conference did discuss this question, and that a certain standpoint was unanimously adopted both as regards the theoretical as well as the practical aspect of the matter. All three States were unanimous in declaring that they were not in principle against the recognition of the Soviet Government, but that they would await events until after an eventual recognition by England and Italy, and that they reserved to themselves freedom of action according to the new situation that would then arise. We have no desire to overestimate the importance of such recognition of Russia, either for Russia or for Europe. The decisive matter will not be the fact of recognition but what will happen after recognition."

This proved to be true, though scarcely in the sense Benesh meant; the turn of events invested it with a curious, mordant irony. For the "decisive matter" was not what happened after the recognition of the Soviet by the MacDonald Government, which was accorded on February 2, 1924, or four days before Benesh made the speech embodied in *Five Years of Czechoslovak Foreign Policy*, but the withdrawal of that recognition, which had not been provided for in his mind, by the Baldwin Government—the second Baldwin Government—in 1925. As for the Belgrade Conference, the three States remained "as they were" respecting Soviet Russia.

The Franco-Czechoslovak Treaty

It was on January 25, 1924, that the Franco-Czechoslovak Treaty was signed in Paris. In its preamble the desire of both parties to it was emphatically stated to be "to respect the international obligations solemnly affirmed in the Covenant of the League of Nations," and "to protect the peace, whose preservation is necessary for the political stability and economic restoration of Europe." Article VI provided, in conformity with the principles laid down in the Covenant, for compulsory arbitration between the two States in the event of a dispute which could not be settled by diplomacy—the first instance of a Great Power, France, accepting without reservations the principle of arbitration. There were no military provisions, but Article II pledged the two States to "agree together as to the measures to be adopted to safeguard their common interests in case the latter are threatened." The Third Article affirmed the intangibility of Austrian independence as laid down in the St. Germain Treaty and in the Geneva Protocols of October 4, 1922, thus proscribing Anschluss, except by the unanimous consent of the Council of the League of Nations. The two next Articles were directed against the restoration of the Habsburgs and of the Hohenzollerns respectively.

Report spoke of secret military annexes, but untruly, for they did not exist. All the same, an important section of French opinion regarded the treaty as another link in the chain of the military alliances of France. Yet it was abundantly evident from the treaty itself that it was little or nothing more than a restatement and a refortification by France and Czechoslovakia of the settlement of Europe under the Peace Treaties, and had no aggressive aims whatsoever. On February 6, 1924, Benesh made a great speech in the Parliament at Prague on this treaty and the general policy he had pursued since 1918. Woven into the texture of part of this book and quoted from in this and preceding chapters, this speech, of which an English version, entitled *Five Years of Czechoslovak Policy*, was published in Prague, must ever remain one of the most illuminating documents in the history not only of Czechoslovakia, but of the Little Entente and Central Europe. It ran to many thousand words, and showed the most careful preparation.

Benesh himself said his speech was designed "equally for abroad and our own public" in its exposition of the Franco-Czechoslovak Treaty, and that it would "put everything in the right light." He had remarked just before: "In the first moment the treaty evoked a very considerable echo. In Italy this soon subsided, especially after the conclusion of the Italo-Yugoslav Treaty. The Little Entente States were acquainted with the matter and accepted it gladly. In England" (where the echo had indeed been very considerable) "I had an opportunity of elucidating the question in interviews with both the old and the present Government and with official circles generally, and all of them appreciated our peaceable intentions, our efforts, and our aims." In his speech he more than once stressed the necessity of maintaining the Anglo-French Entente as the "key for solving the European situation and for safeguarding the European peace for long decades ahead," and as meaning, "in the difficult times in which we now live, peace and quiet in Europe." There was no justification for the statement that the treaty had placed Czechoslovakia "definitely on the side of France against England, in contradistinction to the policy hitherto pursued of keeping an equilibrium between the two countries."

Now Benesh claimed the treaty to be the logical sequel of that policy, and that it would have been signed much earlier but for two things: "First, we expected France and Great Britain to agree on the Guarantee Pact, which had long been the subject of negotiations, and that this pact would become a mainstay of reconstruction and peace for the New Europe, and that we should then be enabled in some form or other to participate in it directly or indirectly and by agreement with France. This, for instance, was the meaning of the efforts made by us at the Genoa Conference. Secondly, we waited till our immediate troubles in Central Europe were removed and until we were consolidated and strong enough, and till we came to agree with our neighbours, so that the treaty with a Power like France would then be nothing but the confirmation of our peace and reconstruction policy, not a menace against or undue pressure on other States—in other words, that it should be an act of peace and consolidation, not of intimidation."

It was pointed out by Benesh that of all the Great Powers, France, with her interests, stood nearest to Czechoslovakia: "Our Republic, adhering to the Peace Treaties, partly because its existence depends on them, partly because they safeguard both its peace and its present condition, has on the whole the same interests as French politics. The interests of the two States are not in conflict anywhere. In sentiment and traditions the two nations are very close. Likewise a correctly conceived European policy leads them both to the establishment of peace in Central Europe and to good relations with Germany; this must, after all, be the ultimate goal of any French or Czechoslovak policy. . . . The political state of affairs has continually found expression during the last five years in the cooperation of the two States. May I say to-day that none of the Big Allies has supported Czechoslovakia in all her political difficulties so much as France during the War and the succeeding years? I am only stating facts." Turning to England, he said: "Our relations with Great Britain have been throughout these five years the best imaginable. Our interests may be distant, but the indirect relations are numerous. The situation can be best expressed in this form: our (Czechoslovak) post-War reconstruction policy, our moderation towards the defeated States, the help given to Austria and Hungary, our relations with Germany, our Russian policy, and general economic interests have brought us into close accord. All this has created much sympathy for us in England, and we must show our appreciation of it in our future acts."

In view of the necessity of preserving the Anglo-French Entente, Benesh went on to remark: "We desire a definitive improvement and clearing up of the relations between France and Great Britain, just because we have concluded the treaty with France. . . . It is not the intention of the policy to make any changes in its line of conduct which has brought it nearer England, and hence it will remain in full harmony with British politics, as heretofore. The treaty with France does not hinder us at all in this respect, and those in England who have criticized us have been greatly mistaken; no doubt they have misunderstood the treaty. To-day the official circles have a correct view of the matter, and British public opinion also is beginning to comprehend the whole question well."

International Situation Improving

Public opinion in England was now inclined to regard the general international situation as improving. The conviction that it was true that the Franco-Czechoslovak Treaty had no secret military clauses had grown, nor was this shaken by the publication in March by the *Berliner Tageblatt* of the text of an alleged secret agreement between France and Czechoslovakia; it was hardly necessary for Prague to issue a denial of the genuineness of the thing. And in its widest aspect the international situation showed, and continued to show, signs of that profound change which became so marked as the year rolled on. If it could not be said that Poincaré's Ruhr policy was an entire failure, it was certain that what France got from it was obtained at enormously disproportionate cost. The Dawes Commission had held its meetings and had come to its conclusions, which were embodied in its Report on April 9, 1924. Put briefly, the findings were that Germany must fulfil the obligations she had undertaken to the utmost of her power as determined by the neutral experts, and, as a corollary, that France must be more moderate and reasonable in her demands.

What was in the wind was apparent some days before, when Poincaré intimated that France was prepared to accept the entrance of Germany into the League of Nations if Germany accepted the Dawes Plan. That opinion in France had gradually undergone something in the nature of a psychological transformation was beyond dispute when, in May, 1924, the Elections in that country went against Poincaré, and Herriot became Prime Minister; a characteristic difference between these statesmen was exhibited in their attitude towards the League of Nations; Herriot attached far greater importance to it than did Poincaré, and in this Herriot had the backing of MacDonald, the British Prime Minister. The result of the Elections in Germany also helped to clarify the general situation by bringing into office a Government which understood that the policy of fulfilment must be adopted and carried out. The sky of Europe, so long overcast, was visibly lightening and brightening; the sun was shining through the clouds when arrangements were made, with the approval of France and Great Britain, for holding a Conference in London in August to adjust reparations.

Bearing on the general position, and particularly on their own, the States of the Little Entente recorded losses and gains, and both had their repercussions, during the spring and early summer of this year. A conference between Rumania and Soviet Russia, which had been in session at Vienna for several days with the object of regulating their relations to each other, completely broke down on April 2, 1924, on the question of Bessarabia, the Soviet refusing to recognize that territory as Rumanian. Though a more favourable result was scarcely to have been expected in the circumstances, Rumania was disappointed and her Press showed displeasure and bitterness, some of which was vented, most mistakenly, on her Little Entente allies, whose newspapers were not slow to reply. As against all this, Rumania had some compensation in the ratification by France of the Bessarabian Treaty of October 28, 1920, which so far had been ratified by Great Britain alone of the Great Allies; Italy and Japan still withheld ratification. The French ratification of this treaty was also a subject of lively comment in the papers, notably in Yugoslavia in certain quarters, this hostility certainly not being mitigated by "incidents" in the Banat caused by Rumanian troops when they were evacuating districts in that region that had been assigned to the neighbouring and allied State.

Italo-Czechoslovak Treaty

It was not altogether surprising that rumour got busy again regarding the relations of the States of the Little Entente among themselves. Among the positive gains for the Little Entente was the negotiation of a Pact of Friendship and Cooperation between Italy and Czechoslovakia by Benesh and Mussolini, the former going to Rome for that purpose in March, 1924, and again in the following May. Touching the latter visit to Mussolini, Benesh was reported to have said that his object on that occasion was to do away with any idea that Czechoslovakia had not just as much reason to be friends with Italy as with France, or with Great Britain for that matter, and to demonstrate that no Great Power would be able to boast of possessing a hegemony or absolute dominion over the Little Entente. The pact was signed at Rome on July 5, 1924, and the ratifications were exchanged at Rome on August 21. Its First Article stated that the two States would "decide in concert on the measures best designed to protect their common interests in the event of their being agreed as to the existence or possibility of a menace," and in Article II they undertook to afford each other "support and assistance" to ensure the maintenance of the situation established by the Treaties of St. Germain, Trianon, and Neuilly and the fulfilment of the obligations specified therein. The Third Article validated the treaty for five years, and the Fourth, the last in a very short document, provided for the communication of the treaty to the League of Nations in accordance with Article XVIII of the Covenant.

Every word of this treaty was in complete agreement with Benesh's policy of treaty-making and with the general policy of the Little Entente. On his way to Rome in May, Benesh had met Nintchitch at Bled, the picturesque Slovene town on the lovely lake of the same name, and had acquainted him fully with the details of this treaty, with which the Yugoslav Minister was in perfect accord as the complement of his own work for cordial relations with Italy. Further progress towards peace and consolidation appeared in various agreements in which one or other of the Little Entente States was interested, as, for example, the Conventions concluded at Bucarest on March 31, which settled outstanding points at issue between Rumania and Hungary, and the Protocol signed at Cracow on May 6 between Czechoslovakia and Poland for better economic and transport facilities in their frontier zone at Spis.

Little Entente Conference at Prague

The next of the regular, periodical conferences of the Little Entente was held at Prague on July 11 and 12, 1924, those attending it being the three Foreign Ministers, Nintchitch for Yugoslavia, Duca for Rumania, and Benesh for Czechoslovakia. Again there was a great gathering of journalists, for the meeting had been preceded by the most extraordinary rumours, among them being nothing less than the dissolution of the Little Entente as its result, owing to divergencies of view respecting Soviet Russia and so forth. A knowledge of the history, aims, and achievements of the Little Entente was still lacking in some quarters, where there was also a failure to understand the improvement which had taken place and was still going forward in the general situation in Europe, and which was favourable for the Little Entente and its policy. According to custom the Ministers in their first session discussed all questions of foreign policy that bore on their States.

The first *communiqué* issued said: "From the very beginning the Little Entente was concerned with maintaining unity between the Great Allies, and it therefore observes with particular satisfaction that agreement for the purpose of settling the question of Reparations is being more and more attained. In the course of discussion, the Ministers placed on record the fact that various incidents of recent occurrence"—this sentence referred to the incidents in the Banat—"did not and could not have any influence on the very close and loyal relations which have existed from the very first between all three States, and therefore Rumania, Yugoslavia, and Czechoslovakia are united as firmly as ever by their common vital interests. The Little Entente continues to be an alliance with a limited scope, but beyond this it aims at maintaining the existing peace, and in this regard it will exert its utmost efforts for the upkeep of this peace in all circumstances."

At their second sitting the three Ministers discussed the Reparations problems in their entirety, and reviewed likewise the question of Inter-Allied Debts; they agreed as to the way in which these difficulties should be approached and settled, the necessity of cooperation on the part of all three countries, and the indispensability of close and permanent contact at the approaching London Conference, as well as on all other occasions when such subjects came up for discussion, in order thus to be able to represent effectively the interests of their countries. From the London Conference the conference passed to the consideration of the agenda of the next meeting of the League of Nations in September, and, as on previous occasions, the Ministers decided to proceed jointly, their views being identical. At the third session they considered more particularly questions on the agenda of the League relating to Disarmament and Agreements as to Mutual Guarantees, and found themselves of one mind in these matters. The Prague Conference was marked by a spirit of sincerity and complete cordiality. In concluding the work of the conference, the representatives of the Little Entente were able to record the fruitful results of a cooperation extending over the past four years, and once more to emphasize the loyal friendship which had always been the basis of their common endeavours for peace and the political and economic reconstruction of Central Europe.

After the close of the conference in the afternoon of July 12, the three Ministers received the journalists, who were addressed first by Nintchitch. Having stated that the *communiqués* issued were not a string of empty phrases, but sincere expressions of facts, the Yugoslav Foreign Minister said he was astonished that some special significance had been attributed to this conference, "not so much on account of the work it has done, as because there was an idea that it would wind up, if not with the termination, at least with the weakening of the Little Entente." On what was the idea based? "On unimportant incidents between us and Rumania, the newspapers on both sides becoming unduly excited over very trivial affairs—an excitement, however, that met with no echo in political circles. The truth is that we (Yugoslavia) and Rumania have concluded in the last few months a number of important agreements, which is the best proof that there is a complete understanding between the two countries. For example, we have settled the question of our frontiers without the intervention of the League of Nations" (the agreement for delimitation was signed at Belgrade on November 24, 1923). Referring to some journals in Yugoslavia that had sought to arouse ill-feeling against the Little Entente, Nintchitch dissociated himself and his Government from all such efforts. While the Little Entente united the common interests of the three States, it granted to each sufficient freedom of action. It was a factor of peace and consolidation in Central Europe, and had exerted a salutary influence even farther afield, as was seen in its collaboration in the reconstruction of Austria and in the satisfactory start made with the reconstruction of Hungary. The Minister next alluded to the Italo-Yugoslav Treaty of Friendship, which had "done much to promote the reconstruction of the whole of Europe." Replying to a question, he stated that the relations between his country and Hungary had considerably improved.

Nintchitch was followed by Duca, who remarked at the outset of his speech: "Although it is alleged that the Little Entente does not exist, or at any rate is in a very precarious condition, I hope that after this conference the whole world will be convinced that the Little Entente is alive and never healthier than at present. It is also alleged that the Little Entente has passed through critical moments, because its members were unable to agree on certain questions"—meaning Bessarabia and Soviet Russia. "With regard to this, I repeat what I told the journalists at the Belgrade Conference: it is not the task of the Little Entente to ensure the agreement of its members on questions which do not come within the scope of their definite aims. It is surprising that some people are continually trying to attribute to the Little Entente a scope of activity different from that which it actually possesses. Thus the Russian question and the recognition of the Soviet did not concern the Little Entente as such, but only each individual member of it separately." Rumania, he said, had no theoretical objection to recognizing Russia; the position of Rumania was governed by the fact that the Soviet would not recognize the present frontiers of Rumania; "as long as this question is not settled, we cannot proceed to the recognition of Russia. Our policy is a policy of peace towards the whole world. As we have achieved our national unity, we have no demands to make on anybody, and we should be happy if we could start regular relations with Russia, as with other States. . . . We have done everything possible in this respect, and it is not our fault if we have not been successful." Replying to a question, the Minister said that if Hungary would take her stand on the Peace Treaties, she would find a neighbour in Rumania prepared to cooperate with her politically and economically. He noted that the relations of the two countries had obviously improved. "We have negotiated concerning the practical carrying out of the Peace Treaties, and on April 16 we concluded conventions of a juridical and practical nature. We have settled the question of War Debts with the Reparations Commission."

Benesh spoke third and last. In answer to questions submitted to him, he stated: "Our negotiations here in Prague on the Russian question were almost on the same lines as those at Belgrade. We placed on record the changes that had occurred in the situation. We took note of the special difficulties confronting Rumania respecting the recognition of Russia, and, further, concluded that the position of Yugoslavia is the same now as at the time of the Belgrade Conference. For myself, I favour the recognition of Russia, and I am waiting only for the moment which will be most opportune in the interests of Czechoslovakia and Europe as a whole. . . . In this question I reserve for myself complete freedom in the choice of that moment. I shall be prepared for the recognition of Russia to-morrow, in a month, or in a year. As I have said, we shall settle this question as demanded by the interests of Czechoslovakia, the Little Entente, and the whole of Europe." Benesh stated that he was in favour of the entry of Germany into the League of Nations, an event which would relax the tension still existing. When the Great Powers had agreed on the Dawes Plan, the moment would arrive, he thought, for settling this matter. He saw a great improvement in Hungary's relations with Czechoslovakia. Czechoslovakia would participate in the Hungarian loan as in the Austrian loan.

"I do not know," he went on, "what more can be expected of

us. We have agreed that the reparation commitments of Austria and Hungary are to be reduced. I hope that authoritative circles in Hungary will take a reasonable view, and I therefore hope that between Hungary and ourselves good neighbourly relations will develop. But we will defend ourselves against acts of malice and will demand that written agreements be respected." Touching the rumours that the Little Entente was breaking up, Benesh said that those who spread them were not aware of what the Little Entente had already achieved. "It came into existence at a time when the internal difficulties of all countries in Central Europe as regards finance, supplies, and communications were at their height. It was then that the idea arose of creating a more peaceful atmosphere. In that way people were stimulated to carry on their work and to create new values, so as to restore the economic position. The policy of the Little Entente was not established at random, but on the basis of the justified interests of the nations concerned. If anyone supposes he can make mischief among us, he is greatly mistaken. The Little Entente has proved that it is capable of commanding respect with regard to its interests." In this connexion Benesh referred to the place given to the Little Entente in the League of Nations.

"Those," he continued, "who speak of a collapse of the Little Entente, do so either from ignorance or ill-will." Questioned about Russia and her possible entry into the League, Benesh said that the Soviet did not wish to join, but if it did, the subject would be considered in relation to recognition, the first condition of which would be for Russia to fulfil her obligations—there was the matter of her pre-War Debts. He thought that the economic position of Russia was serious: "The reconstruction of Russia will be a long and difficult business. Everything will depend on the methods adopted. I have no illusions as to the possible results of recognition nor as to the rapid recovery of Russia. That is all the more reason for establishing regular relations with Russia, so that the process of reconstruction may not be delayed."

Conversations at Ljubljana

In Yugoslavia the Pashitch Government was replaced by one under Davidovitch, with Marinkovitch as Foreign Minister, on July 27, 1924. On his way to Geneva to attend the Council of the League, Benesh stopped at Ljubljana on August 27 to confer with the new Yugoslav Foreign Minister, and went on to Switzerland later that day. On August 28 Duca arrived in the same city, and discussed matters with Marinkovitch. All three Ministers found themselves in complete accord as to the position to be taken by the Little Entente at Geneva; there had really been no doubt as to the identity of their views; the Ljubljana meetings took place rather to enable Benesh and Duca to get into personal communication with Marinkovitch, whose foreign policy was precisely the same as that of Nintchitch, his predecessor, both for the other Little Entente States and the whole international situation. The two official *communiqués* issued were limited to stating that the Ministers maintained the points of view and agreements previously adopted or reached by the Little Entente, as nothing had occurred to modify them. Chief among these was insistence on the military control, and the participation in it of their group, of Austria, Hungary, and Bulgaria. On June 17, 1924, the Council of the League had begun to investigate this question, and in the following month the League's Juridical Committee had started confidential discussions on the subject. The matter was ripe for settlement at the Council's meeting at the end of August.

Other matters considered, doubtless with sincere congratulations, at Ljubljana were the Agreement of the Great Powers, which fortunately had been come to at the London Conference earlier in that month, and the acceptance of the Dawes Plan by all concerned. According to Press reports, Benesh, Duca, and Marinkovitch talked over the way things were going in Bulgaria, whose Government, still under Tsankoff, was greatly exercised by the Communist menace, and not without cause; an increase in the strength, permitted under treaty, of the Bulgarian Army was suggested. When at Ljubljana Marinko-

DR. MARINKOVITCH

vitch also met Bordrero, the Italian Minister at Belgrade, discussed with him the question of the delimitation of the Slovene frontier, and though no protocol was signed, reached an agreement for a friendly settlement as soon as possible. In a statement to the Press, Marinkovitch said that Yugoslav policy in regard to Italy would continue along the line of the Pact of Rome, and would be based on broad views and not on petty chicanery, so that good results would soon be seen. Present at Geneva in September, the three Foreign Ministers of the Little Entente were in constant contact; they united in strongly supporting the Geneva Protocol; in all other questions raised, especially that of the military control of the ex-enemy countries, they acted in concert. On September 27 a system of military control was approved by the League; delegates of the Little Entente worked together on the committees appointed to implement it. Concerning the Soviet, each of the three States preserved its liberty of action, in conformity with the decision at the Belgrade Conference and its reaffirmation at the Prague Conference. Benesh was still waiting for the opportune moment.

In August it might have been thought to have come. Both Great Britain and France had already recognized the Soviet as a *de jure* Government, but in that month the MacDonald Government, after some contradictory steps, had signed various treaties with it, which undoubtedly gave it a prestige it had not possessed before, and gave a hint that other States might move in the same direction. The Balkans, however, plainly indicated something different from all this; there the propaganda and intrigues of the Soviet, not in the least disguised as the Third International, were seen to be in persistent and malignant play. Benesh admitted that the relations between the Third International and the Soviet Government were a serious obstacle in the way of the establishment of regular relations between Russia and other countries. In any case, the fall of the MacDonald Government, largely on the Soviet issue, a few weeks after the Geneva meetings, and the consequent formation of the second Baldwin Government, gave good ground for further pause; in November Austen Chamberlain, the new British Foreign Secretary, in two Notes to the Soviet Chargé d'Affaires in London, intimated that Great Britain definitely rejected the treaties with the Soviet.

The Geneva Protocol

As said above, the Foreign Ministers of the Little Entente worked together at Geneva in complete collaboration, yet reports to the contrary got about; it was said that differences had arisen between Duca and Marinkovitch—differences which found an echo in the *Vreme* and the *Politika* of Belgrade, and of course were not unheard in Bucarest. Referring to this, Duca, on his return home, said in an interview published in the *Indépendance Roumaine*: "During the whole sitting of the League of Nations the most cordial and perfect understanding reigned at Geneva, not only between the Rumanian and Yugoslav delegates, but among all the representatives of the Little Entente. . . . M. Marinkovitch was greatly surprised by the comments of the Belgrade papers, and immediately dispatched a categorical denial of their statements." To the same effect was the re-election of Benesh on October 3 as a member of the Council of the League on the joint candidature of the Little Entente. As the main artisan of the Protocol, he was inevitably one of the greatest figures, if not the greatest, at Geneva.

In the Czechoslovak Parliament at Prague on October 30, 1924, Benesh made a long speech, in which he discussed the Protocol in all its aspects. He described the struggle for the reduction of armaments, which had been proceeding for the past five years, and the efforts put forth in the League of Nations for the same purpose. He pictured the divers views which, in 1922, after long debate between England and France, led to the enunciation of the principle that reduction was possible only if security was certain. Next he came to the Treaty of Mutual Assistance, which, he reminded his hearers, "recognized the need of local and supplementary alliances, such as those of the Little Entente," but which was objected to by some Governments, as they thought it would lead in the end to that grouping of opposed Powers exhibited before the World War, and with a like result. Then followed an elaborate dissertation on the Protocol itself, in the course of which he said that he had defended in the Assemblies of 1921, 1922, and 1923 the Czechoslovak policy of regional alliances: "I have always upheld the need and the legitimacy of such special conventions, but on condition that they were public, strictly defensive, and open to any State desirous of becoming a party to them, always provided, however, that they were not contrary to the spirit of the Covenant; this being the case, they would be instruments for maintaining peace." He pointed out that such alliances would also be a means for assuring the rapid execution of any measures taken under the Protocol. He expressed his conviction that the great principles of the Protocol which had been formulated with such solemnity at Geneva by fifty-four States, who represented three-fourths of the population of the world, could never disappear from international politics.

Turning to other topics, he mentioned that at Geneva he had discussed with Skrzynski all questions pending between Czechoslovakia and Poland; they had agreed to settle them by negotiation and by special commissions. A supplementary treaty of commerce had been concluded with Austria, and he would go shortly to Vienna to sign it—at the same time returning the last visit of the Austrian Chancellor to Prague. He contemplated a commercial treaty with Hungary, which would make relations with that country "absolutely normal." A Customs treaty had been concluded with Italy on October 27. He remarked that the cooperation of the Little Entente delegations with those of Great Britain and France at Geneva had been very close and had fortified their mutual friendship; it was the same with respect to the Italian delegates. He wound up his lengthy review by a glance at Soviet Russia. On his way to Rome, where the Council of the League was about to meet, Benesh negotiated with the new Austrian Foreign Minister, Mataja, in Vienna on December 7, respecting various outstanding matters, and during his stay in Rome he visited Mussolini and discussed reparations with him.

Meanwhile the Davidovitch Government in Yugoslavia had fallen in one of those recurring crises, all too frequent, which marked the continuous struggle between centralists and federalists, now made more bitter by the inflammatory oratory of Stephen Raditch, the Croat peasant leader, on his return from Moscow, where he had been in contact with the Soviet authorities. On November 6, 1924, Pashitch was again in office, and Nintchitch replaced Marinkovitch in the Ministry for Foreign Affairs. In December Tsankoff went from Sofia to Belgrade and exchanged views with Pashitch and Nintchitch to such good effect that the Yugoslav Ministers were able to say that collaboration between their country and Bulgaria was entirely possible on the basis of the treaties. Taking the international situation as a whole, the close of 1924 clearly suggested that the political sky was clearing more and more.

CHAPTER VIII

THE LITTLE ENTENTE AND LOCARNO
1925–1926

EXCEPT as regards Soviet Russia, improvement described in one word the trend of the European situation, in which the Little Entente had its distinctive place, both particular and general, during 1925 and 1926, the two high-lights in the picture being the negotiation and signature of the Locarno series of treaties in the former year and, in the latter, the entry of Germany into the League of Nations, with a permanent seat in its Council. The period thus embraced might be denominated that of Locarno. The amelioration was not always continuous; there were hesitations and even halts, but the undertone was strong and persistent, and the broad movement towards the consolidation of peace went on, despite the checks, with gathering momentum. The tension between France and Great Britain, previously a grave preoccupation of the statesmen of the Little Entente, virtually disappeared. The difficult question of Reparations was held as settled by the Dawes Plan, which came into successful operation, but was in itself incomplete, as the total amount of Germany's liability remained to be determined. Still, German reparations had been relegated to the sphere of economics, where they more properly belonged.

The next big and more difficult problem for solution was that of Security—to which the latest contribution had been the Geneva Protocol, as recorded in the last chapter. At the meeting of the Council of the League at Rome in December, 1924, Great Britain had indicated that she would not accept the Protocol, and at Geneva in March, 1925, she pronounced absolutely against it. This killed the Protocol, and led to further exploration of the problem; a beginning had been made earlier in the same year. The British Government intimated that it thought the solution of the problem was possible only through the conclusion of guarantee pacts between individual interested Powers directly—in other words, regional treaties or defensive alliances. According to an article in the *Gaulois*, March 10, 1925, Benesh, "the principal artisan" of the Protocol, consoled himself for its loss with the idea that these pacts must have the same character as the treaties on which the Little Entente, of which he was "also the principal artisan," was based. Further, he was credited with the project of forming four such pacts: a Western Pact, including England, France, Germany, Belgium, Holland, and Spain; a Central European Pact, covering Poland, Czechoslovakia, Austria, Hungary, Yugoslavia, and Rumania; a Balkan Pact, which might take in Turkey; and a Scandinavian-Baltic Pact; Italy would belong either to the Western or to the Central European group, in consonance with her sympathies or interests. Benesh himself, however, while proclaiming his belief that the Protocol was the best solution of the question of Security, said it would be absurd and stupid to look with disfavour on certain suggestions made by Germany and the consequent negotiations then going on.

These suggestions were contained in a Memorandum, dated February 9, 1925, in which Germany proposed a special Pact of Gurarantee of Peace for Western Europe and arbitration treaties with her neighbours. England, France, Belgium, Italy, Poland, and Czechoslovakia, after some time, accepted these proposals in their broad lines. Two Allied Notes, the one of June 16 and the other of August 24, 1925, carried the negotiations another stage; they were completed at the Conference of Locarno, held from October 5 to 16, 1925, the Final Protocol being signed on the last day of the conference; and the seven interlocking treaties, the outcome of all these proceedings, were signed on December 1, 1925, at the Foreign Office, London, in a memorable scene. The occasion was distinguished by the presence of the British Prime Minister and the Foreign or other Ministers of the various States who were parties to the treaties, as well as Chamberlain, the British Foreign Secretary, who had very largely been instrumental in bringing the negotiations to a successful conclusion. Based on the bilateral principle that if France wanted security, Germany also needed it—this was the lesson taught her by the occupation of the

Ruhr—the Rhineland Pact, the first and most important of the seven treaties, provided for the inviolability, under the guarantee of Great Britain and Italy, of the frontiers of France, Belgium, and Germany as established by the Treaty of Versailles. The four treaties that came next in order provided for arbitration between Germany on the one hand and France, Belgium, Poland, and Czechoslovakia respectively on the other. The sixth and seventh were treaties of reciprocal guarantee between France and Poland and between France and Czechoslovakia. The Rhineland Pact was to come into force after the entry of Germany into the League of Nations, an act that was to seal the seven treaties.

From War to Peace

The general result of Locarno was well summed up in the words "From War to Peace." The atmosphere created was one in which a mentality of peace, not of war, might live and grow. Locarno was thus the greatest step that had so far been taken in the consolidation of the peace of Europe. Yet differences within the League prevented Germany from being received into the Council in March, 1926, as had been expected. This pause in the programme gave an opportunity for a proceeding which caused doubts and apprehensions, namely, the conclusion in Berlin of a treaty between Germany and Soviet Russia which extended the Treaty of Rapallo. It was not till the following September that the German Delegation found its place at Geneva; it was headed by Stresemann, the German Foreign Minister, who had collaborated with Briand and Chamberlain at Locarno, and who represented the bulk of German opinion.

All was well—if Germany was acting in good faith. Her sincere acceptance of the principles of the League was questioned by many who, pointing to the clamour in Germany for the immediate evacuation of the occupied territories, declared that she had entered the League solely for what she could get out of it. They recalled how Hindenburg had been elected President in 1925 and how high German officials had stated that they did not regard the eastern frontiers of Germany as permanent. And much was made of the undeniable orientation of Germany to Soviet Russia, the avowed enemy of the League. But the general disposition was to take Germany on trust and to believe that all was well. Certainly all Europe breathed more freely—except Soviet Russia.

Soviet Russia the Exception

Despite all disparagement, Locarno and its results stood out as the greatest positive achievements for peace since the War. During the period under review Soviet Russia continued to be the chief menace to peace. She filled those two years with threats of war, with her plots, intrigues, and propaganda. Towards the close of 1924 a conspiracy which she had fomented for the subversion of the Republic of Estonia had come to a head at Reval in an outbreak that had, however, been successfully dealt with by the Estonian Government. As already narrated, the Soviet in 1924 was active in the Balkans, particularly in Bulgaria. Vienna was at that time the centre of its operations both for the Baltic and the Balkans. As 1925 opened, Raditch, the leader of the Croat Peasant Party, was arrested at Zagreb, with five of his principal followers, by the Yugoslav Government on charges of sedition and of being in league with Moscow. He had long declined to permit the deputies of his party to take their seats in the Skupshtina at Belgrade; under his guidance the party, originally for Home Rule, and then for a Republic, had affiliated itself with the Peasant International, a Soviet organization. Raditch himself had visited Moscow and the Soviet headquarters in Vienna. Shortly before imprisoning him, the Yugoslav Government suppressed the Croat Peasant Party, "for the sake," it said in a *communiqué*, "of the whole country and especially the Croats, who have not realized the destructive character of the action taken by their leaders." It accompanied these measures with a vigorous campaign throughout Yugoslavia against Communism, but, as was inevitable, these measures still further embroiled the

Serbs and the Croats, though, on the other hand, Communism ceased to be dangerous.

Soviet agents remained active in Bulgaria, and the consequences of their work were seen at Sofia in April, 1925, in an appalling outrage—the explosion of a bomb in the Cathedral, which resulted in the deaths of many people, including the Mayor of the city, several generals, and other prominent persons. This dastardly affair followed hard on an attempt to assassinate the King and the discovery of a plot to bring about a Communist insurrection in North-Western Bulgaria. The Bulgarian Government requested the Allies for permission to strengthen its armed forces against the authors of these outrages and supported its plea with documentary evidence establishing the culpability of the Third International, the other name of the Soviet. It was under the shadow of these events that the chiefs of the Little Entente held their next periodical conference in the second week of May, 1925. But before it took place, Czechoslovakia and Poland had reached a friendly agreement on all points, and treaties had been concluded establishing excellent relations between them.

Polish-Czechoslovak Rapprochement

While attending the meeting of the Council of the League at Geneva in the preceding March—when the Protocol fell through owing to its rejection by Great Britain—Benesh had discussed with Skrzynski, the Polish Foreign Minister, the various matters still unsettled between their respective countries, with a view to their complete liquidation, and had come to an agreement with him, satisfactory to both, which was to be embodied in relevant treaties or conventions. For the signing of these instruments Benesh arrived in Warsaw on April 20, 1925: they took the shape of a Treaty of Commerce and a Treaty of Arbitration, important in themselves, but still more significant as opening a new period of friendly relations between Czechoslovakia and Poland. Nor did its value end there; as Benesh said: "For us and for the whole situation in our neighbourhood and for Europe generally it means a good step forward towards the consolidation of conditions." The *rapprochement* between the two countries was indeed a matter of first-class political importance.

As previously stated (p. 183), attempts to bring this understanding about had been made by Benesh and Skirmunt in 1921, but the treaty they then signed had not been ratified by Poland, and consequently had lapsed. At that time there had been too many issues in dispute, and the temper of the two peoples towards each other was scarcely favourable to a settlement of them. Yet, as was shown at Genoa and elsewhere, the statesmen of the two countries frequently cooperated in political work with marked success. In March–April, 1925, the turn of events in the international situation respecting the question of Security had perhaps hastened the negotiations for a better understanding between the Poles and the Czechoslovaks, but in any case it was unequivocally a good thing. It had a very good Press, especially in France, as was natural. In welcoming this entente, the *Temps* said: "France is indissolubly united with Poland and Czechoslovakia. The *rapprochement* between them can cause her only to rejoice. This *rapprochement* constitutes a new factor in the general political situation in Europe." William Martin, in the *Journal de Genève*, after mentioning that Poland had signed a commercial treaty with Hungary shortly before, thought that it was now possible that Poland might facilitate intercourse between the Czechoslovaks and the Magyars, and in return Czechoslovakia might play an extremely useful rôle with respect to Polish-German relations.

In an interview given to the *Matin*, Benesh said: "Our understanding is an event of political importance in view of the serious nature of the problems of to-day. Negotiations for security have begun. Certain German circles are raising the question of a union with Austria. There are also the troubles in the Balkans and the Bolshevist menace. We are well aware that if the Treaty of Versailles is impaired in one point, the whole fabric of Europe will be in danger. I am in a position to say that Count Skrzynski and myself have agreed to adopt an almost identical attitude towards any proposal for an arbitration treaty which is made to us by Germany." Supplementing this statement, *The Times* Paris Correspondent, on May 3 (published next day), wrote: "President Masaryk, in a separate statement given on the same day (as the Benesh interview in the *Matin*), is reported to have spoken in the same sense, and the representative of the *Matin* says that he was shown on a map of Europe the various points where conflicts are not improbable, and where the entente between Poland and Czechoslovakia may be called on to play a useful part."

The Times Correspondent continued: "So far as can be ascertained here (Paris), the questions which are expected to come in the near future within the purview of the entente between Poland and Czechoslovakia are the following: (1) Silesia, Danzig, and the Corridor—in this Czechoslovakia will support Poland; (2) the Union of Austria and Germany—in this Poland will support the opposition of Czechoslovakia to any such attempt; (3) the situation in the Balkans—here Poland and Czechoslovakia will give their united support to the efforts of Yugoslavia, Greece, and Rumania to create stability, taking into account the peculiar position of Bulgaria; (4) League of Nations affairs—here a united front will be formed by the States of the Little Entente and Poland." To these was added the question of relations with Soviet Russia, towards which the attitude of the "new entente will not necessarily be hostile." With some of these questions Benesh had dealt in a speech on April 1, 1925, in the Foreign Committee of the Czechoslovak Senate at Prague, but he dwelt chiefly on the "Diplomatic Struggle for European Security and the Stabilization of Peace," under which title the speech was published in English. It must be noted that the *rapprochement* between Poland and Czechoslovakia did not bring the former into the Little Entente, but it greatly increased the general interest manifested in the Little Entente's approaching conference.

Little Entente Conference at Bucarest

This conference was held in Bucarest on May 9–11, 1925, and was attended by Duca, Nintchitch, and Benesh, the Foreign

Ministers of the three States, with Bratianu, Rumanian Prime Minister, in the chair at the start. A large concourse of journalists had gathered from all quarters, as on former occasions of a similar character. They were addressed by Duca before the opening of the conference. He told them that neither the question of the recognition of Russia nor that of Poland nor Greece's adhesion to the Little Entente would be discussed at the meeting; the subjects under consideration would be the situation in Bulgaria, the Geneva Protocol, Security, Soviet propaganda, the Hungarian problem, especially in relation to the intensification of the irredentist movement, and the Austrian question—Anschluss. Then he dismissed the journalists for the day. Particular interest was taken in the last topic—the union of Austria with Germany. It was known that Benesh in his speech of April 1 had said categorically that this could and would not be permitted, and that any proposal for a Danubian Federation would be equally barred. But it was also known that speeches had been made during the recent electoral campaign in Germany, such as that of Marx, the Chancellor, on a Greater Germany, and that interviews had been given by Austrian statesmen, as by Ramek, the Austrian Chancellor, which pronounced in favour of Anschluss.

The usual *communiqués* were issued during the conference, and, when its deliberations were concluded, the three Foreign Ministers offered their observations on it to the pressmen who had assembled to hear them. Duca emphasized the complete solidarity of the Little Entente. "I regard this," he said, "as the essential condition for clarifying the international situation, which cannot be considered as alarming, but nevertheless must be watched with great attention. It is necessary for the Little Entente to act to the fullest possible extent as a factor of peace and order in Central Europe. . . . As usual, we discussed all the important questions of international politics. The maintenance of peace on the basis of the Peace Treaties against any attempt at revision is, and will remain, the chief underlying idea of the Little Entente. Such attempts will always meet with energetic opposition from the three States. The Little Entente declares that such questions can in no circumstances be placed on the agenda of international affairs. I do not need to say how great is the satisfaction of Rumania that the *rapprochement* between Poland and Czechoslovakia is so cordial. Rumania has always been anxious that the relations between those two countries should be of the friendliest." He stated that Rumania was always ready to resume relations with Russia and recognize the Soviet Government, but only on condition that the Soviet recognized the present frontiers of Rumania. Referring to the possibility of a Greco-Rumanian alliance, he said he did not know whether such an alliance would come about soon; however, it was possible for relations between two countries to be stronger than alliance, and relations between Rumania and Greece were of that kind.

Nintchitch said: "Nobody who has followed our periodical conferences can help forming the impression that they manifest an immense solidarity." He then dealt specially with the relations between the Little Entente and Bulgaria, Hungary, and Austria respectively. "As regards Bulgaria, as we stated in the *communiqué*, it is our sincere desire to stabilize the situation of that country, which hitherto has appeared to be menaced as the result of internal disturbances. I draw particular attention to the action of the Third International, which makes its influence felt not only in Bulgaria, but in all European countries, although it is particularly strong in Bulgaria, as the Third International considers it the weakest point in Europe. Repeated references have been made to an anti-Communist group under the leadership of England, and it has even been suggested that this group would form the subject of our negotiations. I can assure you that I have had no such negotiations with the Bulgarian Government. Our State is in a position to combat the international Bolshevik danger with its own resources. The struggle which the Bulgarian Government is waging against Bolshevism is a serious one, but I am convinced that Bulgaria has at its disposal adequate resources to cope with Bolshevism, and I therefore regard as unjustified Bulgaria's demand for its army to be increased. The Little Entente is prepared to give Bulgaria moral support, but cannot allow the increase of the standing army, which was permitted till next June, to be continued beyond that date. I consider any extension of the date as dangerous." (The Council of Ambassadors had permitted a temporary increase of the small Bulgarian Army by 8,000 men, voluntarily enlisted, until the end of May.)

"As regards Hungary," Nintchitch went on, "according to our information, the carrying out of the financial and military clauses (under which the sanitation loan had been granted and procured) leaves much to be desired. Count Bethlen's statement (at the Budapest Conference of the Magyar Unionist Party on May 7, 1925), that the acceptance of these clauses was the result of coercion, causes us surprise. A victorious State has the right to demand from the defeated countries adequate assurances which will prevent a new war and guarantee peace. It should also not be forgotten that Hungary applied to the League of Nations for admission, and undertook to respect the Peace Treaties. We shall adopt towards Hungary an attitude in accordance with this. It is in the interest of all the Succession States, and particularly of the Little Entente States, as also of Italy, that the position of Austria should remain as it is." In reply to a question, Nintchitch said that the relations of the Little Entente to Italy left nothing to be desired, and he added that negotiations with Greece, with a view to renewing the old Yugoslav-Greek alliance, were being carried on amicably, and that the results would be for the advantage of both Greece and Yugoslavia.

It was reserved for Benesh to make the most general statement. He began by noting that chance had caused the conference to coincide with important international events: first, with the discussion of the Protocol at Geneva in March; in this matter the Little Entente found itself faced with an entirely new situation, which it had to examine; second, with the German proposals for the Western Pact of Guarantee; here again the Little Entente had to reach agreement and consider the consequences entailed for each of its States; third, with the new direction of German policy; fourth, with the Balkans; and fifth, with the Polish-Czechoslovak Treaties. He said: "In the question of the salvaging of Austria, there has recently been much talk about the union of Austria with Germany and the impossibility of an independent economic existence for Austria. Czechoslovakia has a direct interest in this question, Rumania to a slighter degree. Our standpoint is that the juridical and territorial *status quo* must be maintained in Central Europe; that is, we insist upon the loyal fulfilment of the Peace Treaty. We do not wish to oppress anyone, but only want peace.

"As regards Hungary, I will not go into details, such, for example, as the recent declarations of Count Bethlen. In Hungary there are certain people who are continually agitating. In the face of all that agitation we remain calm, and steadfastly pursue our own line of conduct. As regards the position in the Balkans and Bolshevik propaganda in general, I am of opinion that the Communist danger will diminish. Recently I informed a representative of the *Neue Freie Presse* of my belief that in two years the Communist danger will have completely disappeared. I am still of that opinion. By that I do not mean that the Communist danger is not of immediate importance, but merely that the power of the Communist disruptions is on the point of diminishing. But precisely because the Bolshevik schemes which aim at revolutionizing the whole world have everywhere resulted in failure, their convulsions are becoming more violent. Communism is having recourse to terrorism. For that reason we must be more attentive than ever to Communist action."

He touched briefly on the Geneva Protocol and bilateral or multilateral arbitration treaties, on sanctions and limited pacts of guarantee; in his view it did not matter whether the ideas of the Protocol were realized from below upwards or the other way about. Asked whether the Little Entente intended to enter a protest with the Ambassadors' Conference against extending the period granted to Bulgaria for increasing her army, Benesh replied that there would be no protest, but negotiations would take place. That conference, he recalled, consisted of the representatives of the Great Powers, who were duly concerned for the interests of the Little Entente, and therefore it was not necessary to address a protest to it, but merely to acquaint it with the Little Entente's point of view.

Referring again to Hungary, he stated that when the *communiqué* had announced that in certain contingencies the three States would be obliged to take cognizance of the facts and act accordingly, it made known the fundamental decisions which had been reached. The question of the carrying out of these decisions was, however, one of tactics, and thus was not a matter that could be dealt with publicly. Speaking of the difficulties of Austria, he maintained that she herself must try to cope with them. "As regards the situation," he said, "its difficulties cannot be removed at a moment's notice, as they are the result of the dissolution of the Austro-Hungarian Monarchy, and involve the replacing of the economic entity which that Monarchy constituted by various smaller entities. It will take decades before there is an equilibrium of Austria's social and economic relations. Till then the States of Europe must, if they do not support her, remain in closest cooperation with her. The economic cooperation of the Little Entente with her is one of its duties—a cooperation of advantage to both. In the situation that has arisen since the War new forms must be found, but this has not yet been possible in the short period that has elapsed since the conclusion of peace. I believe that at the moment when the position of Austria becomes stable, the endeavours towards union with Germany, which have recently been on the increase, will disappear. I am convinced that the Austrian Government entertain completely loyal feelings towards the States whose interest it is to maintain the present territorial status."

He went on to remark that he was an opponent of a Danubian Federation, and that such a federation was out of the question because nobody desired it. Anyhow, it was not desirable that there should be a tariff union or a free economic relation between the Succession States. He also stated that he was still anxious for relations with Russia, but, as before, must reserve the choice of a suitable time for the recognition of the Soviet Government.

He made no secret, however, of the fact that the present was less favourable than some earlier moments, for Communism had made a considerable advance in Czechoslovakia and other countries. In the course of an interview Benesh had already expressed the opinion that the general situation of Europe was continually improving and gave no reason for alarm. He thought that there was no fear of a conflict, and that neither the political change in Germany nor Bolshevik propaganda presented any immediate danger.

Towards Locarno

At the June meeting of the Council of the League of Nations at Geneva, discussion turned largely on the question of Security and cognate subjects, such as the proposed arbitration treaties. Concerning these matters Benesh delivered another of his carefully prepared speeches or expositions on June 23, 1925, in the Foreign Affairs Committee of the Czechoslovak Chamber of Deputies at Prague. After emphasizing the importance of the new political understanding between Great Britain and France, he dwelt on the fact that, for the first time since the War, Germany was going to be treated as an equal. He laid stress on the conclusion of arbitration treaties between Germany on the one side and France, Belgium, Poland, and Czechoslovakia on the other, and saw in them another advance of the most distinct kind in the consolidation of peace. Czechoslovakia was anxious not to lose anything guaranteed to her under the Peace Treaties, and it must be made clear that she was included in the negotiations for the Pact of Guarantee to the extent that the security of the western frontier of Germany was dependent on peace and security in the east. In practice this meant that the Czechoslovak alliance with France must not be disturbed in any way owing to the signature of the new pact, and that this must be made part of the pact in some form or other. The arbitration treaties must be concluded as a consequence of and simultaneously with the Western Pact. If Germany accepted the principle laid down in the Allied Note of June 16, negotiations between her and Czechoslovakia could follow and an understanding on arbitration could be reached. Dealing with affairs of particular interest to the Little Entente, Benesh intimated that an agreement had been arrived at with Italy for cooperation on the Austrian question. Two or three weeks previously Bulgaria had been told by the Ambassadors' Conference that she must disband the additional forces that she had been permitted to enroll to deal with internal disturbances; the wishes of the Little Entente were thus respected and satisfied.

The Salonika Question

Negotiations which had been proceeding for some time between Yugoslavia and Greece for a renewal of the alliance of the two States led to a conference that ended in failure in June, 1925. The Greek delegates ascribed this unfortunate result to the claim of the Yugoslav Government to administer the Salonika–Ghevgeli Railway in Greek territory, and thus to convert the "Serb Free Zone" into a Yugoslav port linked by a railway corridor with Southern Serbia. On the other hand, the Yugoslav delegates insisted on the economic necessity of Yugoslav Governmental control of the whole railway system from the Danube to the Aegean.

During the eventful sessions of the League of Nations in September at Geneva, a special conference of the three Foreign Ministers—Benesh, Nintchitch, and Duca, as before—of the Little Entente was held on September 7, 1925; its main business was the consideration of the Security Pact and the arbitration treaties; and the Ministers found themselves in complete agreement. Speaking in the Czechoslovak Parliament on October 31, 1925, Benesh, alluding to this conference, said: "I had the opportunity of discussing these questions with the Ministers Nintchitch and Duca, and I can assure you that the two friendly States consider with us those recent developments with a single eye, and rejoice with us in the marked progress made in the consolidation of Europe and in the new guarantees for our security. The situation has improved for them as for ourselves." The Yugoslav-Greek trouble was also discussed at this Little Entente Conference, and it was decided that the standpoint of Yugoslavia should be supported by the three States jointly, although opinion in League circles was on the whole unfavourable to it. Rentis, the Greek Foreign Minister, who was also at Geneva, had several conversations with Nintchitch, at one of which Briand assisted, the upshot being that negotiations were resumed through the ordinary diplomatic channels. A mixed commission met at Salonika in December, 1925, but after prolonged discussion without result suspended its work in February, 1926. However, the Yugoslavs and the Greeks were in contact again at Geneva in the following month, and the subject was reopened.

Yugoslav Consolidation

It was during the period covered by the clash over Salonika and the Ghevgeli railway that a great change took place in the internal politics of Yugoslavia; it was nothing less than a second reunion of the Serbs and Croats. In March, 1925, Paul Raditch, a nephew of the imprisoned leader of the Croat Peasant Party, made a declaration in favour of complete Yugoslav unity under the Karageorgevitch dynasty. This statement led to negotiations between the Pashitch or Radical Party and Paul Raditch and his Croat supporters, which ended in an agreement for cooperation between the Radicals and the Raditchists, and the formation of a new Government on the basis of a coalition composed of Serbs and Croats, the latter being given four portfolios in the new Cabinet. Immediately after this Cabinet had been sworn in on July 19, 1925, King Alexander signed a decree abandoning the proceedings against Stephen Raditch and the five other Croat leaders who had been arrested with him in the previous January; they were released forthwith.

In a leading article, *The Times* on July 20 observed: "By the outside world the fact that the chief Serbian Party and the chief Croat Party have at last agreed, after years of recrimination, to form a joint Government will be generally regarded as an indication that the Yugoslav peoples are at last beginning to fulfil the best hopes of their reunion." On July 22 Stephen Raditch was in Belgrade, after having had an audience with the King at Bled on the previous day; he declared that he was done for ever with Republicanism or Communism. On November 18, 1925, he was appointed Minister of Education. It was noteworthy that the first occasion on which the Raditchists left the Opposition and voted with the Pashitch Government was when Nintchitch, replying to an interpellation in the Skupshtina on July 13, made an emphatic pronouncement against the union of Austria with Germany. In a strong speech Paul Raditch supported the Foreign Minister.

A week later a Yugoslav Delegation signed at Nettuno a series of conventions, notes, and agreements, nearly thirty in number, which had been elaborated at conferences of Italians and Yugoslavs held at Venice and Florence. Some of these documents dealt with questions arising out of the execution of the Peace Treaties and reaffirmed the territorial status in Central Europe as defined in them, particular mention being made of the banning of the union of Austria with Germany. Other documents related to the rights of Yugoslavs living in Fiume and of Italians domiciled in Dalmatia; a special agreement dealt with disputable matters springing from the division of land in the Fiume area. Other documents again were concerned with the reduction of railway tariffs, the self-government of Yugoslav Orthodox communities in Italy, and so on. These agreements implied one more step towards the consolidation of the peace of Europe, but they were not ratified at the time—and things happened that delayed ratification by the Yugoslav Parliament till 1928. On the ground that the agreements conceded too much to Italy, there was considerable opposition to them both in the Skupshtina and among a large section of the Yugoslav people, who regarded Mussolini, and what were believed to be his plans in the Balkans, with no very friendly eye. Hostility increased and deepened when, in 1926, the question of Albania became acute.

The Locarno Treaties

On October 16, 1925, the Final Protocol concerning the seven interlocking treaties was signed at Locarno. A compromise had been reached between the Allies and Germany respecting the Sixteenth Article of the Covenant of the League of Nations, which solved the last difficulty standing in the way of her entrance into the League. The German Parliament passed and Hindenburg signed the necessary legislative measures. When the treaties were signed in London on December 1, a Collective Note to Germany was appended which embodied what had been agreed to regarding the Covenant's Article XVI —which was interpreted: "The obligations resulting from the said Article on the members of the League must be understood to mean that each State Member of the League is bound to cooperate loyally and effectively in support of the Covenant and in resistance to any act of aggression, to an extent which is compatible with its military situation, and which takes its geographical position into account."

A few days after the conclusion of the sessions at Locarno, Benesh had met Nintchitch at Bled for the purpose of discussing with him all that had been done. Duca was unable to join the two other representatives of the Little Entente, but was kept informed by telegraph of the course of their conversation. On October 30, 1925, Benesh delivered the speech, already referred to, in the Permanent Parliamentary Commission at Prague on the Locarno Treaties; it was afterwards published in French, under the title *Les Accords de Locarno*, by the Orbis Company of Prague, 1925. It sketched the proceedings that had led to the Locarno Conference, and offered a penetrating analysis of the various treaties. He said that he had worked in full harmony with Skrzynski, for whose country Locarno was of great political importance: "The agreements bring to Poland and all the other States a profound appeasement and permit of further consolidation from all points of view." He thought that one result of Locarno would be that there would soon be normal relations with Russia. He believed that another would be an improvement of the situation with respect to Austria and also to Hungary: "I feel sure," he said, "that the attitude of the Little Entente to these States will also be regulated in accordance with the spirit of the Locarno agreements." He hoped that, discarding illusions, the German population of Czechoslovakia would draw a moral from these treaties, namely, to work in peaceful and loyal cooperation with other races in the country.

On November 5 Duca made an important speech in the Senate of the Rumanian Parliament at Bucarest. After referring to the Rumanian alliances with Yugoslavia, Czechoslovakia, and Poland, which had in view the maintenance of the peace of Central Europe, he said that two things still obscured the outlook, one being the attitude of Soviet Russia, and the other the mentality of some of the peoples who had been vanquished in the War. "Russia continued to be enigmatic as to her intentions and very energetic in her activities. Some of the defeated States were unwilling to adapt themselves to the situation created by the War and the triumph of the principle of Nationalities." A certain relaxation, he continued, had been brought about by the Locarno Treaties, but they did not, unfortunately, apply to that part of Europe with which Rumania was most concerned. Although some nations, especially the United States, refused to resume relations with the Soviet on account of its political creed, Rumania did not object to the form of government Russia had chosen to adopt. Rumania was willing, therefore, to renew diplomatic relations with the Soviet, but on the express condition that it recognized Rumania's territorial integrity. Furthermore, Rumania was ready to conclude a permanent non-aggression treaty, and had repeated her offer in this sense at the League of Nations that year. Duca's words met with no response from the Soviet, which, moreover, publicly and decidedly dissociated itself from the Locarno Treaties.

"The Problem of Small Nations" Again

When Benesh was in London for the signing of the treaties, he delivered a lecture at King's College on December 2, 1925, in memory of the tenth anniversary of the foundation of its School of Slavonic Studies. His subject was "The Problem of Small Nations after the World War," and the opening sentences of the lecturer could not but recall that almost exactly ten years had passed since Masaryk had delivered there his first address as a lecturer of the College, his theme being "The Problem of the Small Nations in the European Crisis" (p. 59). Lord Oxford and Asquith was in the chair, and remarked that he occupied it in "belated performance" of a promise made ten years before. In the course of his observations, he spoke of "that artificial and unstable conglomerate, the Austro-Hungarian Empire." Of Benesh he said: "We are honoured to-day by the presence of one of the statesmen who have just signed the greatest and, we believe, the most fruitful international instrument since the conclusion of the Great War. Dr. Benesh has been a foremost figure, not only in nurturing and guiding the infant years of his own State, but also in the counsels of Europe in assisting to bring together the nations in harmonious association alike for political and economic aims. We recognize his services to international amity and peace, we welcome him here wholeheartedly, and we shall listen to his address with interest and respect."

In his exordium Benesh characterized Masaryk's lecture in October, 1915, as a great political event. The movement associated with it had been particularly helped forward by a statement sent by their present chairman, then Mr. Asquith, Prime Minister, whom illness had prevented from taking the chair at the meeting addressed by Masaryk. Benesh proceeded to "pick up the thread of President Masaryk's discourse of that day, point out the further development of the question of the small nations of Europe after the War, and show how President Masaryk himself was able to bring into effect those ideas of which, ten years ago here in London, he was the exponent and upholder." Enlarging on the meaning and philosophy of the War and the idea of the freedom of small nations, Benesh discussed the origins of the War, the idea of Nationalism, and pan-Germanism—a "monstrosity from the point of view of humanitarian philosophy." Turning his attention to the political organization of the nations of Central Europe after the War, he spoke of the difficulties caused by the inclusion of National Minorities in the new and old States, and of the way in which these difficulties had been met by the Minority treaties. States possessing Minorities must, he said, treat them with justice and wisdom; on the other hand, precisely because the Minority problem was not one which applied to a few States, but was of world-wide political significance, the Minorities must themselves realize that what was known as Minority policy must not be carried to extremes; it must have limits, it must be moderate, and could generally be pursued only within reasonable bounds.

Speaking of Austria and Hungary, he said: "Our (Czechoslovak) treaties of alliance with the States of the Little Entente are being progressively transformed into treaties which are intended exclusively for the maintenance of peace and good order in Central Europe and for close economic and cultural cooperation. We hope that just as the spirit of the Locarno treaties will hold sway on the Rhine, so also will it reign on the Danube. Sooner or later there will be a Locarno also for the States of Central Europe. The States forming the Little Entente are already working energetically to this end."

Hungarian Bank-Note Forgeries

What was generally called the affair of the Hungarian Bank-Note Forgeries, which aroused attention and much controversy throughout Europe early in 1926, demonstrated how far the spirit of Locarno was from holding sway over the Danube. The affair began with the arrest in Amsterdam of three Hungarians of good social position on a charge of passing forged thousand-franc notes of the Bank of France in mid-December, 1925. Colonel Jankovitch, one of the three men, said in defence that the notes had been forged and put into circulation from patriotic motives—a statement that threw into an uproar almost at once the whole of Central Europe. The Hungarian Government was compelled to take the matter up. The preliminary police investigation showed that Nadossy, Chief of Police not only in Budapest but of all Hungary, and other Government officials were concerned in the affair; among others implicated was Prince Windischgraetz, a former Minister and intimate adviser of the late Emperor Charles. It was discovered that the forgeries were prepared in the Geographical Institute in Budapest, that is, on official premises.

The affair certainly had a very ugly look, though Bethlen, the Hungarian Prime Minister, denied all complicity on the part of the Hungarian Government in it. In Czechoslovakia, however, the forgeries recalled the forgeries of Czechoslovak bank-notes in the years 1919 to 1921, which involved the Czechoslovak Government in a loss of upwards of thirty million crowns (about £230,000). Substituting dinars for crowns, Yugoslavia had had a somewhat similar experience in 1921. Inquiry traced the root of the mischief to Budapest in both cases. Touching the forgeries of Czechoslovak crowns, the Czechoslovak Government addressed two Notes to the Hungarian Government, on December 22, 1922, and February 15, 1923, respectively, but received no reply, and therefore reserved to itself liberty to take action later if it saw fit. The inquiry into the forgeries of French francs revealed new clues. The Czechoslovak Minister in Budapest, on January 7, 1926, pressed for an answer to the two Notes, and was told on January 28, 1926, that the investigations into the forgeries of Czechoslovak crowns had been suspended for lack of evidence. Now, Nadossy, one of the persons seriously implicated in the French franc forgeries, had been in charge of these investigations; it was he who had announced that they had been suspended; more than that, he had demanded that in the interests of Hungary nothing should be written about the matter.

In view of this, Czechoslovakia desired the Hungarian Government to extend the inquiry into the French franc forgeries so as to include the Czechoslovak crown forgeries. In the Little Entente States, especially Czechoslovakia and Yugoslavia, there was wild excitement, which was reflected in their newspapers. It was stated that the money which would have been realized if the forged franc notes had been disposed of successfully was to have been used in irredentist schemes; there was talk of an "Otto putsch," an "Albrecht putsch," an "Awakening Magyar" putsch, and the like (Otto, the eldest son of the late Emperor Charles; Albrecht, Archduke, a relative of Otto, living in Hungary—both had their partisans among the Magyars; "Awakening Magyars," the name of an irredentist organization). On January 26 *The Times* published an interview which Bethlen had given its Budapest correspondent on the previous day. Bethlen said he hoped it would soon be abundantly clear that the Hungarian Government was not attempting to hide anything, and he stated that a Parliamentary Committee of Inquiry had been set up; it would have the opportunity of investigating all the circumstances and all the evidence; the French police and officials of the Bank of France would collaborate. Referring to the accusations that were being made, Bethlen said: "After all, thirty million francs was not a sum of money which could provide the sinews for any far-reaching plot of an internal character, much less for an international conspiracy." So far nothing had been discovered which incriminated the "Awakening Magyars" as an organization, but it was probable that some of those arrested were members of it. He saw the "origin of the whole affair in the exhausted, sick mentality springing from the many sufferings of the country and in the difficult circumstances in which so many people found themselves. People who before had plenty and now had nothing, and who tried in desperation to find some way out, took even to crime." Excitement over the affair continued unabated for some time. The forgeries and the resultant situation were among the topics discussed at a special conference of the Foreign Ministers of the Little Entente, which was held on February 10, 1926, at Timisoara (Temesvar), Rumania.

Little Entente Conference at Timisoara

When the periodical conferences of the Little Entente were initiated the intention was to hold them semi-annually, but in practice this was difficult, as the convenience of each of its representatives—the three Foreign Ministers—had to be suited for the given date, and this was not always practicable. The Timisoara Conference was arranged in view chiefly of the importance attached to the meeting of the Council of the League of Nations in March, 1926, when it was anticipated that Germany would enter the League. The *communiqué* issued at the close of the day's proceedings intimated that Nintchitch, Benesh, and Duca had passed in review, according to custom, the general political situation, with respect to which their views were identical, and had given particular attention to the questions which were to be debated at the March meeting of the League; a common line of action would be pursued at the Disarmament Conference. Locarno and its consequences were discussed and found concordant with the eminently pacific aims of the Little Entente, which led it to envisage the possibility of consolidating peace in the Balkans still more firmly. The hope was expressed that the "sad affair" of the Hungarian forgeries would in the interest of peace be completely elucidated and that steps would be taken to prevent anything of the kind again. It was the firm desire of the Little Entente to continue, in full solidarity and cordiality, the work of pacification needed in the interests of the three States, and pursued by them for five years without halt, despite international vicissitudes.

After the conference the Ministers received representatives of the Press, who were addressed first by Nintchitch. He said there had been an exchange of views on the general situation. Asked whether the passage in the *communiqué* on the Hungarian forgeries was to be taken as a suggestion that the measures adopted were insufficient, Nintchitch replied: "The matter is only in process of development. In 1920 Yugoslav dinars were forged, but the Magyar authorities then frustrated any attempt at investigation, and the official we sent to help in the inquiry just escaped being murdered. But the same things were apparent then as are apparent now. We are convinced that the present Hungarian Government will shed light on the matter. While we are, of course, most interested in the forged dinar notes, we recognize that the question of the forged franc notes is much more important as being on so much larger a scale. In our opinion the Hungarian people can choose any form of Government, but Hungary must fulfil her undertaking not to permit a Habsburg to ascend the throne." Nintchitch then spoke of a Balkan Pact. Naturally this interested Yugoslavia in the first place. She accepted in principle the idea of the application of the Locarno Agreements to such a pact, but at the moment her relations with Greece and Bulgaria were the more important things to consider, and it was necessary that first of all some questions still pending should be clarified. A Balkan Pact in the spirit of Locarno would make the whole Balkan situation much better, though at present it was good.

Benesh spoke next. He said: "Our present meeting is an extraordinary one. As the Rumanian Foreign Minister was unable to take part in the ordinary periodical conference of the Little Entente, we decided at least to exchange views, and discuss what we would do at the Council of the League before going to it." Touching Locarno, he stated that he had set forth his views fully in a speech in the Czechoslovak Parliament (p. 265). He thought that peace in Western Europe was secured to a large extent by the treaties, and that they would also have a good influence in Central Europe. "The work of Locarno is of great value and ought to be made general by similar agreements for Central and Eastern Europe." Concerning the forgeries, Benesh said he had simply requested from Budapest a reply to the Notes sent three or four years before, and had not yet got it. With regard to the negotiations between Czechoslovakia and Soviet Russia on the question of recognition, he stated that they were going on. "When I left Prague the matter had not been settled." Replying to a question, Benesh said there had been no discussion on admitting another State into the Little Entente.

In his remarks Duca underlined the harmony existing in the Little Entente, and then spoke of the work of this conference in terms very similar to those employed by the two other Ministers. On the question of disarmament he maintained that Rumania's interest was to disarm, as she had accomplished her national unity and wanted nothing more. "But we cannot lose sight of realities," he continued: "we are the neighbours of a great country which is not a member of the League of Nations and which at present refuses to enter it. Therefore, disarmament with us is closely related to our security." Rumania, too, was in principle in favour of a Balkan Pact, but felt that the time was scarcely ripe for it, as there were controversial matters still to be adjusted, as, for example, the differences existing between Yugoslavia and Greece. Paying further tribute to the Little Entente, he said: "During the four years in which I have been Foreign Minister of Rumania I have assisted at numerous conferences dealing with world politics, and I have always felt a satisfaction, and I may add the greatest pride always, in stating that among all vicissitudes the Little Entente constitutes a strong block united by the same interests and the same ideal."

Italo-Yugoslav Relations

Among the subjects connected with the international situation discussed at the Timisoara Conference were the relations of the Little Entente as a whole and of Yugoslavia in particular to Italy. Some weeks earlier Mussolini had made a strong speech, in which he said that German penetration must be repulsed from the Brenner, Italy's northern frontier, and that, if the necessity arose, the flag of Italy might wave beyond the Brenner. What underlay his words was the proposal, or rather suggestion, again adumbrated in certain quarters, that Austria should be united to Germany; he made it perfectly clear that Italy was determinedly opposed to such an idea. This, of course, was in keeping with the policy of the Little Entente, whose orientation, however, was towards France rather than Italy. At this time France and Italy could scarcely be called the best of friends, but the Little Entente, though it could not like the replacement of French leadership in the Balkans by Italian, which seemed to be the aim of Mussolini, yet held without break to its programme of peace all round and general consolidation. That the Italian Army had been greatly improved and strengthened, and had been freshly equipped with munitions and aeroplanes, was a matter of common knowledge, but, after all, it did not appear that Mussolini wanted war, and it seemed that this military refurbishment was to be taken rather as a sign that, as he indicated in what he said on the Upper Adige question, he would stand no nonsense.

To get on terms of real friendship with Italy was among the Little Entente States mainly the concern of Yugoslavia, and, as already recorded, Nintchitch, her Foreign Minister, had already shown himself most desirous of coming to a good understanding with Mussolini—witness the Pact of Rome, 1924, and the Nettuno Conventions, 1925. The latter, however, remained unratified, and this put Nintchitch in a somewhat delicate position; still, Mussolini's uncompromising statement on the pan-German agitation opened the door to further negotiations. On the other hand, the susceptibilities of France *vis-à-vis* the Balkans had to be considered. Nintchitch took both Great Powers into account, first by visiting Rome and Paris immediately afterwards. He arrived in Rome on February 25, saw the King, and had long conversations with Mussolini and the high officials of the Ministry of Foreign Affairs. The burden of their talk was concerned chiefly with precautions to be taken in common against any development favourable to Anschluss, with regard to which their views were identical, as were those of France and the two other Little Entente States.

This identity of views hinted that there might be a new Guarantee Pact of the territorial status in Central and Eastern Europe established by the Peace Treaties and conceived in the spirit of Locarno, a pact in which both France and Italy could join. But since 1924 there had been a project for a Franco-Yugoslav Treaty of the same kind as the existing Franco-Polish and Franco-Czechoslovak Treaties. The Yugoslav Government wished to sign the projected treaty, but Mussolini looked askance at it. From Rome Nintchitch went on to Paris, and negotiated with Briand and the Quai d'Orsay an agreement which was initialled, the final signing of it being postponed, in deference to Mussolini, till there was a new Italo-Yugoslav Treaty; in the upshot there was no such treaty, because Mussolini subordinated the conclusion of any further treaty to the ratification of the Nettuno Agreements by the Skupshtina. Referring to his visits to Rome and Paris, Nintchitch said in the Skupshtina on March 25, 1926: "I have the satisfaction and the pride to state that the foreign policy of Yugoslavia did not have to wait for the Locarno Agreements, but has all along been conceived in the spirit which animates them. The conclusion of the treaties forming the Little Entente, and the signature of the treaty of friendship and cordial collaboration with Italy, have not only consolidated the relations of the contracting States to each other. While confirming the status given by the Peace Treaties to this part of Europe, they have made possible the speedy re-establishment of normal relations among ourselves and the neighbouring States which were our enemies during the War. And, in this order of ideas, we can say that we have done everything we could do." In the meantime the Greek Minister of Foreign Affairs visited Mussolini at Rome, and *communiqués* were published stressing the complete harmony of the views of the Italian and Greek Governments on Balkan policy.

Czechoslovak-Austrian Arbitration Treaty

Amidst other Ministerial comings and goings which preceded the March, 1926, meeting of the League of Nations was the visit paid by Benesh to Vienna, where he arrived on March 4 on his way to Geneva, exchanged visits with the Austrian President, and concluded a treaty of arbitration of the Locarno type and altogether in the spirit of the League of Nations. On being asked by a pressman whether the visit of Nintchitch to Italy would adversely affect Austria or Czechoslovakia, Benesh expressed the opinion that any agreement arrived at by the two countries concerned would contribute to the general peace of Europe, and need by no means be interpreted as being directed against either Austria or Czechoslovakia. Closer economic relations between Czechoslovakia and Austria, he said, were most desirable, but could only be reached by slow and successive steps, because of various divergent interests. Of Hungary, he said that he thought she would enter into a guarantee pact in time, and Czechoslovakia was certainly prepared to meet her half-way. Described as a Treaty of Conciliation and Arbitration, this instrument was signed at Vienna on March 5, 1926; it was ratified on May 31 and registered with the League of Nations on July 28, 1926. It consisted of twenty-one Articles, and was concluded for a period of ten years. It provided for the setting up of a Permanent Conciliation Commission to "elucidate questions in dispute, to collect with that object all necessary information by means of inquiry or otherwise, and to endeavour to bring the Parties to an agreement." If agreement could not be obtained by or through this commission, the subject in dispute was to be referred to the Permanent Court of International Justice. Benesh was in Geneva on August 7, and three days later conferred with Ramek, the Austrian Chancellor, on the commercial agreements between their two countries.

On March 17, 1926, the Assembly of the League in special session at Geneva reported with regret that, owing to the veto of Brazil, no resolution could be passed for the admission of Germany to the League, and expressed the hope that the entry of Germany might be effected at the regular September meeting of the Assembly. It was not alone the failure as regards Germany that made postponement desirable, for there were the differences regarding the composition of the Council, on which agreement was difficult to attain. Though the breakdown produced a general feeling of depression, the meetings at Geneva, stretching as they did over several weeks, gave abundant opportunity for conversations among the Prime Ministers, Foreign Ministers, and other statesmen present which was taken full advantage of. It was rumoured that one result would be a conference of representatives of France, Italy, the Little Entente States, and Austria for the purpose of trying to set up a Central European Pact—a pact distinct from the suggested Balkan Pact, of which much had already been heard. It was known that Nintchitch had made the Salonika railway question a special subject of discussion with Rouphos, the Greek Foreign Minister, at Geneva, and had hopes of reaching agreement with Greece.

The various statesmen returned to their homes in the third week of March.

Particular significance was attached to a visit to Prague of Ramek, the Austrian Chancellor, towards the end of the month, after visiting Berlin, from which he arrived in the Czechoslovak capital on March 30. He was welcomed in both cities; it was noteworthy that the Czechoslovak Press and people, irrespective of race or party, greeted him warmly. He lunched with President Masaryk and had a long talk with Benesh, with whom he dined in the evening. At a Press reception he laid stress on the importance of friendly relations between Austria and Czechoslovakia, and after a reference to the arbitration treaty recently signed in Vienna, said he was confident that this work of peace would soon be crowned with a commercial treaty, the negotiations for which were entering the decisive stage.

Polish-Rumanian Treaty of Guarantee

A Treaty of Guarantee between Poland and Rumania was signed at Bucarest on March 26, 1926. Its Protocol stated that as the Convention of Defensive Alliance (p. 136), which expired on April 3, 1926, had been recognized to have had beneficial results for the cause of peace, the two States agreed to conclude this new treaty for a period of five years. In imitation of the Locarno Treaties it was a regional agreement in conformity with the Covenant of the League, as was shown especially in its Second Article, which ran: "In the event of Poland or Rumania, contrary to the undertakings imposed by Articles XII, XIII, and XV of the Covenant of the League of Nations, being attacked without provocation, Poland and reciprocally Rumania, acting in application of Article XVI of the Covenant of the League of Nations, undertake immediately to lend each other aid and assistance. In the event of the Council of the League of Nations, when dealing with a question brought before it in accordance with the provisions of the Covenant of the League of Nations, being unable to secure the acceptance of its report by all its members other than the Representatives of the parties to the dispute, and in the event of Poland or Rumania being attacked without provocation, Poland or reciprocally Rumania, acting in application of Article XV, paragraph 7, of the Covenant of the League of Nations, will immediately lend each other aid and assistance. Should a dispute of the kind provided for in Article XVII of the Covenant of the League of Nations arise, and Poland or Rumania be attacked without provocation, Poland and reciprocally Rumania undertake immediately to lend each other aid and assistance. The details of application of the above provisions shall be settled by technical agreements."

The Third Article of this treaty provided: "If, in spite of their efforts to maintain peace, the two States are compelled to enter on a defensive war under the terms of the foregoing article and of the First Article (Poland and Rumania undertake to respect and preserve against external aggression the territorial integrity and existing political independence of each other) of this treaty, each undertakes not to negotiate or conclude an armistice or peace without the participation of the other State." Ratifications of this treaty were exchanged at Warsaw on February 9, 1927, and the treaty itself was registered with the League on March 7, 1927. The day after this treaty was signed the Foreign Affairs Committee of the Polish Seym or Parliament, after a debate on the report of Skrzynski on the March meeting of the League, decided to continue to press the Polish claim for a permanent seat on the Council of the League, a claim which was one of the things which caused agitation at that meeting.

On the day after the signing of the treaty between Poland and Rumania there occurred an important change in the political situation in the latter country; it had no connexion, however, with the treaty itself. The Bratianu Government had existed for the full term of four years; a strong administration, it had done much for the internal consolidation of the country; on its resignation King Ferdinand, on the advice of Bratianu, sent for Averescu, who formed a new Government on March 30, 1926, Mitilineu replacing Duca as Foreign Minister. Up to this time Rumania's relations with Italy had been correct rather than cordial; Averescu, who had received part of his military training in Italy, oriented Rumanian foreign policy towards Mussolini,

M. MITILENEU

and soon began negotiations with him for a treaty of friendship, accompanied by an arbitration agreement.

German-Soviet Treaty of Berlin

Surprise, speculation, and even alarm were caused throughout Europe when in mid-April, 1926, *The Times* announced that it had learned "from several excellent sources" that the German Government was negotiating with the Soviet with the object of concluding a treaty designed "to adapt the terms of the treaty concluded between the two Governments at Rapallo in 1922 to the terms of the Locarno Treaty." It stated that the British, French, and Italian Governments had been informed of these negotiations, and said that the new treaty might be described, with "reference to the treaties recently concluded with the Powers of Western and Central Europe, as a 'reinsurance' treaty." Instantly the Press was flooded with denials, conjectures, and comments of all kinds, but it was soon established that the statement of *The Times* was well-founded. The idea of the treaty produced marked dissatisfaction in Paris. The German Government made it known that it regarded the treaty as complementary to and in no way at variance with Locarno; the notion that it was in the nature of a reinsurance treaty was scouted; what was aimed at was asserted to be the creation of a situation in Eastern Europe similar to that created by Locarno in the West, and the keeping of German policy free from either a Western or an Eastern orientation.

A great deal turned on the precise interpretation Germany put on the reservations which she had made respecting Article XVI of the Covenant of the League of Nations, and which had been accepted by the Allies at Locarno (p. 269). With a view to elucidating this and other matters connected with the Soviet-German Treaty, Benesh addressed to some of the Locarno Powers a series of questions. This he did in his capacity as a member of the Council of the League and in the interests equally of Germany and all concerned. The treaty was signed in Berlin on April 24 by Stresemann for Germany and by Krestinsky, Russian Ambassador at Berlin, for the Soviet; its text was published two days later, and with it were two separate Notes signed by Stresemann and Krestinsky respectively. Ratified at Berlin on June 29, 1926, it was registered, together with the two Notes, with the League on August 3, following. Assurances were given from Berlin that no supplementary secret treaty or understanding had come into existence; but that Germany as a whole attached some very special value to the treaty—which was perhaps not altogether apparent on the surface—was demonstrated by its joyful acceptance by all German political parties.

The terms of the treaty were canvassed and scrutinized minutely everywhere; they were severely criticized in France; many observers thought that the plain meaning of the whole business was that Germany had contracted out of Locarno and League obligations in favour of Soviet Russia. In his Note Stresemann had insisted on Germany's loyalty to the pacific principles of the League, but he had at the same time pointed out that when Germany was in the League the question, whether in case of any conflict the Soviet was or was not the aggressor, could not be decided without the assent of Germany. The inference was obvious. However, in the end the Allies accepted the German assurances, and the agitation over the treaty died away. An event of a striking and unexpected character which occurred in Poland about this time drew attention away from the Soviet-German Treaty; this was the *coup d'état* by which Pilsudski established himself in chief power at Warsaw after causing the resignation of Wojcischowski, the Polish President. Pilsudski stated that his purpose was to hasten the internal consolidation of his country and that there would be no change in its foreign policy.

Franco-Rumanian Treaty

A treaty which possessed great interest for the Little Entente was signed at Paris on June 10, 1926, between France and Rumania. Described as a Treaty of Friendship, this instrument had as its First Article an undertaking that France and Rumania would in no case attack or invade each other or resort to war against each other. This stipulation, however, was not to apply to the exercise of legitimate defence, that was to say, resistance to a violation of the undertaking contained in this Article; to action in pursuance of Article XVI of the Covenant of the League of Nations; or to action as the result of a decision taken by the Assembly or Council of the League of Nations in pursuance of Article XV, paragraph 7, of the Covenant of the League of Nations, provided that in this last event the action was directed against a State which was the first to attack. The other Articles were equally within the framework of the League of Nations; for example, Article V ran: "The High Contracting Parties agree to concert their policy in the event of any modification or attempted modification of the political status of the countries of Europe and, subject to such resolutions as may be passed in the matter by the Council or the Assembly of the League of Nations, to confer with one another concerning the attitude to be observed in such an event by each Party." In brief, this treaty was of a type similar to the Franco-Polish and the Franco-Czechoslovak Treaties, but it had a Protocol added to the effect that Rumania, whose sole desire was to work for the development of her internal resources in a spirit of peace and respect for treaties and subject to the maintenance of the *status quo*, confirmed the declaration made at the Genoa Conference on May 17, 1922, at the fifth meeting of the first Commission, by M. I. Bratianu, the President of the Rumanian Delegation, concerning a permanent undertaking of non-aggression as towards Russia, based on the *status quo*. "Rumania is prepared to extend this undertaking to all her neighbours. Rumania interpreted the said undertaking as prohibiting her from making an attack on Russia with her regular forces and similarly from allowing regular troops to be trained on her territory for purposes of an attack on Russia." Accompanying the treaty, which was to remain in force for ten years, was an arbitration agreement of the kind that had now become tolerably familiar. Several months passed before this treaty was made public. It was ratified at Paris on November 8, 1926, and registered with the League on November 22, 1926.

In his brochure entitled *L'Europe balkanique et danubienne de 1925 à 1928*, Mousset suggested that the delay in publishing the treaty was "strange and only explicable by Averescu's wish not to offend Italian susceptibilities." At the Rumanian general elections on May 25 Averescu and his party gained a majority of the seats; under the peculiar electoral law of Rumania this majority was converted into 275 votes out of a total of 387 in the Parliament, whereas in the preceding Parliament the party counted only eight deputies. One of his first acts was to conclude a loan with Italy for two hundred million lire; its terms were onerous, but Rumania was glad to get it to help in stabilizing her currency. Negotiations for the Italo-Rumanian Treaty were pushed on, and at the next Little Entente Conference, which was held at Bled, Yugoslavia, on June 17 and 18, 1926, Mitilineu was in a position to acquaint his colleagues with what was toward between Averescu, his chief, and Mussolini.

Little Entente Conference at Bled

This conference was preceded on June 13 by an event of paramount significance to the Little Entente—the renewal of two of the treaties of defensive alliance on which this political organization had been built. This was effected by the signing on that day at Bucarest of two Protocols, one between Rumania and Czechoslovakia for prolonging the convention concluded by them at Bucarest on Aprii 3, 1921, and the other between Rumania and Yugoslavia for prolonging the convention concluded by them at Belgrade on June 7, 1921. These treaties had been extended by Protocols in 1923 for three years (p. 218); they were now extended in similar language for three years more. There was no need to do anything respecting the Treaty of Alliance between Yugoslavia and Czechoslovakia concluded on August 31, 1922, the remaining Little Entente Treaty, as it still had a year to run. The signing of the two new Protocols was made public immediately, but this did not prevent rumour from proclaiming once more that the Little Entente was on the point of dissolution. Indeed, a lying report was actually published stating that the conference broke up in confusion owing to the dropping by Mitilineu of a "bombshell."

Many journalists had gathered at Bled in view of the continued crisis through which the League of Nations was passing and the admitted importance of the Little Entente as a prime factor in the general international situation thus disturbed. The conference opened in the morning of June 17, and consisted of Nintchitch, who presided, Benesh, and Mitilineu, the Foreign Ministers of the three States. Two *communiqués* were issued, one at the close of the first day's proceedings, and the other at the end of the conference next day. They were couched in very general terms, and gave little positive information—this was given in the speeches made by the three Ministers to the pressmen after the conference was over; but the first *communiqué* stated that there had been an exchange of the ratifications of the two defensive alliances which had been renewed on July 13.

To the journalists Benesh said: "I am entirely satisfied with the results of our discussions. I would emphasize that both Dr. Nintchitch and I are delighted with M. Mitilineu, our new collaborator. We worked for several years with M. Duca, and esteem him for his sincerity and loyalty. In M. Mitilineu we see a man who follows closely in the footsteps of his predecessor, and is as frank and sincere as he. As regards our negotiations, I would first lay stress on the ratification of the two treaties prolonged between ourselves (Czechoslovakia) and Rumania and between Yugoslavia and Rumania respectively as the best refutation of all the misleading rumours which, as usual, have been spread in the Press hostile to us on the occasion of Little Entente Conferences. As regards the League of Nations, we are all of the same opinion on every question, irrespective of whether it concerns each of us or not. It cannot be denied that the League is passing through a crisis. To-day it is a political crisis, last March it was only a constitutional one. The result of the March resolutions was that a special commission drew up a scheme for reorganizing the Council, but the attitude adopted by Brazil and Spain showed that the re-election of non-permanent members would not satisfy the protesting parties and avert the threatened crisis. The Council could not discuss the Brazil question for statutory reasons, but will deal with it in September. The Polish question will come up for discussion, but will probably not occasion difficulties."

Here Benesh broke the thread of his remarks by saying: "At this moment I receive the news that a number of English papers have published a report that the Little Entente has broken up with a feeling of tension among its members. We read similar reports in Vienna papers. This is a characteristic symptom, and it is the duty of individual journalists to combat such unprincipled reporting." Resuming, Benesh went on: "Touching the proceedings of the League of Nations, I may state that at Geneva, before the Council and the Assembly meet, we shall confer together and adopt a final attitude towards any changes which may arise in the situation. As regards Balkan problems, Czechoslovakia will maintain her traditional policy—to sanction the policy pursued by her allies. Conversely, this principle applies to problems of other members of the Little Entente. No special discussion took place on the subject of Russia; the former resolutions of the Little Entente remain good. As for the Soviet-German Treaty (of Berlin), it has already been considered by the Commission of the League, which found nothing objectionable in it, and accordingly we too have no objections to it. The Council has dealt with the question of the Hungarian franc forgeries and passed a resolution that falls in with our wishes. The relations of Czechoslovakia to Hungary are not unsatisfactory, and we are ready to negotiate with her at any moment. The relations of the Little Entente to France are the most amicable, cordial, and loyal possible, and will remain so. The same can be said of its relations with Italy. There are no difficulties between us, nor even the least ground of friction; our common endeavour is the consolidation of Central Europe. Our relations with Poland are cordial. I may add in this connexion that the relations between Czechoslovakia and Poland are now fully and finally stabilized, and that the friendly agreements between us will not be affected by any change of Government." After stating that there had been no negotiations at the conference on economic questions, he said that the day would certainly come when such questions would find a place on their agenda.

Benesh was then asked to express his opinion on an organization, called the Little Entente Press Association (la Petite Entente de la Presse), which had been founded at the Sinaia Conference in 1923, and consisted of the editors of the principal papers published in the three States. It had been established to promote Press collaboration along the lines of the principles governing the Little Entente. The association was in strong force at this Bled Conference, held regular meetings, and subsequently published an illustrated account of its proceedings. Respecting it, Benesh remarked that he thought it a valuable factor for carrying out the ideas and programme of the Little Entente. "Journalists are undoubtedly freer agents than are statesmen, and they can therefore more easily go deeply into the things that bring nations together. The association can do great good as a source of correct information about the Little Entente to foreign countries."

Mitilineu spoke next; he told the journalists that he was annoyed at finding ideas attributed to him in the Press of which he had never dreamed—one such idea was the weakening of the Little Entente. He stressed the fact that on the contrary all the negotiations between the three Foreign Ministers at the conference had been carried on in the most amicable spirit, and that complete agreement had been achieved. Touching the relations of Rumania with Bulgaria, he stated they were neighbourly and satisfactory; as regards the loan Bulgaria was seeking through the League, there was no objection to it if the money were to be used entirely for humanitarian objects (provision for the refugees); but the other Balkan States could not permit the loan to be used for political purposes, as was possible; on this matter Rumania, Yugoslavia, and Greece thought alike. "Rumania," he said, "continues to be on the most cordial terms with Italy, and expression was being given to this by a Treaty of Friendship. The loan to us from Italy will strengthen our relations still further." He thought that a Balkan Pact could be realized only in an atmosphere of absolute confidence, but events were tending that way. The position of Rumania to Russia was the same as before. He concluded with a reference to the League of Nations, and said that the representation of the Little Entente on the Council had been settled without any reservation whatsoever.

Nintchitch, in his turn, said he must begin by severely rebuking the journalists who spread false reports for the purpose of causing a sensation, even if they had no ulterior motives. He did not wish to name the papers that published fictitious statements, as he would not like to embarrass any of their correspondents still at Bled. "As President of this conference I state that all the questions that came before us were settled in complete agreement and almost without discussion. We agreed on our line of action at the League of Nations, and we have decided who will represent the Little Entente in the Council during the coming year. The relations of Italy to the Little Entente were cordial and become increasingly so, as both of us have the same object in view—to stabilize and strengthen peace in Central Europe. All our activities, whether of Italy or the Little Entente, are in perfect harmony, and as often as not this is the result of a preconcerted plan." Referring to Greece, he said that Yugoslav relations with her were of a neighbourly character, both States desiring to settle all questions in dispute in a friendly manner; thus, the question of revenue from Salonika would be arranged at an early date by an amicable agreement. Concerning the loan to Bulgaria, he concurred in what the Rumanian Foreign Minister had said; it seemed to him that the problem posed by the refugees might be solved in some other way. Some newspapers reported that the conference also discussed the komitadji border raids, which were then creating unrest and were credited to the Macedonian organization in Bulgaria, which the Government of that country was unwilling or unable to suppress. These outrages resulted in August in a collective Note of Yugoslavia, Rumania, and Greece to Bulgaria, who sent a conciliatory Reply. In the same month the Finance Committee of the League of Nations agreed in principle to a loan to Bulgaria of £2,500,000 for the purpose of assisting in settling the refugees.

League Crisis Resolved

When September came it was soon evident at Geneva that the League of Nations had passed safely through the crisis that had developed at the March meeting. Everything had been arranged behind the scenes for the entry of Germany and the enlargement of the Council, the defection of Brazil and Spain being accepted. The Assembly—the seventh—was opened on September 6, 1926, by a speech by Benesh, as President of the Council. After reviewing the progress made by the League during the year, he said he was not discouraged by the slow advance towards disarmament; to go quickly might risk failure. He believed that the Locarno Treaties would have a profound effect in pacifying the mind of Europe. He expressed great regret that Brazil and Spain should separate themselves from the League, but trusted they would return. Next day, with Nintchitch as its President, the Assembly admitted Germany into the League by a unanimous vote.

There was something impressive, dramatic, and in a high sense romantic in the fact that it fell to the lot of Nintchitch, a Serbian representing the country which felt the first shock of the World War, to announce this decision—this supreme gesture of reconciliation with the enemy. On September 10 the German Delegation made its inaugural appearance at the Assembly. Two days later the Foreign Ministers of the Little Entente met in a special conference, and agreed to support Rumania for membership of the Council, as, it appeared, they had decided provisionally to do at the recent conference at Bled. Nintchitch had been their candidate for the Presidency of the Assembly. The elections to the Council were held on September 16; Rumania was given a three-year seat and Czechoslovakia a seat for one year; Poland was given a three-year seat and was declared re-eligible, results all most gratifying to the

Little Entente. The re-election of Czechoslovakia was universally regarded as a fitting personal tribute to the value of the services Benesh had rendered to the League and the cause of peace. Meanwhile the Locarno Treaties had been ratified, as was shown on September 14 by the deposit with the Secretariat of the League of documents attesting the ratification of the treaties by the respective Parliaments of the seven signatory States.

Polish-Yugoslav Treaty

During that September there were many negotiations proceeding between the representatives of the various States at the Conference; one result was seen in the signing at Geneva on September 18 of a "Pact of Friendship and Cordial Collaboration between Poland and the Kingdom of the Serbs, Croats, and Slovenes." Its First Article ran: "The continuance of the sincere friendship and good understanding which happily already exist between the Polish Republic and the Kingdom of the Serbs, Croats, and Slovenes is solemnly confirmed." Article IV provided for the early conclusion of an arbitration convention. Time passed, however, and this pact was not ratified. Another Yugoslav Treaty had met with a singular fate in August, 1926. As the result of prolonged conversations the question of the Salonika-Gevgheli Railway had seemed to be settled at last by the signing of a defensive treaty of friendship and conciliation at Athens on August 16, 1926, by Yugoslavia and Greece, in replacement of the treaty of alliance between the two States which had been denounced by Yugoslavia in May, 1924. The new treaty took the form of four conventions which regulated all outstanding questions. Six days after the conventions were signed a *coup d'état* brought the dictatorship of Pangalos to an abrupt close in Greece, and the Government which came into being on his fall declared them to be inacceptable—they were definitively rejected by the Greek Parliament in August, 1927.

Italo-Rumanian Treaty

Meanwhile the negotiations for a treaty between Italy and Rumania, of which Mitilineu had informed the other Little

Entente representatives at the Bled Conference, had been completed. Averescu visited Rome and in the Chigi Palace signed, with Mussolini, on September 16, 1926, a "Pact of Friendship and Cordial Collaboration between Italy and Rumania." Its First Article was: "The High Contracting Parties undertake reciprocally to lend each other their mutual support and cordial cooperation for the maintenance of international order and to ensure respect for and the execution of the undertakings contained in the treaties to which they are signatories." Article II provided: "In the event of international complications and if they are agreed that their common interests are or may be endangered, the High Contracting Parties undertake to confer with one another on the joint measures to be taken to safeguard their interests." And the Third Article said: "Should the security or interests of one of the High Contracting Parties be threatened as a result of violent incursions from without, the other Party undertakes by means of its friendly support to lend the said Party its political and diplomatic assistance, with a view to removing the external cause of such threats." In the Fourth Article Italy and Rumania undertook to "submit to a procedure of conciliation or arbitration" questions in dispute between them which could not be settled by the "normal methods of diplomacy." The treaty was for five years. A Protocol was appended in which it was stated that the Governments of the two States, desiring to strengthen their economic ties, had decided to appoint a Commission to study the practical means of attaining this object. The pact was ratified at Rome on July 18, 1927, and registered with the League on November 1 following.

To the great disappointment of many Rumanians, nothing was said about Bessarabia in the pact. It had been purposely left out, but was dealt with separately in letters exchanged between the Italian and Rumanian Prime Ministers. Mussolini wrote that in the course of their conversations on the pact they had had occasion to examine also the question of the treaty concerning Bessarabia signed in Paris on October 28, 1920. For reasons that he had submitted no mention was made in the pact of this treaty, "the ratification of which," he added, "will take place on the part of the Italian Government only when this can be done without prejudicing the general interests of Italy." In his reply, Averescu noted that "the Italian ratification of the Bessarabian Convention is a question of time and opportunity." Mussolini thought the time and opportunity arrived some six months later; on March 8, 1927, Italy decided to ratify the Bessarabian Convention, but with the addendum that the ratification had no hostile bearing towards Soviet Russia, but was merely the carrying out of the intention manifested when Italy signed that convention.

Two other matters of interest in Balkan affairs claimed attention in October, 1926. At the beginning of the month Nintchitch visited Paris; a few days later Bouroff, the Bulgarian Foreign Minister, visited Rome. It was said that both visits were "devoid of political significance," and they certainly led to no treaties—the Franco-Yugoslav Treaty still existed in the initialled stage. But the Italian Press was justified in drawing the conclusion that Bouroff's visit to Mussolini, coming almost immediately after that of Averescu, could not but enhance the prestige of Italy in the Balkans, a circumstance that had its repercussions in Yugoslavia.

Affair of Hungarian Bank-Note Forgeries Closed

In mid-October, 1926, the Affair of the Hungarian Bank-Note Forgeries reached its close. The wheels of justice had revolved but slowly. As far back as March 1, 1926, the French Minister at Budapest had urged that the trials should be expedited. On the following day a sensation had been caused when the Magyar Minister of Justice read in the Hungarian Parliament a statement made by Meszaros in 1921, according to which it had been the intention, the Hungarian Ministry of War consenting, of the Magyar irredentist societies to invade Czechoslovakia, the funds being provided by the forgery of the Czechoslovak bank-notes. On March 4 proceedings were begun at The Hague respecting Jankovitch and his two comrades, and a fortnight afterwards Jankovitch was sentenced to three years' imprisonment, and the other men to two years' each.

Interest in the affair centred in Hungary much more than in the Hague criminals; there were extraordinary scenes in the Hungarian Parliament; on March 20 a resolution to conclude the debate on the subject, which really involved the question of the responsibility of the Bethlen Government, was passed amid the violent protests of the Opposition; and on March 23, after a speech by Bethlen, the Parliament voted for the majority report of the investigating committee, and rejected the vote of censure on the Government. Nadossy, Windischgraetz, and others implicated in the forgeries were placed on their trials at Budapest early in May, and were found guilty. Nadossy and Windischgraetz were sentenced to four years' imprisonment each and fined ten million crowns apiece, with loss of all political rights. In June the affair came up in the Council of the League of Nations, where it was agreed to transfer the French proposal for investigating the forgeries by an international conference to the hands of a simple financial committee. In the Council Benesh stated—what he and other representatives of the Little Entente had often stated—that he and the Little Entente desired to enter into good neighbourly relations with Hungary. Another proof of this was the starting at Prague at the end of July of negotiations for a tariff agreement; on August 26, 1926, a provisional agreement was come to, dealing with Czechoslovak-Hungarian commercial relations and incorporating the most-favoured-nation clause.

In the meantime Nadossy, Windischgraetz, and the others who had been condemned in May had appealed against their sentences, and were tried again; it was finally disposed of on October 14 when the Royal Curia, the last Court of Appeal in Hungary, reduced some of the sentences—that of Windischgraetz, who was sentened to four years' simple imprisonment instead of four years' hard labour, and that of Nadossy, who was given three and a half years' penal servitude instead of four years, being the chief examples. Bethlen resigned along with his Cabinet after the decisions of the Royal Curia, though the various courts before whom the affair had come had stated that it had been proved that the Government had absolutely no connexion with the crime. Horthy, the Regent, would not accept the resignations, and Bethlen therefore continued in office, but he made some changes in the Cabinet, the most notable being the transfer of Walko from the Ministry of Commerce to that of Foreign Affairs. In any case, what Briand had called the "affair of incredible brigandage" had terminated.

Two Germans Join Czechoslovak Government

It was while this wretched episode was being ended that an event of a very different kind occurred in Czechoslovakia—the entrance of two of her Germans into her Government as Ministers. Owing to the existence of considerable Minorities, internal consolidation continued to be one of the greatest problems confronting the States of the Little Entente, and in the solution of them Czechoslovakia, with her relatively higher development in various directions, continued to be the pioneer. On October 12, 1926, a new Government was formed at Prague under Shvehla as Prime Minister; it consisted mainly of deputies belonging to the Czech Agrarian Party, some Ministers who were experts but without a seat in the Parliament, and Mayr-Harting and Spina, both German Czechoslovak deputies. Of the experts, Benesh was one; he had resigned his seat some months previously because of trouble with his party—the National Socialist—but remained in the Cabinet as Foreign Minister. The two German Ministers were university professors, and came from the German bourgeois groups, which for some time had shown an "activist" tendency in the politics of the country.

The inclusion of these men in the Czechoslovak Government was one of the most significant signs of the times for Central Europe. It was at once a landmark in the consolidation of the Czechoslovak State and of good augury for the stability of the New Europe of the Peace Treaties. Partly the outcome of the spirit of international reconciliation initiated at Locarno and in the conversation at Thoiry in which Briand and Stresemann later participated, it was also the logical result of the wise guidance of President Masaryk. He had long sought to bring about this consummation of his internal policy, the object of which was the unifying of all the races of his land. To a correspondent of the *Matin* he said: "In speaking of Czechoslovakia it is natural to refer to that little revolution which has just taken place in our internal political situation—the recent Parliamentary and Governmental collaboration of Czechs and Germans. It is the first time since the War that in one of the States sprung from the victory, or enlarged by it, a Minority ethnically alien has been called to sit on the council of the Ministers of the country. It is a veritable domestic Locarno. . . . It is certainly an extraordinary coincidence that this change has manifested itself among us at the very moment when a similar change has occurred in the domain of Franco-German relations. The appeal to the Germans in Czechoslovakia, I must say, was dictated by our internal necessities, and though I should not wish to represent it as a Czechoslovak response to Locarno and Thoiry, nevertheless it is impossible not to note the synchronism at such an interesting moment in the life of Europe. It is evident that the same spirit inspired this twofold series of events, so different otherwise in their proportions and bearing." After some remarks on Locarno and Thoiry Masaryk touched on a theme that was a favourite with him: "In my opinion an essential condition for making the policy of Thoiry successful is that France shall pursue it in full accord with England."

Treaty of Tirana

Yugoslavia was less fortunate as regards internal consolidation. The bright hopes associated with the cooperation of the Croat Peasant Party in the Government were justified for a time, but became heavily clouded because of the eccentric actions and extraordinary speeches of Stephen Raditch, its leader. He did not hesitate to criticize the Government of which he was a Minister, and it was with the greatest difficulty that the Radical-Raditch combination continued to exist. In

October, 1926, an incident occurred in which he figured conspicuously and unpleasantly. On the occasion of a visit to Zagreb of a deputation from the Czechoslovak Parliament, Raditch complained that the Croat colours were not to be seen among the flags with which the railway station was decorated, and he interrupted the speech of welcome given by the Prefect to correct the expression "Czechoslovak," which he maintained should be "Czech and Slovak." His Radical colleagues saw in this an attempt to interfere in the politics of another, but friendly and allied, country, as well as an assault on an official of the Government. The Prime Minister, then Uzunovitch, offered to resign, but was prevailed on by King Alexander to remain in office.

A much more serious matter shook the Government when on December 6, 1926, Nintchitch, who had been Foreign Minister almost continuously since the peace, resigned, as a protest against the Treaty of Tirana, signed on November 27, 1926, between Italy and Albania. In this "Pact of Friendship and Security," the First Article ran: "Albania and Italy recognize that any disturbance threatening the political, legal, and territorial *status quo* of Albania is contrary to their common political interests." Article II stated: "In order to safeguard the above-mentioned interests, the High Contracting Parties undertake to afford each other mutual support and cordial cooperation; they also undertake not to conclude with other Powers any political or military agreements prejudicial to the interests of the other Party, including those defined in the present pact." Other Articles provided for conciliation and arbitration procedure, validated the pact for five years, and postulated its registration with the League of Nations. The treaty in effect amounted to a unilateral guarantee by Italy of the territorial integrity of Albania, and might be regarded as taking the place of the declaration of the Conference of Ambassadors on November 9, 1921, entrusting the task of protecting Albania to Italy. The publication of the treaty, which had been signed at Tirana, the Albanian capital, immediately raised a fierce storm in Yugoslavia. In his letter of resignation Nintchitch said: "I have followed the policy which I was convinced was best for my country and which was founded on principles mutually agreed to. I have loyally followed these principles during my whole ministry. But in the last few days an event has occurred which has shaken the confidence on which I based my policy. For this reason I resign as Foreign Minister."

The event alluded to was, of course, the Treaty of Tirana, and the policy was that of conciliation toward Italy; he regarded the treaty as a repudiation by Mussolini of that policy. On December 7 the Yugoslav Government resigned, partly on account of the treaty, and partly owing to the action of Stephen Raditch in connexion with charges of corruption preferred against Pashitch's son and several former Ministers. While engaged in resolving the resultant crisis, Pashitch died suddenly, after an apoplectic seizure, on December 10, 1926. The passing of the "Grand Old Man of Serbia" was the subject of glowing tributes from the whole Press of Yugoslavia. But he was a great Serbian rather than a great Yugoslav. And he left in confusion the party he had founded and so often led to victory; the country was distracted; it was significant that Raditch did not attend the funeral. The parties appeared to be united only in common resentment against the action of Italy. As the year closed this was virtually the only danger threatening the peace of Europe, Soviet Russia always excepted.

CHAPTER IX

THE LITTLE ENTENTE AND THE NORMALIZATION OF EUROPE

1927–1928

MARKED progress towards normality in Europe was the outstanding feature of the period covered by the years 1927–28, especially during its last half-year. This was not, of course, the normality of pre-War Europe, for that had been shattered by the War; it was a post-War normality arising out of and conditioned by the results of the War, the norma or rule being found in the explicit or implicit acceptance of the status imposed by the Peace Treaties, interpreted by the League of Nations, and illuminated by Locarno. The stabilization, the consolidation of peace, for which the nations had been struggling either by means of regional pacts, such as those of the Little Entente, or through the League in a more general manner, was in sight of being achieved—was in fact virtually achieved. It was true that some great problems remained to be solved: disarmament, security, reparations, evacuation of the occupied territories. But the will to solve them, which had been lacking earlier, was the dominant and decisive factor. There was again a Concert of Europe, the big exception being Soviet Russia, as always; there were some lesser exceptions, as, for instance, Hungary, with its "No, no, never!"

Troubles, some of greater significance than others, existed here and there and had still to be composed. It was beyond dispute, however, that Europe as a whole was adjusting herself more and more to the post-War settlement, or in other words was—not "returning to the normal," as that was impossible, but was in process of realizing, establishing, and working under a new normality, having the complete political liquidation of the War in view, and from that as a starting-point going on to solve economic and other questions, which were important and difficult enough, but which would be more easily dealt with thenceforward. Steps in the direction of economic normalization were already to be noted in the success of reconstruction and stabilization loans, in the salvaging of Austria and Hungary, so long one of the chief matters of concern to the Little Entente, and perhaps most of all in the firm fixation of national currencies, as, for instance, the French franc and the Italian lira; before the close of 1928 the exchange or valuta was stable in almost every country of Europe—less Soviet Russia. The abrogation of the Inter-Allied Military Control in ex-enemy States was another characteristic of this period.

In 1927 the international situation had certain fluctuations. If Germany's position in the League and in Europe was established, and the relations of France and Germany to each other continued to improve, despite some momentary interruptions, there were also to be taken into account the prolonged tension between Italy and Yugoslavia, the breaking off by Great Britain of relations with Soviet Russia, and the failure of the Conference, initiated by the United States and held at Geneva, on Naval Disarmament. These latter factors had a depressing effect on the opening of the Assembly of the League in September of that year, but the spirits of its members quickly rallied on assurances being given by the representatives of the Great Powers that there was no real risk of war and that these Powers held steadfastly to the policy of peace. Thus encouraged, the Assembly voted for the Polish resolution against all wars of aggression. Animated discussions on the general question of disarmament resulted in instructions to the Preparatory Commission to expedite its preparations for the conference on this subject, which had already been envisaged by the League, as it was bound to be under Article VIII of the Covenant. Another question, of particular and vital interest to the Little Entente, came up before the Assembly; it was concerned with the Hungarian "optants" in Rumania, and was posed first at the March meeting of the Council; but it could not be said that it seriously affected the general situation, even though it was linked with a campaign for the revision of the Peace Treaties which had developed in some strength during the previous year.

THE KELLOGG PACT

In 1928 much of the time of the League was occupied with discussions of the problems which it had considered in 1927, and undoubtedly progress was made towards normalization. Apart from the League, there were obvious reasons for the acceptance of the New Europe as something definitely static. To vast masses of men the idea of the New Europe of the Peace Treaties—the existing Europe—had become familiar with the passage of the years since the treaties had been concluded—as familiar as had been in its time the idea of the Old Europe before the War. In addition to this quasi-psychological change, there was a wide recognition of the truth that, imperfect in some details as the Peace Treaties might be, the Europe they had so largely created was an infinitely better Europe than that of pre-War days.

Besides the argument for peace and normalization that sprang from this justification of the treaties, there was yet another, in its way even more cogent, which arose from the conviction that any serious attempt to upset the status established by them would inevitably cause another Great War, involving, in all probability, Europe in final irreparable ruin, owing to the absolutely destructive nature of the warfare that would ensue. War was not to be thought of! The professional makers of war, so vociferous in Germany before the War, were silent. The Soviet stood alone in teaching and preaching war. Unquestionably the League gained ground. But the great feature of 1928 had nothing to do with the League, though well in line with its work for peace, and therefore welcomed by it. This was the signing in Paris on August 27, 1928, of what was known as the Briand-Kellogg or, simply, the Kellogg Pact, a multilateral treaty to renounce war as an instrument of national policy.

At first there was some apprehension in Europe that this treaty might in one way or another deprive the League and Locarno of much of their force and persuasive efficacy, but closer acquaintance with it proved that, instead of it being derogatory to them, it was an additional guarantee of peace, and possibly had the further advantage of renewing the association of the United States with Europe in common effort; in all, it was another advance in the process of normalization, in the standardization of the *status quo post* not *ante bellum*, for, as applied to Europe, it could mean nothing else—unless it meant just nothing at all, which no one believed. In effect it enjoined on a Europe that had renounced war as an instrument of national policy to look to the Covenant of the League of Nations, which was part and parcel of the Peace Treaties, for the procedure to be followed if change was sought of the status prescribed by them —to Article XIX of the Covenant; there was no other way out, and as things were it was a very "strait and narrow way." That the Soviet should express a desire to sign the Kellogg Pact was nothing to the point, but was merely in accordance with its peculiar mentality, which found no difficulty in facing both ways when this fitted with its plans. The Soviet continued to ingeminate war, not peace.

Behind all the ideas in men's minds were certain positive facts. The Anglo-French Entente stood none the less firm because Great Britain had extended the Entente to include Germany. The regional treaties, of which those of the Little Entente had been the first, far-shining examples and the Locarno Treaties the most comprehensive, also stood firm; where these were defensive alliances, they remained without alteration. At the close of 1928 Europe was covered with a network of arbitration and conciliation treaties, and of guarantee and mutual security treaties, as well as the Locarno Treaties. Europe was treaty-proofed for peace. Watchfulness, however, was still necessary on the part of its guardians.

Italo-Yugoslav Tension

At the opening of 1927 the area of danger lay in South-Eastern Europe—in the tension of the relations between Italy and Yugoslavia; it had been so acute in December, 1926, as to give some appearance of likelihood to reports then current in some papers that the Little Entente was about to hold a special conference on this subject. No such meeting was held.

It had been arranged that one of the regular conferences was to take place later in the year, and this was adhered to. Yet the Italo-Yugoslav conflict was a matter of grave concern to Czechoslovakia and Rumania, especially to the former because of the Treaty of Alliance of August 31, 1922, with Yugoslavia (p. 199) and the Pact of Cordial Cooperation of July 5, 1924, with Italy (p. 241). In the course of a statement in the Foreign Committee of the Chamber of Deputies, at Prague, Benesh said on February 3, 1927, that arising out of the Treaty of Tirana there were differences of opinion between Italy and Yugoslavia, as had to be admitted. Nothing could be said, however, at that stage about the arguments put forward by one side or the other, as the treaty still formed the subject of negotiations between the interested parties. "Czechoslovakia," he continued, "is the friend and ally of Yugoslavia, and she has also a treaty of friendly cooperation with Italy. We desire that there should be no conflict between the two countries, but that they should reach an understanding at the earliest possible moment." Rumania had likewise treaties with the two countries, and her attitude to them was the same as was that of Czechoslovakia.

At this juncture the internal political situation was unsatisfactory in Yugoslavia, as it had been for months before; there had been six Cabinets in less than a year, and it certainly did not seem to be a time for a foreign policy of adventure, even though all Yugoslavs were a unit as against Italy. It was therefore all the more surprising when an official announcement was made in the third week of March to the effect that the Italian Government had sent a Note to the British, French, and German Governments drawing their attention to military preparations in Yugoslavia for an expedition, on a considerable scale, into Albania, with the object of overthrowing the existing Government of Ahmed Bey Zogu, then President of the Albanian Republic. The Belgrade Government indignantly and categorically denied the accuracy of this statement.

In Belgrade it was asserted that reports of the alleged preparations were being circulated with the intention of providing a pretext for the landing of Italian troops on the Albanian coast. In his Note to London, Paris, and Berlin, Mussolini had stated that he would repel any invasion of Albania. It was not forgotten that rather more than two years before an incursion which had been organized in Yugoslavia had been made into Albania and had succeeded in overturning the Government of that day, under the Premiership of Bishop Fan Noli, who had fled the country; and that the invaders had been led by Zogu, who forthwith had become ruler of the little, troublesome State, and, almost as promptly, had turned his back on Yugoslavia. Considering all these circumstances, it was to be expected that the tension between Italy and Yugoslavia would become still more acute—as it did, despite Mussolini's declaration that his sole desire was peace and the pacific assurances given by the Yugoslav Government both in Belgrade and Rome.

One of the incidents of this time of severe strain was a speech in the Skupshtina by Trumbitch in support of an understanding with Great Britain, "which country," as *The Times* Special Correspondent at Belgrade remarked in his dispatch to that paper on March 21, published next day, "has recently been regarded as the villain of the piece, second only to Italy." It was widely believed that Mussolini had the support of the British Government. Trumbitch's speech had been preceded by a statement by Peritch, then Yugoslav Foreign Minister, in which he said that Yugoslavia desired to live on good terms with Italy, and was willing to allow an inquiry by military experts into the facts of the case. In his observations Trumbitch asked why it was that Italy had not communicated her fears to the Council of the League, which was in session only a few days before she had sent her Note to the Powers.

There was some notion of referring the dispute to the League, but it was dropped. Great Britain, France, and Germany counselled moderation both in Rome and Belgrade. The crisis passed, and in connexion with this Briand, in a speech in the French Chamber on March 22, made the significant statement: "Europe, though still exposed to them, is not now so much at the mercy of incidents as was the case some years ago. All nations, great and small, are now eager and ready to assist in stamping out any beginnings of the flame of war which may arise among them." For all that, the crisis passed away but slowly, and left a feeling of great bitterness throughout Yugoslavia. Peace seemed somewhat precarious, as was manifested in May, when the arrest of an official of the Yugoslav Legation in Tirana by the Albanian Government, on the ground that he was plotting against the security of Albania, led the Yugoslav Government to break off relations with that State. But Great Britain, France, Germany, and on this occasion Italy, intervened at Tirana, found a formula acceptable alike to Yugoslavia and Albania, and succeeded in bringing this controversy to a pacific termination. Naturally the association of Italy with the other Powers in the *démarche* to the Albanian Government had an ameliorating effect upon the situation in Yugoslavia. One result of the Italo-Yugoslav trouble was the reconstruction of the Yugoslav Cabinet in a more broadly national way; the new Ministry took office on April 10, 1927, with Vukitchevitch as Premier and Marinkovitch as Foreign Minister; the Raditchists, however, were not represented in it; yet the real solidarity of Yugoslavia was abundantly evident during the crisis.

Italo-Hungarian Treaty

It was about this time that Hungary came into considerable prominence. Early in January, 1927, the Budapest papers had announced that Bethlen, the Prime Minister, whose position had been greatly strengthened by his victory at the elections in the preceding December, was about to pay a visit to Rome, where he was to confer with Mussolini. On March 3, 1927, in a statement in the Financial Committee of the Hungarian Lower House of Parliament, where the estimates of the Foreign Ministry were being discussed, Bethlen said that the international situation as it stood did not permit the raising of the question of the revision of the Peace Treaties. For himself, he took as his model the policy of Stresemann, and hoped to be successful in securing good relations with the neighbouring States, just as Stresemann had secured them with France. The most important task, he went on to state, for Hungary at the moment was to adjust the question of her access to the sea—which would be through Fiume, and would facilitate friendship between her and Italy.

Almost exactly a month later Bethlen was in Rome, on the invitation of Mussolini, with whom on April 5, 1927, he signed a Treaty of Friendship, Conciliation, and Arbitration between Hungary and Italy. It consisted of five Articles and a Protocol of some length dealing with the procedure of conciliation and arbitration mentioned in the Second Article of the treaty. It was ratified by the two States at Rome on August 8 and registered with the League on November 1, 1927. This treaty was of the same general character as the treaties Italy had made with Czechoslovakia and Rumania, and it was validated for ten years. The conclusions reached by Magyar and Italian experts respecting Fiume as Hungary's access to the sea were embodied in a convention. Yugoslavia had offered Split (Spalato) to Hungary as a port, Greece had suggested Salonika, and Rumania Constanza. Fiume was preferred by the Hungarian Government, but to reach it Hungarian passengers and goods had to cross a stretch of Yugoslav territory, a difficulty which could be surmounted only by a suitable agreement with the Yugoslav Government, which Bethlen was reported as saying he had already secured. The treaty, as was to be expected, had its repercussions.

It was scarcely well received in Yugoslavia, whose people were inclined to speak of her isolation, as she had become surrounded by States in close treaty relations with Italy. Even in Rumania, which State a month before had been deeply gratified by the Italian ratification of the 1920 treaty recognizing the union of Bessarabia with the country, the Italo-Magyar Treaty was not welcomed. Benesh, however, said, when asked his views, that he thought it was natural that Hungary should seek again a place in international politics and try for the necessary support; he could not agree with those who saw in a closer understanding between Italy and Hungary an attack directed against the Little Entente; the two States were only establishing relations which were based on vital interests. In

Hungary there was much rejoicing over the treaty; it was pointed out that, as Bethlen had observed in an interview in the *Lavoro d'Italia*, it was the first friendly treaty concluded by Hungary with one of the former enemy States in which she was accorded equality of diplomatic rank with her cosignatory. In France comment on the treaty was marked by reserve, but there was apparent some apprehension that events had to a certain extent altered the diplomatic situation in Central and South-Eastern Europe.

Little Entente Conference at Jachymov

As had been arranged, a regular Conference of the Little Entente was held on May 13, 14, and 15, 1927, at Jachymov or Joachimsthal, the famous little spa in Northern Bohemia, Czechoslovakia. It was attended by Marinkovitch, Mitilineu, and Benesh, the Foreign Ministers of the three States. Upwards of a hundred journalists from far and near had gathered in the town. As usual on similar occasions, the conference had been preceded by reports in portions of the Press of the impending collapse of the Little Entente, and great interest was taken in its proceedings, but from its beginning to its end there was no sign of the breaking up of the Little Entente; on the contrary, the utmost harmony prevailed. *Communiqués* were issued in the customary fashion of giving information in a very general way. That published on the second day stated that the three Ministers had dealt with the questions of special interest to their States in a "spirit of sincere amity and firm attachment to the idea underlying the policy of the Little Entente" which united the three States, and had kept them in constant association for seven years, besides contributing substantially to the maintenance of peace in Europe.

All the Ministers emphasized the fact that any statement of lack of unity among them or of a termination of the international mission of their alliance was destitute of foundation. "The three States regard it as their duty to preserve the Little Entente unimpaired and to pursue continually their common aims: international union, loyal cooperation with their neighbours, and political consolidation consistent with the ideas and principles of the League of Nations."

At the close of the conference on May 15 the Foreign Ministers of the three States received the representatives of the Press, all anxious to hear what was to be said, the chief topics in their minds being the Italo-Rumanian Treaty, the Italo-Hungarian *rapprochement*, and the strained relations between Italy and Yugoslavia. Italy loomed large in their thoughts as the possible disturber, perhaps destroyer, of the Little Entente, despite the *communiqués*. Of the three Ministers, Mitilineu spoke first and at considerable length; his opening words completely dissipated any notion of the dissolution of the Little Entente.

He said: "At the very outset I am able to confirm the complete agreement and the friendly solidarity of our three States, which form a necessary and indestructible group. It is essential for the whole world to realize that the Little Entente has existed, exists, and will continue to exist, just as exists the permanent community of our interests. If the Little Entente did not exist, it would be necessary to create it. In this respect there is not the slightest divergence in our views. All those who still believe in the possibility of a misunderstanding among us will be disappointed by the further development of the Little Entente, which will confirm what I am telling you." He continued: "The relations of each individual State of the Little Entente, and of the Little Entente as a whole, to France are cordial and firm, in accordance with the most intimate feelings of our three nations and our own as well. On this subject our views differ not at all. The States of the Little Entente and the Little Entente itself are on excellent terms with the other Allies, England and Italy. The friendship of Italy is greatly esteemed by Rumania, as was again manifested recently by the ratification of the Bessarabian Protocol. The relations of Rumania to Germany are sound, and after certain questions have been settled, no reason will remain why Rumania should not come into even closer touch with her. The relations of the Little Entente States to Poland are of the best and are characterized by the alliance of Poland with Rumania. Relations with Austria are good. I am glad to be able to state that she has demonstrated her absolute vitality, of which she daily exhibits additional proofs, and which will still be further safeguarded by economic agreements. As regards relations between Rumania and Austria, I may say that our last Government entered into negotiations with that country for an arbitration agreement. I hope they will soon be concluded and the agreement signed." Questioned about the relations of the Little Entente to Hungary, Mitilineu replied: "It is the sincere desire of us all that every obstacle between the Little Entente and Hungary should be removed. It is clear that the intention of the Little Entente, which pursues a policy based on the fulfilment of the Peace Treaties and the maintenance of the *status quo*, is to ensure general peace in Central Europe.

"Personally I am an advocate of an agreement with Hungary, and I have never made a secret of that fact. I can therefore mention the reasons which postpone the realization of such an agreement. To begin with, it is not our impression that Hungary shares our views, especially as regards the fulfilment of the treaties and the maintenance of the *status quo*. Again, it would be in the interests not only of the Little Entente but also of Hungary to conclude mutual commerical agreements—it is Hungary who has the main interest in this matter. I am happy to see that she is abandoning her policy of isolation. We want all the neighbours of Hungary to be able to negotiate with her and arrive at agreements. If any State of the Little Entente undertakes any arrangements whatever with Hungary, it will do so exclusively in agreement with the two other allied States." Turning to the area of the Balkans, Mitilineu remarked: "We can apparently place on record a real improvement in the relations of Yugoslavia and Rumania on the one hand and Bulgaria on the other. There has been scarcely a single frontier incident throughout the year. We are considering the possibility of concluding with Bulgaria an agreement for good neighbourly relations between us, if the attitude of the Bulgarian Government remains as it is at present. Bulgaria has made application for the abolition of the Inter-Allied Military Control, and I can say that we shall deal with this in a favourable and conciliatory spirit. The relations of the Little Entente with Greece and Turkey are good." From the Balkans the speaker passed to Soviet Russia: he said: "As regards the Soviets, no change has occurred in our views. We are, and we remain, in the same position taken up at our previous conferences—the question is precisely on the same footing as we adopted before, that is, each State of the Little Entente can freely negotiate regarding the possibility of the recognition of the Soviet Government, but this question in the last resort remains a subject for agreement on the part of all three States forming the Little Entente." Asked about the Treaty of Tirana, Mitilineu answered: "We Rumanians are and remain allies of Yugoslavia; we are and remain friends of Italy. From the beginning of the Italo-Yugoslav conflict Rumania has shown a keen desire for a prompt agreement between the two States. M. Marinkovitch also has exhibited a keen desire for reaching an agreement with Italy and for removing obstacles and misunderstandings, and I heartily hope that this desire on the part of Yugoslavia will be shared by the other side." Questioned about Anschluss, Mitilineu said that the question was not urgent and that the attitude of the Little Entente with respect to it had undergone no change whatever.

The Rumanian Foreign Minister had touched on virtually every point of interest, and the two other Foreign Ministers spoke very briefly. Marinkovitch merely said: "We have gone into the questions that concern the Little Entente States, that is, almost all European questions of immediate urgency. We have arrived at the conclusion that the reasons for which the Little Entente was established seven years ago continue to be completely in force. The Little Entente is far from being superfluous; on the contrary, it is still essential not only to the three allied countries forming it, but also for maintaining equilibrium in Central Europe." Benesh informed the pressmen that his task of addressing them had been greatly facilitated, and that he himself enjoyed a considerable advantage, because his colleagues had really said everything there was to say; he was in perfect agreement with them. Laying stress on the need for economic cooperation on the part of the Little Entente States and their neighbours, he said: "We have a duty not only towards our own States, but also to our neighbours and the whole of Europe. Our international function is upheld and will be maintained. The main concern of the Little Entente is to assist in safeguarding peace in Central and South-Eastern Europe and Europe as a whole." Replying to a query, he added: "The constructive function of the Little Entente will be manifested more and more effectively in the future in the realm of mutual economic relations and in the adjustment of relations to neighbouring States."

It must have been evident, even to those who did not wish to see, that the Jachymov Conference was a most successful affair. What was unmistakable was that there had been the frankest discussion *vis-à-vis* Italy, yet before the conference met statements had appeared in certain newspapers to the effect that at the request of Mitilineu the subject was to be excluded from all discussion at it. The speech of Mitilineu himself to the journalists showed the falsity of these statements, and justified the words of the *communiqué* issued by the Belgrade Ministry of Foreign Affairs two or three days before the conference: "No questions can be excluded from discussion between sincere friends and allies." It was not without point that during May 14 the three Ministers, with their staffs and representatives of the Press, motored over to Karlsbad and Marienbad, where they were received by the Queen of Yugoslavia, who was taking a cure there. Nor did it pass unnoticed that soon after the conference Mitilineu paid a visit to Paris, Bucarest papers seeing in it a reassertion of Rumania's traditional policy respecting France. On his return to Belgrade, Marinkovitch told the Press that the chief success of the conference lay in its having dispelled the allegations of the disruption of the Little Entente and of the freedom of its members to join other combinations. He also remarked that the economic relations of the Little Entente must grow and extend to other Central European

States in order to demolish the present system of Chinese walls of prohibitive tariffs and customs.

World Economic Conference

The extreme difficulty, not so much of abolishing these Chinese walls but of even making a breach in them, was illustrated during the same month of May, 1927, by the World Economic Conference held at Geneva. Assembling on May 4, it sat till May 23. This conference was preceded by a variety of publications presenting an analysis of existing economic conditions, which formed a basis for its deliberations and work. The delegates represented the most varied national and class interests, and anything approaching unanimity of opinion was impossible from the start, except in the most general way. Both the United States and Soviet Russia sent delegates. The most important discussions took place in the Commission on Commerce and the Commission on Industry. In the former the feature was the fight between countries advocating free trade, such as England, and those championing protection, such as the United States and most European lands; the one saw the cause of the existing economic crisis in the dislocation of the international distribution of goods and the remedy in the removal of all obstacles, such as tariffs, to international trade; the second saw the cause in the lack of consumption and the remedy in increasing the purchasing power of the masses at home through higher wages and increased production under tariffs.

In the end the commission took the view that further increases in tariffs were undesirable, recommended indeed the gradual reduction of tariffs, and advocated the conclusion of commercial treaties on the most-favoured-nation basis. The Commission on Industry debated international cartels. Here again two groups stood out; on one side were England and Germany, and on the other was France, who, in opposition to them, wanted a great extension of the cartel system. The situation thus disclosed was worsened by the demand put forward by the workers' delegates for the international registration and control of cartels. The French delegates were conciliatory, and the commission succeeded in pacifying the others and in making the question of unemployment and its possible remedies the chief subject of discussion. Less interest was taken in the meetings of the Commission on Agriculture, perhaps for the reason that agricultural output had been much less affected by the post-War economic crisis than had commerce and industry. This commission suggested the extension of the cooperative system, in order to increase direct contact between producer and consumer and to develop cheap agricultural credits.

The best that could be said for this conference was that it did represent a success on the whole for the League of Nations, under whose auspices it was held. It indicated that its policy of pacification was, by making international political questions less acute than they had been before, centring general interest in the economic sphere. The proceedings of this conference were closely scanned throughout the world, and nowhere more closely than in the Little Entente States, which had long been endeavouring to obtain better economic relations with each other and the adjoining States. An instance of success was registered in the signing of a Commerical Agreement on May 31, 1927, between Czechoslovakia and Hungary at Prague. To this end negotiations had begun in January, 1927, and were concluded in May following; the agreement was ratified on August 8, 1927, at Budapest. In April Czechoslovakia and Austria failed to come to terms regarding changes in their commercial agreement, but a new treaty, which was favourable to Austria, was concluded in July following.

Masaryk Re-elected President of Czechoslovakia

On May 27, 1927, an event occurred which was of good omen for the Little Entente, more particularly to Czechoslovakia. This was the re-election of Masaryk as President of the latter. There had never been any real doubt that he was the only possible candidate for the position, though there was some opposition on the part of the Communist Party. In joint session of the House of Deputies and the Senate at Prague he was re-elected on the first ballot. Of the 434 members of the two divisions of the Czechoslovak Parliament present, 274 voted for Masaryk, 54 for Shturc, the Communist selection, 104 votes were blank, and two were spoiled. Masaryk secured 13 votes above the number postulated by the Constitution.

An editorial in *The Times* of May 28, 1927, admirably expressed Czechoslovak sentiment and that of the world in general. It ran: "The people as a whole instinctively recognize him as their leader, the man who, far above the strife of parties, most faithfully represents the national aspirations. Years ago, when Czech or Slovak independence seemed an almost incredible dream, Professor Masaryk instilled into his students a sober faith in the national idea. He thought it necessary then to insist upon vital impulse rather than on political theory, and amid a whirl of contending doctrines, he simply declared that character was of much greater importance to the nation than any political views. His own attitude confirmed his teaching." After summarizing what Masaryk had accomplished during the World War for his country, and recalling his election as its first President, the article continued: "Ever since, he has been the greatest personal asset of the nation. The sober forethought that is the dominating note in the general policy of the Czechoslovak Republic can be traced in very large measure to his counsels, to his clear realization of the character and resources of his people, and to his wide knowledge of the complicated European situation in which the new State is placed. At the age of seventy-seven President Masaryk is full of vigour and unfailing foresight. He has devoted his life to a Cause that is now an Achievement—the Republic of Czechoslovakia. In congratulating him on his re-election, it is permissible to express the hope that this wise European statesman may long be spared to assure the bases of national prosperity in his own country and to achieve that general reconciliation in Central Europe upon which he has set his heart."

It might also have been said that Masaryk's heart had been gladdened by the reconciliation that was going on in Czechoslovakia itself with regard to its component races. This was manifested by the German parties giving their full support to Masaryk in the election; in the Government there were now not only German Czechoslovak Ministers, but also representatives of the aforetime dissident Slovaks.

Death of King Ferdinand

Shortness of duration characterized the meeting of the Council of the League of Nations in June, 1927—it lasted just four days, but important diplomatic conversations took place "behind the front" touching the keeping of the peace of Europe, still somewhat jeopardized by the Italo-Yugoslav conflict and shadowed by the breaking off of relations with the Soviet by Great Britain. The most contentious subject on the agenda of the Council, and that which was of particular interest to the Little Entente, was concerned with the controversy between Rumania and Hungary respecting the "optants"—the landowners in Transylvania who had opted for Magyar Nationality—and the special phase of it before the Council was connected with the powers of the Mixed Arbitral Tribunal to decide or not to decide the question at stake. The commission which had the matter in hand requested the delegates of the two States to ask their respective Governments to make a fresh examination of the question, further consideration of which was postponed, with other things, to the September meeting of the Council.

Before that meeting took place, however, great changes had occurred in Rumania. In May King Ferdinand, who had long been seriously ill, felt that his death was approaching, and asked Averescu to form a Cabinet of National Union in which all Rumanian political parties would be represented. The King had reached the conviction that the formation of a coalition Government on a broad basis was essential in the interests of the country. After a fruitless effort by Averescu to form a coalition, the King dismissed him and replaced him by Prince Stirbey, Administrator of the Crown Domains; but after two weeks the prince retired, and on June 21 Bratianu was again

Prime Minister. Elections were held on July 7 and resulted in 314 seats for Bratianu and the Liberals, the Tsaranist or Peasant Party under Maniu, the next largest group, obtaining only 57 seats.

Titulescu, then Rumanian Minister in London, had accepted office as Foreign Minister in Bratianu's Government, and on July 11 he received a large deputation of Rumanian and foreign journalists, to whom he discoursed on the foreign policy of Rumania and her domestic affairs. He said that Rumania's foreign policy expressed the agreement which existed between her interests and those of Europe as a whole, and every act of that policy was to be interpreted, whether in the past or the future, from that point of view. Rumania earnestly desired peace, but peace was impossible without international order. Rumania therefore had supported with all her energies that Magna Charta which Europe had secured for herself in the Peace Treaties. Rumania had contributed to the solidarity of Europe not merely by words, but by deeds, and that often to her own detriment—a fact which had been gratefully recognized by the League of Nations. In these conditions the line of Rumania's foreign policy was clear: it was to extend and where possible strengthen good relations with all countries without exception; to maintain the mutual bonds uniting the country with the Little Entente and Poland, States which had the same desire and need for peace and order as Rumania; and to collaborate closely with the three great friendly Powers, France, Italy, and England, with whom Rumania was united in indissoluble bonds. Friendship with France had recently been freshly sealed by a treaty, and the same was the case with respect to Italy. Rumania was never unmindful of the help rendered to her in her darkest hour by England. Continuing, Titulescu said that he would use all the experience which more than five years' stay as Rumanian Minister in London had given him to make friendship with Great Britain more and more profound. He concluded by stating that as external affairs depended largely on internal policy, the new Government intended to carry out a programme which might be described briefly as the consolidation of the

Rumanian State, and would work on it with determination but in a spirit of conciliation towards all.

King Ferdinand expired on July 20, 1927, but his death did not occasion a political crisis, his grandson, Prince Michael, a boy of six, son of Prince Carol, who had renounced his claim to the throne, becoming King under a regency composed of his uncle Prince Nicholas, the Patriarch of Rumania, and Buzdugan, the former President of the Court of Cassation, as had been arranged before the demise of Ferdinand. All parties in the State accepted the new situation, and Bratianu remained in power, despite the clamour of the Peasant Party for a dissolution of Parliament and a general election. All parties were at one, however, on the foreign policy of the country and its place in the Little Entente.

Hungarian Optants Question

Replete with interest for all, the September, 1927, meetings of the Council and Assembly of the League of Nations at Geneva, had a profound significance for Rumania, Czechoslovakia, and other States of the New Europe which had carried out policies of agrarian reform—the social side of the transformation effected by the World War and the Peace Treaties. The general question of these agrarian reforms was involved in the particular question of the Hungarian "optants," already referred to above, which again came up for discussion before and by the League. The challenge to Rumania was in effect a challenge to all other States which had established land reform since the War, as it bore on their internal policy, on their right to have such a policy, and in brief on the Sovereignty of each individual State. The claims advanced for the return to the optants of lands expropriated by the Rumanian Government were plainly in derogation of the Sovereignty of Rumania, but were upheld by the Hungarian Government on the ground that these expropriations were contrary to the relevant provisions of the Treaty of Trianon, which was binding on Rumania.

In August, 1922, the Hungarian Government had requested the Ambassadors' Conference to deal with the matter, but was told to take it before the League. In March, 1923, that Government asked the League to declare that the Rumanian agrarian laws were contrary to the treaty and that the land belonging to the optants should be restored to them, with compensation. In the following May representatives of the Rumanian and Hungarian Governments met in Brussels, under the presidency of Adatchi, the League Council representative of Japan, and signed an agreement, under the terms of which it was admitted that the Treaty of Trianon did "not preclude the expropriation of the property of optants for reasons of public welfare, including the social requirements of agrarian reform." The Council of the League adopted this finding. But in December, 1926, the optants brought their claims before the Rumano-Hungarian Mixed Arbitral Tribunal, functioning under the Two-hundred-and-thirty-ninth Article of the treaty, but with its jurisdiction strictly limited to the liquidation of ex-enemy property. The optants now pleaded that the expropriations were war liquidation, and contrary to the Two-hundred-and-fiftieth Article of the treaty. In reply, the Rumanian Government raised the question of the competence of the Tribunal; it also showed that agrarian reform in Rumania began before the War, the Constituent Assembly of May, 1914, having been elected for the purpose of amending the Constitution so as to render agrarian reform possible; that action was deferred because of the War, but was rendered imperative by the menace of Bolshevism; and that no sooner was Rumania evacuated in 1918 than her Government at once proceeded with the reform as a general State policy. In the Regat or Old Kingdom the aristocracy renounced their estates—"one of the most memorable incidents of its kind in modern history," as Seton Watson rightly said in an article on "The Little Entente" which was published in the *Contemporary Review* for November, 1927. In other parts of Rumania the reform not only deprived Hungarians of their lands, but also many Rumanian ecclesiastical and other institutions, such as the Uniate Church, the Academy, and the hospitals of Bucarest, who suffered in precisely the same way.

It was clear, therefore, that the agrarian reform was not a measure of war liquidation. Nevertheless, the Mixed Arbitral Tribunal, by a majority of two votes to one, declared itself competent to hear and determine the question of the optants, and thereupon Rumania withdrew her representative from the Tribunal, so far as the agrarian matter was concerned, as she held that on this point the Tribunal had acted in excess of its authority. Hungary next asked the Council of the League to appoint an arbitrator to replace the Rumanian. In June, 1927, at Geneva, as in the preceding May at London, various meetings took place under League auspices between the interested parties with a view to a settlement, but were unsuccessful. On September 17, 1927, the Committee of the Council of the League which was dealing with the controversy made a unanimous report, Chamberlain being its spokesman; after narrating what the League had already done, the report defined two principles which the acceptance of the Treaty of Trianon made obligatory for Rumania and Hungary: (1) The provisions of the Peace Settlement effected after the War of 1914–18 do not exclude the application to Hungarian nationals, including those who have opted for Hungarian nationality, of a general scheme of agrarian reform; (2) There must be no inequality between Rumanians and Hungarians, either in the terms of the Agrarian Law or in the way in which it is enforced. The case was argued with skill and feeling, Titulescu appearing for Rumania and Apponyi for Hungary, on September 19.

On the previous day Benesh had submitted a Memorandum to the Council dealing with the question. He stressed the fact that while the agrarian reform was being accomplished in Czechoslovakia, the Peace Conference was kept constantly informed of what was being done, and he recalled that at that conference the Hungarians, represented by Apponyi also on that occasion, asked only for pledges that Hungarian subjects would not be treated differently from Czechoslovak subjects. Benesh repelled the Hungarian contention that disputes arising from the reform were within the competence of the Mixed Arbitral Tribunal, for that would mean giving a privileged

M. TITULESCU

position to Hungarian subjects as compared with both Czechoslovaks and foreigners, English, French, and so on, who would not have the right to appeal to a similar tribunal.

In his speech Titulescu pointed out that land reforms like those enacted in Rumania were in operation in neighbouring countries, and he maintained that once a breach was made in the right of a State to carry out its own reforms without interference, the result would be that many cases of claim for alteration in allotment of land would be brought forward in Czechoslovakia, Yugoslavia, Poland, and other States. The consequence of admitting the right of the Tribunal to adjudicate on questions arising out of the reforms would be that Hungarians in Transylvania would be able to obtain relief where Rumanians, who had no right of appeal to it, could not do so. Apponyi made a spirited reply, his chief point being that the Council in its findings was acting on the advice of jurists who did not constitute a court of justice, but were merely legal experts attached to six of the Delegations then in Geneva and did not form a statutory body; he said he thought he could find six other jurists who would give an opposite opinion. Chamberlain remarked that the Council was both a court of law and a court of equity, and was bound to weigh the most general considerations. He said that the Hungarian Government had made no concessions from first to last, and he exhorted it to accept the report. Apponyi, however, would not agree to this. In the end the Council adopted a resolution that the two parties should not be called on to accept at once its findings, but should have till the ensuing December meeting to consider them.

Little Entente Conference at Geneva

While the League was in session the three Foreign Ministers of the Little Entente—Benesh, Titulescu, and Marinkovitch—had met in a special conference on September 2 and 3. They discussed the general situation and reviewed the proceedings of the World Economic Conference. Titulescu referred to the position in Rumania after the death of King Ferdinand, and stated that the situation was now fully cleared up. Marinkovitch spoke of the improvement in the relations between Yugoslavia and Italy, of the Franco-Yugoslav Treaty of Friendship (p. 278), and of relations with Bulgaria being facilitated —all proving that the Little Entente was taking every possible step to strengthen peace and further the consolidation of Central and South-Eastern Europe. The Ministers decided that the Little Entente had no reason to modify its original attitude of disapproval of Anschluss, which in itself was contrary to the Peace Treaties unless accorded by the unanimous vote of the League, in this case an impossibility. The conference welcomed the Polish resolution against all wars of aggression, as they regarded it as a new step towards guaranteeing peace. The Ministers also had before them the action of Lord Rothermere for the revision of the Peace Treaties, and they arrived at the conclusion that there was no reason for the Little Entente's taking official notice of it, as Rothermere was acting as a private person, and the intangibility of the frontiers of the three States was in any case insured.

The "Rothermere Campaign"

What came to be called the Rothermere Campaign had been started by the publication in the *Daily Mail* during June, 1927, of an article signed by Lord Rothermere and entitled "Hungary's Place in the Sun," which attacked the Little Entente States and demanded a revision of the frontiers assigned to Hungary by the Treaty of Trianon. Strongly advocating what he termed a "reasonable rectification" of the Magyar frontiers, he said he did not desire any alteration of the Peace Treaties by violence or intimidation, but he did suggest that financial pressure might be enforced by the exercise of wise caution by banking institutions whose help was invoked by the new States of Central Europe. He invited the British Government to follow the lead which Italy had given to the Powers of Western Europe in holding out a helping hand to Hungary. Though the article failed to excite opinion in Great Britain to any appreciable extent, it did arouse a great deal of comment and feeling throughout Central Europe—favourable, of course, in Hungary and the reverse, as naturally, in the States of the Little Entente, a combination of which Rothermere had expressed the opinion in his article that it was "less aggressive" than of yore and was fast losing international value.

In the Committee of the Czechoslovak Senate, Benesh, replying to a question, said in mid-July that the relations of Czechoslovakia with England were excellent and were becoming ever closer and more cordial; as for Lord Rothermere's article in the *Daily Mail*, he had no intention, he stated, of occupying himself too much with it; a significance was being given it in some quarters which it did not possess. In August Rothermere returned to the attack by publishing over his signature another article in the *Daily Mail*: "Europe's Powder Magazine" was its sensational title, and this was reinforced by a second headline, "Gross Injustices Making for War." In the article he declared that Central Europe was "piled high with the materials of a new conflagration," and that the cause of this was the "partitioning of the Hungarian nation among its neighbours by the Treaty of Trianon, imposed on Hungary in June, 1920." Czechoslovakia was singled out for assault in this flaming article.

On October 25, 1927, in the Commission on Foreign Affairs of the Czechoslovak Chamber of Deputies, Benesh dealt trenchantly with the Rothermere Campaign. His speech was published in French by the Orbis Company of Prague, 1927, under the title *La Situation Internationale et la Politique Étrangère Tchécoslovaque*. After passing in review the general situation, the Geneva meetings, and the position of the disarmament question, he touched on the quarrel between his Government and the Vatican, which was concerned with the John Huss celebrations, and then went on to speak of the optants question and Magyar propaganda.

He said: "During recent months public opinion in Czechoslovakia has been somewhat agitated by a campaign for the revision of the Peace Treaties, a campaign masked by propaganda against the agrarian reform in Central Europe. The object was twofold: (1) By direct action at Geneva in the matter of the Rumano-Hungarian controversy about the optants to procure a decision hostile to the agrarian reform in Rumania and consequently in the other Succession States; (2) To create a spirit hostile to the Treaty of Trianon and prepare the ground for raising, at the moment desired, the question of the revision of that treaty. This campaign has aroused among us much greater interest than it really merits. On the other hand, it has induced demonstrations of attachment to the State and the very idea of the Czechoslovak Republic from all the Slovak Parties from the Right to the Left, demonstrations which are perhaps the most important and the most decisive since the formation of the State. It has also caused a response in favour of the State and the Republic on the part of some of our Minorities. This is a very satisfactory thing which should be noted, particularly in foreign lands." Certainly nothing was more remarkable than the way in which the Slovaks, who had been represented as groaning under the tyranny of the Czechs, rallied to the State, the truth being that on the whole they were much better off as citizens of the Republic than they had ever been under Magyar domination.

After remarking that this campaign was of the same nature as other Magyar propaganda campaigns, he said that all such campaigns failed, because the character and methods of their working, which consisted mostly in a manipulation of the facts and in comments and statements contrary to the truth, were immediately shown up and condemned by everybody. Alluding to the optants question at Geneva, he told how he had supported Titulescu. Continuing, he said: "I call attention to the importance of this question. It is an integral part of a general campaign launched last year with much force in Western Europe, which, starting in certain political and social circles united by common interests, and having gained to its side some international jurists of authority, seeks to overthrow in some countries legislation for agrarian reform, or to undermine its essentials. It would be easy for it to attack other domestic legislation, but the check suffered by it at Geneva will keep it within the desired limits. . . . For the rest, I have no doubt that the campaign will be a complete failure."

Turning to the Rothermere articles, he said: "Of the second objective of this propaganda I shall speak briefly. I state, in view of the fact that it started in London, that the British Government has nothing whatever to do with it. Not only is it not in accordance with the intentions of that Government, but it is in direct opposition to its policy. I mentioned the matter to Sir Austen Chamberlain, the British Foreign Secretary, when we were at Geneva, and he authorized me to state that the policy of the British Empire was defined by his last declaration in the House of Commons, namely, the British Government followed a policy of peace in Europe and held to the existing treaties of peace which Great Britain had signed." On various occasions the British Government, through the Foreign Secretary and also through the Prime Minister, made it clear that it had nothing whatever to do with the Rothermere Campaign.

Benesh next warned his countrymen that such campaigns would reappear or recommence every time there was tension in the international situation; this meant constant vigilance. "You have all seen lately," he observed, "many representations from various quarters in favour of a revision of the Peace Treaties. . . . We have always said, as everybody knows, that these treaties are not perfect, but we have always maintained, and we always maintain, that the present state of things is infinitely better, from the point of view of political and ethical justice, than that which obtained before the War. . . . Everybody is aware that it is impossible to trace frontiers according to this or that political and ethnical ideology, and that in any settlement extremely complex considerations come into play—history and historical rights, economics, the geographical situation, and political and ethnical needs. Everybody knew and took into account the fact that in the States, whether old or new, more or less considerable Minorities would remain—there was not a State which had no ethnical Minorities. This was why there were treaties for the protection of Minorities. But it had never been pretended, even at the Peace Conference, that the Peace Treaties or, for that matter, any other treaties were eternal." Accordingly Article XIX of the Covenant of the League, he pointed out, provided for making changes in the treaties; any State could present to the League a demand for the modification of any treaty; but this demand presupposed that the State making it had observed the principles of the Peace Treaty and of the Covenant, namely, loyalty and the love of peace towards others, was able to prove that the treaty had become out of date, and could show that its policy in general was one characterized by good faith.

He agreed with Lloyd George that modifications of treaties could be obtained peacefully through the procedure of the League in application of Article XIX and in conformity with the conditions therein set forth. But the propaganda that was being made was founded on quite different principles. It assumed a menacing tone, vexed international political life, prevented consolidation, and placed obstacles in the way of ententes between interested States. It did not stop to think that in the majority of the changes it advocated there would be new injustices if they were carried out, nor would it be satisfied with small rectifications. Its real inspiration was hate and enmity; for the most part it was based on "inexactitudes, inaccuracies, false statistics, falsified documents, and statements incorrectly interpreted." It created uncertainty, trouble, and disorder both politically and socially, and spread abroad a bellicose spirit. After this denunciation of the campaign, it was no wonder that Benesh said that the Czechoslovak Government would oppose with the utmost energy all such campaigns. In conclusion, he declared that the Little Entente stood as firmly as ever, and that the three States composing it regarded economic cooperation throughout Central Europe as the question that was most important for them at present; therefore they would give it their attention above everything else.

Macedonian Disturbances

In the autumn of 1927 the area of the Balkans was deeply troubled once more, the chief causes of friction being Macedonia and Albania. The season, however, began well. During the

September League meetings Titulescu and Marinkovitch came to a friendly agreement which regulated the status of Rumanian schools in the Yugoslav part of the Banat, about which there had been disputes; as the *Novosti* of Belgrade observed on September 10, 1927, this settlement was a genuine contribution to the consolidation of the Little Entente and peace in the Balkans. In the same month the general election passed off quietly in Yugoslavia and left the balance of parties but little changed; the Cabinet was reconstituted partially, Vukitchevitch and Marinkovitch remaining Prime Minister and Foreign Minister respectively. The political situation in Rumania was tranquil. The relations of Rumania and Yugoslavia to Bulgaria were good; Marinkovitch's policy was directed towards a real *rapprochement* between Yugoslavia and Bulgaria; his predecessor Peritch had spoken of the ties of kinship that existed between the two States, and his words had been noted in Sofia.

This promising state of affairs was suddenly disturbed by the renewal of outrages by komitadji bands early in October; a Serbian General was murdered at Ishtip by emissaries of the Macedonian Revolutionary Organization, whose headquarters were in Bulgaria; there were other "incidents." The Yugoslav Press demanded the suppression of the organization by the Bulgarian Government; some papers hinted that support was being given to the komitadjis from across the Adriatic. In a semi-official Note the Yugoslav Government drew the attention of Bulgaria to the serious effect the outrages might have on the relations of the two States. Bouroff, the Bulgarian Foreign Minister, affirmed the good will of his Government to Yugoslavia; the Council of Ministers decided to take energetic measures against the Macedonian Organization, and proclaimed martial law on the frontier. In the Bulgarian Parliament Liaptcheff, the Prime Minister, deplored the outrages; "nothing," he said, "could be more disastrous or more dangerous for Bulgaria and the entire Bulgarian nation than these actions, which are the actions of madmen." This language, which required some courage, had good results both in Sofia and Belgrade; and gradually the tension eased.

Franco-Yugoslav Treaty

General attention in the Balkans, as elsewhere, was next paid to the signing, on November 11, 1927, in Paris by Briand and Marinkovitch of the Franco-Yugoslav Treaty of Friendship, which had been negotiated and initialled long before (p. 278). In a telegram to Poincaré, then French Prime Minister, Vukitchevitch expressed his "feelings of deep and sincere joy at this historic event, which will powerfully contribute to the consolidation of general peace." In a statement in the *Temps*, Marinkovitch said that for Yugoslavia it was a question of existence to be friends with France. He remarked that France's attachment to the Little Entente States was as natural as the creation of the Little Entente itself; both in fact were the natural results of the present international conditions of Europe. He added that France pursued no private ends in any of the countries of the Little Entente. He hoped that Yugoslav relations with Italy would be excellent, and it was his view, he declared, that the treaty could serve only to consolidate such relations by confirming once more the eminently pacific intentions of his country. In Italy the treaty was sharply criticized, both France and Yugoslavia being attacked. In Paris it was explained that the signature of the treaty had been put off so long because there had been a hope to extend the scope of the pact—by the inclusion of Italy was the suggestion.

On November 23 Marinkovitch delivered a speech on his foreign policy in the Skupshtina in reply to an Opposition interpellation. He said that his great aim was to maintain and strengthen the system based on the Peace Treaties and to establish a basis for collaboration between all Balkan countries by promoting good relations between them. At Geneva in September he had told the Greek Foreign Minister Michalakopoulos that he was ready to begin fresh negotiations for an agreement with Greece. Touching Bulgaria, he stated that the fact had been established that the Macedonian Organization was sending agents into Yugoslav territory, and he had communicated with the Bulgarian Government on the matter in the hope that it would stop these incursions. Yugoslav relations with Albania had improved. Referring to France, he maintained that Yugoslavia had always represented France and French ideals in that part of the world, and for that reason the signing of the treaty with her was an act of international loyalty. Continuing, he stated he was happy to say that his efforts to obtain the support of Great Britain had not been without result; Yugoslavia had reason to be grateful for the British attitude during recent difficulties, when she had been accused of giving way to nerves and showing a tendency to be aggressive. He wound up by expressing his eagerness to improve the relations of Yugoslavia with Italy; the geographical propinquity of the two countries indicated that they had many interests in common.

Everybody knew, however, that Marinkovitch's policy included friendship with Italy, and that he desired that the Skupshtina should ratify the Nettuno Conventions, the non-ratification of which nettled the Italians. It was therefore unfortunate, to put it mildly, that on the day preceding that on which he delivered this characteristically pacific speech, a second Treaty of Tirana was signed between Italy and Albania, the terms of which apparently were designed to wound Yugoslav susceptibilities. This treaty was one of Defensive Alliance and reinforced the Tirana Treaty of 1926, which had virtually set up an Italian political protectorate over Albania; the new treaty turned that political protectorate practically into a military one for twenty years. It could not but make a bad impression throughout Yugoslavia, nor did it have a good Press outside Italy, being looked on very generally as Mussolini's reply to the Franco-Yugoslav Treaty in a manner inconsistent with the spirit of the League and of Locarno. Though it was not discussed officially at the December meeting of the Council of the League, it was one of the chief topics of conversation at Geneva, but in the meantime what might have become a highly dangerous situation was being mitigated by efforts to bring about a better understanding between France and Italy, which, after a time, were successful. The optants question was not considered at the December Council, but was postponed till the following March, owing to the ill health of Titulescu. In Rumania towards the end of October there had been some appearance of an agitation in favour of Prince Carol; a former Under-Secretary of State was arrested, tried, and acquitted; the country remained calm. On November 25 Bratianu died suddenly after an operation. A great patriot and experienced leader, he had ruled rather than guided his country for many years. He was succeeded as Prime Minister by his brother Vintila, who had long been associated with him in the Government, mainly in finance. Vintila had a difficult task in keeping in power because of the growing strength of the National Peasant or Tsaranist Party, but its opposition to him did not imply any change in Rumania's foreign policy.

As the year came to an end, the most hopeful sign for the further consolidation of peace in Europe was the move towards a Franco-Italian *rapprochement*, a move most gratifying to the Little Entente, and assuredly not less welcome to Great Britain, bent on peace everywhere. It probably smoothed the way for negotiations respecting the Pact of Rome between Italy and Yugoslavia at this time. This treaty (p. 233) ran for five years, but its validity was conditioned by the Article providing for its renewal or denunciation a year in advance of its termination, the date when this was to happen being January 27, 1928. The parties agreed to defer the date for six months, and on January 25, 1928, Bordrero, the Italian Minister to Yugoslavia, and Marinkovitch signed at Belgrade a Protocol extending the treaty in this manner to July 28 following.

The Machine-Guns Incident

On January 3, 1928, *The Times* published a message, to which had been given the headlines: "A Frontier Comedy: Machine-guns as Machinery," from its Vienna Correspondent and dated the previous day; neither the correspondent nor *The Times* appeared to attach to the news any value other than that indicated. The telegram stated that an incident which, but for the numerical preponderance of Hungarian railwaymen over Austrian Customs officials, would doubtless have led to a hand-to-hand conflict on January 1 had been reported from the Hungaro-Austrian frontier at St. Gotthard. The facts were given thus: "An Austrian Customs official, who had failed to compare the contents of five trucks with their consignment bills, afterwards discovered that they contained component parts of machine-guns travelling as machinery. An attempt was immediately made by the Austrian officials to have the wagons shunted back across the frontier, but this the Hungarians prevented. While there is admittedly no law forbidding the importation of munitions of war through Austria into Hungary, apart from any restriction imposed by the Peace Treaty, Austria is entitled to collect a much higher duty for arms than for ordinary machinery, and this in the present instance she will probably have to forgo. Up to December 31 last the Austrian Customs station was on Austrian territory; it had been transferred to the Hungarian side of the frontier yesterday. The consignment of guns had come from Verona, in Italy."

There the message of *The Times* ended, but the affair was far from being closed, for quite another opinion of it, namely, that there had been accidentally uncovered a deliberate attempt on the part of intransigent Hungary to arm herself secretly, caused a great commotion in the Little Entente States and Central Europe generally, and set the Press in full cry. It had been stated in Hungary almost at the start that the five trucks were destined for Warsaw, but this was denied by Poland categorically and at once. Suspicions loomed large, and more than suspicions were voiced. One paper, not without a certain authority, for it was supposed to be officially inspired in Prague, alleged that it had been "ascertained" that this was not the first time that munitions had been smuggled into Hungary, the consignments being sent under false declarations—other forgeries were recalled, such as the recent French franc forged notes—to some firm of forwarding agents beyond the country, the munitions being unloaded in the course of the journey through it. The journals of the Little Entente called loudly and excusably for a thorough inquiry into the facts of the case. The *Viitorul*, the organ of the Rumanian Government, declared in passionate terms for the reinstatement of the Inter-Allied Military Control over Hungarian armaments—it had been withdrawn, the Little Entente consenting, though none too willingly, in 1927—as the only means of safeguarding peace, and it suggested bringing the affair to the notice of the Ambassadors' Conference, the League of Nations, and the Little Entente.

The matter took on a grave aspect. Not unnaturally, considering all that had gone before, the leaders of the Little Entente could not but take a serious view of the business from the beginning, and communications were swiftly exchanged between Prague, Bucarest, and Belgrade, with the result that action was resolved on through the League of Nations, on which had devolved the rôle of the military control of former enemy States. Investigations were being conducted by a joint Austrian and Hungarian Commission, but its work was not regarded as sufficiently exhaustive. On February 1 the representatives of Czechoslovakia, Rumania, and Yugoslavia each presented a Note in Geneva dealing with the affair; in addition the Czechoslovak and Yugoslav Governments sent in a Memorandum to the League Secretariat. All three Notes asked the Council to intervene and re-establish military control over Hungary by virtue of its rights and duties and in accordance with the Treaty of Trianon, with the object of avoiding "more serious incidents and consequences." The Rumanian Note differed from the two other Notes by being prefaced with a statement that "for the moment no real conflict has arisen over this incident between the States directly interested, neither does it wish to accuse or suspect anyone whatever in connexion with it." This language had its reverberations, though these were by no means wholly due to the St. Gotthard affair, but rather were inspired by that hostility to the Little Entente which was always so evident when any occasion offered of questioning its solidarity, no matter how unauthentic the occasion might be—and invariably was.

Italy and Rumania

This form of attack on the Little Entente was now visited on the person of Titulescu. As previously noted, the Rumanian

Foreign Minister was ill when the December, 1927, meeting of the Council of the League was held. The Rumanian side of the optants question was in his very competent hands, and he greatly desired to attend that meeting, as the subject was to come up at it; he intimated that he would be present despite his condition, but the sympathetic Council postponed discussion to its next meeting, which was in March, 1928. After some weeks spent in recuperating, Titulescu began a round of foreign visits with Rome, which he reached on January 24, and where he had a long conversation with Mussolini on the following day. This visit to Rome aroused much interest and even more speculation throughout all Europe; in some quarters the opinion was at once expressed that it connoted nothing more or less than the complete falling away of Rumania from the Little Entente; later it was even stated that a reported delay in the presentation of the Little Entente Note to the Council of the League on the machine-guns incident at St. Gotthard was a result of Titulescu's stay in Rome—a statement which he promptly denied. The fact was that his visit was mainly for the purpose of arranging a commercial treaty between his country and Italy, but it was eminently proper that he should fully examine, as he did, with the Duce the general international situation, with special reference to all questions affecting their two States and those adjacent to them.

Addressing representatives of the foreign Press on January 26, Titulescu declared there was no opposition between the interests of Italy and Rumania, and consequently their friendship was destined to be strengthened. He said that similarly no opposition existed between the policy of loyal and active cooperation of Rumania and Italy and the interests of the Little Entente. Speaking of South-Eastern Europe, he stated that anything which threatened peace in the Balkans was a matter of the greatest concern to Rumania; he did not "hesitate to affirm that the existence of a free and independent Albania" was the safest guarantee of peace in the Balkans; he was convinced that the present difficulties could be resolved "in the light of the great interests common to all civilized nations which ruled all discussions of particular problems." From Rome the Rumanian Foreign Minister went on to Paris, arriving there on February 2.

Despite the drawing together of France and Italy that was proceeding, portions of the French Press had been suspicious of the Roman visit; Titulescu, however, was made welcome by Paris, and had conversations with Poincaré, Briand, Berthelot, and other high personages and officials. In an interview given to the Paris Correspondent of the *Prager Presse*, he said that it was, and would continue to be, the aim of Rumania's foreign policy to secure peace on the basis of the Peace Treaties; to this end Rumania was desirous of collaborating with France, Italy, and Great Britain, as well as with the two other States of the Little Entente. Rumania was anxious to cooperate with former enemies on condition that they were ready to abide by the Peace Treaties. She was an ally of France, Yugoslavia, and Italy, and had therefore an interest in seeing closer relations prevail between these countries; Titulescu stated his belief that relations between Belgrade and Rome would improve and would lead eventually to a treaty of alliance. He particularly stressed the truth that he remained absolutely faithful to the idea of the Little Entente, in which he saw an instrument of peace.

These words found an echo in the Senate at Bucarest on February 4 when Duca, then Rumanian Minister of the Interior, said that his Government regarded the Little Entente as a vital necessity for Rumania; Rumania's foreign policy was not of the weathercock kind. He added that the Little Entente was based not merely on the special interests of its members but on those of all Europe, for otherwise the peace of Central Europe would be continually menaced from Hungary, a country where secret armament and agitation against the Peace Treaties were still carried on.

Little Entente Conference at Geneva

General interest continued in the machine-guns case. Germany in particular watched closely what was being done by the League, as she thought the procedure adopted might form a precedent for the League's action in her own case, should it ever be necessary. There was a singular development in the third week of February; Cheng Lo, the Chinese Minister in Paris and President of the Council, intervened by telegraph to suspend the sale of the machine-gun parts until the investigating machinery of the League was put in motion; Bethlen replied that it was impossible to postpone the sale, and, besides, it was to be held in accordance with the railway regulations. The machine-gun parts, having been made unfit for use, were bought by a local merchant at St. Gotthard for 1,800 pengo, or about £64, but by order of the Hungarian Government the material was left under official control till further notice. The Council met at Geneva on March 5, 1928.

On the preceding day a special conference of the Little Entente took place, those present being Titulescu, Benesh, and Marinkovitch, the Foreign Ministers of the three allied States. Views and information were exchanged. Titulescu gave an account of his recent journey to Rome and the West and its bearings on the situation. The relations between Yugoslavia and Italy were considered with a view to assisting the efforts which were being carried on for a solution of all the questions at issue between these two States. Benesh spoke of a recent visit of Seipel, the Austrian Chancellor, to Prague, where he conversed with him and President Masaryk; the occasion had been a lecture given by Seipel to the Catholic Student Union, and was unconnected with politics, though there could scarcely have been no reference in his talk with the Czechoslovak statesmen to Mussolini's recent outburst regarding the Austrians in South Tirol, in the course of which he spoke of "deeds, not words, next time" should the agitation be renewed. The three Little Entente Ministers also had before them the current phases of the optants question and of the St. Gotthard incident, both of which were to be discussed by the Council. A *communiqué* issued after the close of this conference stated that the Ministers completely agreed in their views.

Bethlen on the same day, addressing his constituents at Debreczen, admitted that it was a matter of vital interest to Hungary to come to an understanding with her neighbours. She was constantly being assured by them that they were ready for an agreement with her, but only on condition, however, that all question of treaty revision was dropped. His answer, and the only one possible, he said, was: "Our aim is not the revision of the Peace Treaty. What we want are new frontiers. Upon the present frontiers no lasting peace can be founded—they are a prison in which we are shut up with the victorious States as gaolers. A sort of Locarno Pact would not assist us; our case is not the same as that of Germany. . . . Germany could renounce a province, whereas we are asked to abandon for ever one-third of our whole race. The Hungarian nation would crucify any statesman willing to sign such a treaty." Continuing, he protested very strongly against the attempt to make use of the St. Gotthard affair as a ground to introduce an investigation, which might well cover an effort for reinstating military control over Hungary. It was to be observed, he said, that no one had accused the Hungarian Government of having ordered the machine-guns; actually Hungary had not "enough weapons for the army of 35,000 men she was authorized to have under the Peace Treaty."

Machine-Guns Affair Closed

First in private and then in public session the Council of the League discussed the machine-guns incident on March 7. On behalf of the Little Entente, Titulescu said they regarded this matter as one of general interest and importance in regard to League procedure. They made accusations against nobody, but they did urge on the League that it should maintain its rights in an affair of this kind. For Hungary, General Tanczos replied at considerable length and gave the Hungarian version of the story. Chamberlain and Briand intervened, the former to suggest the appointment of a committee of three to investigate the whole affair, and the latter to ask, while supporting the suggestion of the British Foreign Secretary, why, after seeing the excitement aroused by the discovery of the trucks and their contents, and after noting the steps taken by the States most nearly concerned, the Hungarian Government had persisted in destroying the material. To this query Tanczos replied that his Government had acted in accordance with administrative practice. On March 10 the Council decided to appoint a Commission of technical experts to elucidate the incident and report to the June session.

On June 7 the Council, after discussing the report, officially settled the affair by expressing regret that the real destination of the machine-guns could not be ascertained, criticized Hungary for her precipitate destruction of the evidence, and once more asserted the right of the Council to order an immediate investigation of incidents of the sort. The reporting committee was thanked for its services—and the matter thus was closed. In a short speech Chamberlain said that the results of the procedure adopted had not been satisfactory, nor had the incident been fully elucidated; he regretted it the more because the Council, in choosing this particular method, had been careful of the susceptibilities of the interested States; a more drastic procedure would have increased ill-feeling; he consoled the Council by remarking that it was a "growing organism, and would learn by experience." The net result of the proceedings of the Council was a warning to Hungary and, of course, other States against similar incidents in the future. thus making them much less likely to occur. This was the view of the Little Entente, whose action in the St. Gotthard affair arose solely from concern for the peace of Central Europe.

Optants Question Again

At the March, 1928, meeting of the League the other subject of particular interest to the Little Entente was the optants question. Prior to the meeting, Rumania had sent a Note to Hungary suggesting that the Hungarian Government should undertake to compensate landowners of Magyar nationality out of the amount due to Rumania by Hungary for reparations. This proposal was not well received in Hungary, yet, if the question had not had a very distinct political as well as legal side, the idea of an increase of compensation to the aggrieved optants appeared to hold in it a solution of the trouble. The Council devoted nearly the whole of March 8 and 9 to a discussion of the subject in all its aspects. As before, Apponyi and Titulescu argued the case for their respective countries, and went over much of the ground that had been covered at the September, 1927, meeting. Apponyi now stressed the legal point that the findings of the Council at that meeting (p. 321) overruled a decision of the Mixed Arbitral Tribunal, a thing the Council did not possess the power to do; he said the Hungarian Government was willing to submit the point to the Court at the Hague, but to this Titulescu refused to agree. On March 9 Chamberlain, *rapporteur* in this matter, opened the proceedings with a fresh proposal—that the Mixed Arbitral Tribunal should be reconstituted by the return to it of the Rumanian representative, who had been withdrawn, and by the addition of two new arbiters chosen from neutral States, thus increasing the number of the arbiters from three to five. Briand and Stresemann spoke in support of Chamberlain's proposal, as did other members of the Council.

Apponyi accepted it unconditionally, but Titulescu did so with reservations; finally, however, he was prevailed on to withdraw his refusal, which his reservations were held to amount to, and he promised to consider the matter in conjunction with his Government, but without much hope evidently that it would act on the proposal. The decision of the Council was a recommendation to Rumania and Hungary to agree to the appointment of two arbiters from neutral countries, and to Rumania to return the Rumanian arbiter to the Mixed Tribunal, but this was prefaced by a statement that the Council had not modified its point of view as expressed in its previous findings. The news of this decision excited the greatest surprise in Rumania, where it was generally regarded as tantamount to a reversal of the Council's action in the previous September. In the Rumanian Parliament Bratianu said that Rumania had considered this question as settled, and was dismayed to find that the present decision of the Council of the League contradicted that of September last. The Chamber unanimously approved the attitude of Titulescu in refusing to accept the decision, which was considered as an encroachment on the sovereign rights of Rumania; Opposition leaders united with Government speakers against it. The Rumanian Press did not fail to point out that Rumania's foreign policy was one of peace, whereas the same could scarcely be said of Hungary after the machine-guns incident and the excessive statements made by Bethlen at Debreczin at the beginning of March. In the other Little Entente States the wisdom of the Council's decision was seriously questioned.

A lively correspondence in the British Press on the subject was an interesting feature of the day, the Hungarian side finding formidable advocates in Lord Buckmaster, Lord Newton, and others, and the Rumanian strong support from Seton Watson and Wickham Steed, the former of whom, replying to the contention of Buckmaster and his friends that the "real and important question involved" in the controversy was the Council's omission to fill the vacancy on the Mixed Arbitral Tribunal, accused them of suppressing the fact that fifteen eminent international lawyers, including three British professors of international law, had endorsed the findings of the September Council, which, therefore, could not be characterized as a "wholly illegitimate proceeding."

On June 8, 1928, the optants question came before the Council once more, and a resolution was unanimously adopted saying that while the Council deeply regretted that Rumania and Hungary had failed to reach agreement, it was of the opinion that the controversy ought to be settled by the States themselves on the basis it had recommended—which got the matter no farther. On August 29 Rumania addressed a Note to Hungary suggesting the appointment of delegates to begin direct negotiations, but on September 7 Hungary replied that she would not do this as, according to the Rumanian interpretation, it would mean the acceptance of the Rumanian conditions and point of view; she preferred to apply again to the Council of the League.

Poland and the Little Entente

A visit paid to Mussolini by Zaleski, Polish Foreign Minister, in April, 1928, appeared to create some misapprehensions respecting the attitude of Poland to the Little Entente. Yet, before leaving Warsaw for Rome, Zaleski stated clearly and unmistakably, in an interview given to the Rumanian Press Bureau, that Polish relations with the Little Entente were excellent. The Polish-Rumanian Alliance, he said, was a political reality, as was the Polish Alliance with France. Poland was united with the Little Entente by the common ideal of maintaining peace on the basis of respect for existing treaties. Though the Treaty of Trianon did not affect Poland directly, she regarded it as a factor in her general policy. Next, Zaleski categorically denied the rumours to the effect that he had said Poland had no interest in the permanence of the frontiers of the Little Entente States; he declared that it would be absurd to take up such a position. Referring to his visit to Italy, he remarked that he had availed himself of an invitation extended to him by the Italian Government, in order to get into direct contact with Mussolini; he wished to renew their personal friendship, begun when he (Zaleski) was Polish Minister at Rome. He expressed his conviction that his visit would do nothing but contribute to the further stabilization of peace.

Nettuno Conventions Ratified

During the spring and summer of 1928 tension persisted between Yugoslavia and Italy, though it was less severe than it had been before. In an interview Mussolini had said in March that he needed peace and had given proof of his pacific intentions; he had concluded and ratified a treaty of friendship with Yugoslavia which she had not ratified, but which he hoped she would ratify. Two months later diplomatic negotiations were resumed in Belgrade, and on May 23 the Yugoslav Government, at a Cabinet meeting, authorized submitting to the Skupshtina the ratification of the treaty to which Mussolini had referred—the Nettuno Conventions (p. 268). The announcement of this action raised a storm of angry protest throughout Yugoslavia, the greater part of the Yugoslav Press being against ratification. *Politika* said that while it was clear what Yugoslavia would lose by the conventions, what she would gain was far from clear; it doubted whether Italy would change her policy of trying to isolate Yugoslavia and secure domination of the Balkans, of interfering in Albania, Bulgaria, and Greece, and of assisting the Magyars in their struggle against the Treaty of Trianon. The whole Opposition was against the idea of ratification, as was perhaps natural enough, as its members represented Croatia, Dalmatia, Bosnia, and Herzegovina, the areas which would suffer most from the unfavourable parts of the conventions, by opening the door to Italian economic and political penetration.

Violent anti-Italian demonstrations were held in Belgrade, Ljubljana, and towns in Dalmatia, rioting being particularly serious in Split (Spalato) and Shibenik (Sebenico), after news had been received of anti-Yugoslav riots in Zara. Anti-Yugoslav demonstrations were held in Rome, Venice, Fiume, and other Italian cities. The Italian Minister in Belgrade, Bordrero, made strong protests against the anti-Italian demonstrations, but the anti-Yugoslav demonstrations had also to be taken into account, and there were protests from, as well as to, Belgrade. Friendship with Italy had long been, as already noted, the policy of Marinkovitch, and, undismayed by what was going on, he told the Skupshtina on May 30 that the conventions would be presented to it for ratification as soon as certain important questions of detail had been settled. He denied all statements asserting that the Government's action had any connexion, as had been alleged, with the loan negotiations then proceeding in London, or that pressure had been applied by Italy or any other country. He stated that during his tenure of the Foreign Ministry the conventions had never been mentioned by the Italian Government, nor had any Power made diplomatic representations to him on the subject. The Yugoslav Government kept its head, as did the Italian; Notes of a conciliatory tenor were exchanged between them; and the tumult slowly died down.

Commenting on the situation, Benesh, in a speech before the Foreign Commission of the Czechoslovak Parliament on June 6, 1928, stated his belief that just as Italy and France were composing their differences, so would Italy and Yugoslavia compose theirs. He knew there were difficulties in the way, but Yugoslavia had given many proofs of her desire for peace which would appeal to Italy, and there was no reason to fear a prolonged conflict or war. "Those," he said, "who fear anything of the kind fail to take into account the solidarity of international relations. To-day, whether in Western Europe, Central Europe, or Southern Europe, no one thinks seriously of an armed conflict, simply for the reason that it would involve political and social suicide. This is why, despite obstacles of any sort whatever, and I do not underestimate their importance, all well-informed political leaders are certain that the Italo-Yugoslav conflict will terminate in an entente. Yugoslavia, for whom the pacific and far-sighted attitude of the Minister Marinkovitch has gained great consideration internationally, will do all she can to reach an agreement. I am persuaded that Italy has every intention of acting in the same way." On the previous day Mussolini, speaking in the Senate at Rome, had enlarged on the improvement in Franco-Italian relations, and had gone on to pay a high tribute to the good will displayed by Marinkovitch; he urged Yugoslavia to believe that Italy did not hate her and did not try to interfere with her pacific advancement.

In the course of his remarks, the Duce said "that, great as was his regard for Sir Austen Chamberlain, the direction of Italian foreign policy was under no authorization or tutelage on the part of the British Foreign Office"—an observation from which students of foreign affairs might infer that, whatever had been the case before, Great Britain was now no supporter of a forward policy by Mussolini.

Solidarity of the Little Entente

Proceeding with his speech in the Foreign Commission of the Czechoslovak Parliament on June 6, Benesh touched on the

Hungarian campaign for the revision of the Treaty of Trianon. This campaign, he said, made no real progress. He stated that he had recently visited London, Paris, and other centres, and there he found it was felt that the revision of the Peace Treaties would provoke such disquietudes and conflicts as would again see Europe transformed into one vast conflagration. Alluding to Rothermere, Benesh said that the attitude of the British Government to the "campaign of the English lord" was expressed when, on May 23, Chamberlain had declared, replying to a question, that it did not identify itself with the Press campaign for the revision of the Treaty of Trianon. Czechoslovakia followed along the course marked out for it, Benesh added, with calm and dignity. Her point of view was that of the Little Entente; "all attempts at weakening" the "robust solidarity of the countries of the Little Entente on all questions appear to us absolutely ridiculous." Its adversaries did not grasp the "real and indestructible solidarity of the interests of the three States, and were blind to the elementary, psychological foundations on which our collaboration reposes."

He concluded: "I shall not speak again of the attempts to break our solidarity, as there is no need to do so, but I permit myself to state that on all Central European questions there reigns among the States of the Little Entente, and between the Ministers Marinkovitch, Titulescu, and myself, a complete unity of views. This may also tell our opponents why we shall continue to advance tranquilly, despite all agitation against our common interests." In his more general remarks, Benesh said that he regarded the Kellogg Pact, which had been under consideration for some months by the Great Powers and other States, as of great importance for strengthening peace, representing as it did a species of concise Geneva Protocol. His entire speech was optimistic, its keynote being that the constructive forces of Europe were far stronger than the destructive.

Little Entente Conference at Bucarest

Postponed on account of the illness of one or other of the Foreign Ministers, a regular Conference of the Little Entente was held at Bucarest on June 20 and 21, the representatives present being Marinkovitch, Benesh, and Titulescu, with Vintila Bratianu, the Rumanian Prime Minister, as chairman at the beginning of the proceedings. More than a year had passed since the last regular conference, and this was held in some quarters as indicating the enfeeblement of the Little Entente. The Bucarest Conference was preceded by a visit of Titulescu to Belgrade during the previous week, the object of which, it was generally supposed, was to strengthen the hands of Marinkovitch in his efforts to improve Yugoslav relations with Italy. While in Belgrade, Titulescu, in a statement to the Press, declared that the Little Entente was "one and indivisible," and that there was no nation with which it did not desire to establish friendly relations. In thanking Titulescu for his services to Yugoslavia at Geneva, Marinkovitch recalled the fact that peace had reigned between the Rumanians and the Yugoslavs for the twelve hundred years in which they had been neighbours, a proof of their pacific disposition.

The conference issued three *communiqués* of the general character usual at such meetings; the second, however, was explicit enough; it ran: "Having taken into consideration all the attempts made for destroying the edifice of peace and the existing international *status quo*, the three States of the Little Entente, conscious of their great mission in Europe of guarding and consolidating, despite all efforts to the contrary, peace in their respective countries, have decided to continue with calm and dignity the policy they have followed in common for ten years, and to oppose with the utmost energy, and by all appropriate and timely means, every attempt to change the international status established by the Treaty of Trianon." The *communiqué* issued at the close of the conference said the Little Entente policy had contributed materially to the peace of Europe, while yielding considerable benefits to the three States. At difficult moments the Little Entente had effectively supported the maintenance of peace in Europe; it had made its voice heard on European questions, and above all in those interesting the League of Nations. Its practical policy had stabilized its relations of friendship with France, England, Poland, and Italy; its relations with Germany had improved since Locarno, and with Austria were very friendly. It hailed with gratification the Kellogg Pact. The *communiqué* concluded by stating that the three Ministers, having considered appropriate methods for improving intensively their economic relations, had agreed to nominate a delegation to study this subject.

More than two hundred pressmen, local and foreign, were in Bucarest for this conference, at the termination of which they were invited to meet the Ministers and interrogate them on current matters. Questioned on the relations of the Little Entente with Germany, Benesh replied: "Each State of the Little Entente is the neighbour of a Great Power, and the two other States sincerely desire perfect relations in each case. Rumania and Yugoslavia desire, like ourselves, to see cordial relations between Czechoslovakia and Germany. In the same way Czechoslovakia and Rumania expect a happy issue from the Italo-Yugoslav negotiations, as, on the other hand, Czechoslovakia and Yugoslavia wish to see peace reign between Russia and Rumania. Respecting Anschluss, Benesh dryly remarked that the question was not urgent; touching the Soviet and Czechoslovakia, he said that the commercial treaty of 1922 had not worked out well, and negotiations were going forward for a new agreement. In his observations, Titulescu said he had nothing new to report regarding Russo-Rumanian relations. Questioned by a Magyar journalist on the application of Article XIX of the Covenant of the League of Nations to the question of the revision of the Peace Treaties, Titulescu replied by asking what it was exactly the Article said—it was that the League of Nations might consider from time to time whether the treaties were no longer applicable, and if they were, whether the international situation and peace were injuriously affected thereby. "Do you know any treaty whatever that may not become inapplicable?" he inquired. "So far as we are concerned, we know of no such treaty. That Article, however, was not inscribed in the Covenant for the purpose of permitting agitation to bring about a situation requiring the application of the Article. We are quite calm about that Article; for its application unanimity is necessary, and yesterday MM. Benesh and Marinkovitch and I voted unanimously *Non possumus!* We did so in the interests of peace, and in order there should be no doubt on the point."

But perhaps the most impressive declaration made by the Ministers was that of Marinkovitch, when asked to speak about the Nettuno Conventions; he said he had submitted their ratification to the Skupshtina because he had the firm conviction that ratification must absolutely take place. "I have made," he said, "this question a point of honour because I think it is in the interests of my country. I do not hesitate to say that if, unfortunately, our Parliament does not ratify the conventions, I shall resign from the Government, because ratification is an essential part of our (Little Entente) programme."

Croats Shot in Belgrade Parliament

Marinkovitch's words had been given a terrible poignancy by the tragedy which had occurred at Belgrade on the day before the conference—the shooting in the Skupshtina by Ratchitch, an ultra-Nationalist Montenegrin deputy of the Radical Party, of Stephen and Paul Raditch, Basaritchek, and other Opposition deputies. Basaritchek was killed outright, Paul Raditch died within an hour, and Stephen Raditch was severely wounded. As previously noted, the tense situation between Italy and Yugoslavia, and in Yugoslavia itself, caused by the Yugoslav Government's determination to have the Nettuno Conventions ratified by the Skupshtina, had eased considerably after the exchange of conciliatory Notes by Italy and Yugoslavia. The Opposition in the Skupshtina, though numerically weak, continued to show their hostility to the Government by a policy of obstruction, the result being that no serious work was accomplished despite extra sittings. Stormy scenes were of frequent occurrence; the shootings on June 20 were their culmination, but the immediate cause of the tragedy was that Ratchitch considered himself to have been insulted beyond pardon by Pernar, a Croatian deputy. Pernar, however, stated that he had been warned that his life was in danger, and Ratchitch, it appeared, had talked of the necessity of suppressing the Opposition by force.

Whatever were the rights of this most unfortunate affair, the inevitable result of the political murders was to arouse the greatest excitement throughout the country and intensify the internal struggle between the Serbians and the Croats, thus making the political situation very difficult. Stephen Raditch, accompanied by Pribitchevitch, with whom he had made an alliance, eventually left Belgrade; the Croat deputies declared they would not return to the capital so long as the Parliament, as constituted, remained there. News, afterwards found to be untrue, of the death of Stephen Raditch had led to riots in Zagreb, with many casualties. Yet the funerals of the murdered deputies on the following day passed without disorder, though some 200,000 Croat peasants were in Zagreb. It was to a distracted land that Marinkovitch returned, but he kept to his purpose and resolve; on June 26 it was announced that not even the shootings would prevent the Government from carrying out its plans.

King Alexander began a series of conferences with the political leaders for a Concentration Cabinet, but the Croats were intransigent. The Government resigned on July 4, and, after several attempts to form a new one, success crowned the efforts of Father Koroshetz, the Slovene leader, who presented his Cabinet to the King on July 27. It was a coalition and included Marinkovitch as Foreign Minister; it contained several representatives of the territories of the former Austro-Hungarian Monarchy, and this made for unification once more. But when the Skupshtina assembled again on August 1, 1928, the whole Opposition absented themselves; Raditch remained irreconcilable; he had been appealed to to form a Government but in vain. To some extent he had recovered from his wound, but he unexpectedly got worse, and died on August 8, sincerely and even passionately mourned by the Croat peasants, who literally adored him. Perhaps a man of genius and certainly a fine orator, he lacked balance, and was capable of the most astounding political somersaults, without apparently inconveniencing himself in the least.

On August 13 the Yugoslav Government pushed through the ratification of the Nettuno Conventions; a fortnight or so earlier Mussolini had given his consent to a second postponement for six months of the date of the renewal of denunciation of the Pact of Rome, and this assisted Marinkovitch's policy. There was no enthusiasm for the ratification; most of those Yugoslavs who approved looked on it as a sacrifice to demonstrate the willingness of their country to make friends with Italy in the sight of the world. They expected some response from Mussolini, but scarcely found it in his patronage of Ahmed Zogu's advancement to royal honours under the style and title of "King of the Albanians" on September 1. Yet Italo-Yugoslav relations had now been regularized, which was in the view of the Little Entente a step in the right direction. The internal consolidation of Yugoslavia was, however, still to seek.

Anschluss Again

That the question of Anschluss was not dead but merely sleeping was shown during the summer of 1928. In his remarks to the journalists at the Bucarest Conference quoted above, Titulescu had pronounced the Little Entente's *Non possumus*. On June 27 Seipel, the Austrian Chancellor, referred to this veto of union between his country and Germany, and said that no economic entente which Austria might be invited to join would be acceptable to her if it did not include Germany. He declared that the Little Entente was really political, and Austria could not accept a position in which she would be entitled to speak from the economic point of view alone. Further, he said that he did not believe that the Central European question could ever be solved while the largest State of Central Europe, which was Germany, had no voice in its solution. These remarks were made after a speech in the Austrian Parliament by Bauer, the Social Democratic leader, who said that so long as there was danger of the return of the Habsburg dynasty or of a demand by Magyar irredentists for reassigning the Burgenland to Hungary, it was necessary for Austria to maintain close relations with the Little Entente, but that this did not at all mean a change in her attitude to Germany.

In July opinion in Austria was still more pronounced. In the fourth week of that month the Tenth German Singers' Festival was held in Vienna, with President Hindenburg of Germany and President Hainisch of Austria as patrons. Some 40,000 singers took part, and twice as many people attended the concerts. During the festival there were many references to the political connexion between Austria and Germany; the festival developed into a demonstration in favour of Anschluss, as Loebe, the President of the German Parliament, who was in Vienna, did not fail to note in the course of a speech at the Rathaus. He maintained that the Germans and Austrians were one people, and wanted to belong to one and the same State; the right of self-determination in this matter could not be denied to seventy million people for ever. Other speakers at the Rathaus meeting echoed his words, which were as vigorously applauded as he had been. References were also made to the need for a closer economic understanding between the German-speaking peoples, thus recalling a resolution passed by the German Reichstag, just before it broke up for the summer, to the effect that it was desirable that commercial negotiations should lead to an economic and Customs Union with Austria, a *Zollverein*, though that as well as Anschluss was barred by the Peace Treaties. There had been in fact a certain drawing together of the two States, inasmuch as the railway traffic regulations and the penal codes of both were identical, and cooperation existed between many German and Austrian semi-official organizations.

The statements of Loebe, of course, attracted great attention throughout Central Europe and Germany; in the latter the Socialist *Vorwärts* said that there had never been the slightest doubt that the Austrian people wanted to be inside the German Republic, and the *Börsen Courier*, the Democratic organ, pointed out that the Reich and Austria were completely German and their union would harm no one, while the Nationalist

Deutsche Allgemeine Zeitung grew sentimental over German music, which had moved the Austrians to rally to the conception of a great united Germany. *Germania* said that officials might on political grounds show restraint about Anschluss, but the rolling stone was in motion, and would be stopped by no diplomatic tricks. It was inevitable that such statements as these, which struck directly at the Peace Treaties, should occasion most unfavourable comments in the Little Entente States and in France. The *Temps* remarked that they put a query mark against the order of the New Europe which arose out of the Allied victory, and represented the mobilization of the most active elements of pan-Germanism against the maintenance of peace. There were some papers and observers who expressed the view that all the talk about Anschluss in Austria was unreal, and that its true object was to draw concessions from the Little Entente by a species of threat. Anyhow, the Little Entente stuck to its veto; and it certainly was the case that Austria had made a wonderful recovery despite her very bad start ten years before, a recovery largely due to the assistance of the Allies and not least of Czechoslovakia, who had come to her help before anyone else.

The League of Nations Indispensable

In September, 1928, the Assembly and the Council of the League of Nations held their meetings at Geneva, fifty States being represented at the Assembly; Spain was again a member; Argentina had an observer; and Costa Rica signified her intention to return. Six Prime Ministers and eighteen Foreign Ministers were present. Everything demonstrated that the League had established itself as an institution, as an integral part of international life, and as an indispensable medium for international intercourse during the nine years of its existence. Everywhere these facts were recognized in Europe and throughout the greater part of the rest of the world; they were evidences of the new normality issuing from the results of the War. Signed six days before the Assembly met on September 3, and exerting a strong influence on the League, the Kellogg

Pact was another witness to the same general truth. The Assembly made some progress respecting the major problems with which it was faced, notably as regards the prevention of war by the formulation of model treaties of arbitration, conciliation, non-aggression, and mutual assistance—all testifying in their way to the same thing. Briand's rejoinder to the German demand for disarmament had to be read in the light of the foundations of this new normalization, namely, the due observance of the Peace Treaties and the international status built on them—the New Europe which Germany, like other ex-enemy States, had to accept and fit herself into. This was the sound doctrine of the Little Entente.

Among other questions before the Assembly was that of National Minorities, the care of which was vested in the Council. In pre-War Europe whole Nationalities, as in Central Europe, had been oppressed, without appeal; in the New Europe the Minorities had right of appeal to the League, as Briand pointed out on September 10 in the debate on this question, which he said the League would not allow to be relegated to the background, but which, at the same time, it would not permit to be raised so as to conduce to the shattering of Governments or the endangering of its own work for peace. The question was not to become an element of unrest and uncertainty in the international situation—an oblique but significant reference to the campaign for the revision of the Peace Treaties. Among other questions coming up at Geneva of special interest to the Little Entente was that of the Hungarian optants, as already mentioned, and also the Bulgarian stabilization loan which it had previously dealt with, and which was now, after it had been raised to five million sterling, finally passed by the Council. No set Conference of the Little Entente was held at Geneva at this time, but its Foreign Ministers, Benesh, Marinkovitch, and Argetoyanu (who had succeeded Titulescu on his resignation on July 30 owing to ill health), were in constant contact with each other, as were their respective Delegations.

Asked for his views on the situation by a correspondent of the *Neue Freie Presse*, Argetoyanu said that only the cooperation of all the States of Europe could improve the lot of the Continent, and that this was the watchword of the Little Entente; he also spoke of a Central European Locarno as one of the aims of Rumania's foreign policy. In its comment on the interview, the Vienna paper noted that the Little Entente had had a definite policy from its inception, and had never deviated from it. How little likely that it would change that policy was shown when, on the last day but one (September 25) of the Assembly—many of its members had left Geneva—Apponyi, the chief Hungarian delegate, attacked the "stereotyping" of the situation created by the Peace Treaties, a "situation no nation that merited that name could possibly accept," he declared, referring to his own nation and its post-War status, which he said prevented it from concluding a pact of non-aggression and mutual assistance. He stated that if he was alive, he would bring the matter up again at the next Assembly—1929. Next morning Rumanian and Czechoslovak delegates replied effectively to hls assault.

Expansion of Czechoslovak-Yugoslav Treaty

But the generally intransigent attitude of Hungary had already had its answer by the signing at Geneva by Benesh and Marinkovitch of a Protocol prolonging the Treaty of Alliance between their two States concluded in 1922 (p. 199), and forming with the treaties concluded between Rumania on the one side, and Yugoslavia and Czechoslovakia on the other, the basis of the Little Entente. Nothing, perhaps, was more significant of the process of normalization going on in Europe than the fact that the prolongation of this highly important treaty passed virtually unnoticed; it was evidently accepted as a matter of course. In another of his detailed expositions of the international situation given on October 4, 1928, to the Foreign Affairs Commission of the Czechoslovak Parliament, and published soon afterwards in French by the Orbis Company of Prague, Benesh said: "The fact of the prolongation of the treaty is, in view of our relations with Yugoslavia, a thing that 'goes of itself,' and is but the confirmation of the fact that the system of the Little Entente, of which our treaty with the Kingdom of the Serbs, Croats, and Slovenes is a link, becomes stronger and stronger." He stated farther on in his speech that negotiations were proceeding for a commercial treaty between his country and Yugoslavia and for a similar treaty between Czechoslovakia and Rumania. Thus, in accordance with one of its fundamental aspects and recent decisions at its conferences, the Little Entente was concentrating on economic cooperation within itself.

Salonika Question Settled

From Geneva Marinkovitch had gone on to Paris, and there, as September was drawing to a close, he met Venizelos, who had come on from Rome after signing with Mussolini an Italo-Greek Treaty of Friendship and Arbitration, which entirely clarified the situation as between their two States. The dramatic return to Athens of the Greek statesman had been endorsed by his countrymen at the polls; his announced policy was to strengthen and stabilize friendly relations with neighbouring States, and in a speech at Salonika on July 22 he had spoken with joy of a *rapprochement* between Greece and Italy. The treaty was similar to other treaties of friendship concluded by Italy, but it was the first of the kind to be negotiated by Greece with another State. In the First Article the Parties agreed on cordial cooperation in maintaining the order established by the treaties of peace of which they were co-signatories, and in seeing to the carrying out of the obligations postulated by these treaties. Not only did the treaty wipe out the Corfu incident, but it accepted the possession by Italy of the Dodecanese Islands; in a statement from Rome to the Greek Press, Venizelos had said categorically that there was no Dodecanese question as between Greece and Italy, the matter being solely one between the inhabitants of the islands and Italy. He told Italian journalists that he would be glad to sign treaties of conciliation and arbitration with Turkey, Bulgaria, Albania, and Yugoslavia. All this showed a clear-eyed, practical appreciation of the growing normalization of Europe.

Marinkovitch and Venizelos came to terms in Paris, the chief result being an agreement respecting Salonika on the basis of the agreement of 1923, which gave Yugoslavia a Free Zone in the port without derogating from Greek sovereignty. Simultaneously with the signature of this new agreement was to be the signing of a Pact of Friendship for five years between the two States, thus regularizing their relations—another normalization.

Decennial Celebrations

Tenth anniversaries of the States of the New Europe signalized the last quarter of 1928. On October 28 Czechoslovakia celebrated with great rejoicings the completion of her first decade of existence and independence. Shortly before she had perfected her internal consolidation by introducing a system of decentralization in the form of Provincial Councils for Bohemia, Moravia and Silesia, Slovakia, and Carpathian Ruthenia, and conferring on them large autonomous powers. In Yugoslavia, whose decennium as the Kingdom of the Serbs, Croats, and Slovenes was attained on December 1, the controversy between the federalists and the centralists persisted, but the King remained a unifying force recognized by both, and the dissident Croats definitively expressed their loyalty to him. In Rumania a change of Government had made Maniu, the leader of the National Peasant or Tsaranist Party, Prime Minister on November 11, and with him was associated Vaida Voyed as Minister of the Interior. These two men had headed the Rumanian National movement in Transylvania before the War, both being members of the Hungarian Parliament; ten years had passed since they and the Transylvanians had voted for union with Rumania, and now the turn of the political wheel had brought them into power again. Maniu, whose Foreign Minister was Minorescu, announced that there would be no change in the foreign policy of the country; he defined it as being the maintenance of existing friendships and alliances and of good relations with neighbouring States.

Ten years had also passed since Jonescu, Pashitch, Benesh,

and Venizelos had discussed in London and Paris the project of forming a political combination of the States of Rumania, Yugoslavia, Czechoslovakia, and Greece—and Poland too. Ten years had elapsed since Jonescu and Venizelos had talked it over in Paris with Masaryk, just become President of Czechoslovakia (p. 86). The representatives of these States collaborated at the Peace Conference, as has been seen. The idea of including Poland and Greece in the organization subsequently dropped, and the Little Entente, as it came universally to be known, was constituted, 1920–21. It had proved its value, above all, as an instrument of peace and consolidation. Its dissolution had been frequently predicted, but events proved these prophecies as false as they were fatuous; in 1928 it was stronger and more firmly established than ever. It had never deviated from its original programme—peace on the basis of the Peace Treaties of the New Europe. It had succeeded in much, but not in everything.

Writing in the *Cheske Slovo* in connexion with the tenth anniversary of Czechoslovakia, Benesh said: "Among the questions not yet settled which must not be forgotten, and which for a long time to come will come to the front again, are Anschluss and the revision of the Treaty of Trianon. I do not believe in the union of Austria with Germany. I believe no longer in the revision of the Treaty of Trianon. Those things cannot be brought about except by war or by the unanimous assent of the interested States. These two dangers, however, will arise from time to time, and we shall have to combat them with all our energy." The veritable voice of the Little Entente!

With the years, as they rolled on, the Little Entente had become increasingly popular in the three States, for their peoples realized to the full that it had contributed to internal pacification as well as European consolidation. In April, 1928, an Inter-Parliamentary Union was founded at Prague; it consisted of groups in the three Parliaments, and had as its object the maintenance and strengthening of the political, economic, and cultural relations of the three countries; visits were exchanged between these Parliamentary groups. In furtherance of this same solidarity, sporting clubs, schools, and so on, also exchanged visits. Various organizations, such as the "Little Entente of Railwaymen" and the "Little Entente of Women," supplemented these efforts. But the most important influence in this direction was exercised by the "Little Entente of the Press," whose formation has been already mentioned. It not only worked continually for a closer and better understanding among the journalists of the three States, but also rendered very great services to the cause by furnishing accurate news and illuminating comment, by contradicting false reports, and by exposing tendentious statements, particularly in the foreign Press.

POSTSCRIPT

January to June, 1929

Increasing difficulties in the political situation in Yugoslavia compelled the resignation of Koroshetz and his Cabinet, and after fruitless efforts by various groups to form a Government King Alexander cut the Gordian knot by proclaiming himself dictator. On January 6, 1929, he issued a royal decree abolishing the "Vidovdan" Constitution, and dismissing the Parliament which had been elected in November, 1927. In announcing the change, he stated: "Parliamentary government, which was always my ideal, as it was that of my unforgettable father, has been so abused by blind party passion that it has prevented every useful development in the State. The people have lost all faith in the institution. In Parliament even the ordinary decencies of social intercourse between parties and individuals have become impossible. It is my sacred duty to preserve the unity of the State by every means in my power. To seek to remove these abuses by fresh elections would be a waste of time and energy. By such methods we have already lost many precious years; we must try other methods and tread new paths." He appointed a Cabinet, with General Zhivkovitch, Commander of the Royal Guard, as Prime Minister; Koroshetz became Minister of Communications, and Marinkovitch was again Foreign Minister, a sign that there would be no marked change in Yugoslav foreign policy. Comment on the action of the King was favourable in the two other States of the Little Entente, the view almost universally expressed in their papers being that it had been inspired by a high sense of duty, and would lead to the more complete unification of the Kingdom of the Serbs, Croats, and Slovenes. The policy of the new Government was definitely Yugoslav, rather than Serbian, Croat or Slovene.

In mid-January Marinkovitch went on sick-leave to Switzerland, and Dr. Kumanudi, Mayor of Belgrade, was appointed Acting Foreign Minister. The Pact of Rome—the Italo-Yugoslav Treaty of Friendship—lapsed in January, no serious effort being apparently made for its renewal. On the other hand, the reopening of the Yugoslav-Bulgar frontier, closed since October, 1927, indicated progress towards consolidating peace in the Balkans—as was also shown in the success at last of the negotiations for the establishment of the Yugoslav Free Zone at Salonika. Early in March six protocols were signed at Geneva by Kumanudi and Cathandaris, the Greek Foreign Minister, who later went to Belgrade, where, after a two hours' audience of King Alexander, he signed on March 27, 1929, with Kumanudi a "Pact of Friendship, Conciliation and Judicial Settlement" between Yugoslavia and Greece.

Early in February Rumania successfully floated a large stabilization loan—another step forward in the new normalization of Europe. The signing by Rumania of the "Litvinoff Protocol" for putting the Kellogg Pact into immediate operation between her and Soviet Russia, together with Poland and the Baltic States, might be taken as another guarantee of the general peace, though it did not imply that the Soviet renounced its claim to Bessarabia. A conference of delegates of the Little Entente met in Bucarest, February 19th–20th, for the purpose of developing economic relations between the three States. A provisional plan of operations was drawn up. An analysis of their trade and commerce was to be undertaken to ascertain where it was possible to purchase from one another commodities hitherto bought elsewhere, and improvements in the intercommunications of the three States were considered. It was suggested that the Little Entente should take action in common respecting economic matters internationally. Another conference was to be held later. Touching the Optants question, no agreement had been reached at the end of May, but meetings of Rumanian and Hungarian delegates had been held at San Remo and Vienna, at which some progress towards a settlement was made. In April Mironescu visited Paris and London, and discussed the policy of his Government in general; he said it desired to establish friendly relations with Hungary, as also with Bulgaria and the Soviet. In the same month a conference took place between Rumania and Yugoslavia at

Belgrade to settle some juridical and economic questions still outstanding.

On March 6, 1929, the Council of the League of Nations discussed the Minorities question, the point of view of the Little Entente being upheld by Titulescu, who endorsed the statement presented by Zaleski for Poland as against that made by Stresemann for Germany. In the course of a speech Chamberlain pointed out that if the Government of a State had obligations respecting its Minorities, these Minorities owed loyal allegiance to the State to which they belonged. The Council instructed Adatchi to draw up a Report in conjunction with Chamberlain and Quinones de Leon; this Committee of Three met in London towards the end of April, and considered the memoranda which had been submitted by various Governments, including those of the Little Entente; the Committee's report was to be placed before the Council in the June session, which it had been agreed was to be held at Madrid, out of compliment to Spain. The Minorities question was also a topic at the regular Little Entente Conference at Belgrade on May 20–22, 1929.

Little Entente Conference at Belgrade

Prior to the conference, King Alexander received in his palace Benesh and Minorescu, the Foreign Ministers of Czechoslovakia and Rumania respectively, together with Kumanudi, his own Acting Foreign Minister, early on May 20th, the first session of the conference, the tenth of the regular series, opening at ten o'clock, immediately afterwards. There was the usual large gathering of journalists, and as usual they were all agog. Grandi, the Italian Foreign Under-Minister, had recently paid a visit to Budapest, and Zaleski, the Polish Foreign Minister, was on his way to that city. Both visits occasioned some comment, a section of the Hungarian Press, backed up by some Italian papers, making the most of that of Mussolini's representative. Then there were the changes that had taken place in the internal politics of two of the allied States—Maniu's Government in Rumania, and the dictatorship of King

Alexander in Yugoslavia. With respect to them Benesh said that the "Little Entente was a group which maintained the ties uniting it quite independently of any alteration in the régime or interior policy of its States." The agenda of the conference was perhaps more extensive than at some other conferences, but, though there was a decidedly striking new departure in one special tripartite treaty, the proceedings had nothing sensational about them. As heretofore, the statesmen of the Little Entente were in perfect harmony in their views, and nothing was more manifest than that the passage of time had but strengthened the alliance of the three States.

A *communiqué* issued on May 20th stated that the three Ministers had considered in particular the general political situation, and afterwards had discussed the Minorities question, respecting which they had agreed on a policy in common at the Madrid meeting of the Council of the League, if it should be brought up there. It was well known that the Little Entente held the same views on this question as did Poland and Greece, and had ranged itself by their side. The *communiqué* also referred to the relations of the Little Entente to neighbouring States, and said that these were developing in a normal manner. For the opening of the conference Kumanudi had received a telegram from Marinkovitch in which the latter expressed his great regret at not being able to attend, and observed that the conference "met at a time when questions that could shake confidence in the maintenance of peace were posed with a light heart, but the real friends of peace understood the importance of the Little Entente, and would see in the conference a fresh manifestation of its vitality and strength." These words had their echo in a statement by Kumanudi who described the Little Entente as a "citadel on which was broken every attempt to disturb that calm and serene atmosphere which was the aspiration of all wise and serious nations." No doubt it was the Minorities question, with revision of the Peace Treaties in the foreground, that was mostly in the minds of these Ministers, but there was also the Optants question, touching which the conference decided to maintain united action. Again, Reparations were to be dealt with in common on the basis of permitting no reduction of the sums due to them.

May 21st was the great day of the conference. The *communiqué* stated that the three Ministers had continued and completed their examination of the general political situation, about which they were in complete agreement. "In accordance with the recommendations of the League of Nations," ran the message, "the Ministers considered a project for a general treaty of conciliation and arbitration on the lines of the model treaty elaborated by the League," thus manifesting their firm will to cooperate with it in the maintenance and consolidation of peace. This highly interesting project was adopted, and the treaty, which affected the three States, was signed in the afternoon—May 21, 1929. Besides this tripartite treaty, the treaties forming the foundation of the Little Entente were prolonged, a new clause being added making renewal automatic at the end of each five-years' period. A good day's work, and this all the more because, as Mironescu pointed out, the tripartite treaty had the added virtue of making entry into the Little Entente by a new State far more simple, since that could now be done by adherence to this treaty, and did not necessitate the conclusion of numerous separate treaties with each of the member States.

On the last day of the conference the Ministers discussed the Soviet question without, however, reaching any decision other than that come to at previous conferences, as was made clear by both Kumanudi and Benesh when they addressed the journalists; each State preserved its freedom of action. At this final session the Ministers agreed to support at Geneva, in September, the candidature of Yugoslavia as member of the Council of the League for the next term. Among other matters dealt with at the conference was the economic question; the Ministers ratified the programme of economic collaboration drawn up for the three States by the experts at Bucarest, and agreed that further similar conferences of experts should be held. In addition, there was an agreement for intellectual collaboration.

As usual, the statements made by the three Ministers outside the conference were of great interest. One of the most notable was uttered by Benesh in the course of a dinner given by General Zhivkovitch, the Yugoslav Prime Minister, in honour of the occasion. Benesh said that about two conferences of the Little Entente had been held each year, and he had been fortunate enough to attend all of them, and "bear witness to the progress made year by year in the consolidation of Europe and the States of the Little Entente. The alliance," he continued, "has passed through several critical periods, and has shown its value as a medium of peace and good order. Despite sceptical prognostications by its opponents, the Little Entente continues to make steady progress and will go on from strength to strength. The work which it has accomplished during the nine years of its existence has been really important." At the same dinner Minorescu looked at the Little Entente from another point of view when he said: "The happy Entente of our three nations, preceded and prepared by their fraternal collaboration on the battle-fields, was born of the imperious need to safeguard the existence and prosperity of our countries. That existence, that prosperity, are bound up in the maintenance of the present Peace; therefore we are united in defending and guaranteeing the Peace Treaties, whose inviolability is the only means of maintaining and assuring the peace of the world. To attempt to touch them would incur the risk of provoking a fresh and terrible cataclysm which would overwhelm the world—with the most frightful consequences to those who had provoked it."

APPENDIX

THE LITTLE ENTENTE TREATIES

I

CONVENTION OF DEFENSIVE ALLIANCE BETWEEN THE KINGDOM OF THE SERBS, CROATS, AND SLOVENES AND THE CZECHOSLOVAK REPUBLIC, SIGNED AT BELGRADE, AUGUST 14, 1920.

FIRMLY resolved to maintain the Peace obtained by so many sacrifices, and provided for by the Covenant of the League of Nations, as well as the situation created by the Treaty concluded at Trianon on June 4, 1920, between the Allied and Associated Powers on the one hand, and Hungary on the other, the President of the Czechoslovak Republic and His Majesty the King of the Serbs, Croats, and Slovenes have agreed to conclude a Defensive Convention.

For this purpose they have nominated as their Plenipotentiary Delegates:—

For the President of the Czechoslovak Republic: M. Edward Benesh, the Minister for Foreign Affairs;

For His Majesty the King of the Serbs, Croats, and Slovenes: M. Momtchilo Nintchitch, Doctor of Law, Minister of Commerce and Industry and acting Minister for Foreign Affairs;

Who, having exchanged their full powers and found them to be in good and due form, have agreed as follows:—

Article 1

In case of an unprovoked attack on the part of Hungary against one of the High Contracting Parties, the other Party agrees to assist in the defence of the Party attacked, in the manner laid down by the arrangement provided for in Article 2 of the present Convention.

Article 2

The competent Technical Authorities of the Czechoslovak Republic and the Kingdom of the Serbs, Croats, and Slovenes shall decide, by mutual agreement, upon the provisions necessary for the execution of the present Convention.

Article 3

Neither of the High Contracting Parties shall conclude an alliance with a third Party without preliminary notice to the other.

Article 4

The present Convention shall be valid for two years from the date of the exchange of ratifications. On the expiration of this period, each of the Contracting Parties shall have the option of denouncing the present Convention. It shall, however, remain in force for six months after the date of denunciation.

Article 5

The present Convention shall be communicated to the League of Nations (Covenant of the League of Nations).

Article 6

The present Convention shall be ratified, and the ratifications shall be exchanged at Belgrade, as soon as possible.

In witness whereof, the Plenipotentiaries named have signed and have affixed their seals thereto.

Done at Belgrade, in duplicate, August 14, 1920.

(*Signed*) MOM. NINTCHITCH. (*Signed*) DR. EDWARD BENESH.

The Ratifications were exchanged at Belgrade, February 10, 1921.

See p. 367 ff. for renewal of this Convention.

II

CONVENTION OF DEFENSIVE ALLIANCE BETWEEN THE KINGDOM OF RUMANIA AND THE CZECHOSLOVAK REPUBLIC, SIGNED AT BUCAREST, APRIL 23, 1921.

Firmly resolved to maintain the peace obtained by so many sacrifices, and provided for by the Covenant of the League of Nations, as well as the situation created by the Treaty concluded at Trianon on June 4, 1920, between the Allied and Associated Powers on the one hand, and Hungary on the other, the President of the Czechoslovak Republic and His Majesty the King of Rumania have agreed to conclude a defensive Convention.

For this purpose they have nominated as their Plenipotentiary Delegates:—

For the President of the Czechoslovak Republic: M. Ferdinand Veverka, Envoy Extraordinary and Minister Plenipotentiary of the Czechoslovak Republic at Bucarest;

For His Majesty the King of Rumania: M. Take Jonescu, His State Minister for Foreign Affairs;

Who, having exchanged their full powers and found them to be in good and due form, have agreed as follows:—

Article 1

In case of an unprovoked attack on the part of Hungary against one of the High Contracting Parties, the other Party agrees to assist in the defence of the Party attacked, in the manner laid down by the arrangement provided for in Article 2 of the present Convention.

Article 2

The competent Technical Authorities of the Czechoslovak Republic and Rumania shall decide by mutual agreement and in a Military Convention to be concluded, upon the provisions necessary for the execution of the present Convention.

Article 3

Neither of the High Contracting Parties shall conclude an alliance with a third Power without preliminary notice to the other.

Article 4

For the purpose of coordinating their efforts to maintain peace, the two Governments undertake to consult together on questions of foreign policy concerning their relations with Hungary.

Article 5

The present Convention shall be valid for two years from the date of the exchange of ratifications. On the expiration of this period, each of the Contracting Parties shall have the option of denouncing the present Convention. It shall, however, remain in force for six months after the date of denunciation.

Article 6

The present Convention shall be communicated to the League of Nations (Covenant of the League of Nations).

Article 7

The present Convention shall be ratified, and the ratifications shall be exchanged at Bucarest as soon as possible.

In witness whereof, the Plenipotentiaries named have signed the present Convention and have affixed their seals thereto.

Done at Bucarest, in duplicate, April 23, 1921.

(*Signed*) DR. FERDINAND VEVERKA. (*Signed*) TAKE JONESCU.

The exchange of ratifications took place at Bucarest, May 27, 1921. The Convention was renewed May 7, 1923, and June 13, 1926.

III

CONVENTION OF DEFENSIVE ALLIANCE BETWEEN THE KINGDOM OF RUMANIA AND THE KINGDOM OF THE SERBS, CROATS, AND SLOVENES, SIGNED AT BELGRADE, JUNE 7, 1921.

Firmly resolved to maintain the peace obtained by so many sacrifices and the order established by the Treaty concluded at Trianon on June 4, 1920, between the Allied and Associated Powers on the one hand and Hungary on the other, as well as the Treaty concluded at Neuilly on November 27, 1919, between the same Powers and Bulgaria, His Majesty the King of the Serbs, Croats, and Slovenes and His Majesty the King of Rumania have agreed to conclude a defensive Convention.

For this purpose they have nominated as their plenipotentiaries:—

For His Majesty the King of the Serbs, Croats, and Slovenes: M. Pashitch, President of the Council, Minister for Foreign Affairs;

For His Majesty the King of Rumania: M. Take Jonescu, His Minister for Foreign Affairs;

Who, having examined together their full powers and found them in order, have concluded the following articles:—

Article 1

In case of an unprovoked attack on the part of Hungary or of Bulgaria or of both these Powers against one of the High Contracting Parties, with the object of subverting the situation created by the Treaty of Peace concluded at Trianon, or by that concluded at Neuilly-sur-Seine, the other Party agrees to assist in the defence of the Party attacked in the manner laid down by the arrangement provided in Article 2 of the present Convention.

Article 2

The competent technical authorities of Rumania and of the Kingdom of the Serbs, Croats, and Slovenes shall by mutual agreement determine in a military Convention, to be concluded as soon as possible, the provisions necessary for the execution of the present Convention.

Article 3

Neither of the High Contracting Parties shall conclude an alliance with a third Power without first giving notice to the other.

Article 4

For the purpose of coordinating their efforts to maintain peace, the two Governments undertake to consult together on questions of foreign policy concerning their relations with Hungary and Bulgaria.

Article 5

The present Convention shall be valid for two years from the date of the exchange of ratifications. On the expiration of this period each of the Contracting Parties shall have the right to denounce the present Convention. It shall, however, remain in force for six months after the date of denunciation.

Article 6

The present Convention shall be communicated to the League of Nations (Covenant of the League of Nations).

Article 7

The present Convention shall be ratified and the ratifications shall be exchanged as soon as possible.

In witness whereof the plenipotentiaries named have signed the present Convention and have affixed their seals thereto.

Done at Belgrade, in duplicate, June 7, 1921.

(*Signed*) TAKE JONESCU. (*Signed*) N. PASHITCH.

Ratifications exchanged at Bucarest, July 8, 1921.

The Convention was renewed on July 7, 1923, and June 13, 1926.

IV

TREATY OF ALLIANCE BETWEEN THE KINGDOM OF THE SERBS, CROATS, AND SLOVENES AND THE CZECHOSLOVAK REPUBLIC, SIGNED AT MARIANSKE LAZNE (MARIENBAD), AUGUST 31, 1922.

The Governments of the Kingdom of the Serbs, Croats, and Slovenes and the Czechoslovak Republic, desirous of prolonging and completing the Agreement concluded between them on August 14, 1920, by new provisions having the following objects: (*a*) the strengthening and maintenance of peace; (*b*) the consolidation and extension of the political and economic bonds between the two States, have accepted, by common agreement, the following Articles.

To this intent there have been appointed as plenipotentiaries, by His Majesty the King of the Serbs, Croats, and Slovenes: His Excellency M. Nik. P. Pashitch, President of the Council of Ministers; by the President of the Czechoslovak Republic: His Excellency Dr. Edward Benesh, President of the Council of Ministers and Minister for Foreign Affairs;

Who, after communicating their full powers, found in good and due form, have agreed as follows:—

Article 1

The Agreement concluded at Belgrade, on August 14, 1920, between the Kingdom of the Serbs, Croats, and Slovenes is prolonged for the duration of the present Convention.

Article 2

The High Contracting Parties take note of the political and military treaties and of the agreements concluded between the Czechoslovak Republic and Rumania, Austria, and Poland on the one hand, and of the similar agreements concluded between the Kingdom of the Serbs, Croats, and Slovenes and Rumania and Italy on the other.

Article 3

The High Contracting Parties will endeavour to establish on a solid foundation all their economic, financial, and transport relations and mutually to ensure the closest cooperation in these relations; for this purpose they will conclude arrangements on these subjects, and particularly a commercial treaty for this purpose.

Article 4

The two High Contracting Parties undertake to give each other in general all possible political and diplomatic support in their international relations; should they consider their common interests to be threatened, they undertake to consider together steps for their protection.

Article 5

The proper authorities of the Kingdom of the Serbs, Croats, and Slovenes and the Czechoslovak Republic shall come to a mutual understanding with a view to taking all the steps necessary for the application of the present Convention.

Article 6

The present Convention shall remain in force for five years from the date on which the instruments of ratification are exchanged. At the expiration of these five years either of the High Contracting Parties shall be free to denounce the present Convention, giving six months' previous notice to the other Party.

Article 7

The present Convention shall be ratified and the instruments of ratification shall be exchanged at Belgrade as soon as possible.

Article 8

The present Convention shall be communicated to the League of Nations.

In faith whereof the two plenipotentiaries have signed the present Convention and have affixed their seals thereto.

Done in duplicate at Marianske Lazne the thirtieth day of August one thousand nine hundred and twenty-two.

(*Signed*) DR. EDWARD BENESH. (*Signed*) NIK. P. PASHITCH.

The exchange of ratifications took place at Belgrade, October 3, 1922. The Treaty was renewed in 1928.

NOTE.—On May 21, 1929, the Little Entente Conference at Belgrade prolonged the Little Entente Treaties for five years, a clause being added making their renewal automatic at the end of each five-years' period.

On the same day the representatives of the Little Entente also signed at Belgrade a tripartite Treaty of Conciliation and Arbitration, on the lines of the model elaborated by the League of Nations.

See p. 361.

BIBLIOGRAPHY

THE body of literature of all sorts on the immediate pre-War period in Europe, on the World War, and on the Peace Conference is simply enormous, and it is growing ever larger. Very much less but still a good deal has been written on Europe since the Conference. The following is a selected list of books, etc., which have been read or consulted:—

AGRARIAN REFORM IN ROUMANIA and the Case of the Hungarian Optants in Transylvania before the League of Nations. 1927.

ASHMEAD-BARTLETT, E. The Tragedy of Central Europe. 1923.

BAKER, RAY STANNARD. Woodrow Wilson and the World Settlement. 1923.

BAERLEIN, HENRY. The Birth of Yugoslavia. 1922.

BENESH, DR. EDWARD. Bohemia's Case for Independence. 1917. My War Memoirs. 1928. Speeches in the Czechoslovak Parliament: The Foreign Policy of Czechoslovakia, January 27, 1921; The Genoa Conference, May 23, 1922; The International Situation, January 30, 1923; Five Years of Czechoslovak Foreign Policy, February 6, 1924; The Foreign Policy of Czechoslovakia, October 30, 1924; The Diplomatic Struggle for European Security and the Stabilization of Peace, April 1, 1925; The Locarno Treaties, October 30, 1925; The International Situation, October 25, 1927; The International Situation, June 6, 1928; Present Problems of Czechoslovakia, October 4, 1928. Articles on "The Little Entente" in the *Encyclopedia Britannica*, *Foreign Affairs*, *Eastern Europe*, etc.

BROZH, ALESH. Three Years of the Czechoslovak Republic. 1921.

BUDAY, DR. LADISLAUS. Dismembered Hungary. 1922.

CABOT, JOHN M. The Racial Conflict in Transylvania. 1926.

CZECHOSLOVAK WHITE BOOKS: Documents diplomatiques concernant les Tentatives de Restauration des Habsbourg sur le trône de Hongrie, 1922; Documents diplomatiques relatifs aux Conventions d'Alliance conclues par la République Tchécoslovaque avec le Royaume des Serbes, Croates et Slovènes et le Royaume de Roumanie, 1923.

DRAGE, GEOFFREY. Austria-Hungary. 1909.

DRAGOMIR, SYLVIUS. The Ethnical Minorities in Transylvania. 1927.

DYBOSKI, ROMAN. Outlines of Polish History. 1925.

EASTERN EUROPE, for December, 1921. Contains an article by Take Jonescu on "The Little Entente," and an article by Dr. Benesh on "The Future of Europe," dealing also with the Little Entente.

EVANS, IFOR L. The Agrarian Revolution in Roumania. 1924.

FILASIEWICZ, STANISLAS. La Question polonaise pendant la Guerre mondiale. 1920.

Gooch, G. P. History of Modern Europe, 1878–1919. 1923.

Hungarian Government. Documents diplomatiques relatifs au detrônement des Habsbourg. The Hungarian Peace Negotiations: an account of the work of the Hungarian Peace Delegation at Neuilly S/S, from January to March, 1920. 4 vols. 1922.

Ivshitch, Milan. Les Problèmes Agraires en Yougoslavie. 1926.

Jaszi, O. Revolution and Counter-Revolution in Hungary. 1924.

Jorga, N. A History of Roumania. 1925.

Lützov, Count. Bohemia. 1910.

Macartney, Maxwell H. H. Five Years of European Chaos. 1923.

Masaryk, President. Has written many important books, of which the most recent are The New Europe (The Slav Standpoint), 1918; and The Making of a State, Memories and Observations, 1914–1918. 1927.

Mousset, Albert. La Petite Entente, Ses Origines, son Histoire, ses Connexions, son Avenir. 1923. Le Royaume Serbe, Croate, Slovène, son Organisation, sa Vie politique, et ses Institutions. 1926. L'Europe balkanique et danubienne de 1925 à 1928. 1928.

Nosek, Vladimir. Independent Bohemia. 1918. The Spirit of Bohemia. 1926.

Nowak, Karl Friedrich. The Collapse of Central Europe. 1924.

Polish Delegation, General Secretariat. Akty i Dokumenty elotyczace Sprawy Granic Polski na Konferencji Pokojowej u Paryzu, 1918–1919. 1920.

Pribram, Alfred Francis. The Secret Treaties of Austria. Austrian Foreign Policy, 1908–1918. 1923.

Schevill, Ferdinand. The Balkan Peninsula and the Near East. 1922.

Seton-Watson, R. W. Has written many important books dealing with Central and South-Eastern Europe, among them being Racial Problems in Hungary. 1908. This was published under the pen-name, "Scotus viator." More recent works, written under his own name, are: The Southern Slav Question and the Habsburg Monarchy, 1911. The Rise of Nationality in the Balkans. 1917. German, Slav, and Magyar. 1916. Europe in the Melting Pot. 1919. Sarajevo. 1926. He edited *The New Europe*, 1916–20, and is one of the editors of the *Slavonic Review*.

Seymour, Charles. The Intimate Papers of Colonel House. Vol. IV. 1928.

Slavonic Review. Particularly II, 6 and V, 15, the latter of which contains a valuable anonymous but obviously inspired article entitled "The Foreign Policy of the Little Entente."

STEED, H. WICKHAM. The Habsburg Monarchy. 1919. Through Thirty Years. 1924.

STREET, C. J. C. Hungary and Democracy. 1923.

SZADICZKY, LOUIS. Revision of the Peace. 1926.

SZASZ, ZSOMBOR DE. The Minorities in Roumanian Transylvania. 1927.

TELEKI, COUNT PAUL. The Evolution of Hungary and its Place in European History. 1925.

TEMPERLEY, HAROLD W. V. History of the Peace Conference of Paris.

TEXTOR, LUCY ELIZABETH. Land Reform in Czechoslovakia. 1923.

TOYNBEE, A. J. Survey of International Affairs. 1925.

WILSON, H. W. The War Guilt. 1928.

INDEX

Political map of Central Europe.

THE LITTLE ENTENTE